NATURAL ACTS
Ohio

NATURAL ACTS
Ohio

BY STEPHEN OSTRANDER

ORANGE FRAZER PRESS
WILMINGTON, OHIO

Library of Congress Catalog
Card Number: 94-066496

ISBN 1-882203-02-X

Published by
Orange Frazer Press
37 1/2 W. Main Street
Box 214
Wilmington, Ohio 45177

DEDICATION

This book is dedicated to my wife, Janine, who nurtures my dreams, and to my children, Catherine and David, whose generation may be served by these words.

CONTENTS

Southeastern Ohio

Central Ohio

Southwestern Ohio

ACKNOWLEDGMENTS

Though writing a book appears to be the product of many hours of solitary confinement with a word processor, it is actually a collaborative effort. I have many collaborators to thank.

Ralph Ramey, former chief of the Division of Natural Areas and Preserves, Ohio Department of Natural Resources, and his staff, notably Nancy Strayer, Guy Denny, Yetty Alley, and Kathy Smith, allowed me to pick their brains and rummage through their files. Michael Hansen, senior geologist at the Division of Geological Survey, made common sense of ancient geological events. I appreciate the help of John B. Klein, Hamilton County Park District; Kim Bork and Pam Menchaca,Toledo Metroparks; Gary Moore, Mac Albin, Leslie Rawlings, Tim Taylor, Julie Gee, and Phil Feldmeier, Columbus Metroparks; Carl Reineman and Brian Parsons, The Holden Arboretum; Ed Quinn and Kent Scott, Lake Metroparks; Bob Hawes, The Wilderness Center; James Schneider and Christine Barnett, Greene County Park District; Christopher Bedel, Edge of Appalachia Preserve; Terry Jaworski, Tom Shisler, and Roy McKenzie, Ohio Historical Society; Joan Heidelberg, Brukner Nature Center; Mary Jo Sage, Cincinnati Nature Center; Alan Cook, The Dawes Arboretum; Richard and Barbara Ganulin; Terry Seidel and Rebecca Richman, Ohio Chapter of The Nature Conservancy; Dan Best, Geauga Park District; Jennifer Grusenmeyer, Vicky Eppley, and Alex Chartle, Dayton Metroparks; and M. Jane Christyson, Doug McRainey, Tom Stanley, Steve Coles, Cleveland Metroparks. To those I have omitted, my apologies. I am humbly indebted to the numerous scientists and writers who have published articles on Ohio's natural wealth; and to Marcy Hawley and John Baskin at Orange Frazer Press, and George Zimmermann, author and chief of the Ohio Office of Travel and Tourism, for being congenial mentors.

Illustrations: Diane Manning

Cover photograph of Cedar Falls/Hocking Hills: Tom Till

Cover design: Brooke Wenstrup

Technical support: Jill Work, Herb Johnson, Mike Houke

PREFACE

In the spring of 1993, as this book unfolded, I had lunch in Columbus with author David Rains Wallace, who wrote about his four-season stay at Chestnut Ridge Metropark in his acclaimed book, *Idle Weeds*. He was back for a while to teach a writing seminar at Ohio State.

We bounced between literary and environmental topics, but when the topic stopped on nature preserves and urban development Wallace briefly sank into despair. He fretted, correctly, about the unremitting human lust for land, natural resources, energy, and dominance. Sighing, he worried aloud about nature preserves. Would they end up being merely managed gardens or zoos? Simply "green" spaces on an urban master plan? Just disjointed biological and genetic warehouses? We shuddered and changed the subject.

Occasionally those dark thoughts followed me as I hiked through more than 100 natural areas in 1993. But at the risk of sounding naive, I confess that I finished my journey more enthusiastic about the status of nature preserves. Their importance to the natural, human world grows daily.

Traditionally, natural areas are seen as places for preserving wildlife, especially endangered species and habitats, and for showing off natural beauty. People go for relaxation, exercise, fun, nature study (casual and professional), and for viewing slices of natural and human history. They also go to breathe that odd and invigorating odor called fresh air.

To me, nature preserves are expressways to the past, umbilical cords to the primeval world that we sometimes long for. They are the repositories of freedom, wildness, chaos, peace, and sanity. They represent the antithesis of life in the city and home.

In nature preserves we begin to restore what Wendell Berry calls "charitable relations between humanity and nature." Here we accept natural processes and biological diversity, a discovery that will help us respect human diversity as well.

These are places of hope, not despair. It is, then, wise for us to invest in them. They may be our only hope.

I confess that what started for me as a field guide to Ohio's natural areas became a celebration of the land. Sometimes, I simply could not restrain my enthusiasm.

The Ice Age glaciers that swept across the northwestern two-thirds of Ohio have been a blessing and a curse. They flattened and massaged the terrain. The streams and fertile soil born from the glaciers sponsored the growth of one of world's great forests. However, the easy topography and rich forest also attracted white settlers, who, in little more than a century had used up most of the bounty.

Yet, Ohio is blessed with an abundance of natural beauty. Its greatest natural asset is its variety of plants, animals, and habitats, an ecological windfall too often taken for granted.

To understand the vitality of such diversity consider that 1,000 different plants flourish in the Oak Openings Preserve near Toledo. Imagine the same kaleidoscope of humanity living in your community—1,000 different ethnic groups, 1,000 different languages, 1,000 different customs, etc.

Ohio boasted greater diversity on the eve of European exploration of North America. At that time 95 percent of the land called Ohio bristled with hardwood trees. Animals such as bison, elk, black bear, mountain lion, and wolf roamed the woods. The small population of native people who lived in harmony with their environment hardly put a dent in the land's natural wealth.

On the eve of the 20th century, however, only about five percent of Ohio could be considered forested. The indigenous population was long gone, so were the animals listed above as well as almost all beavers, deer, turkeys, bald eagles, passenger pigeons, and others.

Seeing the ruin, enlightened people said enough was enough. Ohio's nature preservation movement began in earnest in 1900.

In the ensuing years, state government created parks, forests, and wildlife areas. The Ohio Historical Society acquired valuable sites such as Cedar Bog. Legislation passed in 1917 enabled local governments to establish park districts (metroparks). Meanwhile, private groups, universities, natural history museums, and national conservation organizations such as The Nature Conservancy began buying precious land for preserves.

In the early 1960s, J. Arthur Herrick of Kent State University compiled an inventory of key natural areas for the Ohio Biological Survey. Herrick's list laid the foundation for a state nature preserve network, derived from the passage of the Scenic Rivers Act in 1968 and the Natural Areas Act of 1970. In early 1994, Ohio had 103 state nature preserves, and more were in the works. And because of better stewardship, 25–30 percent of Ohio is forested today.

This does not mean we can relax. Unrelenting human development threatens proposed and existing preserves and parks, right up to their borders. Fowler Woods, Ohio's first state preserve, may have an industrial landfill as a neighbor. Intense development in suburban Columbus has forced deer to flee into Edward S. Thomas preserve. Their overbrowsing has wiped out wildflower communities and the deer themselves have become malnourished and deformed. Columbus metroparks officials are stuck with the "deer problem," though the real problem, of course, is controlling development on the outskirts of a burgeoning city.

What is a nature preserve? It is a special place where endangered and threatened wildlife find refuge, where natural processes continue without interference by humans, where nature can restore the land to its former glory, where humans can find quiet and solitude, and opportunities for hiking, bird watching, nature study, wildlife observation, art, photography, and other "non-consumptive" activities.

Nature preserves may be better understood by knowing what they are not. They are not designed for big crowds. Many offer visitors little more than a hiking trail and a small parking lot. Restrooms, if they exist, are often primitive. Drinking water, also iffy, may flow from a handpump. Picnicking, camping, rock climbing, fishing, hunting, boating, ball playing, bike riding (some exceptions), and swimming are forbidden in preserves, though facilities for these activities may be nearby. Plant gathering, flower and berry picking, mushroom harvesting, fossil and rock collecting—are also not allowed. You are asked not to stray from the footpath and not play a radio. Technically, you cannot climb a tree, snooze in its shade, or skinny-dip, though I am guilty of two of these violations.

This book only describes natural areas open to the public year-round (some exceptions). These include state preserves designated interpretive or scenic, several private nature centers, one state wildlife area, Ohio's only national wildlife refuge, and many of the most striking metroparks. Though metroparks offer various recreational opportunities, some 70–80 percent of the park acreage is expressly set aside for nature. So, they}ve been included in the book. Admission to most of these sites, but not all of them, is free.

Humans cannot just pop in on preserves designated scientific or ruled off-limits. For example, more than half of the state-designated preserves are off-limits. (Usually these are fragile habitats protecting endangered species. Repeated human intrusions could ruin them.) To explore them you must obtain the permission of the owner.

I had the pleasure of hiking most of the preserves during the middle of the week when few humans were around. Some popular preserves, like Clifton Gorge and many metroparks, get crowded on weekends. Folks seeking maximum quiet and solitude should visit preserves on weekdays if possible.

Most preserves have year-round charm. Spring offers the best opportunities to view wildflowers and the arrival of migrating birds. Summer displays nature's full abundance, but it's not necessarily the ripe moment to see forest critters or geological formations. Thanks to its great diversity, Ohio's autumn colors, honestly, have greater range and saturation than New England's. Autumn also is the best time for birding and wildlife observation. Winter is quiet, bare, and geological formations are best seen then.

Helpful hints. Dress appropriately, and wear proper footwear. I always hike with a walking stick, especially during the muddy spring and winter, but many people find staffs a nuisance. I always carry binoculars and field guides. Environmentally safe insect repellent is recommended for summer hikes. Tote water and toilet paper on long hikes, especially if you have children. If nature calls, defecate in a small hole and cover it. Carry out all litter, even cigarette butts. Do not smoke, play radios, shout or talk incessantly, run, or jog on the foot trails.

Quiet, alert, and slow hikers always see more. The status of Ohio's rare and protected plants and animals is determined by the Ohio Department of Natural Resources. The Division of Natural Areas and Preserves keeps track of plants, while the Division of Wildlife monitors animals. I have taken the liberty of reclassifying animals designated "special interest" as being "potentially threatened." The difference between the two is slight.

Strangely, some people think of nature preserves as wild, remote, and forbidding places. Have no fear. There are few dangers, and you won't get lost, if you stick to the trails, and avoid stupid risks (like climbing the rock walls at Conkle's Hollow). Many preserves are less than an hour's drive from some of Ohio's largest cities.

Sometimes, getting to a preserve is half the struggle and half the joy. This book will safely escort you to your destination. Hopefully, you 'll be swept away to common ground. Don't forget to hang on.

Stephen J. Ostrander
January 1994

OF SPECIAL NOTE

Please watch for the symbols throughout this book. They are located at the end of preserve introductions.

Top 12 Wildflower Preserves

You may photograph, admire, and sniff the flowers, but you cannot pick them.

Best Scenic Overlooks and Views

Look, but please don't leap.

Best Birding Preserves

Take binoculars, and travel.

Best Trails for the Physically Challenged

Most metroparks, arboretums, and nature centers feature short paved trails that accommodate wheelchairs. Although most of these trails are scenic and satisfying, only a few venture far from the parking lot and actually enter designated natural areas. Here is a brief list of some of the best paths.

BLACKHAND GORGE STATE NATURE PRESERVE
(*Licking*)—A flat, paved bike path measuring four miles follows an old railroad bed along the wooded shore of the Licking River. 91

SHARON WOODS METROPARK
(*Franklin*)—A paved 3.8-mile trail journeys through the Edward S. Thomas State Nature Preserve located in the park. Travelers must negotiate a few steep ravines. 171

BLACKLICK METROPARK
(*Franklin*)—A half-mile paved path departs from the nature center and loops through the Walter A. Tucker State Nature Preserve and Blacklick Woods, a National Natural Landmark. 96

FOWLER WOODS
(*Richland*)—The flat boardwalk trail wanders through this swamp forest of beeches and maples. 34

Best Outings for Children

You can't go wrong at any of the metroparks, arboretums, or nature centers because they cater to children and young adults. Here are some special selections.

AULLWOOD AUDUBON CENTER
(*Montgomery*)—Combined with a tour of the historical farm, fossil collection spot, and Aullwood Gardens, this site may be the top choice of children and adults. 129

GLEN HELEN NATURE PRESERVE
(*Greene*)—It has everything (nature center, exhibits, hikes, blinds, etc.) but children like the cable bridge and raptor rehab center most of all. 162

ROCKY RIVER RESERVATION
(*Cuyahoga*)—A replica of an ancient, armored shark named Dunk hangs from the ceiling. The nature center also has a deck built over the river. Hiking trails lead to Indian earthworks on a scenic overlook. 26

INDIAN MOUND RESERVE
(*Greene*)—Yes, the kids can climb to the top of the burial mound. Ask them to count the steps as they climb. It keeps them on the trail. 185

BLACKHAND GORGE STATE NATURE PRESERVE
(*Licking*)—The perfect outing for the biking family. The flat, paved trail will satisfy beginners and experts. 91

Top 10 Sites For Geological Wonders

Looking for some terrain? Some rocky cliffs, ledges, outcrops? Some odd formations? Some waterfalls? Try these.

Solitude, Silence, and Slow Pace

These off-the-beaten-track preserves offer solitude, a slower pace, and few distractions. This is where you go to get away from city sounds and the maddening crowd.

Author Favorites

Every preserve is valuable and noteworthy. But these (alphabetical order) are special to me. Your favorites may differ from mine.

NATURAL ACTS

Ohio

"One touch of nature makes the whole world kin"

— **William Shakespeare.**

NORTHEASTERN OHIO

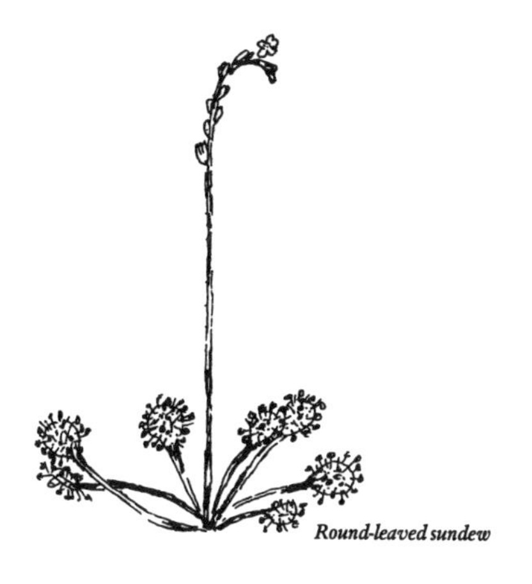
Round-leaved sundew

Though not described in this book, Secrest Arboretum at the Ohio Agricultural Research and Development Center near Wooster can be visited. Mohican State Park and Mohican Memorial State Forest are nearby in southern Ashland County. Try the outdoor recreation facilities at nearby Charles Mill Lake Park, Pleasant Hill Lake Park, and Mohicanville Dam, part of the Muskingum Watershed Conservancy District.

BROWN'S LAKE BOG NATURAL PRESERVE

Here you can clearly see the rings of vegetation that grow around the "eye" of a bog—in this case one of the last unmolested kettle lakes of the Ice Age. Amazingly, this National Natural Landmark was not drained like most of the surrounding land.

Location

Southwestern Wayne County, Clinton Township.

Starting from downtown Wooster, drive south on State Route 3 about eight miles. Turn left (south) on Elyria Road then drive three miles and go right (west) on Brown Road to the small parking lot on the left .8 miles away. Look for the wooden sign.

Ownership

The Ohio Chapter of The Nature Conservancy.

Size & Designation

This 80-acre bog was registered as a National Natural Landmark in April 1967. Dedicated as a scientific state nature preserve in August 1980, it later became an interpretive site.

Access

There is only one way in and one way out of the bog. That is via a soggy path and boardwalk that travels from the parking lot to the bog and back. The walk to the bog is less than a half mile. The boardwalk splits into a "Y" at the bog.

The boardwalk "floats" on a sphagnum moss mat, which explains why it feels like you are walking on a water bed. While the mat feels strong and elastic its thickness may not be uniform. Do not step off the boardwalk (especially on the branches of the Y) because you may sink knee-deep or higher into the bog. You also may destroy fragile plants.

The larger Brown's Lake, to the southeast, is off limits. Insect repellent, long pants, long-sleeved shirts, and ball caps are recommended for visits during the warm months.

For more information contact the Ohio Chapter of The Nature Conservancy, 1504 West First Avenue, Columbus, Ohio 43212; phone (614) 486-4194.

Nearby Natural Attractions

Just a few miles away you will find Shreve Lake and Killbuck Marsh state wildlife areas.

Geology

The bog (once a pond) and adjacent Brown's Lake are perfect examples of kettle lakes formed during the Ice Age. Thousands of years ago a couple of huge iceberg-sized chunks split from the retreating Wisconsinan glacier. The weight of these ice blocks created depressions. Sediment trapped in the glacier fell around the perimeter of the ice chunk, forming a lake bed which filled with melted water. Carbon 14 radioactive dating has concluded that the lakes were formed 10,000–11,000 years ago.

Scientists believe these particular ice blocks melted slowly, perhaps taking a century, because the ponds are framed by a variety of slightly elevated glacial deposits, such as eskers, kames, drumlins, and moraines. (See Siegenthaler Esker State Nature Preserve.)

The ponds benefited from these formations because they acted as a watershed and isolated them from other wetlands which were later drained or polluted.

The bedrock deep below the surface consists of Mississippian-era sandstone and shale some 320 million years old. The ponds are situated above an ancient valley that drained northward. The glaciers that swept across Ohio buried this waterway.

Precipitation running off higher ground fills the bog. Brown's Lake is likewise replenished but it drains southward into Odell Lake in Holmes County.

Scientists rightfully call the soggy, black soil in the bog *muck* (Carlisle muck). It can be 40 inches deep in places which is another reason for staying on the boardwalk. It also feels rubbery when you walk on it. A type of loam soil known as Alexandria silt has taken the higher ground.

Wildlife

If you were a migratory bird, say a Canada goose, flying over the preserve the bog would look like a target with concentric rings of vegetation emanating from a dark brown bull's-eye. The bog shows five distinct plant zones spreading from the bull's-eye of open water.

The first ring is a dense mat of shagnum moss, a rootless plant which floats on the water. The moss intertwines and accumulates into a carpet. It appears to rise and sink like a water bed or quake from the slightest disturbance on the water.

Sphagnum moss makes the bog water highly acidic because it takes in minerals from the water and expels hydrogen which combines with other elements to form acid. The dark brown, almost black, color of the water comes from the tannins that leach from dead leaves that hit the bull's-eye.

Plants which grow on the sphagnum moss mat comprise the next zone. Look for flowers like rose pogonia, marsh cinquefoil, and marsh trefoil. The carnivores—pitcher plant and tiny sundew—thrive here because they prefer acidic environments. They get their daily minimum requirement of nitrogen from the insects they trap.

The mat also supports willow, rosemary, cranberry, leatherleaf, and poison sumac. The roots of these plants spread and connect and have been known to support the weight of adult humans. (Testing this theory in the bog is not advised because people have become entangled in the roots.)

Shrubs like highbush blueberry, winterberry, chokeberry, and poison sumac join trees such as alder and various willows on the shoreline, zone three. Behind it stands the swamp forest zone (swamp oak, ash, maples) adorned in the summer in waist-high ferns named royal, cinnamon, and interrupted.

Skunk cabbage emerges from the muck of this wet forest in the early spring. Its name comes from the foul odor it dispenses. This member of the arum family can produce heat as high as 70º F, enabling it to melt snow at the surface, bake its own pollen and eggs to maturity quickly, and provide warmth for the bees and flies needed to pollinate the plant. Huge amounts of oxygen are consumed by the plant, and the colder the temperature gets, the more oxygen it uses.

The most distant ring is the mixed hardwood forest of oaks, hickory, maple, and other varieties.

Bogs live on borrowed time. If nature is allowed to pass through its stages, the bog will vanish beneath the hardwood forest. That is not likely to happen soon here. It has taken more than 10,000 years for the glacial kettle pond to become a bog, and an equal number of years may be needed for the forest to complete its task.

Bogs are archives that help scientists track the biological past. Things that fall into them rot very slowly. Some materials, like pollen, don't seem to decompose at all. Their long life lets them build layer upon layer of pollen.

Pollen found in a core sample removed from Brown's Lake Bog revealed several climate changes in the area since the Ice Age. A jack pine forest, similar to one found in Labrador today, thrived here on the heels of the retreating glacier. Elephant-like mastodons, elk, giant beaver, and bear probably resided in the area. A warm period 3,000–5,000 years ago brought prairie plants from the Great Plains, but cooler times later enabled a forest resembling a Northern Michigan woods of white pines, hemlock, and oak to develop.

Swarms of airborne dragonflies snag mosquitoes loitering around the rim of the bog. During my visit on a hot, humid evening in June, few mosquitoes attacked me while I examined the bog from the left limb of the "Y." The dragonflies kept the pests away. The mosquitoes returned, however, when I reentered the forest where few dragonflies roam.

History

Early white settlers considered this swamp land worthless. The muck, of course, could not be plowed, and nobody dared to graze here for fear of losing livestock in the mud. Timbering was impossible. The clouds of mosquitoes were almost as impenetrable as the undergrowth. And the place harbored bears, rattlesnakes, and wildcats.

Engineers once tried but failed to build a road through the bog at the beginning of the century. A hunting and fishing club owned the land for many years. Several naturalists exploring the bog, before the boardwalk was built, noted the extreme thickness of the thicket, especially ankle-cutting plants like halberd-leaved tearthumb and stinging nettle, and swarms of mosquitoes.

In 1960 Oliver Diller and John Aughanbaugh published a booklet called the *Flora of Brown's Lake Bog*, listing an amazing constellation of 469 plant species. Their observations, and those of other scientists, heightened interest in preserving the property.

In 1966, The Nature Conservancy bought the site with a loan from the Citizens National Bank of Wooster. The conservation group retired the loan in 1967. The U.S. Department of the Interior listed the preserve as a National Natural Landmark in 1968. A 1980 survey that found the property protected 20 state endangered species prompted the Ohio Department of Natural Resources, Division of Natural Areas and Preserves, to dedicate the place a preserve in September 1980.

Journal

June 19, 1993. This preserve is Ohio's Jurassic Park. It truly has a primordial, almost creepy, ambiance in the summer. Ferns reached my waist. Sudden, startling movements by unseen animals in the underbrush suggested beasts lying in ambush. Will I step into an enormous mutant pitcher plant and never be found?

The birdsong is especially melodious, simultaneously rapturous and haunting. The bullfrogs growled like sputtering outboard motors. Several of them advanced toward me. Their speech became bolder with each hop. These giants broke twigs as they approached. I reached the parking lot feeling exhilarated and relieved.

Large mouth bass

CHAPIN FOREST RESERVATION

You must climb to the top of this flat-topped sandstone summit for the expansive, smiling panorama—the best in northeastern Ohio. On a scorching, cloudless, arid mid-July day, I could easily track the progress of a barge plying Lake Erie some 18 miles away. Clouds stampeded overhead, west to east. This stony knob, also known as Gildersleeve Mountain, has paid a steep price to present this vista. Miners long ago gave the knob the equivalent of a frontal lobotomy, gouging from its north face an enormous block of rock and the forest that covered it. The cliff offering the view is the scar of this quarry. When you finish your blinking at the overlook, explore the pebbly, sandstone ledges and a grand forest of oaks, maples, beech, tulip tree, and hemlock. These, too, should not be overlooked.

Location

Southwestern Lake County, near Kirtland.

From Interstate 90 (or U.S. Route 2) travel south on State Route 306 across the East Branch of the Chagrin River (a state scenic river), pass the Kirtland Temple of the Church of the Latter-Day Saints, to Eagle Road. Here you have a choice. Continue straight on SR 306 and enter the reservation at the Chapin Parkway entrance, or turn right (west) on Eagle Road, then left (south) on Hobart Road, and visit the park from the Pine Lodge and Twin Ponds Picnic Shelter.

Ownership

Under a lease agreement with the Ohio Department of Natural Resources, Division of Forestry, Lake Metroparks manages Chapin Forest Reservation.

Size & Designation

Chapin Forest comprises 390 acres. It is a former state forest.

Nearby Natural Attractions

Within a 10-mile radius you can visit Penitentiary Glen Reservation, another Lake Metropark facility. The Holden Arboretum, Hach-Otis State Nature Preserve, and North Chagrin Reservation, a Cleveland Metropark.

Lake Metroparks also has these reservations—Girdled Road and Hidden Valley—briefly described at the end of the chapter on Penitentiary Glen.

Elsewhere in Lake County, visit Mentor Marsh and Headlands Dunes state nature preserves, and Headlands Beach State Park.

Access

My journey began at the Twin Ponds–Pine Lodge entrance on Hobart Road. Look for a driveway-sized gravel path heading east from the parking lot and the blue blazes of the Buckeye Trail, the main trail through the reservation. Printed guides are available at the trailhead.

The Buckeye Trail and Arbor Lane Trail share the path into the woods. This wide, smooth, moderately challenging trail slowly winds up the hill, generally heading easterly. Several smaller paths branch to the right as you walk—first the Ash Grove Link, then the Parcourse Trail (twice), Ruffed Grouse Trail, Lucky Stone Loop, Mourning Cloak Link, and the Wintergreen Link. Ignore these trails for now, and stay on the main path. We will follow some of these others on the return trip.

As you climb, notice the small outcrops of a pebbly sandstone called Sharon conglomerate. These just whet your appetite for the sights yet to come.

Now follow carefully. Just beyond where the Wintergreen Link joins the main trail, look for unmarked footpaths to the left. These zigzag around trees to steep ledges overlooking the quarry mentioned above and Lake Erie. These ledges are "unofficial" overlooks, not recommended by the park district. I mention them because visitors may think the numerous unmarked paths lead to the designated overlook. They don't.

Caution! There is no fence at the "unofficial" overlook. Approach them slowly and be extremely careful because loose or muddy ground can make footing unsafe. Don't count on the small trees and shrubs on the rim to hold your weight. I urge everybody (children too) to sit or kneel atop the ledge to maintain balance. Do not test your immortality by scaling the 100-foot-high ledges. Climbing them is dangerous, unlawful, and harmful to the wildlife clinging to them. Keep these precautions in mind if you inadvertently find the ledges.

For a safer panorama continue up the trail and follow the footpath to the left to the "official" overlook guarded by a wooden fence. As you scout the horizon, find the bare bluff of Hach-Otis State Nature Preserve (about the 10 or 11 o'clock position).

At this point the main trail descends to the Ledges Picnic Area, a good place to sit a spell. You will find restrooms, drinking water, and picnic tables here.

The Buckeye Trail continues east to another picnic area and places beyond the reservation. We, however, will backtrack slightly, heading back toward the overlook. Midway up the slope take the southern half of the Lucky Stone Loop, which stems left (southerly) from the main trail. This path visits the other jewel of the reservation—the Chapin Ledges composed of the conglomerate described below.

Please view this distinct geological formation from the trail. Climbing through the crevices, gaps, and cracks of the ledges harms the fragile plants growing on the rock and hastens the deterioration of the ledges. Also, one false move on the ledges can lead to an injury. The park district offers guided tours of the ledges for folks who want to seem them closely.

After visiting the ledges, the Lucky Stone Loop returns to the main trail, which you can retrace to the parking lot. I returned via the Ruffed Grouse Trail which heads left a few paces after the Lucky Stone Loop rejoins the main trail. You also can take the Ash Grove Trail from the Ruffed Grouse Trail back to the main path (Arbor Lane Trail). Follow my route for a three-mile roundtrip adventure.

Back at the Twin Ponds Picnic Area you will find drinking water, restrooms, picnic tables, and a ball field. Fishing is permitted in the Twin Ponds (license required). Pine Lodge is the site of education programs, meetings, and cross-country ski rentals.

The reservation is open from 8 a.m.-1/2 hour after sunset. For more information contact Lake Metroparks, 11211 Spear Road, Concord Township, Ohio 44077; phone (216) 639-7275 or 1-800-227-7275.

Geology

The rounded, milky pebbles that you see in the ledges and scattered on the ground are called "lucky stones," though nobody seems to know why they are endowed with good fortune. The stones glisten like pearls in the coarse Sharon conglomerate featured in the ledges and cliffs throughout the forest. Supposedly, the pebble acts as an amulet if tucked into a pocket.

Sharon conglomerate is one of the oldest deposits in the Pennsylvanian geologic period, roughly 300 million years ago. It formed after mountain streams, originating from the north and east, dumped billions of truckloads of gravel along the coast of the ocean then covering Ohio. This deposit stretched out in a wide fan, or delta, larger than the present Mississippi River delta. Over time the sea retreated and the sediment compacted into the coarse sandstone conglomerate.

The quartz pebbles became rounded from the constant tumbling in the quick, ancient streams. Water seeping through joints in the formation created the deep and narrow crevices characteristic of the "ledges." Trees roots sinking into the cracks have contributed to the erosion.

Sharon conglomerate was mined from the abandoned quarry. The rock was pulverized then sifted to separate the pebbles and sand. These products were used in local construction. The foundation of the nearby Kirtland Temple of the Church of the Latter-day Saints, completed in 1836, supposedly is made of this rock.

Sharon conglomerate also has been shaped into marvelous creations at Little Mountain (The Holden Arboretum), Hinckley Reservation (Whipps' Ledges), Nelson-Kennedy Ledges State Park, Gorge Metropark in Cuyahoga Falls, Virginia Kendall Park in the Cuyahoga Valley National Recreation Area, and Lake Katharine State Nature Preserve in Jackson County.

Wildlife

Chapin Forest is a mature woodland packed with beech, oak, maple, and tulip trees. As trail names (Ash Grove and Whispering Pine) imply, ash and pine cover some of the ground, though the latter species was planted years ago for reforestation.

The forest sponsors the growth of wildflowers typical in Ohio—trillium, hepatica, bloodroot, etc. Fragrant wintergreen blossoms along the short trail that carries its name.

Look for deer, flying squirrels, red fox, and barred owls in the woods. Though I failed to flush a ruffed grouse (called a partridge in New York) along the Ruffed Grouse Trail, I did spy a pileated woodpecker clinging to a hickory before it flew away. Fox tracks, faint in the dust beside the trail, pointed to a northerly flight. Chipmunks seem to enjoy running through the cracks, crevices, roots, and pockets of the ledges. Please do not feed them, however.

The fern growing in the cracks of the sandstone is appropriately called rock cap fern, a common plant living in a fragile habitat.

The driveway from the entrance on State Route 306 to the Ledges Picnic Area passes through four types of forest. Red maples dominate first, then beech and sugar maples, followed by red maples again, and oaks at the ledges. See if you see these different communities of life.

History

To save this forest from further logging and mining, Frederic H. Chapin, a Cleveland-area industrialist, purchased Gildersleeve Mountain in 1949 and donated it to the state. The property became Chapin State Forest. The Ohio Division of Forestry used this woodland for some selective cutting and to study the growth of trees. Some trees still bear the faint white-painted numbers of the study trees. The last quarry closed sometime in the 1960s.

Later, Lake Metroparks began leasing the forest from the Ohio Department of Natural Resources. The park district now manages the site as a park and natural area.

Journal

July 17, 1993. It is a clear day, low humidity. I yearn to camp on this quarry ledge tonight and simply watch the stars of the northern sky open after the melon-colored glow of the sunset fades. The blinking lights of barges on Lake Erie would drift in the distance. Perhaps a shooting star will streak across the horizon and fall into the lake.

The ancient people observed celestial luminaries much more than we, especially the shiny bodies that rose and fell on the horizon. They studied the heavens purposefully and reverently. That was how they connected with the cosmos, set their calendars, got their bearings, and followed the rhythms of nature. To them stardom meant the realm and vitality of the eternal nighttime sparks, not some attraction to human celebrities who momentarily glow in the white-hot electronic world. Ask yourself which kind of star—heavenly or earthly—you need.

On the open and bare quarry floor 100 feet below some humans have positioned rocks in a circle. The diameter of the circle is about 10 feet. The darkest stone points north, toward Lake Erie. Is the circle the site of a cult ritual or an extra-terrestial landing site? Ah, if only I could camp on this ledge tonight and learn the answer.

Eastern hemlock

CLEAR FORK GORGE

Some 15,000 years ago, a mighty wall of ice reversed the flow of a river and began creating this V-shaped gorge, Ohio's deepest canyon. The gorge is just one of the natural attractions in this scenic part of the state.

Location

Southern Richland County, Hanover Township.

Exit Interstate 71 at State Route 97 and travel east through Bellville and Butler. SR 97 bisects Mohican Memorial State Forest. About a half mile into the forest (past the Memorial Shrine on the right), turn left on County Road 939 (look for green park signs pointing to the forest headquarters, fire tower, youth camp, etc.), and immediately bear left at the fork. The next 1.2 miles winds to a striking covered bridge that spans the Clear Fork of the Mohican River.

Cross the bridge, turn right and park in the designated area (not the campgrounds). The distance from the interstate to the covered bridge is about 16 miles. Parking is available on the south side of the bridge too.

Ownership

The state preserve, owned by the Ohio Department of Natural Resources, Division of Natural Areas and Preserves, represents a small portion of the gorge. The remainder is held by the Division of Parks and Recreation, and that is the section we will explore.

Size & Designation

Although Clear Fork Gorge State Natural Preserve, located on the south bank of the river, is a scientific preserve and off limits to the public, the gorge can be viewed from trails in Mohican State Park and Mohican Memorial State Forest. The state park encompasses 1,294 acres and five miles of river front, while the state forest comprises 5,109 acres. Clear Fork Gorge was declared a National Natural Landmark by the U.S. Department of the Interior in November 1967.

Nearby Natural Attractions

Mohican Memorial State Forest, Mohican State Park, Malabar Farm State Park, and the Muskingum Watershed Conservancy District all are in the vicinity.

Access

Hike the Hemlock Gorge, Lyons Falls, and Pleasant Hill trails for the best views of the gorge. The covered bridge is a good point of departure.

The Hemlock Gorge Trail begins from the primitive campground on the north bank and follows the river to the state park cabins. The path stays in the floodplain and is flat. The roundtrip will be a little more than four miles.

The Pleasant Hill Trail heads northwest from the bridge, again on the north shore, to the Pleasant Hill Dam, a distance of 3/4 of a mile. Cross the stream above the spillway, climb the stairway to the road, and return via Lyons Falls Trail, which heads off the woods at the bend in the road. The path climbs to the top of the ravine and splits. Bear left (staying along the rim of the gorge) for a 3/4 mile walk back to the bridge.

To visit Little Lyons Falls and Big Lyons Falls, take the loop trail to the right and add a mile to your journey. The detour to the falls returns to the main path. Note the plaque at the end of the trail (near the bridge) commemorating the gorge as a National Natural Landmark.

Scenic overlooks offer quick views of the gorge. Winter is the ideal time to observe the formations. The best vista is east of the covered bridge. Retrace your route toward State Route 97, but bear left at the fork, traveling past the youth camp and fire tower, and park in the next picnic area on the left. The gorge is extremely steep here, so stay in the designated area. Climbing the slope is dangerous and prohibited. The view from Pleasant Hill Dam is less spectacular but worth a peek if you are headed for Mohican State Park Lodge.

The state preserve is located on a precipitous and densely wooded slope on the south bank. You must obtain written permission from the

Division of Natural Areas and Preserves to visit the site.

For more information about the gorge contact: Mohican State Park, 3116 State Route 3, Loudonville Ohio 44842; phone (419) 994-5125; Mohican Memorial State Forest, 3060 County Road 939, Perrysville, Ohio 44864; phone (419) 938-6222; or the Division of Natural Areas and Preserves at (614) 265-6543.

Geology

A geological phenomenon called stream reversal created the beauty of the gorge. Long ago, two rivers originating from the same elevated area flowed in opposite directions. The plateau, in other words, acted like a divide between these two currents.

Around 15,000 years ago the massive wall of the Wisconsinan glacier blocked the flow of the river heading west. A huge lake containing glacial meltwater formed in front of this ice dam. Eventually, the lake water backed up over the divide and poured into the east-flowing river. The stream eroded through the divide, creating the new eastbound channel.

The hourglass shape of the gorge tipped off geologists to the stream reversal theory. Most river valleys widen as they travel downstream. Clear Fork gorge, however, narrows just east of the covered bridge then enlarges again. The divide is located at this pinched point, roughly a half mile downstream from the bridge.

Clear Fork Gorge shows its youth with "V" slopes, rapids, headwater (upstream) erosion, and slump rocks from river bank undercutting. It means the river continues to knife its way through the sandstone and shale bedrock that formed 300 million years ago.

Prominent formations of Blackhand sandstone can be seen in the gorge between the dam and bridge and around Lyons Falls. This thick layer may have been an offshore sand bar protecting part of the vast delta and ocean beach that once stretched for hundreds of miles through what is today eastern Ohio. (See Blackhand Gorge State Nature Preserve.) The marine life thriving in the calm muddy water between the sand bar and delta formed the Wooster shale seen downstream from the bridge.

Waves crashing into the sand bar carried heavier pebbles off the sand bar and deposited them on top of the shale resulting in three distinct strata of conglomerate sandstone. Above them lies a fat layer of Vinton sandstone. The overlook described above is perched on this rock.

Wildlife

See if you can find the various microhabitats in the gorge. The cool, shady lower portion of the south bank supports hemlocks and Canadian yew (relicts from the Ice Age) and red maple with a smattering of yellow birch, mountain maple, and black ash. The top is ruled by oaks, pines, and some black cherry and white ash. Just east of the covered bridge, on an eight-acre plot, grows one of the last unmolested stands of hemlock and white pine in Ohio.

The sunnier north bank contains a panoply of hardwoods—red and white oaks, tulip tree, beech, maple, and sycamore. In the floodplain look for sycamore, hawthorn, various willows, buckeye, and dogwood.

A sample of the wildflowers includes mountain laurel (ridgetops), trailing arbutus, partridgeberry (uncommon), and some unusual hillsiders named shinleaf, wood lily, rattlesnake plaintain, and round-leaved orchid. Fifteen kinds of fern are found here, notably the rare walking fern.

Reptiles and amphibians are represented by box turtles (abundant), dusky salamanders, toads, black rat snakes, and the poisonous copperhead.

Quiet hikers may spot a turkey along the Lyons Falls Trail. During my visit in spring, I spied two great blue herons, plus a kingfisher and an unidentified hawk. Fifteen species of warblers nest in the gorge, particularly the northern parula, hooded, cerulean, and American redstart.

History

The Delaware Indians settled here, hunting and fishing in the gorge. Some of their famous warriors were Janacake, Bill Montour, and Thomas Lyon, who supposedly sought refuge near the waterfalls that bear his name.

The Indians were driven out by white settlers after the War of 1812. John Chapman, better known as Johnny Appleseed, visited here several times to look after his apple orchards. He carved his name in the sandstone wall at Little Lyons Falls, and for a time this graffiti was a tourist attraction. The name has since washed away.

The state began buying land for the state forest in the late 1920s. Pleasant Hill Dam is a flood-control project of the Muskingum Watershed Conservancy District. The impoundment flooded some of the most scenic portions of the gorge.

Clear Fork State Park was created from state forest land in 1949. The name was changed to Mohican State Park in 1966. The U.S. Department of the Interior declared the gorge a National Natural Landmark in 1967.

CLEVELAND METROPARKS

The state's first metropark district started with no money and just three acres of bottomland straddling Rocky River, a parcel donated by a brewer. A revised state law in 1915 enabled counties to fund park districts and to acquire property for park lands. Later that year, the park board hired William Stinchcomb and Frederick Law Olmstead, the son of America's foremost landscape architect in the 19th century, to develop a park plan. The two designers envisioned an interconnecting ring of parks and boulevards around fast-growing Cleveland—a chain of green that has become known as the Emerald Necklace. Today, Cleveland Metroparks comprises 12 reservations totaling 19,000 acres. The parks are free (except special facilities like golf courses, zoo, etc.) and are open every day from 6 a.m.-11 p.m. For more information, contact Cleveland Metroparks, 4101 Fulton Parkway, Cleveland, OH 44144-1923; phone (216) 351-6300.

Mountain maple leaf

- **Bedford Reservation**
- **Lake Isaac Waterfowl Sanctuary**
- **Brecksville Reservation**
- **Hinckley Reservation**
- **Mill Stream Run Reservation**
- **North Chagrin Reservation**
- **Rocky River Reservation**
- **South Chagrin Reservation**

BEDFORD RESERVATION

Tinker's Creek has been tinkering in this valley for many millennia. The awesome hemlock-lined, severe-sloped gorge sculptured by the creek became a National Natural Landmark in 1968.

In summer, the mist churned by the boiling creek stays in the cavity of the canyon until late morning. The forest climbs above the thinning vapors, spills over the rim of the deep cut, and seems to flow, grasp, and grope toward the horizon. For a moment, I forgot that miles of concrete and a million people have got this place surrounded.

Location

Southeastern Cuyahoga County, encircled by the cities of Bedford, Bedford Heights, Walton Hills and Valleyview.

From downtown Cleveland, travel south on Interstate 77, east on Interstate 480, and south on Interstate 271. Exit at Broadway and head north about a mile. Turn left on Northfield Road, right on Union Street, left on Egbert Road, then right at the entrance. Drive on the Gorge Parkway to the Tinker's Creek Scenic Overlook parking lot on the right. (Drive past the tiny overlook between the Egbert and Lost Meadows picnic areas.)

Ownership

Cleveland Metroparks.

Size & Designation

Bedford Reservation encompasses 2,154 acres. Tinker's Creek Gorge is a National Natural Landmark.

Nearby Natural Attractions

Bedford Reservation is one of 12 reservations in the Cleveland Metroparks' "Emerald Necklace." The nearest other jewels from the necklace are Brecksville and South Chagrin reservations. The Cuyahoga Valley National Recreation Area begins a few miles away in Summit County.

Access

Our three-mile trek begins at the scenic overlook and goes east to the Egbert Picnic Area. After letting your mind wander at the promontory, head east (right), along the edge of the woods, to the wide, gravel bridle trail, your route to the picnic area. This path is also the famous Buckeye Trail which circles the state. (Do not confuse this path with the paved All-Purpose Trail across the street.)

After traipsing through a small hollow, you will descend into a small gorge created by Deerlick Creek. A small waterfall can be seen from the trail. About a mile into the trip the trail crosses a run behind Bridle Veil Falls—a good spot for photographs, wading, and a nap. After fording the brook, follow the dirt path, not the wooden steps which climb to the Gorge Parkway.

After the falls, the trail makes a hairpin turn close to the road, rides the rim of a ravine at the left, and crosses the paved road that leads to the Lost Meadow Picnic Area. The path crosses another intermittent brook, ascends a ridge, crosses the parkway and All-Purpose Trail, then skirts the west edge of Shawnee Hills Golf Course.

Ahead the trail splits. Turn left, recross the road, and enter the woods again. The Egbert Picnic Area soon appears on the right. You will find restrooms and drinking water here. Footpaths behind the restrooms lead to a ledge with a westward view into the gorge—a perfect spot to rest tired feet before returning to the car. Be careful near the rim, though, because the rocks can be slippery and loose.

I recommend returning via the same route for a six-mile adventure. However, folks in a hurry can go back along the open All-Purpose Trail which is a little shorter and quicker (because the terrain is gentler and has fewer scenic stops).

The trail is wide and moderately strenuous. Restrooms are located at the picnic areas and Shawnee Hills Golf Course (off Egbert Road), where golfers can try to shoot featherless birdies and eagles on an 18-hole course.

Geology

It has taken Tinker's Creek thousands of years to scour through mounds of till (sand, gravel, clay, etc.) dumped by the Wisconsinan glacier 12,000–15,000 years ago, and through three layers of bedrock ranging from 330–370 million years old, all of them the former floors of shallow, ancient saltwater seas.

The stream falls more than 200 feet on its two-mile passage through the park. The overlook at the start of our trail rests on a cliff 200 feet above the water.

The youngest exposed rock is Berea sandstone, composed of tiny quartz crystals cemented by clay. The crystals shine like diamonds in the sunlight. About 330 million years ago (Mississippian geologic period), currents washing off higher ground to the east and north distributed sand in an ocean in a wide fan. This delta dried and compacted into rock when the sea receded. Huge chunks, or slump rocks, of this sandstone have rolled into the creek, the victims of undercutting, a force where water erosion removes softer rock layers beneath a harder layer causing pieces of the harder rock to split off. Other blocks of slump rock are found along the trail in the ravines of tributaries that flow into Tinker's Creek.

Cleveland shale (350 million years ago), made of extremely small bits of quartz, clay, and mica, lies beneath the sandstone. Waves washing the shore carried these fine sediments into the sea. The rock's black color comes from the murky decayed material of shoreline plants that fell into a late Devonian sea.

In Central Ohio geologists call this formation Ohio shale. Fossils rarely turn up in Ohio shale, but in the Cleveland shale beds in Tinker's Creek geologists have found a rewarding fishing hole.

In 1979, Bob Burns, a geologist from Maple Heights, uncovered a chunk of pyrite (a.k.a. fool's gold) shaped like a shark's skull. The 360 million-year-old beast still had its teeth. The find was a dunkleosteus, an armored fish that grew to lengths of 20–30 feet. A replica of "Dunk" hangs in the nature center at Rocky River Reservation.

At Bridal Veil Falls notice the "ripple" rock, small ridges in shale formed by lapping ocean waves. Please leave the rocks in the stream. Observe, but do not collect.

Downstream, beyond the gorge, the creek has begun to reveal Chagrin shale, bluish-gray and opaque, formed 360 million years ago.

Part of the buried valley of the ancient Dover River runs through the northeast part of the reservation. Like the Cuyahoga River, the Dover River flowed northward, except it refreshed an ocean. In its heydey, the Dover was supposedly deeper than the Cuyahoga River and was one of two major drainage routes in the region. The glaciers that slid over the landscape rerouted the river and filled the valley with glacial till.

Wildlife

Oaks, beech, maples, and their associates dominate the woods on both sides of Tinker's Creek. All totaled, 29 kinds of native trees have sunk their roots here. Others found in the woods include ash, tulip tree, cucumber magnolia, and basswood on the gradual slopes; shag bark hickory joins the oaks on the rim.

The cool, shady gorge allows hemlock and American yew, trees more common in colder climates, to thrive. These arrived in the vanguard of the Wisconsinan glacier. Ohio's gorges and ravines are the only habitats suitable for hemlock and other immigrants from the north woods. Yellow birch also survives on the slopes.

A rare cluster of mountain maple, living at the southernmost extent of its range, grows on a steep slope in the northeast corner of the park. Another tree reaching its northern limit is the redbud, common in Central Ohio and farther south but unusual in Northeast Ohio.

Some winged sumac, also near its northern limit, stands here too. Its leaves become brilliant red in autumn.

The woods also shelters a few old stands of red and white pine, supposedly remnants of an ancient pine forest. Most pines that you will see, however, were planted by humans in this century.

Sycamores, beech, sugar maples, willows—all common inhabitants—prevail in the bottomland.

The reservation protects a number of threatened, rare, or uncommon wildflowers, grasses and ferns: (flowers) helleborne, fringed gentian, large round-leaf orchid (potentially threatened), dwarf crested iris, round-leaf violet, yellow ladies' slippers, twinleaf, tall tickseed, swamp thistle, Indian cucumber root, whorled rosinweed; (grass) scouring-rush; and (ferns) Goldie's, fragile, silvery, rattlesnake, and cutleaf grape.

History

A petroglyph, drawing on rock, found at Poet's Cave along Deerlick Creek, proves that ancient people once inhabited the land.

At the confluence of Tinker's Creek and the Cuyahoga River a few miles to the west, Moravian missionaries established Pilgerruh (Pilgrim's Rest) in 1786. The "black robes" hoped to convert Indians to Christianity.

The creek's namesake, Joseph Tinker, arrived with Moses Cleaveland's surveying party in 1796. He helped plat the holdings of the Connecticut Land Company east of the Cuyahoga River.

Tinker's groundwork led to the construction of grist, woolen, and chairmaking mills which utilized the creek's water power.

Tinker's Creek was one of the first scenic areas chosen for a park by the newly-commissioned Cleveland park board in 1915.

Bedford Glens Park, located on the north bank, became a popular playground before World War II, featuring dances, bowling, picnicking, and sightseeing. It was destroyed by fire in 1944.

Tinker's Creek almost became Lake Shawnee in the early 1960s but a plan to dam the creek was opposed by the park board and conservation groups.

Belted kingfisher

LAKE ISAAC WATERFOWL SANCTUARY (in Big Creek Reservation)

Birds and other creatures find a safe haven in the ponds, marshes, thickets, and bottomland woods that comprise the Lake Isaac Waterfowl Sanctuary in Big Creek Reservation.

Location

Southwestern Cuyahoga County, near Middleburg Heights.

Exit Interstate 71 at State Route 42/Pearl Road. Head north on Pearl Road (toward downtown Cleveland), then turn left (west) on Fowles Road which goes under I-71. Turn left (south) on Big Creek Parkway and almost immediately Lake Isaac appears on the right. Park in the designated area.

Ownership

Cleveland Metroparks.

Size & Designation

Lake Isaac sanctuary comprises about a quarter of the skinny Big Creek Reservation, which encompasses 443 acres.

Nearby Natural Attractions

Big Creek Reservation is one of the gems in the Emerald Necklace managed by Cleveland Metroparks. The other reservations described in this book are Rocky River, Mill Stream Run, Bedford, Brecksville, Hinckley, North Chagrin, and South Chagrin.

Access

Many visitors contentedly view the lake and its waterfowl from the benches behind a long, roadside observation area. But if you get restless, try out the mile-long lasso-shaped trail that starts to the right of the observation platform.

The path traces the north shore of the lake and a meadow on the right. You may catch closeups of ducks on the pond, or startle deer in the pasture. After coursing through a small wooded thicket, the trail splits. The loop in the lasso begins and ends here. I went to the right, walking beneath utility lines, to tiptoe beside a marsh noisy with bullfrogs, songbirds, and the shrieks of unseen feathered creatures hiding among willows and cattails.

After the swamp, the trail reaches railroad tracks and bends to the left (the trail to the right is off limits). Eventually the path enters a wooded area of gnarly locusts, cottonwoods, sycamores, and willows, the floodplain of Baldwin Creek. A bench overlooks the muddy creek from a small bluff, a good spot for birdwatching and resting.

The trail traces the west shore of the lake, but you will never see the water, at least not in the summer, because of a thicket impenetrable to adult humans. Rabbits, feisty terriers, and small, adventurous kids could, of course, negotiate these brambles. The trail returns to the parking lot.

For most of its distance, the gravel path is open, wide, and flat. There's lots of trail room for restless kids. Just try to keep their volume down. I chose to walk quietly in the grass beside the trail to see as much wildlife as possible. It also wanders through a small pine plantation and an old orchard.

Residential subdivisions surround Lake Isaac, and roads choke it from all sides. Busy railroad tracks serve as the western border, and high-flying power lines cut across the property. Try to ignore these distractions. Focus on the details, small scenes, and little miracles when visiting this park.

Geology

Lake Isaac is a glacial pothole created around 12,000 years ago when a huge chunk of ice split from the Wisconsinan ice mass and formed a depression in the land. Water from the melting glacier cube filled the lake. A dam was later constructed to enlarge and stabilize the lake.

Wildlife

Lake Isaac is a haven for waterfowl. Metropark observers have counted as many as 800 birds on the lake—wood ducks, black ducks, mallards, and Canada geese mostly. Great blue herons and green herons are seen occasionally. Other transients such as blue-winged teal, gadwall, pintail, and wigeon fly in during the spring and autumn migrations.

Please observe the signs at the observation platform that urge visitors not to feed the birds. The geese and ducks are not pets.

Fox, deer, mink, raccoons, opossum, and rabbits reside here, along with what sounds like a boat load of bullfrogs. Carp, bluegill, and others swim in the water but snagging them with hook, line, and sinker is unlawful.

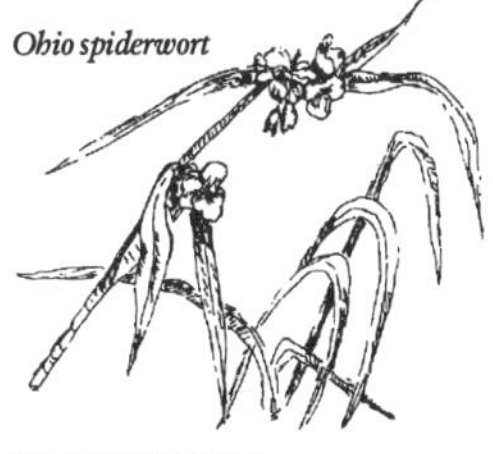
Ohio spiderwort

BRECKSVILLE RESERVATION

Chippewa Creek fashioned a fairy tale, mist-filled gorge of precipitous rock walls before it emptied into the Cuyahoga River. Like mercenary sentries on a castle wall, tall and straight hemlocks, more accustomed to the boreal forests of Canada, protect the crown jewel of this reservation.

Location

Southern Cuyahoga County, near Brecksville.

Leave Interstate 77 at the exit for State Route 82/ Brecksville. Travel east on SR 82, past the intersection with State Route 21 to the entrance on the right. Turn left at the T intersection to Chippewa Creek Drive and park in the lot for the Harriet Keeler Memorial Forest on the right. The trails described below are accessible from here.

Ownership

Cleveland Metroparks.

Size & Designation

The reservation, second largest in the metroparks system, comprises 3,090 acres.

Nearby Natural Attractions

Close to Brecksville Reservation are Bedford, Mill Stream Run, and Hinckley. Furnace Run Metropark is just a few minutes away in Summit County.

Access

Curiosity compels visitors to head for the scenic overlook first. From the parking lot, go across the street and turn left on the paved all-purpose trail to the overlook. After ogling the gorge, walk east (downstream) on the gravel hiking which traces the rim of the gorge. Follow the green blazes of the Chippewa Gorge Trail.

The gorge measures .6 miles, and after walking that distance, the trail descends into the floodplain, exchanging the habitat of hemlock and white oak for the soggy environs of willow and marshland. At the bottom of the hill, a bridal trail joins from the left. A slight detour left down this bridle path takes you to a ford across the creek and an excellent place for wading, photographs, or napping.

The gorge path crosses a suspension bridge built by the Ohio National Guard and returns to the Chippewa Creek Parkway near its intersection with the Valley Parkway. Cross the road to the Chippewa Creek Picnic Area.

Here you have a choice of three trails. (1)Turn right and follow the green blazes if you want to visit the nature center and return to the parking lot. (2)The Valley Stream Trail heads west (left) across Valley Parkway. Just east of the Plateau Picnic Area, a one-way path going to the summit of My Mountain leaves at the left. (3)The red blazes of the Deer Lick Cave Trail go south following Valley Parkway. This four-mile circuit, the longest in the park, basically traces the perimeter of a triangle whose sides are the Valley Parkway, Meadows Drive, and Chippewa Creek Parkway. It traverses scenic ravines and small streams, follows ridgetops, and looks into meadows.

The Buckeye Trail (blue blazes) merges from the left as you reach the Oak Grove Picnic Area. A trail marker notes the distances to Cincinnati—441 miles via the western loop, or 552 miles through eastern Ohio. Headlands Beach, its northern terminus, is a mere 65 miles away.

A bridle trail crosses your path before you reach Deer Lick Cave, a sandstone shelter cave. After crossing Meadows Drive the trail turns north between Sleepy Hollow Golf Course and the road. (The Buckeye Trail splits and continues west.) The path again crosses the road and snakes northward, through the Meadows Picnic Area to the nature center.

Visit the exhibits at the historic nature center before following the yellow then white blazes to the Keeler Memorial and the parking lot. It is open daily from 9:30 a.m.-5 p.m., except on Thanksgiving, Christmas, and New Year's Day. Restrooms and drinking water are available at the nature center. During July and August, visit the park's planted tallgrass prairie (with viewing deck) just west of the nature center. Phone (216) 526-1012.

Less ambitious hikers, or folks pressed for time, can visit Deer Lick Cave by car. Park at the designated spot on Valley Parkway and walk to this site on the foot trails. Frankly, the trail may be at its best in May and October, when wildflowers and autumn leaves put hikers into a trance.

Geology

Chippewa Creek washes over bedrock rich in geological history. The waterfall seen from the scenic overlook tumbles over Berea sandstone, a mere 330 million years old (Mississippian geological period). This gray, tightly-packed rock contains tiny quartz crystals (sand) that were deposited near the shore of a shallow sea. Streams falling from uplands to the east and north brought the sand to the sea. Waves tossed the grains and redistributed them along the shore. Ripple marks (small ridges) showing wave action are often found in Berea sandstone.

Beneath Berea sandstone lie three layers of shale comprising what geologists call the Bedford formation (345 million years old). Color reveals the Bedford layers. Look for the chocolate red strata (iron oxide gives it the rusty tint), followed by a gray layer, then an opalescent shale called Euclid bluestone. The creek runs over a long slab of this beautiful bluestone just upstream from the ford on the bridle trail (the detour from the Chippewa Creek Trail which I described above). Walk barefooted across the bluestone and admire its polished appearance.

Blackish Cleveland shale, also known as Ohio shale, can be seen in the creek. This rock is made of dust-sized particles of quartz, mica, and clay. Scientists think that rotting plants washed into a brackish, shallow ocean and carbonized around 350 million years ago (Late Devonian period). The decay explains the almost black color of the rock.

Near its confluence with the Cuyahoga River, the creek has exposed Chagrin shale of Middle Devonian vintage, 360 million years old.

The unstable slopes are littered with huge boulders called slump rocks, and tortured by narrow and steep ravines cutting perpendicular into the gorge walls. When the creek removed the softer shales, blocks of erosion-resistant sandstone, now unsupported, fell into the valley.

The ancient Dover River used to flow in this area. It drained northeastward into what is now the Atlantic Ocean. During the Ice Age this river system became dammed by ice and its current was reversed into the south-flowing Tuscarawas River. Retreating glaciers dumped dirt into this abandoned valley and its tributaries. This glacier debris, called till (a mixture of sand, gravel, clay, and other stuff), is especially thick around here.

The terrain above the gorge is flat and poorly drained due to a high amount of clay in the soil. (Clay soil does not allow water to seep through it as fast as sandy soil.) Consequently, several marsh ponds have emerged behind the ledge, providing a habitat for aquatic wildlife.

Wildlife

The gorge and creek sponsor a variety of ecosystems which

support a number of rare and unusual plants.

The ancestors of the hemlocks rooted on the rim and slope came here from Canada during the Ice Age when the climate was colder. They thrive here today because the gorge provides the cool, shady environment they need to survive.

Mountain maple, trailing arbutus, and yellow birch, also more common in northern climes, grow in the gorge too. Another rarity found in the gorge is a wildflower called round-leaved orchid (a potentially threatened flower). A small stand of American chestnuts reportedly grows on the north bank.

Some comely white and red oaks, real hunks stretching more than 100 feet into the sky, reside on the flat-topped ridge, sprinkled with black cherry and hickory. Beech and sugar maples prefer the moister slopes. The floodplain downstream from the gorge boasts a marsh and a riverine thicket dominated by sycamore, cottonwood, and willow.

Seven types of ferns grow in the gorge—silver glade, royal, lady, devil's bit, broad buck, crested, and walking fern (a rarity in these parts).

The Deer Lick Trail is surrounded by your favorite hardwoods, spiced here and there by pines and spruces planted during the 1930s by laborers for the Works Progress Administration.

The ponds behind the gorge serve as breeding areas for salamanders and frogs in the spring. Jefferson salamanders, reclusive critters, reside at the Oak Grove Picnic Area pond. When early spring rains fall these tiny creatures leave their burrows for a 2–3 week breeding orgy. They hide in their tunnels for the rest of the year, regaining their strength for the next March downpour.

Look for red-spotted newts and spotted salamanders in the pond across the road from Deer Lick Cave, a good place, I hear, to listen to spring peepers.

From mid-July to Labor Day the flowers in the reservation's "prairie zoo" burst into color. The stars of the show are dense blazing star, prairie dock, coreopsis, bergamot, and boneset. Altogether, some 50 plants grow in this planted prairie.

Cleveland Metroparks began the prairie restoration project next to the nature center in 1976. The prairie protects rare plants and enables visitors to see and learn about this endangered ecosystem.

Seeds collected from 20 locations in northern Ohio were refrigerated for six weeks before planting. A section of the plot is burned each year to curb the encroachment of trees and non-prairie species. (Read the chapters on Bigelow Cemetery, Smith Cemetery, and Milford state nature preserves to learn more about prairies.)

Birders will find an abundance of feathered friends flying about the woods and fields. A 1979 survey found 41 species nesting here, including the cerulean warbler, wood thrush, redstart, red-eyed vireo, cuckoo, belted kingfisher, red-breasted grosbeak, great horned owl, cedar waxwing, Louisiana waterthrush, and three varieties of flycatcher.

History

The men who built the nature center in the 1930s left their mark in the wood. Roman numerals on the beams helped them assemble the building, also known as the trailside museum. Notice the leaf carvings in the black walnut and cherry. Test your observation skills by finding the "ghost leaf," a modified tulip leaf carving.

The trailside museum opened on June 11, 1939. It was built under the auspices of the Works Progress Administration and Civilian Conservation Corps, two federal agencies that hired unemployed men for public works projects during the Depression years. More than 17,000 people visited the museum in 1939. Millions have passed through the doors since then.

Author, teacher, and nature lover Harriet L. Keeler (1846–1921) is remembered by a plaque embedded in a glacial erratic, a granite boulder dropped here by a glacier. The memorial lies along the trail in the 390-acre forest which carries her name. The forest, dedicated in 1990, is bounded by the park roads. Near the tribute a local garden club has erected a deck overlooking the prairie.

Just outside the park on State Route 21 is the Squire (Charles) Rich Home and Museum, managed by the Brecksville Historical Society (for hours call {216} 526-6757). Rich bought 160 acres here in 1835 and 150 acres later. The house he built for $600 was made from trees felled in the nearby forest.

A humbler man lived on the land before Rich. Just north of the museum stands the gravestone of Benjamin Waite, a private in Mosley's Massachusetts Regiment during the Revolutionary War. He died in February 1814.

Journal

Went wading in Chippewa Creek at the ford in the bridle trail. It was near sunset when the shaded rock turns blue. Gentle breezes cooled by hemlocks passed through the gorge. I did not have to be anywhere but here. I rate this a "10."

Whipp's Ledges

HINCKLEY RESERVATION

San Capistrano has its famous swallows, but Hinckley is renowned for its buzzards (turkey vultures). On a Sunday in mid-March, flocks of birdwatchers, tourists, and curiosity seekers outnumber the buzzards who annually return to their ancient roosts in the ledges, caves, and cliffs of this sanctuary.

Location

Northeast Medina County, Hinckley Township.

Leave Interstate 71 at the Brunswick exit and travel east on State Route 303. Go to the village of Hinckley (about 3 miles), turn right (south) on State Route 3 for a little more than half a mile, then left on Bellus Road. The West Drive entrance to the reservation will be about two miles on the right. After a mile on West Drive, turn left at the sign pointing to the Boathouse and Johnson's Picnic Area. Park at the end of this drive in the picnic area.

Ownership

Cleveland Metroparks.

Size & Designation

Hinckley Reservation comprises 2,275 acres.

Nearby Natural Attractions

Hinckley Reservation is one of 12 sites in the Cleveland Metroparks system. The closest reservations are Mill Stream Run, Rocky River, and Brecksville. Lake Medina and Spencer Lake state wildlife areas are located in Medina County.

Access

The route described below goes to Whipp's Ledges, one of the destinations of the buzzards. Unfortunately, gravel hiking and bridle trails are not clearly marked. The blacktopped All-Purpose Trail can be used by visitors in wheelchairs or pushing strollers. This is not a recommended route for undisturbed nature study because bicyclists, joggers, skaters, radio-players, and others also prefer this roadside trail.

From the parking lot, cross the bridge to the paved trail, but take an immediate left down a gravel path. After walking 30 paces look for a painted blue blaze, signifying the Buckeye Trail. Follow these blazes for the next 3/4 mile along the shore of Lake Hinckley.

The trail ends at State Road. Now, turn left and follow the paved All-Purpose Trail across the bridge which spans the East Branch of the Rocky River. Cross State Road and follow the paved driveway which heads to Whipp's Ledges Picnic Area for about 50 feet. At this point, you can play it safe by strolling along the driveway to the shelterhouse in the picnic area, or live on the wild side and trace the stream via a path that begins on the right where an old road enters the woods. If the latter route is chosen, take the road (and other footprints) to its end, then hike the blazed trail up the hillside to the left. The path emerges from the woods behind the restrooms of the picnic area. You will find drinking water there.

The trail to the ledges begins to the right of the shelterhouse, built in 1938 by the Works Progress Administration. The hike to the top of the ledges is short, moderately strenuous, but worth the effort. At the bottom of the ledges, the trail veers left and takes you through the cracks and crevices of the sandstone formation. The rim of the ledge is 350 feet above Hinckley Lake.

Climbing the sheer rock walls is dangerous and forbidden. However, many people, especially children, enjoy climbing the slump rocks. Caution is advised because falls can result in injuries and deaths. Please do not chisel your name in the rock wall.

More decisions. After exploring the ledges you can (1) retrace your steps to the car to complete a hike of 2–2.5 miles, or (2) take the route I concocted. The latter choice is only for hikers confident about their navigational skills.

Choice #2: From the ledges, follow the blue blazes of The Buckeye Trail until you reach a group camping ground (just a few hundred yards behind the ledges). The Buckeye Trail reenters the woods besides the restrooms, but shortly hooks left into the meadow. Walk along the edge of the field (woods on the right) until you reach an old farm lane where the trail goes right (follow the blazes) for about 1,000 feet to another meadow. Here you depart from the Buckeye Trail which heads left along the meadow. Instead, continue straight along the edge of the field with the woods at the right.

In the southwest corner of the meadow, I followed a thin bridle path through a young forest to the edge of a cliff. The path turned right here and traced the rim of the ledge. Soon it crossed a small, spring-fed rill, scouring a picturesque ravine running perpendicular to the ledge, or southwesterly. Use the direction of this ravine (the first one you meet on the rim) for your heading.

The hoofprints I followed descended the bluff into a floodplain and roughly paralleled the southwesterly direction of the ravine. (Not all bridle paths in this neck of the woods will follow that heading, however.) The path crossed the East Branch of the Rocky River at a shallow ford and went along an abandoned road that took me to State Road near the entrance to the Brooklyn YMCA camp.

Now, go right (north) on State Road, then west to the parking area either on the All-Purpose Trail along West Drive, or the lakeshore gravel trail traveled earlier. The overlook on the All-Purpose Trail presents a panorama of Hinckley Lake and the river valley.

The park has eight picnic areas (three reserved), swimming beach, bridle trail (also good for hiking), ballplaying fields, fishing, sledding, cross-country skiing, ice skating, and boating facilities.

Geology

The rock at Whipp's Ledges is made of Sharon conglomerate, a coarse, pebbly sandstone. Some 300 million years ago (during the Pennsylvanian geologic period) swift-flowing streams originating from mountains to the north and east deposited gravel into the sea covering Ohio. This sediment of quartz pebbles piled up in a huge delta bigger than the modern Mississippi River delta. When the ocean receded, the deposit compacted into this rock conglomerate.

The pebbles became smooth and round because they were constantly being tumbled in the streams. Notice the pebbles that litter the ground, changing back to the loose gravel deposit of millennia ago. Humans speed up erosion when they climb the rocks and free pebbles.

Though Sharon conglomerate resists erosion, the East Branch of the Rocky River has eroded through it. Water also has seeped through hairline seams to create the cracks and crevices characteristic of the ledges. Trees growing in the cracks also have widened some of the gaps. House-sized boulders, called slump rocks, have split from the ledge and rolled down the slope. They fell off because softer rock layers (less resistant strata) beneath them eroded away and no longer supported them.

Other scenic examples of Sharon conglomerate can be discovered in nearby Nelson-Kennedy Ledges State Park (Portage County), the Ritchie Ledges in Cuyahoga Valley National Recreation Area (Summit County), Gorge Metropolitan Park in Cuyahoga Falls, Little Mountain (The Holden Arboretum), Chapin Reservation (Lake County), and Lake Katharine State Nature Preserve in Jackson County.

The streams running through the Johnson Picnic Area and north of Worden's Ledges contain rocks with fossils. Maybe you will find the outline of a 300 million-year-old critter at the bottom of this brook.

Wildlife

The buzzards are the main feathered attraction. They begin to arrive in early March (not all at once on Buzzard's Day) from their winter homes, which may be as close as Kentucky or as far away as South America.

The Hinckley Reservation provides an ideal nesting and feeding habitat for this bird. Buzzards lay their eggs on the bare ground of ledges, in recess caves, in hollow trees or at the base of trees growing on the walls of cliffs, or in thickets. The open fields and forest here make suitable hunting grounds. Buzzards fly on warm currents of rising air called thermals which develop above fields.

While they may not be the most beautiful bird, buzzards do have their attributes. Here are some facts about buzzards:

- They dine on death, meaning they pick flesh from the corpses of raccoons, ground hogs, snakes, skunks, turkeys, birds, fish, mice. . . even humans. Not a pretty sight, but as scavengers they hasten nature's process of decay. If starving, vultures may attack small animals, but never humans.
- Buzzards can live as long as 20 years.
- This common bird usually soars at altitudes less than 200 feet when hunting, but when migrating they have been observed at 5,000 feet.
- Buzzards do not have a voice box. They communicate by hissing and grunting. Even though hawks screech while flying, buzzards fly silently.
- To distinguish turkey vultures from hawks while they are airborne, look at the shape of their wing span. A buzzard's six-foot wing span forms a shallow V; the wings of eagles and most hawks are flat.
- Both parents incubate the eggs for a total of 40 days. The young birds are on their own in late August.

Beside buzzards, pheasant and bobwhite quail nest in the meadows. Hinckley Lake and two other ponds attract various species of waterfowl. I observed a great blue heron, wood ducks, mallards, gulls, a yellow warbler, and a belted kingfisher on my walk. White-eyed vireo and the parula warbler, uncommon in northeastern Ohio I have been told, have been identified here.

Hinckley Reservation is 73% forested, a much larger percentage of woods than when it was established more than 60 years ago. Oak, hickory, and white ash grow on the drier, higher ground on top of the ledges, but on the slopes you will find beech and sugar maple communities (mixed with some black cherry), followed by red maple on lower slopes, and sycamore and cottonwood (some huge specimens) in the floodplain.

An impressive stand of chinkapin oak grows on the northeast bank of Hinckley Lake. Stands of various pines and spruces have been planted throughout the reservation. Ginseng, a threatened plant in Ohio, and ostrich fern, uncommon in these parts, thrive here.

Hinckley Lake supports largemouth bass, northern pike, channel catfish, bluegill, white and black crappie, bullhead, and sucker.

History

Today, the Hinckley Reservation is known as a place that protects animals. But for more than a century the area was remembered for the Great Hinckley Hunt, a massacre really, that occurred on Christmas Eve in 1818.

Maddened by wolf and bear attacks on livestock, 600 armed men and boys surrounded the township and slowly closed the noose, killing just about everything that moved on four legs (except hunting dogs) or flew. The exterminators killed 300 deer, 21 bears, just 17 wolves, and many turkeys, foxes, and raccoons. Some versions of the story claim buzzards swooped down on the carcasses, but that is unlikely because the birds would have migrated south by Christmas time. The animal carcasses were divided among the participants.

A gruesome tale of attempted murder surrounds Whipp's Ledges. Robert Whipp came to Hinckley from England in 1848, and, bit by bit, purchased 2,000 acres in the township, including the sandstone cliffs that take his name. However, Whipp's second wife (30 years his junior), her lover, and her brother tried to strangle Whipp with a rope one night. The wife, who had just married Whipp, and her conspirators probably sought the title to his vast land holdings. Whipp survived the attack. His wife and her brother went to jail; the unidentified lover stayed free.

In the 1920s, Hinckley resident George Emmett sought to preserve "the Switzerland of America," an enthusiastic description of the land that he wanted to include in the Emerald Necklace. John F. Johnson joined Emmett's cause and donated 236 acres, 100 of which comprised Hinckley Lake. The East Branch of the Rocky River was dammed in 1926 to create the lake.

Hinckley Reservation harbored another kind of "buzzard," an eccentric named Noble Stuart, a bricklayer, stone mason, and ledge sculptor. Nettie Worden, the daughter of the original landowner, Hiram Worden, was 82 years old when she took Noble Stuart as her third husband.

From 1945–55, in the ledges behind the Worden house, Stuart carved the faces of George Washington, Thomas Jefferson, and baseball great Ty Cobb, as well as a clipper ship, a sphinx, and a Bible with an inscription *IS ALL*. Back at the house, he carved a crucifix, an Indian toting a tomahawk and knife, as well as Romulus and Remus, the mythical founders of Rome.

Everybody thought Nettie's brother, Frank Worden, a monument maker, did the carving, and for awhile the bashful Noble did not let on that he was the artist. Nowadays, such artistry would land you in jail. A trail to the ledges starts at the Worden Heritage Homestead, managed by the Hinckley Historical Society. To get there, turn right from West Drive on to State Road, then right on Ledge Road.

In 1954, state highway planners wanted to build Interstate 71 right over Hinckley Lake and through Whipp's Ledges. Like vultures circling the statehouse, conservationists besieged Governor Frank Lausche with pleas to save the park. They succeeded, and I-71 was moved west around the ledges and the buzzards' roosts.

Cleveland Press reporter Robert Bordner is credited as Hinckley's first buzzard booster. He observed the annual return of the birds in 1957 and inspired hundreds of humans see them in the park. Watching the vultures soon became a tradition.

Two-tailed swallowtail

MILL STREAM RUN RESERVATION

Mill Stream Run, once known as The Gully, has sliced a small and not so scenic gorge through ancient sea beds on its way to the East Branch of the Rocky River. Once the trees leaf, you hardly see the ravine on the hard-to-follow, fast-eroding, and poorly designed trails in this metropark.

Location

Southwestern Cuyahoga County, near Strongsville.

The trails departing from the entrance to the Royalview Picnic Area are described below. This part of the reservation is located off Interstate 71 at the Strongsville/State Route 82 exit. Travel east on SR 82 about a mile, turn right on Valley Parkway, and then right on Royalview Lane (look for the sign) and park in the small two-car lot just over the bridge, on the left, before Royalview Lane bends right.

Ownership

Cleveland Metroparks.

Size & Designation

Mill Stream Run Reservation totals 2,307 acres. The reservation was dedicated in 1976.

Nearby Natural Attractions

Mill Stream Run is one of 12 reservations in the Cleveland Metroparks system, called the "Emerald Necklace."

Access

Several trails wander through the Royalview section of the park. The two best trails (meaning the easiest ones to discern) begin at the parking lot near the entrance. A post, marking the trailhead of a cross-country skiing path, is at the edge of the woods.

A compass might be useful on these walks. Mountain bike ruts tell you are on the right track, though some of them stray off the beaten path.

Trail #1 measures three miles and makes a loop which ends at the entrance bridge, just 100 yards from the trailhead. Trail #2 goes to the picnic area and back, covering nearly two miles.

Follow the path into the woods, staying on the widest and most worn path. In a few hundred yards the trail reaches a crossroads. Trail #1 continues straight (south). Trail #2 goes to right. More on Trail #2 later.

Trail #1 heads south and ascends a ridge that separates Mill Stream Run on the right and a smaller unnamed tributary on the left. Look for a vista on the right where the ridge becomes narrow. The path slowly climbs through woods and reaches the edge of another ridge about a mile into the walk.

At the ruins of an old sugarhouse, the trail turns left (east), crosses a gully, and reaches an oil well. A lane to the right heads south to Drake Road, but you must continue (straight) east. (This spot reportedly is favored by deer, though I did not see any.) Soon, after sloshing across another gully, the trail bends left (north). This marks the highest elevation on the trail, 990 feet, just 170 feet higher than the Rocky River.

Ahead, walk through an old field to a large, hollow white oak at the edge of a ravine. (Hopefully, the old tree still stands.) The trail follows the creek bed before climbing the bank. (A side trail circles into the field on the left and returns to the ravine.) You will probably notice more tire tracks on the trail.

The remaining mile descends slowly north through woods, climbing in and out of a few gullies. When you cross a wooden bridge you are just a few hundred yards from the Rocky River and the bridge at the entrance, the end of this journey.

Trail #2 turns right (west) off Trail #1 at the intersection noted above and heads southwest. Just after the split, it crosses Mill Stream Run, wanders through a stand of pines, then traces a hardwood ridge which overlooks the park's namesake on your left. The trail emerges from the woods near the shelterhouse of the picnic area. Drinking water and toilets are available here. Retrace your steps to the parking lot.

Before driving away, I recommend a stroll along the river. The narrow path begins at the bridge. Unlike the hillside you have just hiked, the soil on the river bank is sandy. In the warm months, quiet walkers may see turtles resting on logs, or great blue herons (bothered more by humans than car traffic) fishing.

Sturdy boots are recommended because the trails are muddy and cross ravines. The terrain, however, is not difficult (though climbing some ravines requires exertion). Essentially, on Trail #2, you climb up a gentle slope, and back down.

A favorite winter attraction at the reservation is The Chalet, a pair of 1,000-foot-long toboggan chutes. In summer, swimmers should head for Wallace Lake. Both attractions are north of these hiking trails.

Geology

Mill Stream Run is one of many currents running perpendicular from the East Branch of the Rocky River. The run has washed away glacial till dropped here 10,000–12,000 years ago by the Wisconsinan ice mass, and exposed bedrock layers of shale and sandstone which began as ocean floors more than 300 million years ago during the Mississippian geologic period.

A slice of this gritty layer cake can be seen on a steep bank of the run about 200 hundreds yards behind the restrooms in the picnic area. Here thin bands of blue-gray siltstone, called Meadville shale, sit atop a strata of

Strongsville sandstone, named after the nearby city. Downstream in the reservation, Rocky River scours over Orangeville shale, a soft, gray crumbly rock. Look for this formation near the Bagley Road (north) entrance.

Winter is the best time to see how the river and the runs have worked the terrain. The floodplain is wide and flat, and when the water rushing down the hillside in tributaries reaches the bottom land, it loses velocity and lets fine grains of sand and clay settle. This erosive action enables wildlife, which thrives in sandy, wet floodplains, to move in.

During the spring flood season the river and the runs overflow their regular banks and follow new channels. Look for these auxiliary channels in the floodplain stage (exposed, dusty tree roots are clues). Large trees that fall into tiny tributaries trap sediments and create a diversion that could change the course of the rill and the distribution of soil and wildlife.

Wildlife

The reservation is a quilt of fragments: here a mature forest of tall oaks; there a habitat for cottonwoods and sycamores; yonder, pines planted decades ago losing their turf to encroaching hardwoods; and elsewhere, saplings of many species compete for space on a hillside that has been hunted, lumbered, farmed, and grazed over the last two centuries.

Fields that were once farmed by human pioneers now sponsor the plant pioneers who will begin the task of changing the land back into a forest. These meadows are undergoing succession, nature's eternal process of returning the land, in stages, to its original state as a hardwood forest.

Mill Stream Run safeguards a threatened wildflower, blunt mountain mint, found in the meadows. North of the run's "run in" with the river, near a grove of pawpaw trees (themselves uncommon in northeastern Ohio), a rare blossom called green dragon, often confused with jack-in-the-pulpit, grows in soggy soil. A green dragon fully unsheathes its pointed "tongue" and extends it several inches, whereas jack-in-the-pulpit just slightly reveals his bitter barb beneath its hood.

Come August, sharp-eyed flower finders can look for nodding ladies' tresses, a small, creamy-white orchid in the damp meadows. On Trail #l, look for wood betony, a kinder name for the lousewort, growing beside a small field near the hollow tree landmark. A healthy community of marsh marigolds (cowslip) emerges in mid-April or early May near the wooden bridge.

You must walk through the meadows during the summer for the butterflies—dozens of varieties, flying about as if confetti rained from the sky. A two-tailed swallowtail landed on me by mistake by the picnic ground. It did not stay long. I had little to offer in the way of food, and my fragrance resembled a livestock pen more than a shadbush blossom, its eventual target.

Birdwatchers know the Rocky River valley is a major corridor for migratory waterfowl and forest birds (warblers). But I had more fun watching some permanent residents engaging in one of nature's jousts. Halfway down the hillside on Trail #2 a bunch of crows shrieked and fussed in the treetops. They were harassing a barred owl. I watched for a moment and saw that the owl was getting the worst of it. So, I clapped my hands. The crows scattered west, the owl, wisely, chose an easterly flight pattern.

If you are lucky you might see a woodcock rising in a field. This game bird, remembered more for its springtime aerial acrobatics than its taste, is trying to make a comeback in Ohio.

History

Farmers and woodsmen found artifacts in these ravines left behind by Indians who lived here 1,000 years ago. The Indians probably hunted game on the hillside and fished in the river. The Erie nation inhabited the area until marauding Iroquois warriors drove them out in 1660. In the mid-18th century Shawnee, Delaware, and Wyandot Indians shared the forests and streams.

White settlers arrived in the early 19th century—families named Sanderson, Southard, Wheller, and Clement. They built farms, a canal, a hamlet, and mills for sawing wood and making wagons, furniture, and baskets. For a while, the town that grew up at the crossroads of Drake and Hunt roads was called Sanderson's Corners, honoring Allison Sanderson, a mill owner. Another small mill town, Slab Hollow, on Howe Road, took its name from the slabs of rock that littered the creeks in the hollows. By the Civil War, steam had replaced running water as a source of power and the mills closed.

Local folks knew this tributary of the Rocky River simply as The Gully. But this name was not suitable for a park in a pastoral suburban setting, so officials came up with Mill Stream Run (ignoring the redundancy of using *stream* and *run* in the name). It became a gem in the *Emerald Necklace* in 1976. The park honors the early mill owners.

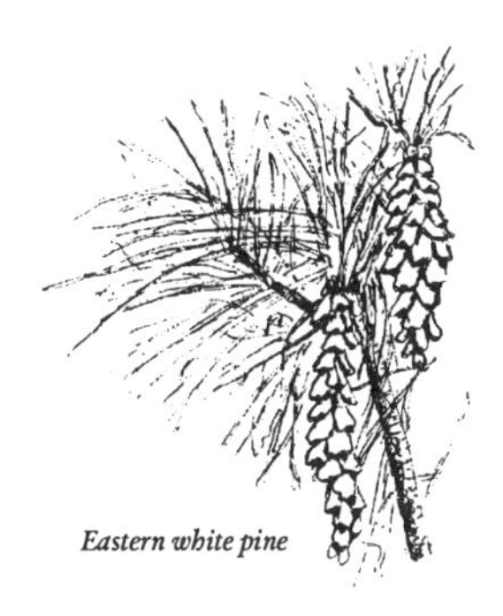
Eastern white pine

NORTH CHAGRIN RESERVATION

Diversity and abundance. The trails in this Cleveland Metropark journey to hemlock-lined ravines, a castle built by a wanna-be English "squire," a beech forest designated a national treasure, a marsh and a river lagoon, a virgin white pine forest, a wildlife sanctuary, oxbows, and the ruins of the nation's first outdoor nature center.

Location

The reservation straddles the boundaries of Cuyahoga and Lake counties and is bounded by the Chagrin River (east), and State Route 6 (Chardon Road) and State Route 91 (SOM Center Road).

Leave Interstate 90 at the exit for Willoughby and State Route 91. Travel on SR 91 south for about a mile, then turn left (east) on SR 6 to the entrance on the right. Take the Buttermilk Falls Parkway to the parking lot at Sanctuary Marsh Nature Center.

Ownership

Cleveland Metroparks.

Size & Designation

The reservation totals 1,912 acres, most of it wooded. The Dr. Arthur B. Williams Memorial Woods has been designated a National Natural Landmark by the U.S. Department of the Interior.

Nearby Natural Attractions

North Chagrin Reservation is one of 12 sites owned by Cleveland Metroparks. The other reservations reviewed in this book are Hinckley (Medina County), South Chagrin, Mill Stream Run, Brecksville, Bedford, Big Creek (Lake Isaac), and Rocky River.

Hach-Otis State Nature Preserve, in Lake County, is just a few miles north of the reservation. In Lake County, you will also find The Holden Arboretum, Chapin Forest Reserve and Penitentiary Glen Metroparks (Lake County), Headlands Dunes and Mentor Marsh state nature preserves, and Headlands Beach State Park.

Access

Sanctuary Marsh Nature Center is centrally located for trails which explore both the northern and southern halves of the reservation. Exhibits in the center explain some of the natural history in the park. Grab a trail map there and guides to certain trails. Restrooms, drinking fountains, and a bookstore called "Earthwords" are located at the center.

The reservation map shows a tangle of trails that only the swiftest sprinter could cover in a day. But we are not in a hurry.

Visitors with limited time can stroll on a trio of brief loop trails—Sanctuary Marsh, Buttermilk Falls, and Wildlife Management—in the Sunset Wildlife Preserve, all near the nature center. (A detailed map of these paths is on the flip side of the reservation map.) The Sanctuary Marsh Trail and All-Purpose Trail (which traces the perimeter of Sunset Wildlife Preserve) are accessible to folks traveling in wheelchairs and strollers.

Folks with big chunks of time can shadow the following paths, or concoct their own. I took the boardwalk across Sanctuary Marsh then lit out for Buttermilk Falls, a bridal-veil-type cascade sprawling over black Cleveland shale. Unfortunately, the scene is scarred by the ill-placed footpath crossing above it. More amazing than the falls is the hairpin bend, or oxbow, that the lanky stream has sculpted out of the bedrock.

The Buttermilk Falls Trail ends at the parkway. Cross the road bridge (look at the oxbow first), then cross the road and walk north (left) a short distance. The entrance to the Hemlock Trail appears on the right berm of the road.

For most of its 1.75-mile distance, the Hemlock Trail traces the bluff of the gorge of Buttermilk Falls Creek, at your right. The path is wide and clearly marked by yellow metal blazes on trees. A bridle trail will be at your left.

As its name suggests, hemlocks preside on the rim of the gorge. You also will walk through an impressive beech-maple forest, and into a few ravines. Before it ends near the Strawberry Pond parking area, the Hemlock Trail crosses the bridle path and joins the Squire's Lane Trail, which heads east led by blue metal blazes (not to be confused with painted blue bars of the Buckeye Trail in the south half of the reservation).

This .75-mile path was used by Feargus B. Squire when he supervised the construction of his weekend retreat. It ends at the Squire's Castle, a good place to rest, picnic, and stretch out on the lawn in front of this miniature English-style castle. Of course, you should snoop around the "castle." (An offshoot from the Squire's Lane Trail, the White Pine Trail, visits one of the last virgin white pine stands in Ohio.)

Now hike the Castle Valley Trail south following white blazes with a castle logo. The trail passes near the River Grove Winter Sports Area and picnic grounds. Just before reaching Ox Lane, it intersects with a bridle path. Here you can turn right (west) and take the bridle path along Ox Lane back to Buttermilk Falls and the nature center, *or* cross the road, wander into the A.B. Williams Memorial Woods, connecting with the Overlook, Sylvan, and Buckeye trails. You will also run into the paved path that returns to the nature center. The journey described above totals at least five miles.

The Overlook and Sylvan trails are interconnecting loop trails in the southern half of the park that visit the Arthur B. Williams Memorial Woods, an undisturbed and enduring beech-maple forest that has been declared a National Natural Landmark by the U.S. Department of the Interior. Self-guiding trail brochures are available for these paths at the nature center.

From Sanctuary Marsh, head east across the parking lot, Buttermilk Falls Parkway, the Forest Picnic Area, and into the woods. The Buckeye Trail soon enters from the right. In a few paces, the Sylvan Trail (yellow blazes) appears on the right. Ignore it for now and keeping walking. The Overlook Trail soon curves to the left. Follow the orange blazes with the bird logo.

A bronze plaque stamped into a granite boulder that was orphaned by the Wisconsinan glacier 10,000 years ago commemorates the landmark and Dr. Williams, the first naturalist for the Cleveland Metroparks. Notice that hemlocks also grow in this beech-maple community. Just beyond this, at a right turn in the trail, the Castle Valley Trail enters the woods. Ahead, look for a log shelterhouse that faces a ravine formed by a tributary of the Chagrin River. I have been told that, in winter, the flat summit of Chapin Forest Reservation (Lake Metroparks), a.k.a. Gildersleeve Mountain, can be seen five miles away.

The Overlook Trail crosses the Buckeye Trail and a bridle path before running into an open area that was the site of the nation's first outdoor nature center, according to Cleveland Metroparks. Several steps beyond, you will take the Sylvan Trail (a half-mile loop) with yellow shields and a maple leaf.

Refer to the Sylvan Trail guide. After crossing the wooden bridge, look for a tall tulip tree, then the cucumber tree sporting the largest leaves among the hardwoods (resembling tobacco leaves), and the Moses Cleaveland Tree (a sugar maple at least 200 years old).

The Chagrin River valley smiles a mile-wide at signpost six. Then you must pay reverence to a tree that absorbed its first sunray when Columbus stepped on the beach of Hispanola—a 500-year-old tupelo, or sour gum. Its deeply-ridged bark, a mark of wisdom were it a human face, reflects the ravages of time. The trail concludes at the path that returns to the starting point.

For those who want to walk the Buckeye Trail (I did not, this time), it travels through the southern half of the park. Beginning at the parking lot near the Wilson Mills Road entrance to the reservation, the Buckeye Trail shares a bridle path that runs alongside Buttermilk Falls Parkway as far as the Forest Picnic Area. Then it goes east through the A.B. Williams Memorial Forest, turns north at Ox Lane, then leaves the park via Rogers Road.

All the trails described above are easy to follow, wide, smooth, and only moderately challenging. For example, young parents toured the Hemlock Trail pushing their baby in a stroller; another father pulled twins in a wagon. The Hemlock and Castle Valley trails are the most strenuous in the group I hiked.

Nature programs for all age groups are held throughout the year at the nature center and adjacent nature education building. Call the nature center at (216) 473-3370 for a schedule.

The reservation has five picnic areas (two reservable), winter sports areas, and a paved all-purpose trail which is accessible to handicapped visitors.

Geology

The Chagrin River winds northward along the east boundary of the preserve. When you explore the reservation, drive along the Chagrin River Road and notice the sweeping turns in the river. The pond at Squire's Castle and the lagoons across the road once formed an "oxbow," or a bend in the river shaped like a thin-necked human head. One day the current breached the neck and formed a new channel. The abandoned, or decapitated, oxbow became a pond, recharged every so often by a flood or runoff from nearby slopes. Other oxbows are along the road, though most are marshes.

For centuries the river and its ravine-forming tributaries have been eating away till (gravel, sand, clay, etc.) left behind by the Wisconsinan glacier some 12,000 years ago. The soil is known as Volusia clay loam, an unproductive turf for agricultural crops, which may explain why the big trees here still stand.

At Buttermilk Falls, the creek has gnawed down to the bone–black Cleveland shale–and shaped a charming, bending, and steep gorge visible from the Buttermilk Falls, Hemlock, and Hickory Fox trails. The gorge is maybe 100–120 feet deep. Other trails visit east-running ravines too, but the one at Buttermilk Falls is the most dramatic.

The Cleveland (or Ohio) shale washed by the falls is about 350 million years old. It is made of tiny bits of quartz, mica, and clay, as well as decayed plant material which gives the rock its black color. The deposit once was the bed of a shallow sea, perhaps a few feet deep and prone to receiving fallen and rotting plants.

Wildlife

North Chagrin Reservation may be best known for its huge trees and the late-blooming naturalist who matured under their limbs.

Arthur B. Williams was 56 years old when he became the first naturalist for the Cleveland Metroparks in 1930. Before that the Yale-educated Williams, a New Jersey native, had toiled in the real estate business, perhaps for 20 years. He also had studied law.

But nature became his game later in life. In 1931, Williams opened what is believed to be the first trailside museum in the U.S. in the middle of the ancient forest that now carries his name. Two years later he told the park board, "Here on the very edge of the old Appalachian plateau, under these great beech and sugar maple trees, are to be found perhaps a greater profusion of early spring wildflowers than in any other of the park reserves. The fact that the forest has been left undisturbed, means also that birds and other animals live here in great numbers–at certain times seeming to occupy every available niche."

In 1935, he received his Ph.D. from Western Reserve University. His thesis was based on his in-depth study of the beech-maple-hemlock forest at North Chagrin. (You might obtain a copy from the Cleveland Museum of Natural History.)

Williams retired in 1950, and died the next year. The park board immediately dedicated a portion of the beech-maple-hemlock forest in his honor. Twenty-three years later Williams again was saluted when the U.S. Department of the Interior designated his beloved forest a National Natural Landmark.

Enough of hardwoods. The reservation also protects one of only a handful of untouched white pine forests in the state. (Take the White Pine Trail off the Squire's Loop Trail to see it.) This "softwood" was prized for ships' masts in the 18th and 19th centuries, but somehow, to our good fortune, the axemen missed this stand.

The park, of course, attracts the usual collection of birds–owls, hawks, warblers, bluebirds, woodpeckers, etc. I have learned on the sly that the prothonotary warbler, which every birder wants to mark off on the checklist, is often seen in a spot the locals call "The Swamp," south of the merger of Ox Lane and Chagrin River Road. Look for tree swallows there too.

Geese, ducks, and other waterfowl favor Sanctuary Marsh and Sunset Pond near the nature center. The boardwalk which spans the marsh is a great lookout, as is the observation deck on the southeast shore of Sunset Pond. You are apt to observe frogs, turtles, water lilies, and all sorts of dragonflies from these vantage points.

History

The pint-sized palace called Squire's Castle was supposed to be the digs of the gatekeeper who would guard the real mansion Feargus B. Squire wanted to build in the forest out back. Squire's Lane Trail traces the path to this would-be castle.

Instead, the stone house became a weekend retreat for Squire, an English-born oilman whose rags-to-riches determination earned him a vice-presidency at Standard Oil of Ohio, along with Frank Rockefeller, brother of company founder John D. Rockefeller. The "castle" had several small bedrooms, living areas, a large kitchen with a porch, and the master's library or "hunting" room. The stone for the castle was quarried from the 525 acres he had acquired.

Squire, a quiet and aloof man, supposedly enjoyed the solitude of his country rookery. "Supposedly" because rumors claim the Squire's solitude–self-imposed or not–stemmed from his wife's refusal to establish a home so far from the social and cultural world of Cleveland. Anyway, Squire gave up the place after he retired in 1909. But he did erect that dream castle–Cobblestone Garth–in Wickliffe next to all the others on Millionaire's Row. Squire sold the property in 1922. Three years later Cleveland Metroparks bought it as the focus for North Chagrin Reservation.

Journal

Summer, 1993. A.B. Williams did not become a naturalist until age 56, proving again that you can teach an old dog new tricks—or that new life springs from old bark.

Bittersweet nightshade

ROCKY RIVER RESERVATION

The Rocky River has spent the last 12,000 years carving an Olympic bobsled trail through this reservation. In doing so, it has unearthed the creatures that lived here long before the dinosaurs.

The ancient people who settled along the river repelled aggressors behind fortifications they built on the heights. Surely they were struck by the beauty too, and considered dying to defend their land. This was their holy place.

Location

Western Cuyahoga County, stretching from Lake Erie to the Ohio Turnpike. This guide focuses on the trails around the nature interpretation center in the north Rocky River Reservation.

To get there, exit Interstate 480 at Grayton Road and go south toward Hopkins Airport. Turn right at the traffic signal on to Brookpark Road, then drive past the Lewis Research Center and the across the bridge. Continue on Brookpark Road, turn left on Clague Road, then right on Mastick Road. The entrance to the reservation, Shepard Lane, will appear on the left in about a half mile. Shepard Lane descends into the valley and ends at Valley Parkway. Turn right on this road, then right again into the parking lot of the nature center.

Ownership

Cleveland Metroparks.

Size & Designation

Rocky River Reservation is the largest jewel in the Emerald Necklace, encompassing 3,432 acres.

Nearby Natural Attractions

Rocky River is one of 12 sites in the Cleveland Metroparks network. The other reservations included here are Mill Stream Run, Big Creek (Lake Isaac), Brecksville, Bedford, Hinckley, North Chagrin, and South Chagrin.

Access

Begin your visit at the nature center which has exhibits on wildlife, fossils, and geology. Kids will especially enjoy "Dunk," the 20-foot-long reproduction of a dunkleosteous, a prehistoric shark. (More on Dunk later.) Step onto the observation deck for an introduction to the steep cliffs and the river, which flows beneath the porch. Restrooms and drinking water are available.

Before leaving, pick up the Woodlands Trails brochure describing four nearby trails, and the Fort Hill guide if you intend to hike this trail. Both are at the reception desk.

The Fort Hill Trail climbs to the top of the bluff you just observed from the deck. From the nature center, take the path blazed with an arrowhead on red (Fort Hill Trail) and a duck on blue (West Channel Pond Trail). It heads left along the edge of West Channel Pond. At the far end of the pond, bear left at the "Y" and follow the red blazes up a steep slope aided by three sets of stairs. There are benches to give weary bodies places to rest or to observe the wildlife.

When you scale the summit you will have climbed 90 feet and reached the same altitude as downtown Cleveland. In June, thankfully, the leaves obscure the skyscrapers. Follow the trail to the edge of the cliff where the view is refreshing and inspiring.

The Indian earthworks are located on the triangular eastern tip of the hill. Look for three rolls or waves in the ground. Return to the nature center by descending the stairway.

The Fort Hill Trail is 1.3 miles long. Climbing the cliff is dangerous and prohibited. Signs warning visitors of the hazards have been defaced or removed and should be replaced.

Now stroll on the other half of the West Channel Pond Trail and the flat Wildlife Management Trail, measuring 1.5 miles. Again, follow the blue blazes of the West Channel Pond, this time on the east side of the pond, past the intersection with the Mt. Pleasant Trail (yellow blazes), to the brown blazes of the Wildlife Management Trail. Deer tracks appear on the brown blazes.

This easy, wide path heads straight west past a pond, the Pilger Amphitheater, a service road, and on to an intersection with a path arriving from the left. This is the Wildlife Management Trail completing its rectangular-shaped loop. You will return to this spot whichever path you follow. The trail draws a rectangle, goes past a cattail marsh, a small pond, a meadow, an old orchard, a grove of staghorn sumac, and pine stands. Backtrack to the starting point.

The lasso-shaped Mt. Pleasant Trail (yellow blazes with the outline of pines) heads north off the West Channel Pond Trail. It crosses Shepard Lane, and climbs Mt. Pleasant. The loop begins after the first set of stairs. Return to the nature center after completing the loop. This walk measures 1.5 miles.

I also recommend the bridle trail, running along the river east of Valley Parkway. Take off your shoes and wade in the river. (Swimming is forbidden, but wading is okay.) Many folks park at nearby Cedar Point Picnic Area and strike out for Arrowhead Island, seen from the deck at the nature center.

Visitors in wheelchairs can negotiate the trail through the Ron Hauser Memorial Wildflower Garden, located between the nature center and the parking lot, or the paved All-Purpose Trail.

Energetic hikers can traipse south several miles via the All-Purpose or bridle trails to Berea Falls, or you can drive there. Here the East Branch of the Rocky River tumbles over sandstone aptly named Berea sandstone.

Geology

The Rocky River is a ribbon of erosion, neatly exposing chunks of ancient ocean beds and more than 300 million years of geological history from its source in Summit County (East Branch) to its mouth at Lake Erie.

In the Hinckley Reservation (northeast Medina County), the river has uncovered thick layers of Sharon conglomerate, a pebbly sandstone a mere 300 million years old. Downstream, winding through Mill Stream Run Reservation, it has revealed Meadville shale (thin-layered, gray-colored), Strongsville sandstone, and Orangeville shale which easily crumbles. These former ocean floors go back roughly 330 million years (late Mississippian geologic period).

At Berea Falls (Rocky River South Reservation), the river falls over a fat layer of gray Berea sandstone composed of tiny quartz grains cemented by clay. The sand was probably deposited in a shallow sea in a delta-like pattern by currents washing off higher ground to the north and east. The formation is cross-bedded (arc-like, or criss-cross deposits), and shows the direction of the shifting currents that carried the sediments to their positions.

Berea sandstone resists erosion. That cannot be said of the reddish shale (Bedford formation) beneath it. The backsplash of the waterfall keeps eating away the softer shale, a process called undercutting, and forms a recess cave beneath the sandstone. Eventually, huge chunks of unsupported sandstone will fall into the river. Undercutting occurs on the banks of the river too. The river earned its name from the sandstone boulders at the bottom of Berea Falls.

Alongside the nature center, the current flows over Cleveland shale, flaky and almost black in color because it holds a lot of decayed matter. The floor of the shallow sea that covered this area 350 million years ago (late Devonian Period) must have been a black, slimy ooze. Before it empties into Lake Erie, the river washes over older rock called Chagrin shale, created perhaps 360 million years ago.

Today, the east and west branches of the Rocky River merge at Cedar Point Road, a half mile south of the nature center. Years ago, however, the west branch looped westerly and joined the east branch a little farther downstream, probably near Shepard Lane. West Channel Pond and the ponds and marshes that you see along the Wildlife Management Trail were once the path of the west branch.

A thin strip of land once connected Fort Hill with Cedar Point Hill to the south. The west branch eventually washed over this barrier and was pulled into the channel of the east branch. This action is called stream piracy. Vegetation moved into the abandoned loop which has evolved into a wetland of ponds and marshes. The old channel would be refreshed from time to time when the river overflowed its bank during floods. An impoundment built by metroparks in the 1970s controls the water level in this vacated channel.

Wildlife

Long before dinosaurs there was "Dunk," a bone-plated bottom-feeding arthodire. Dunk, short for Dunkleosteous terrelli, was king of the Devonian sea some 400 million years ago. Dunk reached lengths of 45–50 feet. The shark feasted on crustaceans.

Dunk's fossilized remains turned up in the Cleveland shale cliff upstream from the nature center and others like him in other locations in northern Ohio. A replica of the beast hangs in the nature center.

The Rocky River valley is an important corridor for migrating birds—various ducks, and warblers. Green, great blue, black-crowned, and yellow-crowned herons have been observed here, along with spotted sandpipers and red-breasted nuthatches, the latter a rarity in these parts. The bluffs on the Fort Hill Trail and the meadow and marsh on the Wildlife Management Trail are prime birding spots.

In the Ron Hauser Memorial Wildflower Garden, named for a local resident who was fond of the wildflowers in the reservation, look for red and white baneberry, foam flower, turtlehead, Soloman's seal, false rue anemone, Jacob's ladder, and seven types of ferns. The garden is located next to the nature center.

Elsewhere, you will find blossoms such as bittersweet nightshade, Dutchman's breeches, wild ginger, Virginia bluebells, jack-in-the-pulpit, blue cohosh, yellow adder's tongue, and others.

Trees typically found in the floodplain (sycamore, willow, cottonwood), on slopes (red oak, sugar maples), in shady areas (beech), and ridge tops (oak and hickory) grow in abundance here.

Ohio buckeye trees and black maple, uncommon around here, also grow in the bottomland. Pines and spruces planted 60 years ago have matured and live in groves scattered throughout the reservation. Wild black cherry and various locusts thrive in large numbers.

History

Native Americans (Whittlesey Tradition) lived on this site, perhaps from 1000–1640. They lived in the valley, farmed the floodplain, and used the river for fishing and transportation. Arrowheads, bannerstones, and other artifacts of these people have been unearthed in the area.

Fort Hill and Mt. Pleasant became places for defense, worship, and perhaps burial. Fort Hill may have been impregnable for a time. The fortifications on the hill are located where the two branches of the river pinched. The strip of land between the streams may have been only 30–50 feet wide. Because the hill was nearly surrounded by 90-foot vertical slopes, attackers had to advance up this heavily defended, steep-sided isthmus. Battles also may have been fought on Mt. Pleasant, where a suspected burial mound is located.

The Erie tribe also settled here. They may have abandoned the site after stream piracy (see Geology) made Fort Hill vulnerable, or when Iroquois warriors drove them off during the colonial period.

White settlers attracted to the river's water power began arriving in the early 19th century. The names of nearby roads remind us of these pioneers. James Ruple (Ruple Road) and seven brothers dug in here. Calvin and Charlotte Spafford (Spafford Road joins Ruble Road south of the nature center) were related to Amos Spafford, a member of Moses Cleaveland's surveying team. The ruins of Joel Lawrence's grist mill, built in 1832, can be seen across the street from the Cedar Point Picnic Area. Lawrence was a constable in 1827.

The Frostville Museum on Cedar Point Road depicts the life of these early settlers. You can walk to the museum, run by the Olmstead Historical Society ({216} 777-0059), on a service road from the southeast corner of the Wildlife Management Trail.

Gen. William Tecumseh Sherman visited the valley after the Civil War and declared it was as beautiful as the most scenic valleys in Europe.

In the 1910s, businessmen with homes overlooking the river began a campaign to protect the area from commercial and industrial exploitation. This led to the creation in 1912 of a county park board, the predecessor of the Cleveland Metropolitan Park Board of 1915. That year Frederick Law Olmstead, son of the country's most renowned landscape architect, explored Rocky River for the board.

In 1951, the park board battled the Ohio Turnpike Commission, which planned to route the Ohio Turnpike through the reservation. A compromise reached the following year moved the turnpike north, saving a mature forest and limiting destruction to the reservation.

Downy woodpecker

SOUTH CHAGRIN RESERVATION

Late at night, when nobody was looking, Henry Church, a blacksmith and spiritualist, crept down to the Chagrin River and chiseled figures in the sandstone wall that faced the river. Was he talking to the ghost of an Indian maiden, or just retouching the gorge with a few strokes of his file? Try as he did, this early graffiti artist could not improve on the beauty the Chagrin River has sculpted over the millennia.

Location

Southeastern Cuyahoga County, near Bentleyville.

Leave Interstate 271 at the exit for U.S. Route 422 and travel east. Turn left on the Hawthorn Parkway which deadends at the Squaw Rock Picnic Area.

Ownership

Cleveland Metroparks.

Size & Designation

South Chagrin Reservation totals 1,879 acres. The Chagrin River carries the state scenic river designation.

Nearby Natural Attractions

South Chagrin Reservation is one of the gems in the Emerald Necklace, a chain of parks managed by Cleveland Metroparks. The other reservations reviewed in this book are North Chagrin, Bedford, Hinckley, Big Creek (Lake Isaac), Mill Stream Run, Rocky River, and Brecksville.

Access

The mile-long journey to Squaw Rock, the site of Henry Church's clandestine carving, slides down a hemlock-rimmed gorge with high sandstone walls to a charming waterfall, and through dark and secluded ravines and shelter caves once used by ancient people.

Study the trail map at the end of the parking lot before departing. I followed the "low road" to the waterfalls where on a hot summer day visitors cool off by wading in the stream. Farther upstream, you will arrive at the famous Squaw Rock. Ahead, the trail stops at a rocky porch.

At this spot the little boy in me took over and I hopped into the river and stepped on stones upstream to another cascade, which can be reached from the Quarry Rock Picnic Area off Liberty Road.

Use the steps behind the porch to start the climb out of the steep ravine. En route to the rim, a gap in the trail appears at a ravine. You will have to cross this rugged little canyon to resume the journey. This part of the hike can be tricky and difficult, so be careful.

At the junction at the top, follow the worn path to the right if you want to return to the car. There is a brief loop trail at the left that goes around a pond. The main trail winds through hemlocks and oaks back to the parking lot. You will find restrooms and picnic tables there.

Another short, pleasant hike begins from a parking lot on the road to Sulfur Springs Picnic Area. Go west on Hawthorne Parkway, then right (north) on Sulfur Springs Drive. Turn into the drive for the Sulfur Springs and park in the small lot on the left near the entrance (not in the picnic area). Follow the bridle trail at the right which heads south through hardwoods. This path also is the Buckeye Trail (blue blazes). Near the Hawthorne Parkway, the trail curves north and descends into a valley. Near the bottom of the hill, look for a narrow footpath to the right with a sign that forbids horses on it. This thin trail follows Sulfur Springs Brook to a tiny waterfall in the Sulfur Springs Picnic Area. Kids will love wading and exploring the stream at this location.

Now, go to the far end of the picnic area and see the spectacular oxbow bend the creek has meticulously chiseled from shale. Return to the car via the driveway.

You can walk to the Sulfur Springs from Squaw Rock. At the intersection above Squaw Rock continue straight (not right) through woods and follow a service road to Arbor Lane. The bridle path on the other side of the lane crosses Hawthorne Parkway, picks up the Buckeye Trail from the left, crosses and recrosses Sulfur Springs Brook. At this spot, you can take the footpath (remember the "no horses allowed" sign) to the picnic grounds, or stay on the bridle path/Buckeye Trail to the driveway. You figure out the best route.

Geology

The walls lining the river gorge and perpendicular ravines in the Squaw Rock area are made Berea sandstone, a compressed, gray rock composed of miniscule quartz crystals bonded by clay. This thick strata originated in the Mississippian geologic period, 320–340 million years ago, when a sea covered Ohio.

Ripples (wavy ridges) appear in the formation and it is cross-bedded, indicating that the fine sand was put in place by currents shifting in direction. The features also show that the Berea sand was dumped in shallow water, perhaps just offshore. Later, the land lifted, the ocean vanished, and other sediment buried the sand which eventually hardened into rock.

Squaw Rock is a chunk of Berea sandstone that fell off the wall. These huge boulders are called slump rocks. Berea sandstone (named after the nearby Cuyahoga County city) was extensively quarried for buildings, canals, bridge foundations, and gravestones (one of Henry Church's specialties). Quarry Rock Picnic Area, as you might have guessed, was the site of a sandstone mine when Henry Church was a boy.

Here the sandstone lies atop shale—specifically Chagrin shale—a flaky, blue-gray bedrock created back in the Devonian days, roughly 375 million years ago. A warm, clear, skinny sea glistened over Ohio in those days. Chagrin shale is made of the extremely fine particles of quartz, mica, and clay, as well as dark organic matter, essentially decayed trees and plants which gives the rock its dark complexion. Chagrin shale is at its best at the oxbow (described above) in Sulfur Springs Picnic Area.

Just north of the park the two forks of the Chagrin River merge. The branch flowing through the park is the as the Aurora or South Branch.

Wildlife

The hemlocks that I have already mentioned are remnants of the Ice Age. They came here in advance of the Wisconsinan glacier some 15,000 years ago and stayed behind in the cool, shady ravines. Another orphaned tree of the north woods, the mountain maple, also flourishes around Squaw Rock.

South Chagrin also protects the only known stand of sweet birch in the metroparks system as well as these species considered uncommon in Ohio—yellow birch, river birch, cucumber tree, bigtooth aspen, and American chestnut (potentially threatened species in Ohio).

Of course, you will see various oaks occupying the drier and higher ground, as well as beech and maples. The bottomland produces sycamore, cottonwood, and willows. Red, Scotch, Austrian, and Norway pines appear in clusters, but these were all planted during previous reforestation programs. You will also find dogwood, black locust, hawthorn, black cherry, and hickory in these woods.

A small arboretum, off Arbor Lane, sponsors a collection of native and naturalized trees.

Perspicacious birders should keep their eyes peeled in the hemlocks for a chance glimpse of the black-throated warbler, a bird more common in the northern boreal woods. Also try to spot the red-shouldered hawk, pileated woodpecker, American redstart, downy woodpecker, red-eyed vireo, northern oriole, Louisiana waterthrush, and chestnut-sided warbler.

A 1980 survey found 36 varieties of wildflowers in the park, though there may be more. These include harbinger of spring, red trillium, yellow mandarin, squirrel corn, and bishop's cap.

Sulfur Springs Brook is the only trout stream in the park district. The waterway is stocked and managed by the metroparks and University School.

History

The sandstone rock that reveals the ancient seas also holds the secrets of humankind.

In 1885, Henry Church could chisel an Indian woman in a slump rock. Today, of course, he would be thrown in jail for defacing park property.

Church was born in Chagrin Falls in 1836. One newspaper account said he was only the second white child born in that community. His father taught him to be a blacksmith, a practical trade, but Henry had the inclinations of an artist too. He played the bass viola and harp in an orchestra, and taught himself to sculpt and paint. Part of his self-education was journeying on a train to Cleveland to watch Archibald Willard paint "The Spirit of '76."

Contemporaries call the folk artist a philosopher, even though he did not publish a book of his thoughts, nor announce any great idea. The moniker probably stems from his pursuit of spiritualism (he went to seances in Chagrin Falls), and his reputation among locals as an eccentric.

Around 1885, so the story goes, Church sneaked down to the river at night (two miles distance) and carved figures in a sandstone boulders. It was difficult work by the dim light of a lantern. On one face of the rock he chiseled what appears to be a serpent, a quiver of arrows, wildcat, skeleton, eagle, shield, flag, and the most discernible figure—an Indian woman, or squaw.

He started on the east face of the boulder with a log cabin and U.S. Capitol. When two neighbors discovered his secret, he abandoned the project and never gave anybody a clue about the significance of the figures. One critic surmised that "Squaw Rock" represented the "rape of the Indians by the white man." Others suggested a historical theme, depicting life in America from the time of Indians and ravenous beasts, to the coming of civilization and democracy. I have jumped to my own conclusion about the motifs in the rock. (See Journal.)

Church did finish sculptures and show them to admirers. Some are displayed at the Western Reserve Historical Society in Cleveland. The sandstone probably came from local quarries. His most famous in the collection shows a small child leading a lion and lamb. It was his tombstone, and he was buried beneath it in 1908.

Cleveland Metroparks acquired the land containing Squaw Rock in 1925. A trail to the attraction was built in 1931, and the rock has been reinforced with a concrete support. Still, it faces the vagaries of the Chagrin River and the elements.

In 1980, Church received the recognition he tried to avoid in his lifetime when the Whitney Museum in New York City featured his work in an exhibit with other American artists.

As noted, Dr. David Brose, a Case Western Reserve University and Cleveland Museum of Natural History archeologist, did unearth the bones and teeth of a small woman a short distance from

Squaw Rock in 1975. (Actually, the scientist's son, who found some artifacts on the surface, prompted the dig.) Radiocarbon tests put the woman's age at 8,000–10,000 years. She was laid on hemlock boughs at the back of a shelter cave, suggesting that she had died during childbirth and been placed there by comrades who eventually moved on. The discovery indicates that the climate and habitat of the area, which was still influenced by the glacier to the north, could support humans—and their spirits.

Brose also discovered arrowheads, tools, and other artifacts dating back to 3500 B.C. These items were probably used by hunters who established temporary camps in the caves.

The Cleveland Natural Science Club built Look About Lodge in the reservation off Miles Road. In 1967, a former Boy Scout camp was added to the park.

Journal

July 1993. It dawned on me when I read a news clip about Dr. Brose's investigations. Brose found the skeleton; Church the soul. I suggest that Church, a spiritualist, was communicating with the spirit of the ancient woman while he tapped on the rock. The Stone Age lady was telling the Industrial Age man her story.

Church stumbled on the spirit while he was hiking to the nearby quarry. His nosy, non-believing neighbors interrupted the seance, requiring Church and the apparition to flee and be silent. I rest my case! Is the spirit still there, hovering in the ravine, restlessly searching for the bones that have been removed?

Beaver

EAGLE CREEK STATE NATURE PRESERVE

Some 12,000 years ago, this spot was shaped by the Wisconsinan glacier and the meltwater that poured from its snout. Today, beavers, once extinct in the area, are nature's primary movers and shakers in this preserve.

Giant ferns, carnivorous plants, rare salamanders, even flying insects with names like "bird-dropping moth" and "the bride," are residents. Eagle Creek is a cornucopia and a kaleidoscope of life. ★

Location

Northeastern Portage County, Nelson Township.

From Garrettsville head northeast toward Nelson on Center Road for about 2.5 miles. Then go right (south) one mile on Hopkins Road. The parking lot will be on the right (west) side of Hopkins Road.

From State Route 305 in Nelson go south, briefly, on Parkman Road, then almost immediately bear right (southwest) on Center Road, then left (south) on Hopkins Road.

Ownership

Ohio Department of Nature Resources, Division of Natural Areas and Preserves.

Size & Designation

This 441.3 acre preserve was dedicated on April 18, 1974 as a state interpretive preserve.

Nearby Natural Attractions

Nelson-Kennedy Ledges State Park is just a few miles away. Portage County also boasts Tinker's Creek, Marsh Wetlands, and Frame Lake/Herrick Fen state nature preserves as well as West Branch and Tinker's Creek state parks, and Berlin Lake Wildlife Area.

Access

The path from the parking lot across a field leads to the

trailhead of two trails. Heading right at this "T" is the 1.5-mile, lasso-shaped Clubmoss Trail. The 2.5-mile Beaver Run Trail branches to the left and journeys to the Beech Ridge Trail, a 3/4-mile loop.

After heading north, the Clubmoss Trail reaches a fork, the start of its loop. Take the left fork which traces the shore of a beaver pond and stops at an observation blind, an ideal spot for viewing wildlife. From here, the path continues along the edge of the pond then swings right, and wanders through a new forest and recovering field. A small bog appears on your right just before you reach the start of the loop. Look for skunk cabbage in the bog in late February.

The Beaver Run Trail heads south from the trailhead and stays on high ground as it follows one of the tributaries of Eagle Creek. Notice the swamp to your right as you start. One side trail stemming to the right leads to the mire. Don't attempt to walk across the swamp. Humans were not made for this terrain.

This path gets skinny in places. Watch out for roots!

Near the southeast corner of the preserve, the trail turns right (west), crosses two tributaries and Eagle Creek itself. (The latter stream via a wooden bridge.) Take a breather on the bridge.

Continue ahead to the Beech Ridge Trail, which circles around a small buttonbush pond. Return to civilization via the Beaver Run Trail. This walk on flat, wooded terrain covers about 4.5 miles.

The preserve is open from sunup to sundown everyday. Restrooms and drinking water are not available at this site. Pack a canteen if you plan to hike all the trails. Preserve brochures, with a trail map, are stuffed in a wooden pocket on the bulletin board.

Nature education programs are regularly held at the preserve. Check the schedule at the bulletin board in the parking lot or contact the Ohio Department of Natural Resources, Division of Natural Areas and Preserves, Fountain Square, Building F-1, Columbus, Ohio 43224-1331; phone (614) 265-6453.

Geology

Eagle Creek, once known as Silver Creek, flows off a sandstone escarpment located west and a little north of the preserve. The sandstone dates back some 330 million years, to the Mississippian geological period.

The current runs over this bedrock to just east of Garrettsville, a mile west of the preserve. Here, the creek begins a serpentine route across a wide, flat floodplain. It now courses slowly over glacial till, an amalgamation of sand, gravel, silt, clay, and boulders deposited by the Wisconsinan glacier about 12,000 years ago.

The abundance of life is indebted to the purity of water in Eagle Creek. After a heavy rain, however, the streams swell and the water becomes turbid with silt. During times of high water the stream may overflow its banks and carve new channels, or temporarily fill old ones. Silt settles in the calmer channels and pools and enriches the floodplain.

The indomitable beaver has influenced the course of Eagle Creek and some of its branches and tributaries. Their dams slow the pace of streams, and create ponds which collect silt and provide a new habitat for waterfowl.

Blocks of ice which split from the retreating glacier formed the small bogs. Till encircled the ice chunks as they sank into the ground. Water melting off the ice filled the depressions, or pools. Precipitation running off the surrounding higher ground refills the bogs.

Wildlife

The lustrous, soft, and chestnut-colored fur of the beaver inspired European exploration into the interior of North America. Its pelts were highly prized in Europe and in the New World.

In Ohio, the beaver was gone by 1830, the victim of two centuries of intense trapping and pioneering. Later, a ban on trapping enabled beavers to recolonize eastern Ohio. Today, they live in just about every suitable watershed east of Interstate 71 (with some exceptions, of course), and controlled trapping has resumed.

Rookie observers may confuse beavers and muskrats. Beavers have paddles for tails and webbed hind feet while muskrats have long, tapered, rat-like tails and unwebbed feet. These distinctions, however, cannot be detected if the animal is swimming.

In their adult stage, beavers are bigger than muskrats, averaging 35 pounds and stretching more than two feet, compared to three pounds and 10 inches for the muskrat. Beavers build intricate dome-shaped lodges of twigs, branches, and mud (though on swift streams they may live along the bank). Muskrats use whatever vegetation is available, usually cattails and grasses.

The beaver's industriousness is famous. A life history on the critter, published by ODNR's Division of Wildlife, says, "Besides man, beaver are perhaps the only mammals able to alter the environment to suit their needs." One amazing beaver dam in Columbiana County measured 1,200 feet, almost a quarter mile. Most dams are much smaller, 50-200 feet long. Sometimes their dams flood cropland, an annoyance to farmers.

All you ever might see of other animals are their tracks. In contrast, the presence of beaver is obvious. Like human construction sites, the beaver's workplace is messy. Look for (1) gnawed and girdled trees with bite-sized wood chips strewn on the ground; (2) neatly clipped branches and sticks stripped of bark, either floating in water or laying beside fallen trees; and (3) grooves or troughs on pond banks where they slide into the water.

Beavers have been known to deforest shorelines of saplings and small trees. Sometimes they tackle huge trees 100 feet or more from shore. They feed at night, dining mainly on the bark and twigs of aspen, poplar, birch, willow, maple, cottonwood, and alder.

This swift swimmer is a cautious and alert plodder on land. To observe them you must move slowly and quietly to their habitat well before dusk and stay motionless in the bushes. If you are detected, they will slap their tail on the surface of the pond, a clap that will echo across the marsh.

The beaver is not the only celebrity at Eagle Creek. The list of protected plants includes the bug-eating pitcher plant (threatened) and round-leaved sundew (potentially threatened) which both snare insects. Buckbean (threatened), catberry, tawny cottongrass, Virginia chainfern, long sedge, large cranberry, and grass-pink (the latter all potentially threatened) find refuge in the preserve.

Cottonsedge, common in the arctic tundra, grows here at its southern limit. Winterberry holly, another northerner, likes the sphagnum bogs. Try to find Venus' looking glass, partridgeberry, yellow fawn lily, cardinal flower, arrow-leaved tearthumb, purple trillium, golden saxifrage, and hawkweed. All totaled, 93 kinds of wildflowers and grasses grow at Eagle Creek.

Ostrich ferns rise to heights of five feet. It is one of 20 ferns (and allies) recorded here. Fern fanciers should search for the crested wood fern. Clubmoss, or creeping pine, is abundant along the Clubmoss Trail. It spreads like a net in the litter layer, the bed of accumulated leaves on the ground.

Don't forget the woody plants—100 varieties en masse. North-facing slopes sponsor the members associated with a beech-maple forest, while the south-facing ridges, warmer and drier, favor the oak community. Less common hardwoods include cucumber magnolia and yellow birch. Basswood (linden), American elm, black maple, white ash, and dogwood fill out the roster.

Eagle Creek protects the blue-spotted (endangered) and four-toed (potentially threatened) salamanders, and the spotted turtle, also potentially threatened.

A survey done by Tom S. Cooperrider of Kent State University in the mid-1970s turned up hundreds of moths and butterflies (lepidoptera) flitting around Eagle Creek. Here are a few. Enjoy their colorful names, as well as their colorful wings. To lepidopterists, my apologies.

- Galium sphinx—only the second sighting in Ohio at the time.
- Agreeable tiger moth—content when eating dandelion, pigweed.
- Smeared dagger moth—a flying assassin.
- The Herald—winters in caves.
- Oldwife underwing—better than being underfoot.
- The sweetheart—loves willows and poplars.
- Girlfriend underwing—rubs her boyfriend's antennae in oaks.
- Bird-dropping moth—named for its diet, not what it drops.
- Lost owlet—eats woolgrass when not disoriented.
- The Bride—honeymoons at Eagle Creek.
- The Penitent—repentant smeared dagger moths.

Eagle Creek gets its name from the bald eagle, an endangered bird which may have lived in the swamp at one time. These days, you are much more likely to see geese, ducks, herons, hawks, owls, and songbirds. And you might get a glimpse of deer, raccoon, opossum, skunk, and fox.

History

The Ohio Chapter of The Nature Conservancy bought 328 acres of this property, much of it cropland, for $36,000 in 1972. The Ohio Department of Natural Resources designated it a scenic preserve on April 19, 1974, but upgraded it to an interpretive preserve on August 29, 1977.

Using federal funds, ODNR purchased the site from the conservancy, plus additional acreage.

Journal

Mid-October 1993. I have trekked every trail but have found no fresh evidence of beavers. That's like going to Disneyland and not seeing Mickey Mouse. Unlike the Disney star who answers every curtain call, the beavers at Eagle Creek can come and go as they please, punch their own clock, and build at their own pace.

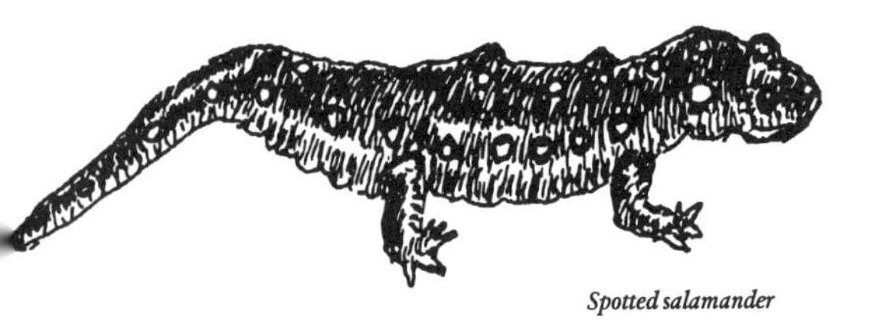

Spotted salamander

FOWLER WOODS STATE NATURE PRESERVE

Beeches and maples, a hundred feet tall and a century old, have raised the roof of this shady, old swamp forest. But in the heart of this wildness, in dark and murky waters, an impenetrable buttonbush swamp use keeps the tall timbers at bay.

Location

Northeast Richland County, Butler Township.

From downtown Mansfield, go north 16 miles on State Route 13, then east 1.1 miles on Noble Road, and finally south .2 mile on Olivesburg-Fitchville Road. The parking lot will be on the right.

Ownership

Ohio Department of Natural Resources, Division of Natural Areas and Preserves.

Size & Designation

Fowler Woods totals 133.4 acres. It became an interpretive preserve on May 16, 1973, the first state-designated preserve.

Nearby Natural Attractions

Malabar Farm State Park is located in southeastern Richland County. Also try Mohican State Park, and Mohican State Forest (Clear Fork Gorge) in Ashland County.

Access

Two trails traverse the grounds, and an observation tower, hidden in the trees, overlooks the buttonbush swamp. Total mileage—two miles.

The Beechdrop Trail is a 1.3-mile boardwalk, making it one of the few preserves accessible to disabled visitors. Folks who like to sink their feet into the ground can walk the mostly earthen, 6/10-mile Crataegus Trail, a lobe off the Beechdrop Trail that swings around the southeast corner of the parcel. (Crataegus is the generic word for hawthorn, a common tree in that neck of the woods.)

The 40-foot observation deck stands at the end of a cul-de-sac that extends from Beechdrop Trail. If that is your first destination, go straight (right) from the bulletin board, which stands just beyond the parking lot, and head into the woods. To walk a perimeter, continue on to the Beechdrop Trail, then turn right on the Crataegus Trail.

Built-in benches promote a slower pace and serve as peaceful viewing and listening platforms. Fowler Woods, far from a towns and major highways, is a quiet place that may soon disappear if a proposed regional landfill becomes a reality on neighboring property.

The woods is open from dawn to dusk every day. Naturalist-led programs are occasionally held here. For information contact the Ohio Department of Natural Resources, Division of Natural Areas and Preserves, Fountain Square, Building F-1, Columbus, Ohio 43224-1331; phone (614) 265-6453.

Geology

As you drive here, you'll probably note the flat to gently undulating terrain. This topography was shaped by the Illinoian and Wisconsinan glaciers, the last one covering Ohio about 15,000 years ago.

As they melted, the glaciers left behind a mixture of clay, sand, gravel, and rocks called till, which served as the base for soil. This deposit buried valleys, rerouted streams, and gave the land its definition.

One type of glacial formation is an end moraine, marking the spot where the wall of the glacier stalled for a while and left till piled up in a long ridge. Much of Fowler Woods grows atop the St. John's moraine, a mile-wide, hummocky belt stretching across the northern part of the county. The area explored by the Crataegus Trail, however, lies on a ground moraine, where a finer till has been evenly spread by an advancing glacier. Ground moraines create flatter terrain. Just a mile south of the preserve the Mississinewa end moraine rises.

You will not find extreme topography in the preserve, just little rises and almost imperceptible changes in elevation (30–40 feet). The bedrock 100–150 feet beneath the surface is shale and sandstone made some 330 million years ago during the Mississippian geologic period.

The preserve contains blends of two kinds of soil—the Pewamo-Bennington and Bennington-Cardington types. Pewamo-Bennington soil, high in clay, occupies most of the preserve, except along Noble Road. The dark, poorly-drained Pewamo soil sustains the swamps, with the light-colored Bennington soil on the knolls and ridges. Cardington soils are found on a few slopes.

Wildlife

Spring brings wave after wave of wildflowers, blossoming on nature's ingenious staggered schedule. Almost 200 varieties have been counted, notably marsh marigold, golden saxifrage, watercress, and yellow water crowfoot. Look for the beechdrop (hence the name of the trail) rising from the roots of beech trees from August to October. Dwarf ginseng, unusual in Ohio, thrives here in thick communities. Gifted nature-lovers, though, will search for these miracles: yellow fawn lily, stitchwork, henbit, common cleavers, king devil, enchanter's nightshade, and moonseed vine.

Now turn to ferns. At last count, 16 varieties covered the forest floor.

American beech and sugar maple dominate the scene, sinking their roots on higher ground. Some of these giants are two centuries old. Ash and red maple have spread out in the poorly drained swamp forest. An amazing assortment of trees and shrubs flourish here, 58 kinds, including four species of oak, and three types of dogwood and ash. Fowler Woods is the only state preserve protecting a grove of balm-of-Gilead, a poplar rare in Ohio whose offspring sprout from roots.

About 80 acres of the 133-acre preserve is forested, with 50 acres classified as mature. The rest is former farm land in the various vegetative stages of reverting to a forest, a process called natural succession.

The forest abounds with common furry critters and popular songbirds and warblers. Sharp eyes might spot a red-tailed, sharp-shinned (potentially threatened), or Cooper's hawk. At dusk, listen for the hoot of a barred owl. Turkey vultures, commonly seen circling overhead during the day, may roost in the tall beeches in the evening.

A good birding spot is the observation tower overlooking the buttonbush swamp. From this podium, you can conduct the revelry of spring peepers and chorus frogs (two of eight species of frogs and toads) whose song echoes through the preserve.

In the good old days of the 19th century, Fowler Woods boasted a great blue heron rookery of 150 nests, one of the biggest nesting areas in the state. Unfortunately, the birds abandoned the site many years ago.

The place also once overflowed with massasauga rattlesnakes, but these also have disappeared. Eight kinds of snakes live there now, such as the rare northern copperbelly (not to be confused with the poisonous copperhead).

Four kinds of woodland salamanders have found a rich life in the woods. The giant among them is the spotted salamander, which can grow to seven inches.

History

The clouds of mosquitoes and swampy terrain has kept Fowler Woods safe from human development. It is the only place left in the region to remind us of the immense forest that greeted the first humans.

Though much of the surrounding area had been settled, these woods were not claimed until August 1832 when John Dobbin bought the tract from the government. The deed carried President Andrew Jackson's signature. For many decades the intersection of Noble and Olivesburg-Fitchville roads was known as Dobbin's Corners.

Chester and Hettie Fowler acquired the farm in 1917, and lived there until 1962. They left 50 acres of the woods untouched, the section referred to as the old growth forest, and resisted several lucrative bids from lumber companies. In 1970 the Fowlers asked ODNR forester Jack Basinger to examine the woods. Basinger recommended that the forest be preserved, so in 1971 the state bought the farm from the Fowler family. ODNR dedicated the site an interpretive preserve on May 16, 1973, the first state natural area.

Though Fowler Woods has avoided the ax it might not miss the cutting odor of rotting garbage. In 1993 conservationists were challenging construction of a 280-acre regional landfill right next door to the preserve. The dump, they argued, would desecrate the woods.

Journal

May 13, 1993. I returned to my car and found a leaflet under a wiper blade. A bold black headline—SAVE FOWLER WOODS—filled the top of the page. I wanted more facts but whoever published it failed to put an address and phone number.

Imagine that. A landfill beside this ancient woods. Trees trimmed

with litter clinging to their limbs. Bird nests made from coffee stirrers, dental floss, and tissue. The roar and gas fumes of bulldozers and dump trucks. I see dust rising from the tires of these earth shakers and coating the autumn leaves of sugar maples, changing their bright, translucent orange hue into a chalky pastel. Instead of smelling the fresh salad scent of the forest, the fart of human plunder will taint the air.

I went back into the woods, closed my eyes beneath a beech, and dreamed I was in the Modern Museum of Art in New York City surrounded by the masterpieces of impressionist painters. When I removed the roof and walls of the gallery, the clamor, dirt, and distractions of Manhattan rushed in to ruin the dream.

Fowler Woods is a living museum and a sacred place. Its roof and walls have been the silent open spaces that surround it. The landfill will pierce these walls and raise the roof. It cannot remain blessed unless it remains whole. Our ancestors did not encounter the stench of garbage, hills of refuse, nor clouds of dust when they entered this domain. Nor should we.

Enough preaching. I need a phone number to save Fowler Woods. (In the Sixties, they always put phone numbers on flyers. How else could you find out how to stop the war or where to find free love?) I search the leaflet again. Nothing. I crumple the leaflet into a ball and toss it into a can at the beginning of the litter stream.

Shrubby cinquefoil

FRAME LAKE—J. ARTHUR HERRICK FEN STATE NATURE PRESERVE

A Nature Conservancy naturalist called this preserve a "mosaic of wetland communities." Indeed, a rare tamarack fen, a cattail pond, a lake, and a moist sedge meadow are all bunched together in this sanctuary. Some of Ohio's rarest plants and animals reside here. Oddly, acid-loving flora sprout from hummocks right beside plants that thrive in the alkaline water which trickles from mounds of dirt deposited by a glacier.

Location

Western Portage County.

From Streetsboro head south on State Route 43. A quarter mile south of the intersection of SR 43 and S R 303, go right 2.2 miles on Seasons Road. Just beyond a railroad crossing, turn left on a gravel road which serves as the northern boundary of the preserve. Pull into the small parking lot on the right.

From Kent, go north on Hudson Road, left (west) on Ravenna Road, and right (north) on Seasons Road.

Leave the RV at home because it might sink deep into the sod of this small, sloped, sometimes soggy parking lot. Motorists should inspect the lot before parking, and drive slowly at the narrow bridge before the preserve.

Ownership

The preserve is owned jointly by Kent State University and the Ohio Chapter of The Nature Conservancy. The conservancy manages the site.

Size & Designation

The preserve encompasses 126 acres. Some 110 acres has been designated an interpretive preserve by the Ohio Department of Natural Resources, Division of Natural Areas and Preserves.

Nearby Natural Attractions

To the north, just minutes away, are Tinker's Creek State Park and Tinker's Creek State Nature Preserve. (The railroad that you cross en route to the fen serves as the western boundary of Tinker's Creek preserve.) Elsewhere in Portage County, visit Marsh Wetlands and Eagle Creek state nature preserves, West Branch and Nelson-Kennedy Ledges state parks, and Berlin Lake State Wildlife Area.

Access

A trail leads from the parking lot across a meadow to the marsh that surrounds Frame Lake. The path continues east and loops around a beech-maple forest in the northeast corner of the preserve. Backtrack from the start of the loop to return to the parking lot.

A boardwalk covers part of the trail, but expect wet, muddy shoes because the path is soggy most of the year. Please stay on the path! Summertime visitors should expect swarms of mosquitoes.

The Nature Conservancy schedules field trips to the preserve. For more information contact the Ohio Chapter of The Nature Conservancy, 1504 West First Avenue, Columbus, Ohio 43212; phone (614) 486-4194.

Geology

The preserve lies atop an ancient river valley buried by till, a mixture of unsorted gravel, sand, silt, and clay, dumped by the Wisconsinan ice sheet about 12,000 years ago. The hills are called kames which formed when till poured through a hole on the top of the glacier like sand through an hourglass.

Water bleeding from the base of the kames created the fen that wraps Frame Lake. Since groundwater is not affected by sun or wind its temperature stays constant, around 54º F. The kames contain limestone (calcite) deposits, which accounts for the alkalinity of the water.

Fens are spring-fed wetlands that flush, or flow. Water leaves this fen through a natural outlet that flows toward the parking lot. (See Cedar Bog State Nature Preserve to learn more about a fen.)

Frame Lake and the small ponds or bogs scattered throughout the wetland are man-made, constructed by previous property owners.

Wildlife

The tamarack, or American larch, is a rare and potentially threatened plant in Ohio. It is a common resident in the northern woods of Canada, but in northern Ohio it lives at the extreme southern edge of its natural range.

Like hemlocks and arborvitae, tamaracks probably marched south in the vanguard of the glacier. Although the glacier eventually withdrew, a few clusters of tamaracks stayed behind, having found suitable cool habitats. The tree likes an open wetland where it will not be crowded out by encroaching maples or black ash.

Unlike pines and spruces, a tamarack (also a conifer) drops its needles in autumn. A tamarack's cones (thumbnail-sized) and needles (rarely more than an inch) are smaller than those of the European larch, a non-native tree more widely distributed.

Various sedges (marsh grasses) took root in the marly water along with sphagnum moss, a spongy moss which spread as the fen matured. As it accumulated, the moss built acidic hummocks which attracted round-leaved sundew (potentially threatened) and large cranberry. These acid-loving plants also share the fen with alder-leaved buckthorn (growing in thickets) and shrubby cinquefoil. Both seek alkaline soils.

A healthy stand of wild calla, a potentially endangered member of the arum family, thrives in a bog in the northeast corner of the preserve. The endangered bayberry survives here at the western edge of its range. Pioneers boiled the berries, then skimmed the wax that floated to the top of the kettle for candles.

The wetland is a paradise for the spotted turtle and four-toed salamander (both potentially threatened), as well as the smooth green snake, a rarity. You might see muskrat lodges among the cattails, but the animals themselves are reclusive. Waterfowl—notably Canada geese, wood ducks, and mallards—head for the lake.

History

J. Arthur Herrick was one of the founders of the modern nature preservation movement in Ohio. For 16 years, beginning in 1958, Herrick, a biologist at Kent State University, compiled lists of natural areas for the Ohio Biological Survey.

Herrick's 1965 inventory included 212 areas. It grew to 580 sites in 1974. Most of the areas are now protected.

Frame Lake, located a few miles north of the KSU campus, was one of Herrick's favorite sites. He persuaded the university and conservancy to buy the land from H.C. Frame.

Frame purchased the place in 1940, and sometime in the early 1950s deepened and enlarged an existing man-made pond to create a lake for waterfowl.

Barred owl

HACH-OTIS STATE NATURE PRESERVE

The trail meanders through a land of giants—100-foot-tall oaks, beeches, maples, and hemlocks, all of them surpassing two centuries of life on Earth. The mammoth tulip trees are all straight as a board. Their limbs branch far above any human's reach, none lower than 50 feet from the ground. Suddenly the land opens to a commanding view—a living diorama. Slithering below, like a mud-colored snake, the Chagrin River slides along its tortured, wrinkled, and gouged riverbank littered with fallen trees, boulders, and some errantly tossed beer cans. Looking deep and faraway, other clay-packed bluffs trace the zigzag course of this eternal reptile.

Location

Western Lake County, Willoughby Township.

From Interstate 90, exit at State Route 91 and travel south .8 miles to U.S. Route 6. Take Route 6 east 1.2 miles, then go north on SR 174 just a few hundred feet to Skyline Drive, which deadends at the preserve's parking lot in .3 miles.

Ownership

The Cleveland Audubon Society owns the preserve but the Ohio Department of Natural Resources, Division of Natural Areas and Preserves manages it.

Size & Designation

The 82.4-acre sanctuary was designated an interpretive nature preserve on July 1, 1977. Audubon members call it a sanctuary.

Nearby Natural Attractions

North Chagrin Reservation (Cleveland Metropark), The Holden Arboretum, Chapin Forest Reservation, and Penitentiary Glen Reservation, the latter two sites managed by Lake Metroparks, are just a few miles from Hach-Otis preserve. Elsewhere in Lake County, visit Headland Dunes and Mentor Marsh state nature preserves and Headlands Beach State Park. The Chagrin and Grand rivers, both state designated scenic rivers, flow through Lake County.

Access

Two loop trails branch from a boardwalk that originates in the parking lot. One footpath explores the north half of the preserve (to the left), while the other, slightly longer path, curls to the south.

Both trails travel on relatively flat terrain through the tall trees, along the edge of ravines, and to the bluffs overlooking the river. A stairway assists hikers across one ravine on the South Trail, the most challenging of the paths.

Warning! The rim of the cliff, composed of clay and loose soil, is unstable, especially in late winter thaws and after heavy rains. Do not lean on the "loose tooth" trees whose exposed roots dangle over the rim. They could fall into the valley with you clinging to the roots. Climbing the riverbank is perilous and prohibited.

The parking lot will accommodate 28 autos, so there's plenty of room for the RV. Toilets and picnic tables will not be found here. A bulletin board at the trailhead describes the preserve.

Hach-Otis is open every day from sunup to sundown. Nature programs on wildflowers, trees, and other topics are held here by Audubon members and ODNR naturalists. For more information on the preserve contact the Ohio Department of Natural Resources, Division of Natural Areas and Preserves, Fountain Square, Bldg. F-1, Columbus, Ohio 43224-1331; phone (614) 265-6453.

Geology

The Chagrin River is re-excavating a valley that was entombed by the debris (clay, sand, boulders, etc.) of the last continental ice mass, the Wisconsinan glacier. Meltwater flowing off the retreating glacier (roughly 12,000 years ago) took the path of least resistance, in this case the ancient river system. Since then, it has been eating away the glacial gravel and underlying bedrock.

The 150-foot bluff smiles on a gallery which reveals the erosive energy and artistry of the Chagrin River. The current already has swept away the glacial spread of sandy, gritty topsoil and the thick layer of clay beneath it. The flaky, blue-gray bedrock underneath the clay is Chagrin shale, a product of the Devonian period some 350–370 million years ago. This rock, once the bed of a shallow and murky sea, appears in thin-plated layers and erodes rather easily too. (The shale disappears beneath the bluff midway around the bend).

Precipitation assists the arching arm of the Chagrin. Rain and melting snow make the bluff more unstable by undermining the lip and carving gullies en route to the river. Each year a little more of the bluff falls into the river.

Notice how tributaries also have cut steep V-shaped ravines into the riverbank. These smaller and intermittent streams break down the bluff from other angles.

All of these activities show a tortured landscape along the slope of the bluff. Mudslides, gaping gullies, and turret-like detached columns and knife-edged ridges of turf balancing a tree or two are characteristic of the terrain. Trees entangled like pickup sticks block the mouths of the ravines.

The bluff at Hach-Otis preserve faces east, at the bottom of a horseshoe-shaped bend in the river. Trace the course of the river upstream and downstream, and see that more bluffs, looking in other directions, rise in the distance. Directly across the river, however, the land is flat and occupied by homes. Some residences rest on stilts because the lowland is washed by floodwater.

Someday, perhaps, an enraged Chagrin River will carve a new channel across the points at the top of the horseshoe. The current below the bluff would then become a mere trickle, or a pond, or a marsh, or a dried up, abandoned river channel. Speculation, of course, but possible.

Wildlife

Except for coltsfoot and a few weeds, not much grows on the harsh, unsettled slope of the river bluff. Behind the precipice, though, grows a luxuriant forest of husky beeches, sugar maples, oaks, tulip trees, and hemlocks, the latter hiding in the shady and cool ravines. Many of these giant specimens rise 100 feet, well above the canopy of the understory trees.

Astute observers can detect the hand of man in this mature woodland. The forest was last timbered in the 1870s, and the few remaining stumps attest to the size of those fallen trees. The veterans mentioned above mostly grow near the ravines—a landscape too difficult for the lumberjacks.

Many sugar maples were tapped for their sap in the 1920s. Some of the aged beeches near the rim of the bluff still show the initials and blazes (trail signs) of pioneer trappers.

John Lillich of Willoughby Hills, an Audubon member and the local expert on the sanctuary, once counted 36 different kinds of warblers in the sanctuary (and he doesn't consider himself a devoted birder). During the spring migration these boisterous beauties accumulate in the ravines and wait for the wind blowing from Lake Erie to subside before continuing their flight to Canada.

Birders should be at the east-facing bluff at sunrise, says Lillich, because many species like to bask in the early morning sun. You may see barred and great horned owls, sharp-shinned hawks (potentially threatened), kingfishers, and pileated woodpeckers (who feast on ants).

As you might imagine, wildflowers put on quite a show. See if you can spot red trillium (toadshade), squirrel corn, wild leek, trailing arbutus, jack-in-the-pulpit, foam flower, partridgeberry (an evergreen shrub), fringed gentian (potentially threatened), and Wood's hellebore, a threatened species. Squawroot, a scaly, pine cone-like parasite that rises above the roots of the red oak, populates the floor in great numbers in early June.

On scheduled night hikes during a full moon, Lillich often takes his charges to see a luminous fungus called foxfire.

Another character to spot is the mourning cloak, a butterfly with purplish-black wings fringed with blue dots and yellow lace. In June, look for the male sunning himself on a fallen log or tree limb. He may begin a spiralling courtship flight to the treetops. At that altitude he folds his wings and dives back to his perch and waits for a mate.

Most mourning cloaks hibernate during the winter, though some may migrate. They may leave their cozy quarters on balmy winter days. This popular bug may be the longest living butterfly in its adult stage—10 months.

History

Back in the 1940s, Mr. & Mrs. Edward Hach, longtime members of the Burroughs Nature Club, decided they did not want the cherished woodlot on their farm to fall into the wrong hands. So, in 1944 they gave 26 acres to the Cleveland Bird Club, the predecessor of the Cleveland Audubon Society. The sanctuary has been open to the public since 1944.

A few years later, C.W. Shipman, a naturalist who participated in the Hach transaction, persuaded Harrison G. Otis to sell about 55 acres of his Beech Hills Farm to Harold T. Clark. The local philanthropist (Clark) then donated the property to the bird club, completing the dimensions of the sanctuary.

The Ohio Department of Natural Resources dedicated the site as an interpretive preserve on June 23, 1977.

Journal

Being a shameless entrepeneur, I told a couple at the overlook to buy this book. During our chat, I learned these lifelong Ohioans had never heard of the Hocking Hills!. That's like a New Yorker not knowing about Central Park! I would have* given *them a book had it been ready.

Beach pea

HEADLANDS DUNES STATE NATURE PRESERVE

Headland Dunes is the beach we all dream about—tall, windswept sand dunes, grasses rustling in the sea breeze, shorebirds tiptoeing at the edge of a wave. It is all that we have left of an ocean shoreline which long ago edged into the heartland of North America. Today, Headland Dunes is the last and best beach resort in Ohio—for wildlife.

Location

Lake County, Painesville Township.

The preserve is located at the east end of Headlands Beach State Park. From State Route 2, travel north on State Route 44 which ends at the state park entrance. Turn right and drive to the easternmost end of the state beach and park near the beach. To the right of a park concession and bathhouse look for the wooden sign designating the entrance to the preserve. Near this sign is another marking the northern terminus of the Buckeye Trail. There are several paths. Follow the one with the interpretive sign.

Ownership

Ohio Department of Natural Resources, Division of Natural Areas and Preserves.

Size & Designation

Headlands Dunes is a 16-acre ecological research preserve, dedicated on May 13, 1976.

Nearby Natural Attractions

Combine a walk along the dunes with a visit to nearby Mentor Marsh and Hach-Otis state nature preserves, The Holden Arboretum, North Chagrin Reservation (Cleveland Metropark), Chapin Forest Reservation, and Penitentiary Glen Reservation (Lake Metroparks). The Chagrin and Grand rivers, both state designated scenic rivers, flow through Lake County.

Access

The preserve is open daily during daylight hours. Drinking water, restrooms, and picnic grounds are available at the state park. Please observe the preserve from the beach (defined below) or along paths originating from the parking lot.

From the state park, you can reach the preserve by simply walking east along the shore toward the lighthouse. The preserve begins where grassy dunes begin.

Please do not walk across the fragile dunes, or make new paths. Sunbathing, picnicking, and recreation activities are prohibited in the preserve (essentially the dunes and grassy area behind them). Pursue those activities at the longest and best state park beach in Ohio.

A few unmarked paths (not really trails) wander through the preserve. Officially, these paths are off limits, but visitors unknowingly follow them anyway. Walk lightly and in single file if you take these paths.

The pier roughly marks the east boundary of the preserve. And if you have hiked to the pier you might as well explore the Coast Guard lighthouse. Children will enjoy this little adventure and challenge. *Two cautions*: the rocks are uneven; and don't become a statistic by diving from the lighthouse where the currents are unpredictable.

Geology

Around 12,000 years ago, this beach was part of the Atlantic seacoast. At that time the mile-high Wisconsinan glacier rested north of the Lake Erie shoreline. Its weight caused the land to sink. Northeast of here a lobe of the ice mass held back the ocean. However, when this ice dike broke saltwater rushed through the St. Lawrence valley and filled the basin. The new body of water was called the St. Lawrence Sea.

It did not take long for Atlantic seacoast plants to colonize the beach of this new sea. Eventually, though, the glacier melted and the land rebounded, probably around 10,000 years ago. The sea went out the same way it came in—through the St. Lawrence valley—and left its coastal plants to fend for themselves on the shore of a freshwater sea.

Natural shaping of the Lake Erie shoreline by wind and waves was interrupted in 1827 when the federal government built piers at Fairport Harbor, at the mouth of the Grand River. The piers acted as big sand traps. Sand transported on eastbound currents parallel to the shore (longshore currents) got caught by the west pier and enlarged the beach. Today's shoreline, west of the pier and lighthouse, is a half mile farther into Lake Erie than its 1827 position. The breakwater will continue to "beach" sand until the shoreline reaches its tip.

Ecologically speaking, the beach is located between open water and sand dunes. It changes daily due to the forces of waves, currents, wind, and humans.

Scientists have divided the beach into three zones. The wet, packed sand constantly washed by waves is the lower beach. Human footprints left on the lower beach are well-defined and provide clues about the size, age, gait, direction, and pace of the walker until they are erased by a wave. The middle beach remains undisturbed until a thunderstorm rolls waves upon it. The sand here is dry and loose; footprints lose their shape and speak fewer truths. Only the severest storms touch the third zone of a beach where the sand is looser, and finer than the middle zone, and probably warmer. Your feet sink in this sand. The footprint is a mere depression.

The line of debris that has washed upon the shore marks the end of the boundary between beach and dune, between two habitats.

Wildlife

Science puts things into categories, and makes distinctions. Dunes are no exception. Like beaches, dunes have zones; the foredune, interdunal, secondary, and backdunes.

The foredune, or primary zone, located just above the drift line (debris), is inhospitable, and rather desert-like. Only plants which can tolerate scorching sun, dry wind, blowing sand, and arid, infertile soil survive here.

Species like beach grass and beach pea (isolated from the Atlantic shore), switchgrass, winged pigweed, sand dropseed, purple sand grass, and wild bean will be the first squatters on the foredune. Characteristically, these plants have deep-spreading roots (perhaps 20 feet into the soil), succulent (sacs) stems or leaves, leathery textures, and leaves that curl or fold to retain moisture. They trap blowing sand, and thus build up the dune. The grasses grow skyward quickly (several feet high) ensuring they are not buried by the sand they capture.

These pioneers stabilize the dune, provide some shade, and enrich the soil when they die. They set the stage for poison ivy, grape vines, and wafer ash (a shrub).

Canada wild-rye and wild bean, plants uncommon in northeastern Ohio grow thickly here. Western xerophytes (varieties used to dry habitats such as clammy weed, four-o'clock, winged pigweed, sand dropseed) have staked their easternmost range at Headlands Dunes. And other Atlantic coast species—sea rocket, seaside spurge, purple sand grass—recall the ancient salty sea that once bathed this shore.

Typically, the interdunal area behind the foredune is a marsh, followed by secondary dunes and backdunes. Eventually, willow, cottonwood, and black oak move into the back zones.

Other creatures live in the dunes. Fowler's toad, one of only two toad species native to Ohio, hops around here. You will see them in great numbers near the interdunal ponds during the spring breeding frenzy. In early June, the little buggers leave the water and head for the woods.

In good years, monarch butterflies flock to the beach. Like many waterfowl, these migrants rest and refuel on the dunes before venturing across Lake Erie.

History

Not many sandy beaches and dunes existed along Lake Erie's southern shore, between Sandusky Bay and Dunkirk, New York, when white settlers began to colonize the Great Lakes. After nearly two centuries of "beach improvements" only a handful of these precious habitats survive. Headlands Dunes is one of the last. Mentor Headlands, west of the preserve, has a small beach-dune community.

The effort to save the dunes from "beach improvement" became more urgent when scientists discovered its plants live isolated from their kin on the Atlantic coast.

White baneberry

THE HOLDEN ARBORETUM

This cultivated setting of neatly trimmed lawns and carefully manicured gardens also protects national natural landmarks, a fairy-tale forest, and a river valley buried and rerouted by a glacier. ★

- **Little Mountain**
- **Stebbins Gulch**
- **Bole Forest**
- **Pierson Creek Valley**

Location

Lake County, near Kirtland.

Leave Interstate 90 at Exit 193 (Mentor) and travel south on State Route 306. At the bottom of the hill (less than a mile), cross the East Branch of the Chagrin River and turn left on Kirtland-Chardon Road. Go about 3.5 miles (past the Newell Whitney Museum and Penitentiary Glen Reservation) then turn left on Sperry Road. The entrance to the arboretum will be on the left in 1.5 miles.

Ownership

The Holden Arboretum, independent and not-for-profit.

Size & Designation

The Holden Arboretum encompasses 3,100 acres, including Stebbins Gulch (425 acres) and Little Mountain (175 acres). Stebbins Gulch, Bole Forest, and Hanging Rock Farm, sites owned by the arboretum, have been listed on the National Registry of Natural Landmarks by the U.S. Department of the Interior.

Nearby Natural Attractions

Lake County is loaded with nature delights. Just a few minutes from the arboretum are Penitentiary Glen and Chapin Forest, both Lake County metroparks. Other

Lake metroparks briefly described in the book are Girdled Road and Hidden Valley.

Three state nature preserves—Mentor Marsh, Headlands Dunes, and Hach-Otis Sanctuary—are located in the county, along with North Chagrin Reservation, a Cleveland metropark.

History

The arboretum is beholden to Albert Fairchild Holden, a mining engineer who at his death in 1913, at age 46, was president of the Island Creek Coal Company, and managing director of both the U.S. Smelting, Mining & Refining Company and the American Zinc, Lead, and Smelting Company.

After the death of his wife, Katharine, and 12-year-old daughter, Elizabeth, Holden established a memorial fund to finance an arboretum. Holden had a keen interest in geology, botany, and ornithology. His sister, Roberta Holden Bole, persuaded him to establish the arboretum in Cleveland. Holden had thought of donating the money to the Arnold Arboretum at Harvard University.

In 1931, after two original sites proved unsuitable, the arboretum took root on 100 acres donated by Benjamin P. and Roberta Holden Bole.

Since its founding, the arboretum has received enthusiastic and generous support from contributors, neighbors, and volunteers. The arboretum now manages 3,100 acres, presides over 4,801 different plants, pays a staff of 51 full time and 26 part time and seasonal employees, holds more than 240 education programs and 105 hikes a year, and claims a membership of more than 7,200 families.

The Warren H. Corning Visitor Center honors a contributor and lifetime volunteer. The Thayer Center remembers Holden's daughter, Katharine Holden Thayer.

Access

The arboretum has blazed more than 20 miles of trails, some easy walks through gardens; others, strenuous journeys through off-premises gorges.

I recommend four trails. The Pierson Creek valley loop (3 miles) and Bole Forest Trail (.75 miles) begin on the main grounds and are described below. Access to Stebbins Gulch and Little Mountain is restricted to naturalist-led hikes, usually held on weekends. These gems are not located on the main grounds, and a fee is charged for the hikes. Call or write for a schedule of these interpretive walks.

First stop should be the Warren H. Corning Visitor Center to pick up a trail map and guide to the plant collections. The visitor center offers refreshments, the Treehouse gift shop, restrooms, nature exhibits, a 7,500-volume natural history library, and classroom for the numerous educational programs held year-round.

Visit the various gardens while you are here. The staff at the visitor center can tell you the blooming schedule of the collections, and point you in the right direction.

The arboretum is open Tuesday–Sunday from 10 a.m.–5 p.m. It is closed on Monday. Admission is $2.50 for adults, $1.75 for children ages 6–15 and for senior citizens. Children under age six can visit for free.

For more information contact The Holden Arboretum, 9500 Sperry Road, Mentor, Ohio 44060; phone (216) 946-4400 or 256-1110.

Wild oats

LITTLE MOUNTAIN

Little Mountain owes its appeal to the geological and dramatic forces that first built the bedrock, and then began tearing it down. These natural forces continue to work their magic on this precious place.

The summit is an enchanting maze of warty ledges, narrow cracks, and dark and sonorous passages topped by lofty, pointed pines. You'll expect to be startled by a troll on the trail.

Geology

Little Mountain consists of three rocky knobs in an L-shaped formation. The tallest and southernmost knob (1,266 feet in elevation) rests in Geauga County. Directly north, on the county line, is the middle-sized knob, elevation 1,244 feet. The shortest (1,240 feet) and smallest one lies to the northeast in Lake County.

The "mountain" stands on the northern edge of a peninsula-shaped ridge jutting from the Appalachian Plateau. Gildersleeve Knob (Chapin Forest Reservation) and Thompson Ledges also form this edge. Because all three knobs are now isolated from their main geological formation they are called outliers. Each is capped by a speckled band of sandstone called Sharon conglomerate.

The origin of the conglomerate dates back to the Pennsylvanian geological period, roughly 300 million years ago. Swollen and speedy streams falling from a mountain range to the north and east (the predecessor of the Appalachian Mountains) transported massive amounts of gravel and sand into the sea that spread across Ohio at the time. The sediments formed a broad delta with extending fingers, supposedly larger than the modern Mississippi delta.

The streams were swift enough to toss quartz pebbles in their currents. They are the white pebbles, called "lucky stones," found in Sharon conglomerate.

Later, the ocean withdrew, the land uplifted, and the exposed delta hardened into a rock. The layer of Sharon conglomerate is about 100 feet thick on the tallest knob, but it was probably much larger before erosion began its work. Sharon conglomerate is classified as a resistant rock because it resists erosion better than softer layers like shale.

Shale and siltstone, members of the Cuyahoga Formation which dates back to the Mississippian period some 330–335 million years ago, lay beneath the conglomerate caprock. These layers remain hidden beneath the gentle slope that you climb to reach the ledges on Little Mountain. Still deeper are Berea sandstone, Bedford shales and siltstone, and Ohio shale. These layers once served as the floors of ancient oceans.

Younger Pennsylvanian-age rock once capped the conglomerate (as it still does in southern Geauga County) but erosion has slowly and patiently washed it away. The water which kept flowing off the Appalachian Plateau (feeding the Grand, Chagrin, and Cuyahoga rivers) eventually cut through the resistant Sharon and Berea sandstone. Then the river systems removed the softer shales and widened their valleys. Little Mountain and the other knobs, situated between these preglacial rivers, either missed or withstood the full fury of the currents.

The continental ice sheets that followed chipped away at Little Mountain too. They scoured and leveled off its top, drove ice wedges into thin cracks to make gaping crevices, and lifted boulders 30 feet in diameter and deposited them several miles away. The last glacier, the Wisconsinan, coated the outliers with a layer of till (unsorted rock debris) as it withdrew some 12,000 years ago. Its meltwater probably flossed through the crevices and channels in mad torrents. In the ensuing years much of the glacial till has washed away.

Through resistant to erosion, Sharon conglomerate soaks in water like a sponge. The liquid slowly seeps through the sandstone, but when it gets to the impenetrable Cuyahoga shale it flows laterally to the surface. That explains the appearance of little springs at the base of Little Mountain.

Because of its higher elevation (nearly 700 feet above Lake Erie) Little Mountain receives a heavy dose of snow, nearly twice as much as Cleveland. The snow hastens erosion and nourishes the ground for wildlife.

Wildlife

A number of microhabitats defined by geology and climate makes Little Mountain a remarkable place for nature study.

Rock outcrops, ledges, and shallow soil usually make an austere environment for vegetation, but Little Mountain's heavy year-round shower of rain and snow enables plants to thrive.

Warty rock faces and cracks, nourished by the abundant water, sponsor the growth of clubmosses and ferns such as shining clubmoss, Christmas fern, hayscented fern, and common polypody fern.

Most striking are the eastern hemlocks, white pines, and yellow birches, species much more typical in the woods north of Ohio. Notice how the roots of these trees have slithered over the ledges, grasped boulders and cracks. Some roots have even bridged a crevice by snaking over a toppled mate.

The origin of the white pines has inspired debate. They are the same size and age, suggesting that they sprouted as a group simultaneously after a natural disturbance, such as a fire or a terrific storm, cleared a space for them on the hill. This theory discounts the claim that the pioneering pines, like the hemlocks (represented by seedlings to giants), are remnants of the Ice Age surviving in this colder microenvironment.

A beech-maple forest grows on the lower slopes of Little Mountain. This community is more typical in the surrounding region. Other trees live here too, including black gum, white ash, cucumber magnolia, oak (chestnut, red, scarlet, and white), tulip tree, and alternate-leaved dogwood.

Botanists in the 19th century listed several rare species growing here—trailing arbutus, mountain maple, one-sided pyrola, pipsissewa, and rattlesnake plantain—but they are no longer seen. Disease wiped out the American chestnut community, though shoots still pop up from rotting stumps.

Some of the wildflowers are wild sarsaparilla, fairybells, wintergreen, Solomon's plume, wild oats, and white snakeroot. Look for blueberry, witch hazel, and huckleberry, and let your nose take you to honeysuckle (two kinds).

The winter wren (endangered), Acadian flycatcher, solitary vireo, indigo bunting, and blackthroated green warbler offer challenges for birders.

The usual collection of four-legged creatures populate the peaks—deer (overabundant), fox, raccoon, opossum, woodchuck, squirrel, and chipmunk. Two centuries ago, the woods still harbored elk, bear, wolf, and panther (a.k.a. mountain lion, wildcat, cougar, puma). The last bear on Little Mountain, a 400-pound beast, was killed by hunters in 1825.

History

No evidence has been uncovered to suggest that Native Americans settled on Little Mountain, nor that they considered it a spiritual sanctuary. Doubtless, many of them explored the rock formations and hunted on the slopes.

Captain Truman Griswold of Mentor supposedly was the first known white man on Little Mountain, probably in 1810. Ashbel Messenger built a cabin here in 1815. One time, he reached his home just ahead of pursuing wolves who caught the scent of his bloodstained foot.

For a while, early settlers eked out a living by farming, milling, or lumbering. In 1831, Simeon Reynolds, a pioneer, turned Little Mountain into a resort when he built a hotel on his property. More hotels and private clubs attracted tourists to the site during the next 90 years.

The Little Mountain Club, founded in 1872 by Cleveland millionaire Randall P. Wade, boasted John D. Rockefeller, U.S. Senator H. B. Payne, and soon-to-be U.S. President James A. Garfield as members.

The hotels were gone by the mid-1920s, and Ralph T. King, a member of the club, bought most of the mountain. Over the years, his descendents, and other landowners, have donated land encompassing Little Mountain to The Holden Arboretum. A sign at the trailhead honors Fanny and Ralph King. The arboretum owns 172 acres of Little Mountain, but the preserve is surrounded by new homes.

Wild geranium

STEBBINS GULCH

I must admit at the outset that Stebbins Gulch was the most sublime natural area I visited in northeastern Ohio. Defying its semi-suburban location, this quiet, hidden refuge offers the feeling of remoteness, timelessness, and suspense.

Geology

Stebbins Gulch sounds like it belongs in some God-forsaken, parched piece of desert in the Old West. A place where crotchety, dusty, bone-tired miners named Grubstake chip at rocks for bits of precious metals. I like to think some ornery conservationist purposely called this green, pristine place a gulch just to scare away developers.

Gulch refers to a steep-sided, V-shaped valley, what we Ohioans would call a gorge or ravine. It got to be a gulch because of Stebbins Run, the waterway that "runs" through it.

Stebbins Run has been on the job since the retreating Wisconsinan glacier began spewing meltwater here some 12,000 years ago. The meltwater first washed away till—the gravel, sand, and clay deposited here by the ice sheet—then tackled the bedrock.

In the arboretum's section of the gulch, it has sliced through 300-million-year-old Orangeville shale (Cuyahoga Formation) of the Mississippian Period, and older Berea sandstone, also of the Mississippian Period. Now it is working on still older Bedford (Mississippian) and Cleveland (Devonian Period) shales, and if it gets through them, it will reach Chagrin shale, some 370 million years old (Devonian Period).

All of these bedrocks were deposited on the floor of the ancient oceans that covered Ohio. The sediments which compose these layers (mud, silt, and sand) were carried into the shallow seas by streams falling off a mountain chain, the predecessor of the Appalachian Mountains.

The creek descends 100 feet through the preserve, a gradient rivaling the mountain streams in the Appalachians. Hikers will be treated to a pair of small waterfalls tumbling over shale, splendid sights any time of the year.

This peaceful run becomes a untamed torrent when the snow melts and after heavy rains. During these high waters, it lifts rocks and boulders, uproots trees, carrying the debris downstream.

When you hike through this gorge, look for the round or elliptical concretions embedded in horizontal layers of shale. Scientists think concretions started as pieces of organic matter (a piece of a tree branch perhaps) which attracted minerals, such as iron, and other sediments. They grew in layers, like pearls or onions. Weathering and erosion loosens them and they roll into the creek bed.

The ice that transforms the gulch into a dazzling crystal palace in the winter also tears down the rock. The cycle of freezing and thawing weakens rock and sends boulders crashing into the stream.

Stebbins Run has cut beneath the groundwater table in places. Water "bleeds" from the cliffs, or trickles out as springs, and refreshes the stream.

In summer, the steep walls of this gaping abyss retain cool air and shade the creek. The temperature hardly ever goes above 75ºF. The cliffs block the Arctic wind in the winter, thus moderating temperatures.

Wildlife

The cool microclimate of Stebbins Gulch (totaling 425 acres) allows trees more typical of forests farther north to survive. These plants include eastern hemlock, yellow birch, and rarities like mountain maple and Canada yew (dwindling in number because it is a favorite snack of the overpopulated deer colony). These tend to grow on the slopes, terraces, and ravine edge.

Elsewhere, you will find chestnut oak dominating the drier bluffs, beech and sugar maples on the level uplands, as well as basswood, wild black cherry, and tupelo.

Because of its ruggedness, much of Stebbins Gulch missed the effects of ax, plow, and grazing livestock. The northern side of the gulch retains fragments of the old growth forest that greeted Native Americans and white settlers.

Folks fond of wildflowers can brighten their eyes on wild columbine (clinging to rocks), shinleaf pyrola (a wintergreen containing a pain reliever), miterwort, Canada mayflower, partridgeberry (creeping on the ground), turtleheads (it looks like its name), and others.

Like Little Mountain, Stebbins Gulch abounds with ferns. Some kinds, like polypody fern and walking fern, stick to certain boulders. Other ferns, notably silvery glade and fancy, grow just about everywhere.

Three Ohio-endangered birds—the dark-eyed junco, winter wren, and Canada warbler—reside here, along with the eastern wood pewee, Louisiana waterthrush, eastern phoebe, and others.

While you are tramping along the stream, try to spot the mountain dusky salamander and brook lamprey, the latter endangered in this state.

History

Charles S. Prosser of the Ohio Geological Survey reported in 1912 that "This glen is the most interesting geological locality in Chardon Township and one well worthy of careful study."

Stebbins Gulch was added to the National Registry of Natural Landmarks in 1968 by the U.S. Department of Interior.

Journal

A compelling place, this gulch. The walk upstream is an obstacle course of fallen timbers, slippery rocks, and thick vegetation. Delightful chaos. Don't come if you like your nature well-groomed. This gulch looks like it was road hard and put away wet."

Jack-in-the-pulpit

BOLE FOREST

Bole Forest compensates its lack of geological attractions by presenting one of the finest beech-maple forests in northeastern Ohio.

Access

The path to Bole Woods begins on the east side of Lotus Pond. It heads east across Sperry Road. The loop starts just after you cross the road. The path circles through this mature beech-maple forest and returns to Sperry Road. Retrace your steps to Lotus Pond and hike other trails. The walk measures about 3/4 miles.

Geology

Bole Forest lies on a thick bed of glacial till deposited here about 12,000 years ago by the Wisconsinan glacier. The land gently slopes eastward to the East Branch of the Chagrin River, which brushes one corner of the 70-acre preserve.

Although there are no enchanting ledges here and no slit exposing bedrock, the rich humus soil that has accumulated makes this ground a perfect site for the propagation of giant trees.

Wildlife

Towering sugar maple and American beech dominate the setting. Many are more than 30 inches in diameter at breast height and sport crowns of 100 feet.

Not to be outdone, individual tulip trees, tupelos, and oaks (mostly red) reach similar proportions. Buxom examples of wild black cherry, basswood (also called linden), white ash, cucumber magnolia, eastern hemlock, sycamore, black walnut, eastern cottonwood, yellow birch, and American elm also are present if you look carefully.

As you walk through the forest, notice the straightness of the giants. Many do not have branches below the 75-foot mark. In a mature forest competition among seedlings is fierce. Theirs is a race to the sky. Those who grow erect earn the most sunlight and blossom quickly. In Bole Forest, a corps of seedlings and saplings, representing all species, stands ready to replace the veterans who fall.

Wildflowers bloom in their staggered schedule from April to October. Many varieties carpet this forest floor, such as wild chervil, cleavers, barberry, Virginia waterleaf, spotted touch-me-not, jack-in-the-pulpit, great lobelia, wood sorrel, bouncing bet, Indian pipe, and blue cohosh.

History

Bole Forest honors Mr. & Mrs. Benjamin P. Bole, relatives of the arboretum's founder, Albert Fairchild Holden. In 1931, the Boles donated 100 acres of their land to get the arboretum started. The forest and adjacent Hanging Rock Farm, another national natural landmark in the arboretum's holdings, once belonged to the Bole family.

The U.S. Department of the Interior added the beech-maple forest and farm to the National Registry of Natural Landmarks in November 1967.

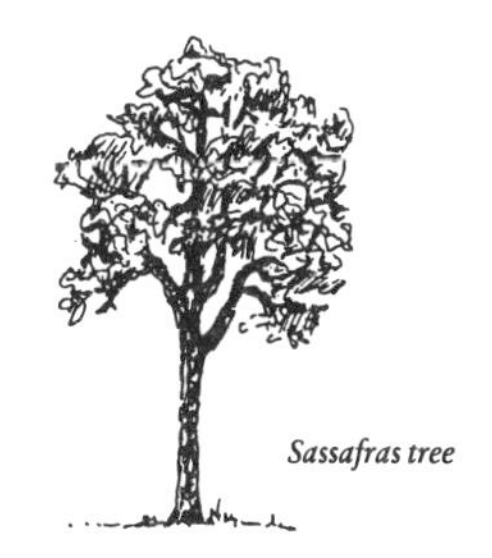

Sassafras tree

PIERSON CREEK VALLEY

Someday, Pierson Creek will hit rock bottom again. Not in our lifetime, of course, but someday. Like a determined spider who keeps repairing its storm damaged web, Pierson Creek again threads its way through a valley which a glacier used for a dumping ground many millennia ago..

Access

The ramble through the Pierson Creek valley measures about 3 miles. From the shelter house behind the Thayer Center, climb down the steps, cross a creek, and turn right on the Woodland Trail. This path traces the south shore of Foster Pond.

Just beyond the pond, turn right on a path shared by Pierson Creek Loop and the Old Valley Trail. As you approach the stairs that descend into the gorge, the trail splits. Bear right on the Pierson Creek Loop, heading downstream. This loop trail swings northwest, descends a stairway, crosses the creek, bends southeast, and merges again with the Old Valley Trail.

This combined Pierson Creek and Old Valley path wanders through the woods on the west bank of the creek. Eventually, it recrosses the creek and reaches The Boardwalk, which offers a closeup view of the creekside habitat.

Climb the other side of the valley via stairs and head for the double-deck observation tower that overlooks Buttonbush Bog. Return to the shelter house via the Woodland (swinging around the bog) and the Blueberry Pond trails.

Geology

Some 75,000 years ago, Pierson Creek Valley was part of a larger, swifter river system that flowed northward into a lake that preceded Lake Erie. Back in those days the valley was deeper and wider, and boasted higher waterfalls. Then the monster Wisconsinan glacier filled the valley with gravel, boulders, and other rubble and sealed it in ice for centuries.

When the monster began to withdraw to its polar origins, about 12,000 years ago, its meltwater followed the easiest path, the buried valleys. The glacier that entombed the river also renewed its life.

Several rivulets which fall and merge at the southern edge of the arboretum's land form Pierson Creek. The creek drops swiftly now (120 feet per mile) and builds up enough steam to shape the land. Tributaries running in steep "V" gullies feed the northbound stream. The mouths of some of these feeders are choked with sand and clay, evidence of the rapid and relentless pace of erosion.

Notice the "slumping" in the valley. Gravity and groundwater combine to detach huge blocks of earth from valley (or gully) walls and slide them toward the stream. The trees and plants growing on these clay-sand slumps go along for the ride. Most of the time the trees topple into the stream, but occasionally one will keep its balance on the miniature mudslides.

Pierson Creek is elastic and everchanging. Spring rains, fallen trees, slumping, debris dams, and the like reroute the course of the channel, sometimes dramatically.

The absence of waterfalls (except near the headwaters) and bedrock outcrops in the valley proves the stream still tosses over till (glacially transported sediment). It also reveals its age, 12,000 years old or thereabouts. The current curls around granite boulders (delivered by the glacier from Canada) and foams over fallen trees, but these cannot be considered waterfalls. The mud-stained water tells us that erosion is working fast. Nobody knows when Pierson Creek will reach rock bottom.

Wildlife

The flora and fauna of the valley unfolds at The Boardwalk, an offshoot of the Pierson Creek Loop. Obtain a plant checklist at the visitor center.

Fifteen kinds of ferns and their allies can be examined, such as scouring rush, ostrich, silvery glade, and Goldie's wood ferns. Some of these are tucked into tiny spots

There are 42 varieties of wildflowers on the checklist. Bring your field guides and look for fairy candles, great merrybells spotted touch-me-not, false mermaid weed, and others.

Several kinds of hardwood communities face the creek. The oak-maple group dominates in some places with towering sugar maples, white and red oaks, and hickories (shagbark, pignut, and bitternut).

The floodplain forest contains a blend of sugar maple, black walnut (creekside), tulip tree, some beech, basswood, ash, cucumber magnolia, and sassafras.

History

Pierson Creek takes its name from a local family of early settlers.The creek supposedly originates on Pierson Knob.

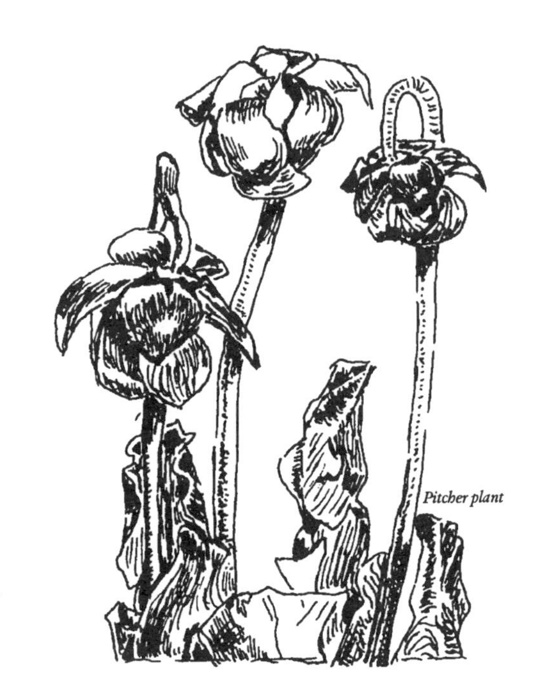
Pitcher plant

JACKSON BOG STATE NATURE PRESERVE

This tiny wetland, a slim relict of the Ice Age, safeguards 23 rare plants and one protected reptile. One rarity, the carnivorous pitcher plant, prefers acidic bogs, but here, and in only one other place in Ohio, it thrives in an alkaline fen. Jackson Bog also may be the only place in Ohio where the hooded ladies' tresses still survives.

Location

Northwestern Stark County, Jackson Township.

From Canton, go about eight miles northwest on State Route 687. A half mile west of the intersection with State Route 241, turn into a driveway to the Jackson Township community park and the offices of the Jackson Local Board of Education. Follow signs to the new recreation facility and park the car on the left side of the parking lot.

Ownership

Jackson Bog is the property of the Jackson Local School District. The site is managed by the Ohio Department of Natural Resources, Division of Natural Areas and Preserves.

Size & Designation

This 5.7 acre fen became an interpretive nature preserve on December 12, 1980.

Nearby Natural Attractions

Visit The Wilderness Center, Quail Hollow State Park, and Berlin Lake State Wildlife Area, all in Stark County.

Access

Two routes to the bog are now open. Face the playground in the park. To your left, at the bottom of a slope, you will find a path along the edge of the mowed park. Follow this path a few hundred yards, past a natural pool, to the wooden signs at the entrance of the preserve. Ignore, for now, the trail to the right.

Walk into the bog through this gateway. The path swings to the left. A boardwalk soon carries you over the fen located beneath a small ridge.

At the eastern border, the route curves left again, climbs the small hill, and swings left to the entrance signs. Retrace your steps to the parking lot.

The journey is hardly a mile-long walk with two small swells to ascend. In fact, the walk through the preserve is so short you are apt to ask yourself, "Is that all there is?" Force yourself to travel slowly and to study details.

You can also explore the trails through the community park west of the preserve. Those trails, as you face the preserve entrance sign, are to your right.

A longer path to the preserve begins at the edge of the woods beyond the picnic shelter in the park. In the second small picnic area along this trail (marked by a tall white oak), take the trail that bears left down the ridge.

At the bottom, an arrow on a wooden post points to a grassy path going left. This trail also leads to the entrance of the preserve. (Remember, the entrance to the preserve is marked by two wooden signs.) The trail to the right of the post visits other spots in the elongated wetland (including a stream) which are not in the preserve. This trail is also open to the public.

Jackson Bog preserve is open everyday from dawn to dusk. For more information, contact the Ohio Department of Natural Resources, Division of Natural Areas and Preserves, Fountain Square, Building F-1, Columbus, Ohio 43224-1331; phone (614) 265-6453.

Geology

Try to imagine two enormous lobes of a continental glacier draped like a stage curtain over northeastern Ohio some 14,000 years ago. Jackson Bog is tucked right in the crotch of these looping lobes.

For decades, torrents of water carried tons of gravel and sand to the edge of these melting lobes. Here the sediment in the meltwater, called till, poured into holes, pits, and crevices at the front of the stationary glacier (like sand falling in an hourglass). When the ice finally disappeared the till formed mounds and conical-shaped hills called kames. The bumpy terrain in the Akron–Canton area is a broad band of glacial kames.

Water melting off the retreating glacier kept the ground saturated. The newly deposited gravel showed an amazing capacity to retain water in underground aquifers. Jackson Bog is situated right where this groundwater surfaces as a spring, in this case at the base of a kame.

Actually, Jackson Bog is a fen, which is a spring-fed wetland, usually with alkaline soil. Water in a fen flows, though imperceptibly. In contrast, precipitation recharges a bog, and water leaves by evaporation.

The water that seeps into Jackson "Fen" is alkaline because the gravel it passes through before surfacing contains limestone. As the groundwater percolates through the gravel it dissolves some of the limey substances in the limestone and becomes enriched with calcium and magnesium bicarbonates. At the surface, calcium carbonate precipitates (separates from water) and makes an ash-colored mud called marl.

The rain and snow that permeate through the glacial gravel replenishes the aquifer, which, in turn, feeds the fen. Prolonged drought, pollution of the aquifer, or further human development could disrupt this natural cycle and ruin the fen environment.

Wildlife

During the Ice Age, plants that typically grew in Canadian bogs colonized this cool, wet area. Temperatures warmed after glaciation and plants from southern climes (the ones we commonly see today) gradually replaced the northern (boreal) vegetation. However, in a few pockets of suitable habitat some northern bog plants held on. One of these microhabitats is Jackson Bog.

A fen is a rather difficult environment for plants. Few plants can flourish in high alkaline (pH 8–9) soil, plus the spring water is always cool (54ºF) and low in oxygen. Scientists called these inhospitable characteristics "limiting factors." The limiting factors in the preserve resemble those found in a glacial environment.

This fen is subtly divided into vegetation zones, defined by their proximity to the alkaline seeps.

- The open marl zone lies closest to the springs and only tough low-growing sedges and grasses seem to thrive there. Some specialized plants flourish, notably false asphodel (potentially threatened), round-leaved sundew (potentially threatened), pitcher plant (threatened), grass-of-Parnassus, and Kalm's lobelia. Supposedly, Ohio's largest pitcher plant patch persists in this preserve. The flower usually dwells in an acidic environment.

- The sedge-meadow zone, farther from the springs, has developed a thin layer of sedge peat which supports taller plants and shrubby cinquefoil, a common shrub in a fen. The peat layer seems to float or quake.
- As the sedge and peat accumulate, a shrub-meadow zone develops. It is farthest from the spring and appears to be a transition area between fen and shrub-swamp habitats. This zone has clusters of tall shrubs like alder, willow, poison sumac, and dogwood, with a few elms or red maples.

The preserve may be the only Ohio home for the hooded ladies' tresses. That species, plus another rarity living here called the small purple foxglove, are endangered plants.

Other protected plants sinking roots include threatened species like the round-fruited pinweed, highbush-cranberry, flat-leaved bladderwort, and variegated scouring-rush; and potentially threatened species such as tall manna-grass, tufted hairgrass, Baltic rush, small fringed gentian, long-beaked and autumn willows, Leggett's pinweed, marsh arrow grass, and six sedges (little yellow, twig-rush, Crawe's, yellow, fen, prairie).

History

The wetland has been known as Stewart Bog, Kettle Lake Bog, and Timken Bog, depending on the property owner. In 1975 Jackson Township unveiled a master plan for a park near the wetland. This prompted the ODNR and others to protect the fen. In 1980, the Division of Natural Areas and Preserves dedicated less than six acres of Jackson Bog as an interpretive preserve.

Cucumber magnolia

KYLE WOODS STATE NATURE PRESERVE

Except for maple sugaring, this hardwood forest, a remnant of the original Ohio woods, has hardly been disturbed by humans since the turn of the century.

Location

Central Mahoning County, Canfield Township.

Kyle Woods borders the eastbound land of the Ohio Turnpike, but you cannot get to the preserve from this four-laner. Instead, exit State Route 11 at U.S. Route 224 (Canfield). Go east on SR 224 (Boardman-Canfield Road) a little more than three miles, then turn right (south) on Tippecanoe Road at a traffic light. Just beyond the spot where the Ohio Turnpike passes overhead, turn right and take your first left, a driveway that climbs to the preserve parking lot.

Ownership

Ohio Department of Natural Resources, Division of Natural Areas and Preserves.

Size & Designation

This 81.9-acre woodlot was dedicated as an interpretive nature preserve on May 14, 1983.

Nearby Natural Attractions

Mill Creek Metropolitan Park District has several facilities in Mahoning County. Phone (216) 743-7275). Berlin Lake State Wildlife Area is located at the western edge of the county.

Access

The preserve is open daily during daylight hours. The mile-long, lasso-shaped Sugarbush Trail that visits a meadow and mature forest begins at the parking lot. Sections of the woods remain swampy year-round, so wear appropriate footwear. Restrooms and drinking water are not available at this site.

For more information about the preserve, contact the Ohio Department of Natural Resources, Division of Natural Areas & Preserves, Fountain Square, Building F-1, Columbus, Ohio 43224-1331; phone (614) 265-6453.

Loghurst Farms, once part of the Kyle estate, is located next to the preserve. This Western Reserve Historical Society site is open to the public from Memorial Day through October. Hours are 10 a.m.-5 p.m. Tuesday-Saturday, and noon to 5 p.m. on Sunday. Admission is $3 for adults, $2 for children under age 12.

For information about Loghurst Farm call the Western Reserve Historical Society at (216) 721-5722 or (216) 666-3711 (the society's Hale Farm site).

Geology

This lush forest grows atop a thick layer of glacial till, a salad of sand, gravel, boulders, silt, and clay. The Wisconsinan ice mass deposited the dirt when it scoured this landscape about 12,000 years ago.

The preserve lies on flat terrain above the Mill Creek Valley. The tiny rills that trickle from the site fill tributaries of Mill Creek which joins the Mahoning River in Youngstown.

Wildlife

The Ohio Department of Natural Resources says the "Big Woods" part of the preserve is "representative of the original forest in Mahoning County." In other words, Kyle Woods is about the best forest you are going to find in this heavily-populated, highly industrialized county. Supposedly the Big Woods has hardly been disturbed since the mid-19th century, and not at all since 1903 (except for tapping maples for syrup).

Though American beech and several members of the maple clan dominate the scene, some 25 types of trees actually thrive here, making the preserve a more complex habitat than it seems. Some sources call this woods a mixed mesophytic forest because of the diversity of species.

The preserve also protects sizable specimens of tulip tree, cucumber magnolia, wild black cherry, black gum, ash, white and red oak, sourgum, and shagbark hickory. Apple trees also grow in the meadow.

Spring begins with the joys of large-flowered trillium, spring beauties, Solomon's seal, trout lilies, and others. The striking pale green-yellow blossoms of the cucumber magnolia tree open in May-June, but the scent of these beauties can be foul. Just as attractive (if you are open-minded) are the tree's scaly, dark red cones, seen August to October.

The meadows brighten with wildflowers, especially asters, goldenrod, milkweed, thistle, and berry patches attract birds. Here, in late summer, you might catch a buck deer polishing his new antlers by rubbing them against the trunk of a sapling. He has hundreds to choose from for the task. Another meadow inhabitant, the eastern bluebird may streak by, its blue flight contrasting with an overcast sky.

Fox, fox squirrel, deer, opossum, and raccoon are among the forest dwellers. Great horned owls and red-tailed hawks nest in the tall trees. The usual cast of warblers occupies the canopy in the spring. When the tree canopy closes in late spring and shades the woods in a greenish tint, you are more apt to hear these songbirds than see them.

History

In 1803, Conrad Neff built a sturdy stagecoach inn on this site using black walnut logs from the forest. The inn became a stopover on the Cleveland-to-Pittsburgh road. Later, Jacob Barnes, an abolitionist, bought the place. It became a "station," an inn of sorts, on the Underground Railroad, a network of safehouses for runaway slaves seeking freedom before the Civil War.

Arthur Kyle purchased the log house in 1903. Though he farmed much of the property, the Big Woods was left alone, except for the late winter extraction of maple syrup. This activity continued into the 1950s, and relicts of the sugarhouse can still be seen in the woods by keen observers. The northwest corner of the preserve was farmed until the 1970s.

In February 1977, about the time sap begins to flow in the sugarbush, Miss Josephine Kyle, a retired physical education teacher, and donated 53 acres of "Loghurst Farm" to the Ohio Department of Natural Resources, in memory of her father. She gave the family's log home, the oldest and largest structure of its kind in the area, to the Western Reserve Historical Society in 1978. The historical site is open for visitors during the warm months.

Kyle Woods preserve opened to the public in October 1981, but was not formerly dedicated until May 14, 1983. With the help of the Ohio Chapter of The Nature Conservancy ODNR purchased an additional 29 acres.

Journal

Kyle Woods is charming throughout the year, but my mid-October hike with the sugar maple leaves ablaze was glorious. Even seedlings no higher than my knees splashed an orange richer than the famed maples of Vermont.

Canada goose

PENITENTIARY GLEN RESERVATION

The only penitentiary here is a rock-bottomed, steep-walled gorge which, like a prison, is easy to get into, but hard to get out of. Actually, Penitentiary Glen offers freedom from the humdrum of daily rigors. The charm of the place may get locked up in your heart.

Location

Southwestern Lake County, in Kirtland.

Exit Interstate 90 and travel south on State Route 306. After crossing the East Branch of the Chagrin River, a state scenic river, bear left on Kirtland-Chardon Road (follow the signs). The entrance will be on the right, after a long climb.

Ownership

Lake Metroparks.

Size & Designation

Penitentiary Glen totals 360 acres, much of it wooded.

Nearby Natural Attractions

Just a few minutes away are Chapin Forest Reservation, also managed by Lake Metroparks, The Holden Arboretum, Hach-Otis, Mentor Marsh, and Headlands Dunes state nature preserves, and North Chagrin Reservation, a Cleveland metropark.

Lake Metroparks also invites you to explore Hidden Valley Reservation and Girdled Road Reservation, described briefly in this section. Also, try Hell's Hollow, Hogback Ridge, Paine Falls, Indian Point, Lakeshore, and Veteran's Park.

Elsewhere in Lake County visit Mentor Marsh and Headlands Dunes state nature preserves and Headlands Beach State Park.

Access

This natural area has four miles of trails through a variety of habitats. Its modern nature center has exhibits for youngsters, an auditorium, gift shop, restrooms (outside access too), and classrooms. Nature programs are held here regularly.

There are two special attractions. One is the wildlife center—part wildlife hospital, part zoo for injured critters, part educational facility for humans. The rehab center is open to the public.

The other oddity is the Penitentiary Glen Railroad, a pint-sized steam railroad, operated by full-sized members of the Lake Shore Live Steamers (toy railroads, not cooked clams) Club. The railroad cars are big enough to pull people on free rides to the gorge during the warm months. The schedule, like this attraction, may be irregular, so call the park beforehand.

Pick up a trail guide at the nature center and follow the Rabbit Run Loop which leaves from the parking lot. Just after entering the woods, the trail splits. Take the left fork, the trailhead of the mile-long Gorge Rim Loop. The tracks of the miniature railroad will be at your left. The gravel and partially boarded path heads southwest to Penitentiary Gorge and turns right (northwest) following the hemlock-lined gorge rim. Skip the shortcut trail to the right and continue ahead to the side trail at the left which descends into the steep gorge to Stoney Brook Falls. This is your only view of the bottom of the ravine. Please stay within the fenced overlook. Naturalist-guided walks into the ravine are held every Sunday for folks who want to frolic in Stoney Brook. If you count the steps, notice that it will take you longer to count all 141 of them as you return to the rim.

Back on the top, the trail continues along the rim, then curves right into a forest of tall hardwoods. You will find a bench in the middle of the woods—a fine spot to rest (especially in autumn) and to watch wildlife.

The Gorge Rim Loop again collides with the west leg of the Rabbit Run Loop near the edge of the woods. I turned right here, staying on the Gorge Rim Trail, preferring the shade cast by young trees on a hot summer day to the east leg of the Rabbit Run Loop which leaves the woods and wanders back to the parking lot through the field along Kirtland-Chardon Road. Turn left at the trailhead of the Gorge Rim

Loop and return to the starting point.

The Gorge Rim and Rabbit Run loops are smooth, wide, and the terrain is relatively flat with some slight rolls. The side trail to diminutive Stoney Brook Falls is steep, but aided by steps (count them). You will walk a little more than a mile on this journey.

For topside views into the gorge and to visit a bird-filled meadow, take the paved Glen Meadow Loop which begins at the outdoor amphitheater located between the nature center and wildlife center. Bear right at the first junction and enter the hemlock woods. Stop at the overlook on the right for the best view of the gorge.

Farther ahead, the path circles a landscaped wildflower garden. The pavement ends here. You can also see the ruins of the former summer cottage of the Halle family.

The old driveway heading south from the wildflower garden is the trail leading to the Bobolink Loop. This path soon turns right, crosses Stoney Brook at the head of the gorge, and climbs a wooded ridge to a "T" intersection in a meadow recovering from decades of farming.

Turn right here and trace the edge of the woods. In a few hundred yards a path at the right leads to another overlook above the gorge. The Bobolink Loop follows the pasture edge for awhile, ducks into the woods briefly, then winds through the meadow. Turn right at the next intersection, recross the creek, and return to the paved Glen Meadow Loop at the wildflower garden.

Just beyond the overlook, turn right and follow the west leg of the Glen Meadow Loop. This path cuts across a field and snakes between an open man-made marsh and pond. An observation deck faces the marsh. This wheelchair and stroller trail returns to the nature center. This latter journey over the Glen Meadow and Bobolink trails covers a little more than 1.5 miles. Add a quarter mile if you snoop among the Halle ruins.

Children will enjoy the exhibits and nature programs inside the new nature center, as well as the adjacent wildlife center. Explain to them that the tethered birds are injured and would not live long in their natural habitat.

For more information about Penitentiary Glen, contact Lake Metroparks, 11211 Spear Road, Concord Township, Ohio 44077; or call (216) 256-1404 or 1-800-227-7275.

Geology

Like a freedom-hungry prisoner who has been sawing the iron bars of his cell with dental floss, tiny Stoney Brook has been scratching at the bedrock that has confined it in Penitentiary Gorge for a thousand years. So far, it has removed layers of Berea sandstone and Bedford formation (shale and siltstone), both products of the Mississippian geologic period 345–320 million years ago.

You will best see sandstone overhangs and other odd shapes from the overlook near the wildflower garden (Glen Meadow Loop). Halfway through its high-walled dungeon, Stoney Brook tumbles about 20 feet over Bedford rock (Stoney Brook Falls via the Gorge Rim Loop). Downstream, it cuts into older, Devonian-aged rocks—Cleveland and Chagrin shales—once the sediment of a shallow, murky sea. You cannot see these latter strata from a trail. Take one of the scheduled naturalist-led hikes for a closer look of these formations, and other curiosities in the gorge.

Stoney Brook does not appear to be a current created by glacial outwash, the water melting from an ancient glacier. It may have started as rain or snowmelt running off higher ground south of the reservation. As it flowed north, it found a depression or crack in bedrock and began its scouring action.

In the forest encircled by the Gorge Rim Loop, you will see many boulders looking out of place. These huge stones, called "erratics," are part of the rubble left behind by the melting Wisconsinan ice mass which passed over this surface some 12,000 years ago. The erratics are the tombstones of that mile-high body of ice.

Wildlife

The tall hemlocks that carpet the rim and gorge walls are remnants, or refugees, of the Ice Age. This species of the cold northwoods arrived in the vanguard of the glaciers. When the climate warmed and the ice mass retreated to the polar caps, the surviving hemlocks found refuge in the cool, shady ravines in Ohio. Another tree of the northern clime, mountain maple, grows in a patch on the south side of the gorge. Look for its white foamy flowers in the spring.

The realm of the hardwoods lies beyond the rim. Some stout red oaks thrive in the forest alongside buxom maples, chestnut oak, tupelos and some beech and hickory. (Study them at the trailside bench on the Gorge Rim Loop.)

A recovering forest of young trees, berry patches, and vines is characteristic along the edges of fields and mature forests. The Rabbit Run, Bobolink, and Glen Meadow trails visit these habitats that are on the road to becoming full-bloom forests again.

Wildflowers brighten the forest floor in the spring. One of them is the small whorled pogonia, a state and national endangered plant. Stemless lady slipper, round-leaved violet (stemless yellow blossom), and trailing arbutus are some of the members of this colorful ensemble. In summer, Indian pipe and squawroot are abundant beneath the shady canopy.

The forest attracts warblers of several varieties, as well as scarlet tanager, rose-breasted grosbeak, and pileated woodpecker. As you could have guessed, bobolinks have nested in the meadow encircled by the Bobolink Loop. Their ecstatic, raspy song is a favorite of many birders. In summer, the male appears to be dressed in a tuxedo, black-bellied with white plumage on top, with an orange brushstroke on the back of the neck. Also look for bluebirds and tree swallows in this habitat.

Waterfowl—Canada geese and ducks mostly—can be seen in the marsh and pond behind the nature center. Occasionally great blue and green herons appear. Naturalists expect more birds will call these newly created wetlands home in the future.

History

Sam and Blanche Halle, owners of the Cleveland department store chain, bought this farm (180 acres) in 1912 and built a weekend and summer cottage above the gorge for the family. Farming continued until after World War II.

Lake Metroparks obtained the Halle property in the mid-1970s. The former horse stable served as the nature center until a new building was completed in 1992.

HIDDEN VALLEY RESERVATION

Some of Ohio's rarest plants and animals hide in this 109-acre preserve on the south bank of the Grand River, a state-designated scenic river. Mountain rice grass and the northern waterthrush, both state endangered and more common north of Ohio, survive here along with sweet scented plantain, a state threatened plant.

North America's smallest owl and a state-protected bird, the saw-whet owl (a mere 7"-8" in height), roosts in the hemlocks that grow along Griswold Creek which forms the west boundary of the park. At the last count, some 46 species of birds use the site.

Seventeen kinds of amphibians (among them the spotted, silvery, slimy, and Jefferson salamanders, mountain duskies, red spotted newts, wood frogs, and spring peepers) live here, most of them in a buttonbush swamp or along the river.

A trail following the river leaves from the parking lot. Another, leaving from Klasen Road, leads to a scenic overlook at the point of an arrowhead-shaped ridge.

Location

Eastern Lake County, Madison Township.

From Interstate 90, travel south on State Route 528. Look for the entrance on the right just after you cross the Grand River bridge. Or turn right on Klasen Road, and bear right to the parking lot. Restrooms, drinking water, canoe landing, picnic tables, playground, sledding hill, and fishing areas are found here.

GIRDLED ROAD RESERVATION

Eighty-three percent of this sprawling reservation is forested, ruled by a mature beech-birch-maple community. Big Creek, a tributary of the Grand River, shapes the northwest boundary and serves as a corridor for migrating birds.

Two potentially threatened plants—hobblebush and Carolina spring beauty—exist in the nooks and crannies of the ravines. Other plants considered to be rarities in the region—mountain maple, harbinger of spring, fire cherry, narrow-leaved spleenwort, and three kinds of sedges—also sink their roots here.

Birders have identified 74 species in the park, including the yellow-billed cuckoo, least flycatcher, Canada warbler, Carolina wren, and wild turkey—all of them considered uncommon regional residents.

Girdled Road, forming the north boundary of the park, is part of an early 19th-century road connecting newly founded Cleveland to Pennsylvania. Road developers marked the route by girdling trees (stripping their bark), a procedure that eventually killed the trees.

Location

Concord Township, Lake County.

The entrance is located at the south end of the property on Radcliffe Road, east of State Route 608 (Concord-Hambden Road). Here you will find a loop trail, picnic tables, water, restrooms, and other recreational amenities. The Buckeye Trail follows Big Creek on the west side of the site. An east-west side trail links the Buckeye Trail to the reservation's multi-use loop trail.

Beaver lodge

MARSH WETLANDS STATE NATURE PRESERVE

Let's face it. You've got to love swamps to come here. It's no place for humans. I could not shake the uneasy feeling that a dozen pair of eyes observed my every footfall. This trackless, dense, and impenetrable swamp filters water headed for the Cuyahoga River, and shelters an abundance of plants and animals. It is the realm of the noble beaver, and creatures that live in the murky waters.

Location

Northern Portage County, within the Mantua city limits. State Route 44, which links the county seats of Chardon (Geauga County) and Ravenna (Portage County), bisects Mantua.

At the traffic light in Mantua, go east on High Street. Just past a large brick structure, the Mantua Service Department, look for a mowed field on the right. A buried tile over a ditch serves as the driveway. Drive into the field and park near the wooden sign at the edge of the grass. If you drive to the crossroads with Peck Road, you have gone about 100 yards too far.

Marsh Wetlands often is mistaken for Mantua Bog State Nature Preserve. The two preserves are neighbors. Marsh Wetlands lies at the southwestern corner of the intersection of High Street and Peck Road, while Mantua Bog is located in the southeastern corner. Mantua Bog, a National Natural Landmark, can be visited only with written permission from the Division of Natural Areas and Preserves.

Ownership

Ohio Department of Natural Resources, Division of Wildlife.

Size & Designation

Marsh Wetlands, a recent addition to the state nature preserve system, totals 152 acres. It is open to the public. Though managed by the Division of Wildlife, hunting and trapping are prohibited in the preserve, because it is in the city limits of Mantua.

Nearby Natural Attractions

Frame/Herrick Bog, Eagle Creek, and Tinker's Creek state nature preserves are located in Portage County. So are Tinker's Creek, West Branch, and Nelson-Kennedy Ledges state parks.

Access

Frankly, only come here if you have no other place to go, or if you want to seek a special wetland habitat. Trails have not been constructed in Marsh Wetlands. Still, you can venture along the northern edge of the swamp on an elevated, abandoned railroad bed. Head west, parallel to High Street, toward the center of Mantua.

I recommend side trips off the rail bed for closer views of the wetland. Wear rubber boots and pants to safeguard against water, bugs, and briars. Look for gaps in the thickets and follow deer trails. Unfortunately, litter has been tossed over the side of the rail bed, now serving as the route of a petroleum pipeline.

You can follow the railroad bed all the way to a park in Mantua and back to the car for a mile or so ramble.

Or wander into the marsh via the Cuyahoga River (upper portion), which is a state scenic river.

Geology & Wildlife

In this area the Cuyahoga River flows over flat to rolling terrain and washes glacial till (sand, gravel, silt, boulders) deposited here 12,000 years ago by the Wisconsinan glacier.

The wetlands that flank the river on its journey through Mantua provide refuge for many rare and protected plants and animals. Beavers have built numerous lodges in Marsh Wetlands Preserve. Waterfowl, reptiles, snakes, and muskrats are common. Tracks indicate the presence of whitetailed deer and raccoons.

ODNR has yet to conduct an in depth plant and animal survey of this preserve.

Red-winged blackbird

MENTOR MARSH STATE NATURE PRESERVE

Once a lake bed, then a river channel, Mentor Marsh thrives as one of the last freshwater marshes in northeastern Ohio. Soggy soil and dense plant life have kept humans out of this wetland. Now it serves as a perfect home for a wide assortment of swamp creatures. ★

Location

Lake County, City of Mentor.

Exit State Route 2 at State Route 44 and travel north toward Lake Erie. SR 44, which forms the eastern boundary of the preserve, ends at Headlands Drive, the northeast boundary. State Route 283 roughly forms the southern boundary. Corduroy Road, off SR 283, crosses the marsh and takes visitors to the Marsh House, the preserve's visitor center.

Ownership

Mentor Marsh is jointly owned and managed by the Ohio Department of Natural Resources, Division of Natural Areas and Preserves, and the Cleveland Museum of Natural History.

Size & Designation

This swamp-forest encompasses 643.7 acres. It has been designated a state interpretive nature preserve, Ohio's first, and is a National Natural Landmark, designated by the U.S. Department of the Interior in 1964.

Nearby Natural Attractions

Lake County teems with nature preserves. Headlands Beach State Park and Headlands Dunes State Nature Preserve abut Mentor Marsh. Also visit Hach-Otis State Nature Preserve, North Chagrin Reservation (a Cleveland Metropark), The Holden Arboretum, and these Lake Metroparks: Chapin Forest, Penitentiary Glen, Hidden Valley, and Girdled Road.

Access

Hiking is permitted on four trails during daylight hours. Boats are prohibited in the marsh. The longest and most challenging trail, the two-mile Zimmerman Trail, runs from a parking lot on Headland Drive (west of SR 44) to another parking lot at the end of Rosemary Lane (Morton Park) in Mentor. It follows the path of the ancient river, first southerly then westerly, passing through hardwood stands, around hummocks, and along the edge of the marsh. It crosses shallow ravines and rills. Portions of the path could be flooded.

The one-third mile, boardwalked Wake Robin Trail goes straight into the marsh from a parking lot on Woodbridge Drive. This path will keep you dry and take you deep into the marsh. A few paces west, also on Woodbridge Drive, is the Carl and Mary Newhous Overlook, a paved path just one-tenth of a mile long. Folks in wheelchairs or pushing strollers might fancy this view.

The Kerven Trail starts at Marsh House, the nature center on Corduroy Road. This .75-mile lasso-shaped trail leads through a forest and a field and traces the south shore of the marsh. Portions of this trail also can be soggy.

Marsh House is usually open noon to 5 p.m. on weekends during the warm months. Trail maps can be found beside the parking lot. Nature programs are held for groups by appointment. For information about nature programs contact the Mentor Marsh Nature Center, 5185 Corduroy Road, Mentor, Ohio 44060; phone (216) 257-0777.

Also contact the Ohio Department of Natural Resources, Division of Natural Areas and Preserves, Fountain Square, Building F-1, Columbus, Ohio 43224-1331; phone (614) 265-6453.

Geology

Just within the last 12,000 years or so, this area has been a lake bed, a dry plain, a river, and now a marsh. A marsh is a wetland found beside a large lake or an ocean, usually with lagoons wide enough for a canoe and featuring many plant and animal habitats.

About 10,000-12,000 years back, east of here, an enormous dam of ice blocked melting Wisconsinan glacier water from escaping through the Niagara-St. Lawrence valleys. The water backed up behind this ice dike and formed Lake Warren, whose shoreline was 100 feet higher that Lake Erie's. (U.S. Route 20 in Northeastern Ohio follows the beach ridges of this ancient lake.)

One day the ice dam collapsed and Lake Warren drained into the Atlantic Ocean, leaving the Mentor area high and dry. Now comes the Grand River. The current starts in the high ground (the Allegheny Plateau) to the east, then heads across a flat lake plain, curling, bending, and snaking its way to Lake Erie.

Back then, Lake Erie drew its shoreline farther north. The Grand River meandered in the flatlands close to that shoreline. At present-day Fairport, the river S-hooked west, then south for a mile, and west again for three miles through a neck to Lake Erie. Gradually, wind and waves eroded the shoreline southward, choking the neck and river mouth. Meanwhile, the big west-to-south riverbend near Fairport kept eroding the bank northward, toward the approaching lakeshore.

Nobody knows exactly, but one day (before white settlement) the riverbank at the big bend collapsed, either run over by a flood, or beaten down by waves during a violent storm. In either case, the Grand River had a new outlet to Lake Erie.

The abandoned river channel filled with silt and sediment from decaying plants, and evolved into a lush marsh abounding with plants and animals preferring an aquatic environment. Black Brook and Heisley Creek, former tributaries to the Grand River, freshen the marsh. Though plugged at the surface, water from the marsh still seeps westward through sand into the lake.

Wildlife

The mask of the marsh has changed several times since the rerouting of the Grand River. Had it been left alone, the marsh might have been a woods today.

Shortly after its abandonment, submerged plants (the stringy weeds that stick to oars and paddles), water lilies, and water lotus moved into the shallows. The ruins of these plants and the silt they collected set the stage for cattails, bulrushes, and sedges (grasslike plants) which grew inward from the shore and shrunk the ponds. This is probably how the marsh looked in the 1850s when disappointed settlers reported that the area lacked trees.

Meanwhile, buttonbush, alder, and willow took root in the soggy soil at the edge of the marsh. Then elm, ash, red maple, and pin oak—the swamp forest trees—colonized the old river banks and marched into the swamp itself. By the 1950s, only a small pool of the open marsh had not been overwhelmed by the trees. The natural process that transforms a wetland into a woods was on the road to completion.

However, in the late 1950s, the forest beside Black Brook began to die. Soon, some 225 acres of forest had been wiped out and cattails made a comeback. Naturalists discovered that pollution (runoff) from a nearby salt mine, and higher Lake Erie water levels killed the forest. The stumps protruding above the water like funereal statuary remind us of the former woodland.

The saltier water enabled the long-stemmed plume grass, which reaches heights of 10 feet, to become the dominate marsh flora. Beavers colonized the marsh in 1973. Their dams raised the water level, choking a red maple-pin oak community along the northeast shore. A few clusters of these trees survive on higher ground.

Buttonbush, alder, and black willow continue to thrive near open water in the northeast section. On the old river banks look for beech and sugar maple. A small mixed oak swamp forest, uncommon in the Lake Erie region, still exists along the eastern border of the preserve.

The marsh is a bird-admirers' paradise. Some 200 different kinds of birds—both permanent residents and migratory species—have been counted at Mentor Marsh. Expert birders might record as many 125 species during peak days of the spring and fall migrations. You are more apt to hear some birds than to see them, so thick is the vegetation and so shy the birds. These recluses include the long-billed marsh wren and the Virginia and king rails.

Migratory waterfowl such as ducks, coots, teals, and gallinules feast in the calm, shallow water, while geese and others dine in deeper channels. Great blue herons tiptoe on the edges for frogs and small fry. The dead stumps mentioned above serve as homes for bluebirds, wood ducks, red-headed woodpeckers, and the prothonotary warbler. Bitterns, killdeer, and varieties of shorebirds also can be seen. And everywhere, red-winged blackbirds perch on cattails while marsh wrens scurry among the reeds. Swallows perform their aerial acrobatics above the pond. Northern harriers (marsh hawk) and an occasional osprey fly in higher patterns over the preserve.

And what would a swamp be without snakes—queen, ribbon, and northern water snake—but none are poisonous. Spring peepers and bullfrogs share their melodies. Careful observers might see a mink, red fox, weasel, raccoon, or opossum on an evening food binge. Those dome-shaped dwellings of cattails and grass belong to muskrats, sometimes seen near trails.

History

In the 1930s, Charles Shipman, a chemist, advocated saving the marsh and nearby Headlands Beach. Shipman's message laid the groundwork for the 1951 state purchase of 125 acres for Headlands Beach State Park. A portion of this acquisition included a tip of the marsh (Shipman Pond) and was dedicated Shipman Wildlife Memorial in 1956.

In the early 1960s, local conservation groups hooked up with the Cleveland Museum of Natural History and the Ohio Chapter of The Nature Conservancy (TNC) to block plans for a boating and water skiing park at the site.

In 1965 the Morton Salt Company gave the state surface rights to 320 acres, followed by a 90-acre donation by Diamond-Shamrock Company. Later, the local Mentor Marsh Committee and TNC bought 80 acres of swamp forest targeted for logging.

The Cleveland Museum of Natural History later became custodian of this "living museum."

Mentor Marsh was one of the nation's first National Natural Landmarks, a designation granted by the U.S. Department of the Interior in 1964. On May 10, 1973 the marsh became a state nature preserve.

SUMMIT COUNTY METROPARKS

Thanks to generous benefactors and clever purchases by the park district, a dozen legacies of natural and human history have been preserved in this industrialized and urban county. Vegetation is reclaiming the structures of human industries—dams, races, barns—found on the sites. The growth, a green bandage, ends the sense of loss and reconnects humans to their natural past. Admission to the 12 metroparks is free. They are open 8 a.m.-11 p.m. For more information, contact the Metroparks Serving Summit County, 975 Treat Line Road, Akron, Ohio 44313; phone (216) 867-5511.

- **Furnace Run Metropark**
- **Gorge Metropark**
- **O'Neil Woods Metropark**
- **Firestone Metropark**
- **Goodyear Heights Metropark**

Raccoon

FURNACE RUN

Though it has been disturbed by the construction of two major highways and a row of steel towers toting power lines, Furnace Run Metro Park is bouncing back, attracting beaver and deer and heron once again.

Location

Northwestern Summit Coun- County, Richfield Township.

Northbound travelers on Interstate 77 can take the State Route 21/Ohio Turnpike (Brecksville Road) exit. (There is no exit here for southbound cars.) The exit lane travels north, so you will have to turn around in nearby parking lots and head south on Brecksville Road (SR 21). Go under I-77, ignore the southbound ramp for I-77, and take the next right, Townsend Road. The park entrance will be on the right in a mile.

From the Ohio Turnpike, exit at SR 21 (Gate 11) and go south 1 mile to Townsend Road, then turn right to the park entrance.

Ownership

Summit County Metroparks.

Size & Designation

Furnace Run Metropark comprises 890 acres, almost all of it being a deciduous forest.

Nearby Natural Attractions

Furnace Run is one of 12 metroparks serving Summit County. Hampton Hills,

Firestone, Gorge, and O'Neil Woods metroparks are briefly described below. Children may especially enjoy the F.A. Seiberling Naturealm, the park district's nature center.

While in Summit County, visit Portage Lakes State Park and the Cuyahoga Valley National Recreation Area.

Access

The trailhead for nature paths totaling 3.2 miles is located at the end of a short trail that begins to the left of the Brushwood Shelter. Brushwood Lake, beside the shelter, grew behind an old mill dam blocking Rock Creek.

You have choices at the trailhead, where you will find maps in a wooden box. A left turn follows the 1.2-mile Rock Creek Trail which heads north through hardwoods with I-77 on the right and the creek on the left. At the north boundary (Ohio Turnpike) the path crosses the creek and ambles south through a forest of pines, spruce, and encroaching hardwoods. It finishes in a picnic area north of the shelter. A shortcut appears about a third of the way along the trail and shortens the hike.

Old Mill Trail, a mile long, goes to the right (south) and soon comes to a fork. Here you will see a memorial to Charles Francis Brush Jr., the namesake of the shelter and lake. The right fork descends a small hill and stays in the floodplain of Furnace Run heading south. This path also is the eastern leg of the Buttonwood Trail. The high road, or left fork, winds south through a beech-maple forest, and is the more scenic walk. The two arms of the Old Mill Trail converge in the south end of the area.

At this junction, bear left following the Buttonwood Trail, upstream along the creek. The limbs of sycamore, walnut, buttonbush, willow, and cottonwoods shade the small pools in the creek. The path slides past the lake, and enters the parking lot. Wooden trail posts help you find the way. You will find some benches along the way—places to rest feet, watch wildlife, or lace children's muddy shoes.

The trails are wide and easy to follow. There are a few brief steep climbs up and down creek banks, nothing too strenuous. You'll be crossing streams on stepping stones, but after a heavy rain the current is likely to wash over these steps. Be prepared for muddy trails and wet feet.

More than two-thirds of the park is off limits to the public. Here, wildlife gets a breather from the intrusions of humans. Much of that land is roughly bordered by I-77 on the west, Boston Mills Road, Black Road, and State Route 303. These oak-hickory tracts can be explored during the annual "Stream Stomp." To find when you can go stomping, contact Metroparks of Summit County, 975 Treaty Line Road, Akron, Ohio 44313; phone (216) 867-5511.

You can peek into this forbidden zone while tiptoeing on the half-mile H.S. Wagner Daffodil Trail, located off Brush Road. This trail is especially beautiful when the daffodils bloom in early spring.

The park is open daily from 8 a.m.–11 p.m. Brushwood Lake is open for ice skating in winter, and the hill beside the parking lot can be used for winter sledding.

Recently modernized Brushwood Shelter accommodates 100 people. It has a food service area, and restrooms. Call the park office for reservations and fees.

Geology

Geologically speaking, you won't find narrow gorges, cliffs, or ledges along the hiking trails. Instead, study the smaller scenes—stream bank erosion which exposes roots and topples trees; sand and gravel beaches on the bends; and pools deep enough for tiny fish.

In the protected (non-public) area of the park the terrain is steeper and more rugged. Tributaries pouring into Furnace Run have carved several ravines.

Wildlife

Canada geese, almost as common as pigeons, and ducks of several varieties float on Brushwood Lake. Occasionally, a great blue heron will wade in the creek, hunting for tasty morsels. The park attracts a fair number of warblers in the warm months, and protects permanent residents such as owls, bluejays, sparrows, and cardinals.

Trees associated with an oak-hickory forest dominate the higher ground above Furnace Run in the protected area of the park. The hiking trails, however, traipse through the land of beeches and maples, with sycamore, willow, and walnut clinging to stream banks.

You will find groves of pines and spruces scattered throughout the park. Many were planted in the 1930s and have grown to maturity.

From time to time, beavers will establish a colony along the creek. I found deer and raccoon tracks on the trail, and I hear that fox run wild in the hollows.

History

Furnace Run Metropark took shape in 1929 when the family of Charles Francis Brush Jr. donated 272 acres to the newly formed Akron Metropolitan Park District. It was opened that year, one of the first in the park district.

Park development hastened during the Depression

years (1930s) when work crews from the Civilian Conservation Corps built trails, roads, bridges, and other structures.

Brushwood Lake was a favorite swimming hole until construction of the Ohio Turnpike and other human developments upstream speeded up erosion. The park district recently scooped out the muck so that waterfowl and ice skaters could return.

Tulip Tree leaf

GORGE METROPARK

Gorge Metropark lets visitors peek into a gorge which exposes pages of geological and human history.

Location

At the border of Akron and Cuyahoga Falls in Summit County.

Exit State Route 8 at Howe Road then go south to Front Street. The park entrance is off Front Street near the bridge over the river.

Ownership

Summit County Metroparks.

Size & Designation

The park encompasses 205 acres.

Nearby Natural Attractions

See Furnace Run.

Access

Two trails, each covering 1.8 miles, emerge from the parking lot. The Gorge Trail, a loop path, heads west, beyond the dam, and visits the Mary Campbell Cave, a channel cut through sandstone called Chuckery Race, and the narrow gorge itself. It returns to the parking lot.

The Glens Trail travels east on the north bank of the river, and finishes at Front Street. Retrace your steps to the parking lot.

Geology

For 12,000 years, the Cuyahoga River has been slicing through this chasm. It has already washed away the glacial topsoil and a thick layer of pebbly, 300 million-year-old Sharon conglomerate. Now it is working on sheets of shale. Several springs spill from the ledges, but don't drink the water.

See Chapin Forest Reservation and The Holden Arboretum (Little Mountain) for more information on Sharon conglomerate.

Wildlife

You will see oak, blackgum, tulip trees, yellow birch, and bunches of spring wildflowers nourishing themselves on the valley walls. Don't expect to see a wide variety of flying and four-legged creatures here, except for the mainstays who endure urban environments. However, spring and fall migratory birds can be spotted in this protected corridor.

History

In 1759, little Mary Campbell was abducted in Pennsylvania by Delaware Indians and brought to the cave here to live with Chief Netawatwees. Mary went home, five years later, at the end of the French-Indian War.

In 1844, workers began cutting a channel through the sandstone, a project called the Chuckery Race. Water flowing in the race was supposed to bring prosperity to a new boomtown called Summit City. The city went bust, but the race got listed on the National Register of Historic Places.

From 1882 to the 1920s, folks flew on the roller coaster and kicked up their heels at High Bridge Glens Park, located here. The Northern Ohio Traction and Light Company, the forerunner of Ohio Edison, gave 144 acres of land to the park district in 1930.

Ruffed grouse

O'NEIL WOODS METROPARK

This hilly park offers scenic views of Summit County, and its trail explores forest, meadow, floodplain, and creek.

Location

Bath Township, Summit County.

The entrance is on Martin Road. Park in the Lone Pine Picnic Area.

Ownership

Summit County Metroparks.

Size & Designation

O'Neil Woods totals 274 acres.

Nearby Natural Attractions

See Furnace Run.

Access

Deer Run Trail, a 1.8-mile loop path, begins and ends at the Lone Pine Picnic Area (where toilets also are located). This path heads south along a narrow ridgetop before crossing Bath Road and swooping into the Yellow Creek Valley. It follows the creek, then bends north to the trailhead.

Geology

Hilly terrain sets off the park. Yellow Creek flows over a shale bed and drains into the Cuyahoga River to the east.

Wildlife

Oaks prevail on the ridges but along Yellow Creek the black walnut, sycamore, eastern cottonwood, and black willow spread their branches. Ferns and wildflowers are especially abundant in the forest. The hiking trail visits one of the few alder swamps in the county.

The park is known for its deer, which quiet hikers are apt to see in the leafless months. The many habitats provide shelter for a thriving collection of birds, notably ruffed grouse and barred owls (oaks and ridges), woodcocks and bluebirds (meadows), kingfishers (creek), as well as song sparrows.

History

The family of William and Grace O'Neil donated their family farm to the park district in 1972. The O'Neils founded the General Tire & Rubber Company. For two decades, beginning in the 1930s, the farm served as a family and weekend retreat for horseback riding and gentleman farming.

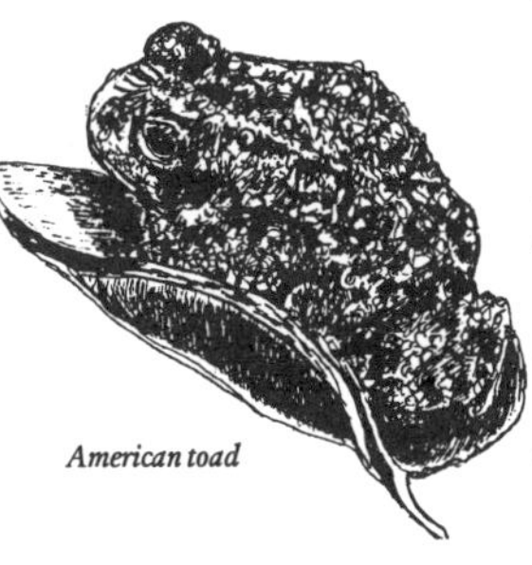

American toad

FIRESTONE METROPARK

Boasting a river, two ponds, a marsh, and a race, Firestone Metropark is a wetland paradise.

Location

Summit County, just south of Akron.

Entrances are located on Axline Avenue, Warner Road, and two on Harrington Road.

Ownership

Summit County Metroparks.

Size & Designation

The park totals 255 acres.

Nearby Natural Attractions

See Furnace Run.

Access

The 1.6-mile Willow Trail is accessible from each entrance. Start at the Little Turtle Pond and Spring Pond entrance off Harrington Road. Little Turtle Pond is a popular fishing hole for anglers 15 years and younger.

The Willow Trail starts its loop in the parking lot, passes the ponds, follows the Tuscarawas River, visits the Axline Avenue Picnic Area, traces Tuscarawas Race and the river, crosses the Tuscarawas Picnic Area, then runs along the shore of the swamp back to the starting point.

Wildlife

More than 175 species of birds have been counted in this park of many habitats. The creek and ponds sponsor fish, crayfish, turtles, frogs, salamanders and other aquatic creatures. Look for fox, raccoons, muskrats, skunks, mice, and voles in the swamp and wet meadows.

History

Some 189 acres of land was given to the park district in 1949 by the Firestone Tire and Rubber Company. The place had been a dairy farm.

The Tuscarawas Race, a channel built in the 19th century to fill the Ohio Canal, runs through the south section of the park.

Sarsaparilla

GOODYEAR HEIGHTS METROPARK

Oaks and other hardwoods are slowly pushing out the Scotch pines that were planted 60 years ago. Anglers and birdwatchers will satisfy their natural desires around Alder Pond.

Location

Summit County, Akron.

From Interstate 76, head north on SR 91 (Darrow Road), turn left on Newton Street, then right on Frazier Avenue.

Ownership

Summit County Metroparks

Size & Designation

This metropark comprises 410 acres.

Nearby Natural Attractions

See Furnace Run.

Access

Anglers will make a beeline to Alder Pond via the half-mile Lake Trail (toilets nearby). Midway to the pond, the Alder Trail (1.8 miles) goes off to the right. This trail soon splits again. The Alder Trail goes left (north) and shares the path with the Piney Woods Trail. Go right at the next intersection, eastbound on Piney Woods Trail.

Piney Woods Trail (two miles) journeys through a growing hardwood forest, a pine plantation on the east side of park, and back to the Alder Trail. Turn left (south) when you reach this last junction, and return to the trailhead. Don't let the fitness trail confuse you.

Wildlife

Trees more typical of the woods of northeastern Ohio are replacing the pines that relief workers planted in the 1930s. In one area on the north side of the park, acidic soil allows sassafras trees to flourish above a mat of sarsaparilla.

Some areas of Alder Pond are becoming bog-like, sponsoring colonies of yellow birch and cattail. Muskrats, who live in cattail lodges, Canada geese, and mallard ducks call the pond home.

History

The Goodyear Tire & Rubber Company and Gilbert Waltz donated the land in 1930.

Eastern meadowlark

SWINE CREEK RESERVATION

Old-timers say the creek was named by pioneer farmers who slept easy knowing their foraging hogs would not run away from this valley. First, no sensible hog would ever stray far from the Mother Lode of acorns and other mast crops that rained upon this landscape. Second, not even an athletic hog could reach the rim of the ravines after pigging out on the nuts. Today, local Amish confine their swine in traditional barnyard quarters. The quiet, old-fashioned ways of these farmers wrap the reservation in silence and harmony.

Location

Southeastern Geauga County, Middlefield Township.

Leave Middlefield, heading south on State Route 608. A couple of miles outside of town, SR 608 deadends into State Route 528. Drive straight across SR 528 onto Old State Road, then immediately turn left to Swine Creek Road. Turn left on Hayes Road, and another left at the park entrance. Bear right (north) at the first intersection and park at the Woods Edge Picnic Area.

Ownership

Geauga Park District.

Size & Designation

Swine Creek Reservation encompasses 331 acres.

Nearby Natural Attractions

The reservation is the second largest of seven sites managed by the park district. The other locations are Big Creek Park (briefly described below), Whitlam Woods, W.C. Best Preserve, Eldon Russell Park, Bessie Benner Metzenbaum Park, and Burton Wetlands. Also visit, in

Geauga County, Punderson State Park, and Auburn Marsh, East Branch Reservoir, and Hambden Orchard state wildlife areas.

Access

Ten trails totaling six miles visit nearly every nook and cranny in the reservation. Look for trail maps at a parking lot next to the trailhead for the Siltstone Trail. Instead of going right to the Woods Edge Picnic Area, bear left after entering and pull into the first parking lot at the right.

I recommend the creekside trails. Starting at the Woods Edge Picnic Area, head south on the wide, smooth Wagon Trail. Ignore the first two paths branching to the left. These are the north and south legs of the Siltstone Trail. Instead, leave the Wagon Trail at the third path, the Valley Trail. This declivitous path also shoots to the left.

The Valley Trail follows an unnamed tributary of Swine Creek downstream through a steep hollow. Near the southern border of the north section of the park, the trail crosses the rill and swings north up a long ridge. Near the summit, the Valley Trail rejoins the Wagon Trail. Bear right on the Wagon Trail if you want to return to car. Go left to reach the Gray Fox, Sugarbush, and Meadowlark trails. The Woods Edge picnic spot offers restrooms, drinking water, playground, and picnic tables.

Swine Creek can be experienced from the Valley Shelter Picnic Area on the southside of Swine Creek Road, east of Hayes Road. Take the mile-long Razorback Trail across the creek and a meadow. Bear left at the first fork and head downstream. Go right at the next junction and climb the slope to a railroad grade. Here the path swings right. Just follow the trail back to the first fork. Retrace your steps to the picnic area to exit.

Swine Creek Lodge opens on Sunday afternoons during the winter. Stop by for a hot beverage and a warm fire. Cross-country ski trails abound. If you get tired of hiking or skiing, hop on the wagon pulled by a team of Clydesdale horses (weekends only). Some 30 acres of the forest is a sugarbush where maple syrup drips into buckets in March. Visitors can watch the sugar making process at the Sugarhouse, open on March weekends. Follow the path to the Sugarhouse from the Woods Edge Picnic Area. Anglers can fish for bass and bluegill at Killdeer and Lodge ponds. Swimming and wading are not allowed, however.

Drive carefully! Amish folk on foot and in horse-drawn carriages own the road, too. Be wary of pets and livestock in the road.

The park is open daily from 6 a.m.–11 p.m. Nature programs are held year-round. For more information contact the Geauga Park District, 9160 Robinson Road, Chardon, OH 44024; phone (216) 286-9504.

Geology

The "gems" in Swine Creek are "lucky stones," pearly white pebbles of quartz found in Sharon conglomerate, a type of sandstone made during the Pennsylvanian geological period some 300 million years ago. Truth is, the "gems" are either the leftovers of a lobe of overlaying conglomerate that has eroded away, or they have been carried here by the current of Swine Creek. (See The Holden Arboretum for more on Sharon conglomerate.)

The steep slopes swelling above Swine Creek and its tributaries are primarily composed of thick strata of clay deposited by the Wisconsinan glacier about 12,000 years ago. Notice the "slumps," or huge blocks, of clay that have broken from the slope.

Wildlife

Fear not. Wild swine (boars) do not roam in these woods. You are more likely to see deer, fox, mink, and birds, notably eastern meadowlark, bobolink, horned lark, ruffed grouse, snow bunting, screech owl, Savannah sparrow, and killdeer.

Cottonwood, walnut, sycamore, and willow shade Swine Creek where the long-legged great blue heron and plunging kingfisher hunt for fish. Beech, maple, wild black cherry, white and red oak, and wild azalea occupy the slopes and ridges.

Spring brings the eruption of wildflowers led by large-flowered trillium, various violets, columbine, bee balm (or Oswego tea), and lobelia.

History

The reservation used to be part of a 1,200-acre hunting preserve owned by Windsor Ford, a well-to-do man from Mesopotamia.

Ford sold the sugarbush, lodge and pond areas (268 acres) to the park district in 1977. The park district later bought 63 acres along Swine Creek, raising the total acreage to 331.

BIG CREEK PARK

Scenic Big Creek, its slopes coated by a fur of beeches, hemlocks, and maples, bisects this 642-acre wooded tract.

Location

Northern Geauga County, a few miles north of Chardon.

Choose from among three entrances: Robinson Road (main entrance) Wood in Road, and Ravenna Road.

Ownership

Geauga Park District.

Size & Designation

Big Creek Park preserves 642 acres and serves as the park district headquarters.

Nearby Natural Attractions

See Swine Creek Reservation.

Access

A network of 11 trails (6.4 miles) and a section of the Buckeye Trail carry visitors to the attractions in the park. The Donald W. Meyer Center has nature exhibits, classrooms, and a wildlife feeding area. Campground (permit), fishing ponds, and four picnic areas are available.

Geology & Wildlife

The tributaries feeding Big Creek have cut impressive ravines, giving the park some steep relief and bedrock outcrops. Hemlocks populate the cool, shady slopes. The spring wildflower show in this forest is especially colorful. The place also attracts the warblers and songbirds who spend their winter in the tropics.

History

The Great Depression ruined Samuel Livingston Mather's dream of building a posh resort at this place. In 1955, he donated 505 acres (of his original 1,000-acre holding) to the state. The park district began leasing the land in 1965, and obtained title in 1990.

Bullfrog

TINKER'S CREEK STATE NATURE PRESERVE

Like meandering Tinker's Creek, the serpentine trail snaking through this isolated wetland takes you into the realm of beavers, waterfowl, dragonflies, and bullfrogs. It's a cornucopia of pond, marsh, forest, and stream creatures.

Location

Border of Summit and Portage counties, Twinsburg and Streetsboro townships.

From Hudson or Aurora, motor down the Hudson-Aurora Road to Old Mill Road and head west 1.6 miles to the preserve.

Exit Interstate 480 at Frost Road and take an immediate left across from the filling station. Turn right at the next intersection (half mile away) on to Hudson-Aurora Road, go past the entrance to Tinker's Creek State Park, then turn left (west) on Old Mill Road. The parking lot is located on the north side of the road. Seven Ponds Trail begins across the street, near the railroad tracks.

Ownership

Ohio Department of Natural Resources, Division of Parks and Recreation owns the land. The Division of Natural Areas and Preserves manages the site.

Size & Designation

This 786-acre marsh became a scenic nature preserve on December 27, 1974.

Nearby Natural Attractions

Tinker's Creek State Park, West Branch State Park, Frame Lake-Herrick Fen and Eagle Creek state nature preserves, Nelson-Kennedy Ledges State Park, and Berlin Lake Wildlife Area are all in Portage County. Portage Lakes State Park is located in Summit County.

Access

Seven Ponds Trail parallels the railroad at first and cuts through a pine plantation. In the pines the trail splits. The trail to the left is the half-mile Lonesome Pond Loop Trail. Hikers with limited time can take this route to get a taste of the preserve.

To see all seven ponds, stay on the Seven Ponds Trail. After visiting two ponds on the left and two on the right the trail splits again. (You will find restrooms to the left.) The path to the right goes through a stand of hardwoods on a peninsula that juts into the marsh. The path ends at the southernmost tip of this peninsula. Return to the intersection and visit the observation deck which overlooks the sprawling marsh and small pond. The current, winding below the deck and winding around the peninsula, is Tinker's Creek.

Return to the main trail and head northward with ponds on the left and the marsh on the right. In the pines, bear right to visit Lonesome Pond, or take the left to return to the parking lot. The southern bank of Lonesome Pond has a long view of the marsh, and the interlocking branches of shrubs have formed tunnels of greenery.

Though insect repellent, long pants, long-sleeved shirts and ball caps are recommended for summer hikes, I was never bothered by mosquitoes (late June) thanks to thousands of hungry dragonflies who cleared the air of the pests. The daring buggers even buzzed under the brim of my hat, literally snagging mosquitoes heading for my brow.

Seven Ponds Trail measures 1.75 miles and is easy to follow. Keep in mind that the terrain, though flat, can be muddy and slippery. A drinking fountain, located between the first and second ponds, was not working when I visited.

The preserve is open daily from dawn to dusk. For more information contact the Ohio Department of Natural Resources, Division of Natural Areas and Preserves, Fountain Square, Building F-1, Columbus, Ohio 43224-1331; phone (614) 265-6453.

Geology

Tinker's Creek originates from higher ground in northern Portage County and snakes across a high plateau leveled by a glacier 15,000 years ago. Consequently, water flows and drains slowly here, and much of the land is a fertile, sprawling peat swamp and marsh. (After this slow start, Tinker's Creek boils through a deep gorge in the Bedford Reservation a few miles downstream, creating one of the nation's natural landmarks.)

Human handiwork enlarged an existing wetland. The railroad grade built a century ago along the western boundary of the preserve acted as a dam and turned fields into shallow ponds and mires. Tinker's Creek is a remnant of that large swamp.

Much of the wetland has been drained for farming and other enterprises. The seven ponds in the preserve all are man-made.

Wildlife

Tinker's Creek preserve teems with life. Around the time the place became a nature preserve, Dr. David Waller of Kent State University identified 188 species of birds, proof of the swamp's value as a habitat. Waller's sightings included rarities like the bald eagle, the American and least bitterns, loggerhead shrike, and king rail, all endangered; the sharp-shinned hawk, red-shouldered hawk, Virginia rail, purple martin, and sora, all "special interest" or potentially threatened. Others have seen the endangered black tern. Some of these protected birds can still be observed here.

You may also spot several varieties of flycatchers, the Louisiana waterthrush, wood duck, scarlet tanager, yellow, cerulean, and blackburnian warblers, common loon, osprey, American coot, and great horned owl. The preserve is a perfect location to view the spring and autumn migrations of birds.

The preserve safeguards three threatened plants (spotted pondweed, highbush cranberry, and crinkled hairgrass) and five potentially threatened—prickly bog sedge, long sedge, prairie sedge, catberry, and swamp oats.

Fifty-five kinds of wildflowers have been identified. Test your skills looking for dwarf St. John's-wort, lesser toadflax, wild licorice, hog peanut, Canadian dwarf cinquefoil (five fingers), mad dog skullcap, turtlehead, bottle gentian, northern arrowwood, pickerelweed, meadow sweet, and wild cucumber.

Ferns named groundpine, bracken, sensitive, rattlesnake, and marsh grew here in the mid-1970s. You might see royal fern, too.

The preserve protects snapping turtles, four-toed salamanders, and snakes. Deer, fox, mink, weasel, raccoon, squirrel, and chipmunk live here. Several cottontail rabbits bounced into the underbrush on my approach.

Lepidopterists are rewarded by the 241 species of butterflies and moths counted here in 1986 by Dr. Roy W. Rings of the Ohio Agricultural Research and Development Center in Wooster. The red admiral, little wood satyr, promethea moth, and the rare hesitant dagger moth have been observed flitting about. (Is the latter moth rare because he hesitates to use his dagger?)

Trees have not been forgotten. They are represented by white pine (planted), hawthorn, ash, slippery elm, alder, red osier, willows, aspen, beech, black cherry, red maple, oaks (swamp white, red, pin, and chinkapin), dogwood, and others. Cattails as big as trees are prolific, and buttonbush are everywhere.

History

This area has been heavily trapped (beaver, muskrat, and mink being the main targets), hunted, and fished. Recently fired shotgun shells found along the trail attest that hunting, an illegal activity in the preserve, still occasionally occurs here.

The preserve land once was part of the adjoining state park. Two decades ago 786 acres of the state park became a designated nature preserve.

Journal

June 1993. Just as I entered woods on a narrow strip of land a loud clap echoed through the preserve. It was the alarm of a beaver. The creature had slapped the still marsh waters with his paddle-like tail. Ripples on the pond next to the railroad tracks revealed the location of the sentry. I searched for the beaver through my binoculars.

A second, louder crack sounded, the splash about 100 yards from the first one. A few ducks scattered, then a heron, then silence fell upon the marsh again.

The by-products of the beaver's work—gnawed saplings and shrubs, stripped branches, girdled trees, piles of wood chips—litter the banks of Tinker's Creek and the ponds. Beavers also have tampered with this oasis. Their projects slow the current of the creek. These incessant builders can transform a landscape faster than any other animal, except humans.

White oak

THE WILDERNESS CENTER

The trails in this recovering land wander through woodlots of 300-year-old hardwoods, by groves of sweet-scented pines, across floodplains, around duck ponds and forest pools, and beside tallgrass prairies and the remnant of an Ice Age lake. The diversity of habitats and well-devised trail system make the Wilderness Center an ideal nature outing. Surrounded by Amish farms, rolling hills, and sleepy small towns, this natural area keeps its distance from the rattle of urban life.

Location

Southwestern Stark County, Sugar Creek Township.

From Wilmot, the nearest village, drive northwesterly on State Route 250. After crossing the bridge over Sugar Creek (about a mile out of Wilmot) turn right (north) on Alabama Avenue. The entrance to the center's headquarters will be on the left. Park in the lower lot if you intend to stay beyond 5 p.m.

Although the Sigrist Woods, Sugar Creek, Fox Creek trails, and Pioneer Path can be reached from paths leaving from the Interpretive Building, you can continue north on Alabama Avenue to small parking lots for these trails.

The road becomes gravel beyond the entrance to the center. The parking lot for the Sigrist Woods, Fox Creek, and Sugar Creek trails is on the right, with the lot for the Pioneer Path ahead on the left.

One of the center's satellites, Zoar Woods, is open to the public. Located in northern Tuscarawas County, exit Interstate 77 at Bolivar, travel east on State Route 212 to Zoar, south on County Road 82 about three miles, then west (right turn) on Township Road 380 to a lane that leads to the parking lot. Look for a sign at the entrance of the driveway.

Please drive carefully. Amish residents traveling by horse-drawn buggy, or on foot, have a right to the road. Proceed slowly at the top of hills, and around blind curves.

Ownership

The Wilderness Center is a nonprofit nature education and research center supported by memberships, donations, and bequests.

Size & Designation

The Wilderness Center comprises seven tracts of land totaling 883.5 acres in three counties. Sigrist Woods has been designated an Ohio Natural Landmark.

Nearby Natural Attractions

In Stark County, visit Jackson Bog State Nature Preserve and Quail Hollow State Park.

Access

Six trails at the main site (578 acres) offer seven miles of hiking pleasure. They are open daily from dawn to dusk.

I started with the 3/4-mile Sigrist Woods Trail. From the designated parking lot (see above) follow the boardwalk across Fox Creek and its floodplain to the loop, which circles a hill of giant trees and returns to the boardwalk. It's an easy walk. The Fox Creek (3/4 miles) and Sugar Creek (1 mile) trails are accessible from this location.

Since I intended to hike past 5 p.m., I drove to the lower parking lot at the Interpretive Building. I chose the Pond Trail (1.25 miles), a path enhanced by constructed landmarks. It begins on the west side (left side) of the driveway near the parking lot.

The path descends to Wilderness Lake, a 7.5-acre pond. Here, you will find a covered observation pier. After passing through a pine grove, the trail climbs a gentle slope to a looming tower, a stalwart structure some 23 feet tall holding a large platform. Check out the view of Wilderness Lake and the surrounding countryside. Next, the trail travels to a bird blind beside a woodland pond. This is a good spot to observe waterfowl and other critters. Ahead, in a beech forest, the trail splits. The path to the right returns to the Interpretive Building. I went left, through the beeches, and joined the Belden & Blake Wilderness Walk (1.5 miles).

Notice that oaks dominate the higher elevations on this trail. Bear left at the next fork, where trails to the right trace a shortcut and return to the parking lots. The Wilderness path heads north, then turns left (west) before swinging east.

With sunset approaching, I had to ignore the Pioneer Path, which shoots off to the left (north) from the Wilderness trail. Eventually, the path swings south, crosses an intermittent stream, and welcomes the shortcut trail from the right. Here, I went straight and watched a pair of whitetails (mother and daughter, I suspect) watch me.

Ahead, on the left, is a brief path leading to a marsh. An interpretive sign explains how silt which eroded from surrounding slopes filled in a lake and converted it into the forest swamp. Soon the trail leaves the woods, traces the edge of a planted prairie, and empties into the parking lot. The combined trails measured about 3.5 miles. This ramble is hilly and moderately challenging.

The Zoar Woods site (194 acres) has a 1.5-mile loop trail that winds through a hardwood forest which has been resting and regrowing for a century. Midway the path climbs to an overlook, actually the summit of a 60-foot high strip mine. The pond below fills a mining pit reclaimed in the late 1980s. In 20 years, perhaps, this setting may look more natural. In other words, the best is yet to come.

Trail maps are available in the lobby of the Interpretive Building, open Tuesday through Saturday from 9 a.m.–5 p.m., and Sunday from 1–5 p.m. The building is closed on Mondays, New Year's Eve, New Year's Day, Presidents' Day, Thanksgiving, Christmas Eve, and Christmas. It stays open on Easter, Memorial Day, Independence Day, and Labor Day, but closes on the Tuesday following these holidays. The building has restrooms, wildlife exhibits, a wildlife window (bird feeders), gift shop, planetarium, meeting rooms, and administrative offices.

The Wilderness Center is a popular magnet for cross-country skiers. It hosts several special interest clubs (birding, photography, astronomy, woodcarvers, etc.) for members. A small, fulltime staff is bolstered by volunteer members.

For information about the center, activities, and membership, contact The Wilderness Center, 9877 Alabama Ave., SW, P.O. Box 202, Wilmot, Ohio 44689-0202; phone (216) 359-5235.

Geology

The holdings of The Wilderness Center have a split personality, geologically speaking. The headquarters site and four smaller tracts (not open to the public) are located at the edge of a region that has been covered by one or more continental glaciers in the last million years of so. These lie in "glaciated" Ohio, which comprises about two-thirds of the state.

Zoar Woods (Tuscarawas County) and the center's Doughty Property (Holmes County, no trails) have not been frozen by glaciers. These are found in "unglaciated" Ohio, largely eastern Ohio south of this location, as well as Pike

County and parts of Adams and Brown counties.

The last glacier, the Wisconsinan (15,000 years ago) deposited thick bands of debris called till (sand, gravel, boulders, silt, clay) over the land. It brought with it large boulders from Canada, called erratics. You can see them lying alone in the forest. Most of these orphans are composed of igneous rock, such as granite.

In northeastern Ohio the glacier's influence dipped halfway into Holmes County, covered all of Stark County except for southeastern quarter, and blanketed the northern half of Columbiana County.

The torrents of meltwater that poured from these ice masses created rivers and streams, the erosive agents which have shaped this land. Today, the currents are mainly refreshed by precipitation that runs off the neighboring hills and slopes.

The primary streams in the main preserve are Sugar Creek, forming the southeast boundary, and Fox Creek, which bisects the main site and runs southeasterly into Sugar Creek.

One interesting spot is the marsh located east of the Wilderness Walk and north of the prairie. This former Ice Age lake used to be recharged by water descending from surrounding slopes. However, silt carried by the runoff filled the lake and enabled vegetation to gain control. Water and silt still collect in the basin.

Wilderness Lake, the pond south of the interpretive center, is man-made. An earthen dike on the east shore contains the water and serves as a footpath.

As noted above, coal was mined from the Zoar Woods property. Coal is a fossil fuel, meaning it originated from accumulated vegetation that grew here during the Pennsylvanian and Mississippian geological periods some 285–345 million years ago. Coal, in other words, is an old tropical forest (the so-called Carboniferous Forest) compacted into black, combustible rock.

Scientists depict the Carboniferous Forest as a lush swamp forest. Trees that fell into the stagnant swamp quickly became waterlogged and sank to the bottom where rotting ceased. The trees piled up in this swamp.

The bottom layer is first pressed into peat, then lignite, bituminous coal, and in rare instances anthracite coal. Each form becomes more compact and contains less and less water. For instance, peat is about 40 percent water, while coal is five percent. After compression, anthracite may be only $^{1}/_{25}$th its original size. Bituminous coal, the kind found in Ohio, is 80 percent carbon.

Coal cannot form without accumulation and compression (the latter occurring because of the former). Other ancient swamp forests did not transform into coal because bacteria immediately decayed the fallen vegetation. As a result, there was no accumulation, no compression, and no coal.

According to a brochure published by the center, Zoarites, members of the nearby Zoar utopian settlement (1817–1898), also extracted iron ore from the mine for handmade crafts and tools.

Wildlife

Sigrist Woods is the crown jewel of the center. It is one of this state's few unbroken links to its natural, or primeval, past. Its existence is an eccentricity, an appropriate description considering the personality of its former protector.

This 30-acre woods is a climax forest, meaning it has fully matured and become self-perpetuating. Barring any major human or natural disturbances, the characteristics of the woods should not change much over time.

Three-hundred-year-old oaks (red and white mostly), sugar maples, beeches, hickories, and sycamores stand over the woods. Their intertwining branches high above the ground close the forest canopy (roof) by late spring, leaving the floor in perpetual shade for nearly five months.

Beneath them rise stately basswoods, black walnut, wild black cherry, sourgum, and white ash. Still lower, hornbeam, dogwood, ironwood (also known as blue beech and musclewood), maple-leaved viburnum, and spicebush occupy the understory. Buxom specimens of willow and elm grow beside huge sycamores in the nearby floodplain.

In all honesty, Sigrist Woods cannot be called a virgin woods because humans have soiled the spot with saws and livestock—though not enough to substantially alter its natural integrity. Soon the signs of earlier selective logging (sawed stumps) and grazing will disappear.

Elsewhere in the preserve, a "second growth" forest is reaching maturity. Second growth refers to a woodlot previously logged. Here, oaks and hickories claim the higher and drier ridges, with beech and maples dominating the slopes. Groves of various pines, planted years ago, offer some refreshing green in the winter.

Due to past woodland grazing, the wildflower show is not especially spectacular. Still, count large-flowered trillium, dogtooth (trout) lily, Solomon's seal, and Virginia bluebells among the collection. The center is planning a wildflower restoration program.

The Wilderness Center, so it claims, was the second preserve in Ohio to plant a tallgrass prairie. The meadows total 20 acres and feature floral beauties called blazing star (abundant), coreopsis, sunflower, and prairie coneflower. An amazing collection of ferns (and their associates), some 37 varieties, grows at Zoar Woods.

Snakes, 13 kinds (none poisonous), find refuge in the center's holdings.

Birds typically observed in Northeastern Ohio will be seen here. Warblers and other songbirds arrive in the spring and build nests in the tree canopy. Red-tailed hawks are common, and red-shouldered and broad-winged hawks occasionally fly by during migrations.

At dusk listen for the hoots of great horned, screech, and barred owls. Once in awhile a barn owl (endangered) appears. Long-eared owls, designated a special interest (potentially threatened) bird in Ohio, have been seen hiding in the pines, both at the main site and at Zoar Woods. They probably come here during the winter.

Ruffed grouse and wild turkey live in the woods but are seldom seen. Canada geese, various ducks, and a occasional swan settle on the pond, mostly during spring and autumn migration times.

The usual cast of creatures reside in woods and meadows—squirrels, deer, raccoons, skunks, foxes, and ground hogs (where the center's property borders farmland). Muskrat and beaver hide in the wetlands, and coyotes have been spotted. A river otter (endangered in this state) released by the Ohio Department of Natural Resources has been seen once, but there is no evidence that it has become a permanent resident. The bobcat, another endangered animal, roams in the neighborhood, but has not yet appeared at the preserve.

History

The Wilderness Center was established in 1964, largely on abandoned farmland and recovering woodlots.

Arrowheads and fragments of other artifacts found on the property indicate that the Ancient People (paleo and woodland Indians) probably hunted here, but no camp or village has been discovered.

White settlers began trickling in around 1810. By 1830 most of the land had been purchased and cleared for cultivation and grazing.

Religious separatists from Germany sought refuge and isolation in northern Tuscarawas County in the second decade of the 19th century. In 1817, they established the village of Zoar, a communal settlement. As noted above, they mined iron ore and coal from mines at Zoar Woods. They also paid for their land, some 5,000 acres, by contracting sections of the Ohio-Erie Canal. Ironically, the commune's isolation ended when the canal opened in 1832.

The community fell into a slow decline following the 1853 death of its leader, Joseph Bimeler. The last members sold their remaining holdings in 1898.

Sigrist Woods takes its name from its former owner, Charles Sigrist, a bonafide and likeable eccentric, who lived, as eccentrics do, alone. Sigrist's peculiarities fed many tales. Folks still wonder why he preserved a sheep's head in a jar.

Another curiosity is why he never chopped down the woods. Of course, his contemporaries who asked that question never sat in the shade beneath one of Charley's giant trees. Once, apparently, he did sign away the trees, but when the loggers arrived he changed his mind and chased them away. Bless the eccentrics.

Journal

October 1993. I watch the low-angled rays of the sun brighten the autumn leaves that float motionless on a small woodland pond. The steady beams, thinned to ribbons by hundreds of trees that stand between the pond and the light source, briefly turn the leaves into shards of gold. This treasure dissolves when the sun falls behind a flat, gun-blue cloud on the horizon.

The scene reminds me that the best is yet to come to The Wilderness Center. The prairie promises to ripen fuller next year, and the forest will continue its task of reclaiming its former glory, both here at the main site and at Zoar Woods.

SOUTHEASTERN OHIO

Partridgeberry

CONKLES HOLLOW STATE NATURE PRESERVE

Something pulls me into the gorge at Conkles Hollow. Maybe it's the bold, massive cliffs, the noble hemlocks or the misty caves. Conkles Hollow, tucked away in a crease of the scenic Hocking Hills, conjures up a fairy-tale place of dragons and armored princes. Once captured by its spell, you'll learn why this hollow is hallowed ground. ★ 🔭 🍒

Location

Southwest Hocking County.

The preserve straddles the border of Benton and Laurel townships, some 18 miles from your starting point on State Route 33. The easiest route is to head south from Rockbridge and follow State Route 374 as its zigzags and snakes through Hocking State Forest and Hocking Hills State Park. From SR 374, turn left on Big Pine Road (look for the sign), which takes you to the preserve's entrance about two-tenths of a mile away.

From Logan, take SR 664 south to SR 374. Head west on SR 664/374, past Old Man's Cave in Hocking Hills State Park. Stay on SR 374 when it splits from SR 664 west of the park's lodge, then turn right on Big Pine Road.

Ownership

This preserve is co-owned by the Divisions of Forestry and Parks and Recreation, both in the Ohio Department of Natural Resources. The Division of Natural Areas and Preserves manages the facility.

Size & Designation

This 87-acre scenic nature preserve was dedicated on April 22, 1977.

Nearby Natural Attractions

Hocking County is a prime destination for nature lovers lured by the Hocking Hills State Park (Old Man's Cave, Ash Cave, Cedar Falls, Rock House, Cantwell Cliffs), Rockbridge State Nature Preserve, Lake Logan State Park, and Hocking State Forest.

Access

Indulge your first impulse and walk into the gorge. From the parking lot, cross the iron foot bridge, visit the information board (where brochures may be tucked into a box), then take the Gorge Trail straight ahead along the stream.

The Gorge Trail is a mile round trip walk over relatively flat terrain. As you go deeper into the gorge, the rocks, boulders, tree roots, and logs on the trail offer a bit of challenge—but these are the kinds of obstacles youngsters love to climb. Foot bridges span the creek in several locations.

Halfway along the trail, you will notice a path to the right. It leads to a feature called Diagonal Cave, a recess cave and seasonal waterfall. Many hikers take this detour, though its route is not shown on the brochure map.

Slump Rock, a huge sandstone boulder that rolled off the cliff, appears two-thirds along the way. Next comes the tallest and most impressive cliff, rising 210 feet above the creek. The Gorge Trail ends at the throne of a petite waterfall you have heard since Slump Rock. Retrace your path to the starting point.

Now go topside for a hawk's view into the hollow. The rim trail takes you to some of most splendid views in Ohio, and I highly recommend it.

Let's remember these precautions before departing. The hike to the rim, whichever path you follow, begins and ends with a very steep and demanding hike. Take a breather when necessary—don't press it. The trail levels out once you reach the top, though a few gentle dips lie ahead.

Stay on the trail! You are probably tired of hearing that warning, but here it may save your life. The cliffs can be dangerous! Careless hikers have fallen to their death from these heights! Loose and slippery rocks and soils, and unsecured rocks and trees at the cliff edge may not support your weight.

Be extremely cautious at overlooks, especially after rain or snow. To maintain balance *crawl* on the ledges, and don't make sudden movements. *Don't let children horseplay or run on the overlooks. Don't allow youngsters to run on this trail, or escape from your view.* They can easily trip on tree roots, rocks, and slippery soil, and wind up a casualty.

Climbing waterfalls and cliffs is perilous, foolish, unlawful. Scaling them is *not* as easy as it looks.

Now, with safety in mind, enjoy the Rim Trail, a two-mile loop that traces the rim on both sides of the gorge. Let's begin on the East Rim Trail, which presents the most commanding panoramas. It starts to the right of the information board. The trail immediately begins with a strenuous climb, aided partly with wooden stairs, to the top of the east rim.

The gorge valley unfolds below through several vistas on the East Rim Trail. Two of these overlooks are must stops for photographers and binocular bearers. You will know these overlooks when you see them. (Photographers using tripods should move slowly on these overlooks and work on their knees or in a seated position. Avoid sudden movements that send you or your equipment into the pit.)

Gradually, the ravine narrows. An observation deck near the end of the East Rim Trail gives a striking view of a 95-foot waterfall, a series of cascades in a shady, hemlock glen. Here, signs advise hikers of the dangers of climbing the waterfall.

After crossing the stream via a footbridge (look for the little waterfall at the right) the path becomes the West Rim Trail. Though the West Rim Trail has fewer expansive overlooks, it does offer glimpses into a trio of shady horseshoe-shaped canyons lined with pine and hemlock trees. The traffic on nearby State Route 374, at your right, may be a distraction (unless you enjoy such references to urban civilization).

White pines planted 60 years ago offer solitude, a soft mat for a nap, and a fresh, pine scent. The walk concludes with a steep descent into the valley along switchbacks and stairs.

Conkles Hollow is open every day, from first to last light. Drinking water (well), latrines, and picnic tables can be found in the parking area and along the driveway. Please throw away your litter in a container. Read the interpretive trail signs to learn more about the ecology of the preserve.

Check out the information board for a schedule of naturalist programs held in the preserve. For more information contact the Ohio Department of Natural Resources, Division of Natural Areas and Preserves, Fountain Square, Building F-1, Columbus, Ohio 43224-1331; phone (614) 265-6453.

Geology

Let's back up some 350 million years when rivers and streams ran off steep Alps-like peaks (today's rounded Appalachian Mountains) in the east and emptied into an inland sea that covered most of Ohio. These swift mountain streams deposited coarse sand and finer sediment in a long, irregular shaped delta that went across much of what today is eastern Ohio.

Later, the ocean vanished and the land heaved upward. The sand in the delta dried and compressed into a rock called Blackhand sandstone. (See Blackhand Gorge State Nature Preserve.) The thickness of the sandstone layer ranges from 85–250 feet, but in the gorge at Conkles Hollow it measures 200 feet. In the ensuing years, erosion has removed overlaying sediment and shaped the sandstone into the gorges, rock shelters (recess caves), knobs, and natural bridges typical in the Hocking Hills.

The Blackhand formation has three zones in Conkles Hollow. The rim layer is firmly cemented and withstands erosion better than the middle layer which is crossbedded (see explanation below) and more susceptible to erosion. Notice the gouged out caves at this level. Another firmly cemented stratum, about 100 feet thick, comprises the lower zone.

Beneath the towering, cream-colored cliff in the gorge, you may notice a bluish-gray rock in the stream. This is Cuyahoga shale, a product of the Mississippian geological period, 345–320 million years ago. A thin layer of coarse, pebbly sandstone, called conglomerate, lies above the Blackhand sandstone in places.

The cascades in Conkles Hollow let you visualize a process called undercutting, which has carved waterfalls as diminutive as the one at the end of the Gorge Trail and as mighty as Niagara Falls. For thousands of years the nameless rill that has tumbled southward through the hollow and into Big Pine Creek (near the trailhead) has fallen over a ledge of Blackhand sandstone into a pool. Spray and backwash from the splashing current ate away the rock behind the waterfall and formed a recess cave.

For undercutting to work the rock layer behind the pool must be "less resistant," meaning it erodes faster than the "resistant" strata on the top. Though most of the rock in the gorge is Blackhand sandstone, some layers are less resistant than others. That explains the series of waterfalls at the crotch of the gorge. A well-cemented, resistant layer sits above a less resistant strata. Beneath that plane is another resistant layer, and so on.

Also, observe the cross-bedded layers in the big cliffs. Cross-bedded refers to the archlike layers (typical of delta deposits) that lie at acute angles beneath the horizontal layer. The angles in cross-bedded rock show the direction of the water current at the time of deposition. These cross-beds are less resistant to erosion.

Undercutting, or sapping, weakens support beneath the precipice and causes chunks of the resistant cap to break off and crash into the valley. Some of the flat slabs of rock piled in the creek bed may be the victims of undercutting.

Study the coarse sand beneath the waterfall at the end of the Gorge Trail. It will give you some idea what the beach and delta of the inland sea must have looked like 350 million years ago.

Along the Gorge Trail look for rock shelters (caves) in the walls, car-sized boulders (Slump Rock) detached from the cliffs, and the pitted facades. These show erosion at work.

Conkles Hollow is a box canyon—or an open-ended ravine enclosed by steep, vertical walls. The only way out is the way you got in.

Wildlife

If you step into the gorge after working up a sweat walking the rim trail, a shiver might run down your spine. The temperature is cooler here because the cliffs and tall trees shade the valley floor.

In the cool nooks and crannies, plants commonly found in chillier northern climates, such as hemlock, Canada yew, teaberry, and partridgeberry, have thrived for thousands of years. They arrived like pioneers some 14,000 years ago in the vanguard of the Wisconsinan glacier, which drove to within six miles of the preserve.

Sections of the gorge look like some Greek god dumped a box of giant pickup sticks on the scene. These hemlocks and hardwoods fell in 1982 and 1985, the victims of violent storms which uprooted hundreds of trees. They will be left there to provide shelter for critters, and to slowly decay and return nutrients to the soil, as nature intended. In the gaps opened by the fallen trees, young tulip trees and sweet birch stretch skyward.

Ferns and mosses, several varieties, spread out on the gorge floor. One type found here is the endangered triangle grape fern.

Four plants listed as threatened can be found on the grounds: radiate sedge, pale green panic grass, pipsissewa (a relative of wintergreen), and a wildflower called round-leaved catchfly. Ten species are potentially threatened, notably the long-beech fern and the rock club moss (both reasons enough for not climbing the rocks, their preferred habitat).

Atop the sun-exposed ridges where drier and thinner soil prevails, chestnut oak and Virginia pine grow in clusters. You also will find large specimens of tulip tree, beech, and assorted hardwoods. Blueberry, black huckleberry, and mountain laurel have wedged their way into cracks on exposed walls. Deerberry, serviceberry, sourwood, and three kinds of hickory (shagbark, mockernut, and kingnut) also grow in the preserve.

The footbridge leading from the parking lot to the trailhead crosses Big Pine Creek whose fertile floodplain sponsors one of the best stands of river birch in Ohio.

The preserve is home for many creatures typical of the Ohio woods. The northern copperhead, a poisonous snake, has been seen slithering in these parts but your chances of spotting one are remote.

History

Hunters of the ancient Adena and Fort Ancient cultures probably camped under the overhangs, or cornered their quarry in the box canyon. Wyandots and Shawnees shared these hunting grounds, which were situated close to a trail that connected Central Ohio and West Virginia.

The preserve takes its name from W.J. Conkle who carved his name into the west wall in 1794 or 1797. The inscription "A.O. Cow 1898" appeared beneath it, and both names were reportedly framed in a rectangle of stars. Unfortunately, the engravings were pilfered or dissolved by erosion.

A descendant claims W.J. Conkle came to Ohio from Germany at his father's request. Generations of the Conkle family have inhabited, toiled, and died in the area. Several descendants still live nearby, two centuries after W.J. Conkle left his mark on the rock of ages.

The state bought the prize for its scenic beauty in 1925. During the Depression years the Civilian Conservation Corps planted pines on the grounds. You can see them, now mature, on the rim trails. The gorge was dedicated as a scenic nature preserve on April 22, 1977.

Red fox

MARIE J. DESONIER STATE NATURE PRESERVE

This is a place of silence, far from any city. If you seek solitude and quiet you have come to the right place. This remote preserve in the hills of Southeastern Ohio protects several kinds of habitat, and hikers will find the trails challenging. ᶻᶻᶻ

Location

Southeastern Athens County, Carthage Township.

The closest village is Coolville. From there, head west on State Route 50 for nearly four miles and turn right on County Road 56, the second right after the split of routes 50 and 7. (The road destination sign was not standing when I visited in April 1993.) Travel .3 of a mile and turn left on County Road 65 (also known as Jordan Run Road). The gate to the preserve will be on your left in .7 of a mile. A sign says to park beside the gate if the parking lot gate is closed.

Ownership

Ohio Department of Natural Resources, Division of Natural Areas and Preserves.

Size & Designation

The preserve encloses 491 acres. It was designated an interpretive site on March 26, 1975.

Nearby Natural Attractions

You will find Burr Oak and Strouds Run state parks in Athens County, as well as four state wildlife areas—Sunday Creek, Trimble, Fox Lake, and Waterloo Experiment Station—and Gifford State Forest.

Access

The two-mile Oak Ridge Trail climbs steep terrain and takes you through various habitats, from recovering farm fields to woods of tall timbers.

I started by heading south, or upstream, along Jordan Run and one of its tributaries. The gate on the right blocks the path to an old gravel mine (called a borrow). The trail turns right and begins a steady climb up a ridge densely covered by young hardwoods. Eventually you will reach the junction of the Oak Ridge and High Meadow trails. You are now at the highest point on the trail. The High Meadow Trail, just a half mile, descends to the "borrow" and Jordan Run. I skipped this path and continued on the Oak Ridge Trail to the left.

The trail dips into a tiny ravine but soon rises again into a healthy oak forest. Look to your left for a meadow (a good spot to surprise some deer). The echoes of waterfalls rise from the ravine to the right. Unfortunately, these spills cannot be seen from the trail. During the dry summer months the flow shrinks to a trickle, and the echo dissolves.

A foot bridge spans a seasonal creek that drops into a ravine. The trail follows another ridge, the teasing sound of waterfalls now on your right, then falls to the valley of Jordan Run and returns to the parking lot.

Though there is little chance of getting lost, a trail map posted on the bulletin board in the parking area would be helpful for visitors who like to know the lay of the land. Hiking is forbidden in the portion of the preserve which lies on the east side of County Road 65.

Desonier benefits from its remoteness and steep terrain. It is one of those rare places where the sounds of nature can be heard without distractions.

The preserve is open daily during daylight hours. For more information call the Ohio Department of Natural Resources, Division of Natural Areas and Preserves, Fountain Square, Building F-1, Columbus, Ohio 43224-1331; phone (614) 265-6543.

Geology

Study the winding course of Jordan Run and its feeders. Notice how the current erodes the outside bank of the stream and piles gravel and sand on the inside bank, making bigger loops. All sorts of beachcombing critters—deer, raccoon, fox, turtles, snakes—patrol on these pebbly pads.

Jordan Run, which bisects the preserve, straightens when it hits bedrock. The preserve lies atop layers of shale and sandstone of the Pennsylvanian and Permian periods (225–320 million years ago).

After a heavy rain a half dozen small rivulets tumble 30 feet over ledges in the ravine on the north side of the site. You can hear the hollow echo of these little wonders (but cannot see them) from the Oak Ridge Trail. It has taken these tiny creeks many centuries to create the steep terrain and ravines. The topography in the preserve varies from 680–900 feet in elevation.

Wildlife

The preserve is noted for its diverse vegetative habitats, ranging from abandoned farm fields in various stages of succession (the continuous restorative process of one species being replaced by another) to lush beech-maple stands in the deep hollows and oak-hickory woods on the higher and drier slopes. Dense areas covered by young trees (hawthorn, dogwood, redbud, sumac), competing hardwoods and shrubs surround the mature woodlots. Open lots and crop lands border the property.

The cornucopia includes 81 varieties of wildflowers (notably "at risk" species like Virginia meadow-beauty, green adder's mouth, weak aster, American mistletoe), and 54 species of woody plants, according to a mid-1970s inventory. Ferns are also abundant.

As you would expect amidst such diversity, songbirds are abundant—29 species counted back in 1975. Numerous ruffed grouse have found a home here. Dusky salamanders and red-spotted newts reside in the creek beds.

History

The preserve is named after its former owner, Marie Josephine Desonier, who as a World War II Army nurse known as Captain Stein or Stone served on General Dwight Eisenhower's staff as a public health and refugee advisor. She was the first Allied woman soldier to see the horrors at Buchenwald concentration camp. Later, she served as a consultant to General Douglas MacArthur, head of the Allied occupation forces in postwar Japan.

After the war she married an Army officer named Desonier, settled down in Athens County, and held administrative and teaching posts in local hospitals. She was crowned Mrs. Nelsonville in 1955 and competed for the Mrs. America title. A newspaper story appearing at the time reported that her maiden name was Isselstein.

Marie Desonier bought 301 acres (about 60 percent of the land that became the preserve) in 1930 for $2,000. She sold it to her brother, Henry Stein, in 1966. She died in 1968. Henry Stein gave the tract to ODNR for a nature preserve in his sister's honor in the early 1970s. The preserve was dedicated in 1975, and ODNR purchased four adjoining parcels totaling 189 acres in 1980.

A threat to the preserve's quietude in 1986 drew local conservation groups out of their silence. The preserve's advocates protested a plan to reroute State Route 50 to within a few hundred yards of the refuge. Petitions condemning the plan (400 signatures) were sent to ODNR and other government agencies. Route 50 stayed on its old course.

Journal

April 28. The remains of a fox, reduced to a skeleton and a few patches of fur, lay right in the middle of the Oak Ridge Trail, just a few paces from Jordan Run. The carcass had been there awhile, judging by how the bones had begun to sink into the soft earth and the lack of flesh. Scavengers usually scatter the bones of dead animals, but not this one. This skeleton remained intact, frozen like a fossil, posed in the middle of a stride.

How did it die? No signs of a scuffle, every bone in its place. A gunshot from the road? Disease? Did a flood drop it there? Could it have just died on the trail of old age, starvation, or weariness? I have sometimes felt like this fellow looks.

Marie Desonier remains a secret herself. Why three different maiden names—Stein, Stone, Esselsrein? Did the newspapers err? Did she change her name during the war to conceal her German ancestry? She undoubtedly witnessed many of the dark horrors of the war. Perhaps this wooded land in Ohio let her briefly forget them.

This is a perfect place to contemplate death and mystery. Seclusion. Silence. The right setting for an episode of "Murder, She Wrote," or an old "Twilight Zone". Maybe an Alfred Hitchcock movie, "The Birds." Dusk might be the best time for something unusual to happen. Shadows start to fall. Quiet sets in before the night sounds begin. Gee, I've been here quite a while. There are more stops to make before I head home. Where's my stick? Where's my car?

Red maple leaf

DYSART WOODS

This is one of only a few places in Ohio that looks anything like the primeval forest that nourished the Indians and greeted the first white settlers 300 years ago. Much of the land surrounding these woods has been strip-mined for coal, clear-cut for timber, and grazed by livestock, making the ancient trees more precious. How did the lumberjack's axe and farmer's plow miss these woods? zzz

Location

Central Belmont County, Smith Township.

From Exit 208 on Interstate 70 head south on State Route 149 for about 2.5 miles. Turn left on State Route 147, which goes through Belmont. Continue on SR 147 southeast about four miles then turn right when you see the Dysart Woods Laboratory sign. That road is Township 234, but you will bear right immediately on Township 194, and travel past the caretaker's residence on the left into the preserve. Park in the designated area on the left.

Ownership

Ohio University.

Size & Designation

The property consists of 455 acres, though the virgin woods comprises about 50 acres. Dysart Woods was designated a National Natural Landmark by the U.S. Department of the Interior in 1967.

Nearby Natural Attractions

Camping and picnicking facilities are available at nearby Barkcamp State Park, in Belmont County.

Access

The two virgin woods stand in ravines, separated by a ridge of younger hardwoods. Township Road 194 bisects this ridge. Two trails depart near the parking lot on the east side of TR194.

Start on the Blue Trail (look for blue-blazed posts) which begins in the corner of the parking lot and descends through the immature forest into the ravine where the big trees grow. After crossing a brook, turn right and take the path that loops around the southeast corner of the ancient forest. The path returns to the ford. From here continue straight (north) on the east bank of the creek to the road.

The Red Trail begins across the street, though its entrance requires bending under arching raspberry branches. This route descends through a young woodlot into another ravine hiding the other patch of undisturbed woods. After crossing two rills the path climbs a ridge and loops through the northwest portion of the preserve. Look for the giant tulip tree (a.k.a. tulip poplar, whitewood) said to the biggest of its kind in the state, with a circumference of 15 feet and a height of 130 feet. The Red Trail spans another creek then snakes its way up a slope to the parking lot.

This hilly, challenging route covers about two miles. The narrow trails here are less developed, or more natural (take your pick) than paths in other preserves. Behemoths that have fallen across trails remain whole, uncut by chain saw. These huge trunks and limbs that block the path like twisted dinosaurs may challenge adults, but kids will like climbing over them. The obstacles add to the adventure and let you feel the size of the slumbering giants.

Seekers of solitude and silence will enjoy this remote place. You will hear forest sounds mostly, and the activities of nearby farms. You will not find restrooms or other human comforts in the grassy parking lot. Not a bad place—the parking lot—to spread out a blanket for a picnic or snooze. Just make sure you take all your belongings with you.

For more information contact Ohio University, Department of Environmental and Plant Biology, P.O. Box 869, Athens, Ohio 45701-0869; phone (614) 593-1000.

Geology

Dysart Woods grows atop shales and sandstones formed during the Permian geologic period, 285–225 million years ago. Deposits of coal, some near the surface others hundreds of feet below, also run through here.

The coal seams recall another great primeval forest, known as the Carboniferous Forest, which reigned here about 310–280 million years ago, during the late Pennsylvanian and early Permian geologic periods. The Carboniferous Forest was a luxuriant swamp woods growing on the coast of a warm, shallow sea. The dead leaves and branches of this forest accumulated in thick layers. Eventually, the ocean level rose, and buried and choked the forest under water, clay, and sand. These heavy sediments squeezed the decaying vegetation into "black gold." Ironically, the nuggets of that ancient forest may undermine Dysart Woods.

Wildlife

Dysart Woods is one of the best places in the Eastern U.S. to study forest life and plant succession, or the changes in the types of plants living at a specific location. Biologists call Dysart Woods a mixed mesophytic forest, meaning that a kaleidoscope of trees—in this case, various oaks, beech, tulip tree, sugar maple, and other hardwoods—will share the site.

Some white oaks reach skyward to 170 feet and boast 48-inch diameters. You will also see stout wild black cherry, white ash, beech, and sour gum trees.

When these hardwoods fully leaf in late spring they will close the canopy, and virtually block sunlight from reaching the forest floor. Shade tolerant beech and maple seedlings can grow in this dark environment but not sun thirsty oaks and tulip trees.

When old trees fall, sunlight rushes to the ground faster than water leaking from a corrupted dam. The seedlings and saplings who bathe in this light race to fill the vacancy in the sky.

Earlier stages of plant succession are underway at this refuge. Notice how pioneer shrubs and trees (raspberry, chokeberry, redbud, hawthorns, alder, sassafras) have invaded meadows. These will be replaced by other species, followed by the blend of oaks, hickories, and the beech-maple stands.

Colonies of mushrooms and fungi are ubiquitous, especially at the base of trees and rotting giants. Besides adding beauty and color to the forest, they advance the life-cycle of the forest by breaking down the life-giving nutrients in the decaying vegetation. Look at their delicate features, but do not trample them.

The woods provide shelter for the birds and furry animals typical in these parts. As you enter the woods listen for woodpeckers tapping on trees. Pay special notice to the holes in trees. You might see a wood duck, raccoon, or some other critter peeking at you.

History

The Dysarts descend from Miles Hart who moved to Belmont County from Pennsylvania in 1813. Hart's granddaughter married Henderson Dysart. The succeeding generations cleared much of their land slowly, all except two woodlots which were allowed to stay in their pristine state. (The fact that logging on steep ravines was difficult was probably a factor in the decision.)

The Ohio Chapter of The Nature Conservancy bought the 455-acre farm from the Dysart family when it learned the forest might be logged. When funds ran low, Ohio University agreed in 1966 to pick up the remaining payments and to protect the parcel as a nature preserve and field research laboratory.

In April 1967 the U.S. Department of the Interior recognized Dysart Woods as a National Natural Landmark because it contained one of the last virgin deciduous forests in the eastern U.S. The commemorative plaque is set in a stone on the caretaker's lawn.

The preserve has become an outdoor education and nature study facility for local high school and college students, as well as scientists. Scientists from around the world make pilgrimages to Dysart Woods.

Coal mining—or the removal of the carboniferous forest that previously grew here—has been the biggest threat to Dysart Woods recently. Although the creation of a buffer zone around the preserve in 1970 has halted the encroachment of surface strip mining, underground mining, particularly long-wall mining, may irreversibly harm this priceless habitat.

Extracting the coal could alter the water table in the area and parch the soil. Surface disturbances associated with underground mining—higher dust levels, truck traffic, vibrations in the ground, and unnatural water runoff—could put stress on the vegetation.

Worse yet, long-wall mining (the PAC-Man-like burrowing through underground coal seams) causes the ground to actually sink or collapse into the earth. This sudden shifting, called subsidence, could uproot 300-year-old trees and reduce Dysart Woods to a pile of pickup sticks.

Journal

June 4. Deer again. I spot two does as I reach the crest of a ridge on the Red Trail. They loitered for 10 minutes then high-tailed it. I continued on the trail thinking about the deer, occasionally looking over my shoulder for them in case they doubled back.

When I reached Interstate 70 I realized that the deer had distracted me from my business of locating the champion tulip tree on the Red Trail. I never did see it. For all I knew the famous tree was the one I hid behind to watch the whitetails. Next time I'll find it, deer or no deer.

Dysart Woods recalls the seamless forest observed by Sayward Luckett, a pioneer woman in Conrad Richter's novel The Trees. *Looking upon the Ohio landscape from a hilltop, Sayward "reckoned that her father had fetched them unbeknownst to the Western ocean, and what lay beneath was the sun glittering on green-black water. Then she saw what they looked down on was a dark illimitable expanse of wilderness. It was a sea of solid treetops broken only by some gash where deep beneath the foliage an unknown stream made its way. As far as the eye could reach, this lonely forest sea rolled on and on till its faint blue billows broke against an incredibly distant horizon."*

Bobcat

LAKE KATHARINE STATE NATURE PRESERVE

A lost colony of endangered bigleaf magnolia, separated from its Kentucky kin by several hilly counties, struggles on the banks of Salt Creek. It is an oddity, a survivor, found nowhere else in Ohio. Altogether the sprawling Lake Katharine preserve guards 20 endangered species, including a diminutive petal called roundleaf catchfly, and the seldom-seen bobcat. Lake Katharine has some of the best hiking trails in the state. ★

Location

Western Jackson County, Liberty Township.

From Jackson, travel two miles west on State Street (which becomes County Road 76 outside of town), then turn right on County Road 85 (Smith Road). The road ends at the parking lot where you will find the buildings of old Camp Arrowhead.

To reach the boat launch (see fishing and boating restrictions below), travel north on State Route 35, go left on County Road 84, then immediately right on County Road 59 (Rock Run Road). Turn left on County Road 59A which ends at the preserve manager's home. Park in designated areas. You will not find destination signs on this route.

Ownership

Ohio Department of Natural Resources, Division of Natural Areas and Preserves.

Size & Designation

Boasting 1,850 acres, Lake Katharine is the largest state-owned preserve. Half of it has been designated interpretive for public visits. The remaining half has been reserved for scientific study. The preserve also is known as the Edwin A. Jones & James J. McKitterick Memorial Wildlife Sanctuary, named after the previous owners of the land.

Nearby Natural Attractions

Jackson Lake State Park, Cooper Hollow Wildlife Area, and Liberty Wildlife Area lie within Jackson County. Lake Alma State Park, just north of Wellston, straddles the border of Jackson and Vinton counties.

Access

Three well-designed trails wind through the preserve. However, only one of them, the Pine Ridge Trail, follows the lakeshore, although only for a few paces.

Stop at the information board near the parking lot for a brochure and trail map. The figure-eight route described below takes you on a walk of about 5.5 miles.

Face the lodge of old Camp Arrowhead. The path to the right (east) is the starting point. Shortly after entering the woods a sign pointing to the Salt Creek Trail points to the right. Skip this trail for now and continue to the intersection of the Calico Bush Trail, heading left, and the Pine Ridge Trail, pointing right. Take the Pine Ridge Trail (2.5 miles), which crosses a wooden bridge over Rock Run and follows Little Salt Creek. Note the gorge cliffs at your left.

The trail loops to the left and ascends the ridge, here dominated by hardwoods. When the path reaches the rim of the gorge it passes through a Virginia pine forest (hence the trail name) and then a healthy grove of hemlocks, where you may flush a ruffed grouse or deer. Several overlooks peak into the ravine and bring you close to the giant hemlocks and tulip trees that tickle the chin of the rim. Along this path, observe the diminutive waterfalls and the recess caves, believed to be Indian encampments at one time.

A word about safety. *Be careful near the edge of the 150-foot cliffs.* A fall could be fatal. You will not find handrails or fences. The soil, rocks, and trees near the edge may not support your weight. Climbing the rock walls is prohibited in order to protect your life as well as the fragile habitat.

Eventually, you will reach a wooden bridge that spans a brook (really the spillway from Lake Katharine). Study the waterfalls at the left, then dash to the dam that forms the eastern shore of Lake Katherine. This will be your only view of the lake from a trail.

The route turns east as it climbs the southern slope of the gorge. Near the crest the trail splits. Take the left fork, or the mile-long Calico Bush Trail. (The Pine Ridge Trail returns to the parking lot, just a few hundred feet away.)

The Calico Bush Trail follows Rock Run (the impounded creek) on the south bank, giving you a great look at the steep northern walls. (ODNR has written an interpretive guide for the Calico Bush Trail. It might be available at the information board in the parking lot.) The path merges again with the Pine Ridge Trail, near the confluence of Rock Run and Little Salt Creek. Here turn right, and backtrack on Pine Ridge Trail to the Salt Creek Trail, pointing left.

The Salt Creek Trail, built by the Youth Conservation Corps in the late 1970s, takes you along the sandstone (actually Sharon conglomerate) wall facing Little Salt Creek. Boardwalks and stairs assist the hiker on this challenging walk. At one point the path squeezes between the cliff and a slump rock, a huge boulder that broke away from the fortress. Study the magnificent rock formations seen on this trail.

Stay left at the next fork, unless you want to take the Shortcut Trail back to the parking lot. The Salt Creek Trail continues southward along the stream, then loops and climbs the ridge and joins the Shortcut Trail. This path returns to the starting point.

From time to time, winter storms and flooding have closed trails. The closures will be posted at the information board. The preserve is open daily from dawn to dusk. For more information contact the Ohio Department of Natural Resources, Division of Natural Areas and Preserves, Fountain Square, Building F-1, Columbus, Ohio 43224-1331; phone (614) 266453.

Fishing and Boating

Lake Katharine's bulky bass (seven pounders) and her bluegills and crappie have been exciting fishermen for years. Some anglers claim they have snagged panfish as big as a dinner plate.

Katharine, however, plays hard to get, which adds to her mystique as a fishing hot spot. Only five permits are issued per day for Friday, Saturday, Sunday or Monday, from April to October. The lake remains boat-free the rest of the year. Call the preserve office at (614) 286-2487 on the last Friday of each month between 8 a.m. and 5 p.m. to make a reservation. You are entitled to only one reservation per call, and only one reservation per month. The permit is good for only one boat, and one day. If you change your plans and fail to cancel your permit within 24 hours, you will forfeit lake privileges for a year.

The boat launch area has 10 parking spaces but you must carry (not drag) the boat down a steep 110-yard path to the lake, a strenuous task for solo anglers. Motorized watercraft are not allowed. Non-fishing boaters can certainly use the lake. Call the preserve office for the rules governing lake use.

For more information, call the preserve at (614) 286-2487 or the Ohio Department of Natural Resources, Division of Natural Areas and Preserves at (614) 265-6543.

Geology

The cliffs at Lake Katharine preserve are composed of Sharon conglomerate, a type of sandstone studded with round, white quartz pebbles called lucky stones.

During the Pennsylvanian geologic period, some 300 million years ago, swift rivers and streams rushing off high peaks to the east (the predecessors of the Appalachian Mountains) washed gravel into the inland sea that inundated most of Ohio at the time. This deposit accumulated in a broad delta that stretched across eastern Ohio. After the land uplifted and the sea dried this conglomerate compressed into rock. Iron-rich water that washed over and seeped into the deposits firmly cemented them.

You can easily see the quartz pebbles embedded in the cliff walls. Their roundness resulted from the agitation in the ancient streams. The beds of these gravel deposits were never uniform.

Study the bedrock carefully for a while. (Trail post #5 on Calico Bush Trail offers a close-up.) The sculpting has been done by the process called differential weathering. It works when water soaks into the rocks and dissolves the areas not permeated with iron cement. Pebbles weakened by weathering pop out of the facades and lay in piles beneath the walls, and sometimes on the trails.

In winter the water that has seeped into the rock freezes and expands, thus creating cracks. Some cracks enlarge and eventually break slabs off the cliff. The cracks and pocks provide homes for lichens, mosses, and ferns which assist erosion.

Differential weathering occurs fastest where the iron is weakly concentrated in the rock. The lumps, burls, swirls, and knobs on the rock indicate iron-saturated spots that have defeated weathering.

Over time Little Salt Creek and Rock Run have worn down the formations. The walls also show other scars of erosion—recess caves and honeycombs. The powerful forces of erosion that formed these gorges established habitats that enabled some plants to extend their range of existence.

Wildlife

The ravines, ridges and floodplains are sanctuaries for some 20 plants listed as endangered, threatened, or potentially threatened. An endangered wildflower called Sampson's snakeroot lives here, along with butterfly pea, a threatened species. Several grasses and a spiny shrub bearing black berries called devil's walking stick (or Hercules-club) are among the potentially threatened. The latter plant, like others in this choice habitat, thrive at the northern edge of their range.

Two snakes observed here, the rough green snake and the black king snake, are rare in Ohio.

Although the Wisconsinan glacier never reached Jackson County (its deepest local penetration being southeastern Ross County) plants from northern regions which marched ahead of the ice mass, notably hemlock, found a suitable microclimate in the cool, shaded ravines.

Lake Katharine marks the northern boundary of the endangered bigleaf magnolia, a flowering tree commonly found in the southern Appalachian highlands but only in one location in Ohio. A colony of about 2,000 bigleaf magnolias, a remnant flora of the ancient Teays River Valley, grows along the Salt Creek Trail. Only about 50 have reached seed-producing maturity.

The tree's kissing cousin, the umbrella magnolia, is more abundant here, but still potentially threatened in Ohio. This tree also reaches the fringe of its range in the preserve.

Leaf design distinguishes them. Umbrella magnolia leaves taper at the stem and are slightly smaller than the "bigleaf" which has twin lobes at the base of the leaf.

You cannot miss these beauties when their creamy-white and fragrant petals unfold in the spring. Later, they will drop seed pods resembling pine cones. In late autumn and winter their huge tobacco-sized leaves cover the floodplain. The bigleaf has green buds; the umbrella brown buds.

The preserve boasts a prominent collection of hardwoods—tulip tree, oaks (chestnut, white, red, black, scarlet, shingle), sycamore, cottonwood, some beech, hickory, and others.

Ferns brighten the cool, shady places. Christmas fern, so-called because it stays green in winter and sports an ear resembling a yuletide stocking on its leaf, appears everywhere. You also find common polypody (cliff faces), as well as wood, fancy, evergreen wood, and maidenhair (horseshoe-shaped frond) ferns.

The interpretive guide for the Calico Bush Trail encourages you to focus on the work of lichens and mosses. These hardy pioneers inhabit rocks and rotting logs, places where no other plants chose to live. Slowly, they decompose rocks and rot, and prepare the ground for larger plants.

The calico bush, better known as mountain laurel, blooms in June along the Calico Bush and Pine Ridge trails. Also look for these uncommon blossoms along this path: mountain watercress, starflowers, puttyroot, and stemless lady's slipper.

Another rarity found here, the potentially threatened roundleaf catchfly, struggles at the base of the cliffs. Blueberries and wintergreen, an evergreen with white flowers and red berries, cling to the lip of the cliffs.

Quiet, slow walkers may see deer, turkeys, and perhaps the bobcats (endangered) known to live here. Spotted salamanders may dart across the boardwalks or race on top of the rocks. Years ago a timber rattlesnake was spotted but you are unlikely to find this reclusive critter.

Look for the telltale signs of a beaver colony along the lakeshore—gnawed tree branches stripped of their bark, girdled trees, inch-long chips near stumps, sticks chiseled to pencil points. The lake contains prize bass and panfish for anglers given permission to fish.

History

The preserve is named for Katharine M. Jones, wife of Edwin Jones, a former owner of the property. Jones, president of the Globe Iron Company in Jackson, and his partner, James McKitterick bought the land during the mid-1940s. The duo constructed a 260-foot long earthen dam across Rock Run Gorge in 1946, and a lodge, blockhouse, and residence, all for the opening of Camp Arrowhead in 1947. The summer camp for boys operated for 18 years.

The Girl Scouts last used Camp Arrowhead in 1970. The Ohio Department of Natural Resources acquired it in August 1976 and dedicated it as a nature preserve in July 1977.

Rockbridge

ROCKBRIDGE STATE NATURE PRESERVE

When the spring wildflowers bloom in early May, the natural arch becomes a rainbow, glowing like some half-buried celestial halo A thin thread of water, working at its eternal pace, chiseled Rockbridge in the Hocking Hills.

Location

This jewel is found in Hocking County, on the border Good Hope and Marion townships, near the village of Rockbridge (about five miles northwest of Logan).

Exit State Route 33 at Crawford-Starner Road and immediately turn right onto Dalton Road (Township 503) which curves left and deadends at the preserve parking lot.

Ownership

Ohio Department of Natural Resources, Division of Natural Areas and Preserves.

Size & Designation

This 99.3-acre geological wonder was designated as an interpretive nature preserve on June 21, 1978.

Nearby Natural Attractions

After visiting Rockbridge, go see Hocking Hills and Lake Logan state parks, and Conkles Hollow State Nature Preserve, all located in Hocking County.

Access

The Nature Bridge Trail gently ascends from the parking lot, following an old fencerow. Read the preserve rules on the information board before trekking. Upon entering the corner of a meadow the Natural Bridge Trail turns left (north) along a ridge. The Beech Ridge Trail goes straight. Either trail leads to the stone arch.

The Natural Bridge Trail traces the edge of the meadow and descends to a stream and the bridge. The hillier Beech Ridge Trail follows the southern property line down to a stream. Then it goes up a ridge, and swings north on a ridge spine and connects with the Natural Bridge Trail.

After visiting the natural arch, continue on the Natural Bridge Trail, above the south bank of the creek, to view the Hocking River. I recommend going to the bridge via the Natural Bridge Trail, and returning along the Beech Ridge Trail. Walk all of it for a 1.75- mile hike. Both trails climb moderate slopes.

Canoeists paddling on the Hocking River can beach their boats at the designated landing and walk to the arch.

Tempting as it may be, *do not walk across the rock!* Falling from it will cause injury or death. There also is a chance that your weight will damage or weaken the span.

Climbing the rock walls also is prohibited and risky to you and wildlife. Remember that wildflowers, small animals, fungi, and tree roots thrive on the cliffs. Footing can be slippery and hazardous at the bank of the Hocking River, especially during the spring when the current is high and swift.

The cold, leafless months are best for studying the geological features. But the setting may be at its best at two times during the year—spring (late April and early May) and autumn.

Naturalist programs are held here periodically. Check the information board in the parking lot. For more information contact the Ohio Department of Natural Resources, Division of Natural Areas and Preserves, Fountain Square, Building F-1, Columbus, Ohio 43224-1331; phone (614) 265-6453.

Geology

Rockbridge is the largest of 40 known natural bridges in Ohio. It measures 100 feet in length, and arches 50 feet across a narrow hollow. The width varies from 5–20 feet, with a thickness of around five feet. Rockbridge's only rival is Ladd natural bridge, also a state preserve, located in Washington County. The Ladd preserve is not open to the public.

The Rockbridge stone arch, comprised of 300-million year-old Blackhand sandstone, started as a typical recess cave, like Ash Cave or Old Man's Cave in Hocking Hills State Park, with water falling over its overhanging lip. (See Conkles Hollow and Blackhand Gorge.) The sandstone on the top, tightly cemented by iron and silica, has resisted erosion. The lower strata, on the other hand, were weakly cemented, enabling the backsplash of the waterfall to hollow out a cave beneath the caprock.

The woodland stream also ate away the cement along a north-south running seam, or crack, in the caprock behind the lip. Eventually, the rock behind the fracture weakened and collapsed, creating a hole. Erosion by the stream widened the gap, leaving a solitary band of sandstone to bridge the ravine.

A 50-foot cascade still tumbles over the recessed ledge, though during the dry summer months the current shrinks to a thread. The tributary ends its journey at the Hocking River, which forms the eastern boundary of the preserve just 100 yards from the bridge.

Wildlife

Elderberry groves and pawpaw trees (noted for their banana-shaped fruit) line the path from the parking lot (along with other species). The meadow shows the typical characteristics of an open area changing into a forest, a transition called succession. As you might expect, Beech Ridge Trail traverses a knoll dominated by beech, oak, maple, and hickory. The land was logged during the 1930s, so this woodlot is called a second-growth forest.

Careful observers may spot deer, ruffed grouse, turkey, beaver, and fox in the preserve. Tracks indicate that raccoons and skunks live here too.

Dozens of common wildflowers carpet the floor, including creeping trailing arbutus, pale Indian pipe, dwarf iris, stonecrop, Joe-pye weed, and Roman ragweed. Great rhododendron and the green adder's mouth, its habitat diminishing, offer a few blossoms.

History

The rock bridge has been a favorite destination for picnickers. In the 1840s, passengers traveling on the Hocking Valley Canal, which ran beside the river between Lancaster and Logan, insisted on stopping here. Some families rented boats, paddled to the river landing, and dined under the arch. In the early 20th century, the Columbus, Hocking Valley and Toledo Railroad, operating on the opposite river bank, stopped at Rockbridge. Canoeists still land here to enjoy the scenery.

Zora Crawford, a former owner, reported that his son once drove a tractor over the bridge (but only once), and that another daredevil crossed it with a horse and buggy. Performing those feats today could cost you your life, a stiff fine, or jail time.

The Ohio Department of Natural Resources, Division of Natural Areas and Preserves bought half of the site in 1978 and quickly designated it a scenic preserve. Another forested tract, east of the Beechwood Trail and bordering the river, was added in 1990.

Polypody ferns

SHALLENBERGER STATE NATURE PRESERVE

The hills around Lancaster look as if a fist, deep within the Earth, punched rock through the crust and left the rubble in dome-shaped piles. These are called knobs. One of them, Allen Knob, crowned by chestnut oaks and mountain laurel, presides over Shallenberger State Nature Preserve.

Location

Central Fairfield County, Hocking Township.

From Lancaster, go 2.5 miles southwest on State Route 22, then 1/4 mile north (right turn) on Beck's Knob Road.

Ownership

Ohio Department of Natural Resources, Division of Natural Areas and Preserves.

Size & Designation

The "knob," comprising 87.5 acres, became a scenic nature preserve on May 15, 1973.

Access

The trail from the parking lot quickly comes to a fork. Take the right branch, the Arrowhead Trail, which leads to the summits of both Allen and Ruble knobs. Arrowhead Trail goes along the southern base of Allen Knob to the Overlook Trail which climbs a steep grade to the top of the hill, some 270 feet above Hunter's Run. The stream runs parallel to the northern property line.

After exploring the summit, backtrack to Arrowhead Trail and continue northeast toward Ruble Knob. A cutoff trail going left to the Honeysuckle Trail soon appears, but stay right to reach Ruble Knob. (The Arrowhead and Honeysuckle trails merge at the bottom of Ruble Knob.) After investigating Ruble Knob return via the Honeysuckle Trail, which winds around the north slopes of the knobs before joining with the trail to the parking lot. Figure on walking two miles.

The trails to the summits become steep. Nevertheless, they are worth the exertion because the views of the surrounding farmland are splendid. Rock climbing is prohibited and can be dangerous to humans and the fragile plants clinging to the rocks. You can visit every day during daylight hours. Naturalists-led educational programs are held here throughout the year.

For more information contact the Ohio Department of Natural Resources, Division of Natural Areas and Preserves, Fountain Square, Building F-1, Columbus, Ohio 43224-1331; phone (614) 265-6453.

Nearby Natural Attractions

Elsewhere in Fairfield County, hike the trails at Wahkeena Nature Preserve, Walter A. Tucker State Nature Preserve (Blacklick Metropark), and Chestnut Ridge Metropark, or visit Buckeye Lake State Park.

Geology

Forces above the surface, not a powerful subterranean fist, actually created these knobs. Some 325 million years ago (near the end of the Mississippian geological period) a shallow inland sea covered the area. Rivers and streams filling this ocean deposited sand in a huge delta at the western margin of the Appalachian Plateau. In some places these layers of sand were 500 feet thick. Overlaying layers of mud and sediment compressed the sand, while water rich in iron oxide glued the grains. The product was a rock commonly called

Blackhand sandstone. (See Blackhand Gorge.)

Eventually, the land gently uplifted, the ocean disappeared, and rivers changed current. During the next 300 million years rain, wind, and sun beat down the layers above the sandstone, then the sandstone itself, creating the rocky knobs, gorges, cascades, caves, outcrops, and rock bridges characteristic of southeastern Ohio.

Stop along the Arrowhead Trail to feel the gritty texture of the boulders that have rolled off of the knob, and notice the cracks in the facades caused by weathering. The iron oxide which cemented the sand gives the rock its orange tint. A curious depression on the top of Allen Knob, suggesting a quarry at one time, becomes a tiny pond during the spring.

Though the summits of the knobs narrowly avoided a collision with the mile-thick Wisconsinan glacier some 12,000 years ago, the ice mass did bulldoze gravel and sand around the bases of the knolls. This glacial feature, called an end moraine, has influenced the plant life at Shallenberger preserve.

Wildlife

On the tops of the unglaciated knobs, where the soil is skinny and dry, chestnut oaks reign beside mountain laurel, a flowering shrub typical in the Appalachians. Here it grows on the south and west sides. The mountain laurel's pinkish blossoms appear from late May to mid-July. Also on the crest, look for ferns like polypody, ebony spleenwort, and walking fern.

Below the rocky tops, in the fertile moraine deposits, grows a forest of white and red oaks, red and sugar maples, American beech, wild black cherry, hickory, elm, white ash, tupelo, tulip tree, honey locust, and black walnut. Wildflowers commonly seen in this type of forest (mixed mesophytic) brighten the floor in the spring and summer. Some of them are foam flower, purple dead nettle, small-flowered crowfoot, cut-leaved toothwort, and mouse-eared chickweed.

Tracks in the snow after an all-night storm showed that deer, squirrels, fox, mice, and raccoons had been active at sunrise. Birders can find tanagers, vireos, warblers, hawks, owls, the horned lark, and other common species.

History

Local Native American tribes no doubt had explored the knobs. One of their major trails, just four miles north of the park, became Coonpath Road.

Hunter's Run honors a Kentucky-born Revolutionary War captain named Joseph Hunter, believed to be the first permanent white settler in Fairfield County in 1797. (Some 800 people attended an outdoor drama reenacting Hunter's settlement, staged in the preserve in September 1988.)

Pioneers following Hunter cleared this land in the early 19th century. Their gravestones in a nearby cemetery may have been quarried from these knobs.

The Fairfield County Commissioners received the property when its owner and preservationist, Jay M. Shallenberger, died in 1971. Grazing continued on several acres near the parking lot until 1973 when the commissioners turned over the site to the Ohio Department of Natural Resources. Remnants of an orchard still stand in the northwest corner of the preserve.

Journal

March 1993. When I reached the crest of Allen Knob, two days after a March snowstorm, a pair of turkey vultures took wing and hovered on thermals for 20 minutes. They took turns eyeing me and tracing figure-eights in the wind. One had lost a couple of wing feathers.

They flew toward another knob, but returned to their roost when I reached Ruble Knob. The gap in the wing span of one bird identified them as the pair I had seen earlier.

On the ride home, I listened to a radio broadcast about the throngs of people who had attended Hinckley's annual celebration for its returning buzzards. (See Hinckley Reservation.) I wondered if their encounter with the vultures was as close as mine.

Deer had walked unhurriedly through the preserve in the early morning. Tracks showed that the small herd had split at the knob; some circled north while a pair wandered south. They regrouped in the northwest corner of the preserve and browsed for food. Their tracks drew blue shadows in the powdery snow.

I hope I can decipher my children's days this well when they become teenagers.

Green heron

WAHKEENA NATURE PRESERVE

This place was not "wahkeena" (a Yakima word meaning "most beautiful") when Carmen Warner received it as a wedding present in 1931. Except for a few whiskers growing on a wart (trees surviving on a rocky knob) the property suffered from deforestation and neglect. But Carmen (Hambleton) Warner was a determined gardener and birdwatcher. In no time, she transformed this treeless farmland into a sanctuary befitting its name.

Location

Southeastern Fairfield County, Berne Township.

From downtown Lancaster, travel on State Route 33 southeast about six miles. Turn right at the "Wahkeena" sign onto Old Logan Road (County Road 86), then take the second right in one mile to Pump Station Road (Township 274). The preserve will be on your right in about 1.5 miles.

Ownership

Ohio Historical Society.

Size & Designation

Wahkeena (say Waw-KEE-nuh) Nature Preserve totals 150 acres. It is a state historical site.

Access

First stop should be the lodge, the former Warner residence, which has been converted into a nature education center with permanent exhibits. Pick up a trail guide while you are there.

The brief Shelter Trail (just a half mile) follows a hemlock-lined path and creek to a shelter house built by the Warners. Here you can cross a foot bridge and return to the lodge on the other side of the creek or continue on the mile-long Casa Burro Trail.

From the shelter house the Casa Burro Trail passes an impressive stand of tulip trees and other hardwoods. The trail circles left and climbs a steep ridge, then descends the hill. The journey ends with a walk through a pine grove. *Signs along the trail warn that a rifle range is not far away!* Stay on the trail.

Also, walk the boardwalk trail through a marsh (west of the lake), visit the observation blind overlooking Lake Odonata, and study the marsh (once a pond) and old gardens east of the lodge. These latter paths wander through the backyard of Wahkeena.

From April through October, Wahkeena is open daily from 8 a.m.–4:30 p.m. Permission is required for visits from November through March. Admission is $2 per vehicle, payable at the lodge.

A fulltime, on-site naturalist offers education programs for schools and nature groups in this open-air classroom. Scientists also use the preserve as an outdoor laboratory. For information on nature study programs, contact the preserve manager at (614) 746-8695 or the Ohio Historical Society, 1982 Velma Avenue, Columbus, Ohio 43211; phone (614) 297-2300.

Nearby Natural Attractions

In Fairfield County, go to Shallenberger and Walter A. Tucker (Blacklick Metropark) state nature preserves, Chestnut Ridge Metropark, and Buckeye Lake State Park.

Geology

Wahkeena is another preserve located at the "edge" of glaciation. (Also see Chestnut Ridge Metropark and Shallenberger State Nature

Preserve.) The various glaciers that scoured much of Ohio during the Ice Age just missed this spot. A lobe of the last mighty ice mass, the Wisconsinan glacier (about 12,000 years ago), extended down the Hocking River Valley but quit at the village of Sugar Grove, just a mile east of the preserve.

The cliffs and bedrock outcrops in the preserve are made of Blackhand sandstone. Some 350 million years ago sand deposited here by the waves of an inland sea and by streams rushing off mountains to the east became compressed into rock. Later, the land rose and exposed the sandstone to the erosive power of water, sun, and wind. These forces carved the rock into the formations typical in the Hocking Hills. (Also read Blackhand Gorge and Conkles Hollow.)

The house-size boulders near the lodge are called float rocks. Erosion split these chunks of sandstone from the outcrops. They rolled down the ridge and rested where you see them.

Look for the natural springs where groundwater surfaces and flows into creeks.

Wildlife

This once-naked land now teems with wildlife. During a recent spring 100 species of birds and 15 different mammals were spotted. Warblers favor Wahkeena's woods, and even the rare prothonotary warbler has been seen, its golden breast streaking through the brush like a sunbeam. Lucky observers may find a pileated woodpecker. I observed a cerulean warbler above the boardwalk trail.

Thirty species of fern, the most common being Christmas fern, carpet the ground. Search for the delicate maidenhair fern during your visit.

Eight varieties of orchids thrive here, including some favorites like showy orchids and pink lady's slipper. Rhododendron and mountain laurel also grace the grounds.

The trees in the forest are young, say 60–65 years old. Many were planted by the Warners, who also let natural succession take its course too. The hemlocks that line the Shelter Trail probably were transplanted from another location in the preserve. These are relicts from the last glacier which promoted the migration of trees and plants common in Canada to Ohio.

Graceful dragonflies and damselflies hover over Lake Odonata whose name honors the taxonomic order of these insects. Frogs and turtles are abundant on the shores of the lake and marshes.

A bird checklist and brochures explaining Wahkeena's geology, ferns, trees, and wildflowers are available at the nature center for a small fee.

History

Wahkeena pays tribute to the creative forces of Carmen Warner, as well as nature's. She was a devoted gardener and an avid ornithologist, the latter interest inherited from her father James Chase Hambleton, first president of the Columbus Audubon Society.

After receiving the tired 94-acre farm in 1931, the Warners planted trees, and built a lodge, three lakes, a footbridge, a corral and barn for pet burros, bird feeders, and a shelter house in the woods. Additional land purchases increased the holding to 150 acres. Topsoil was dumped on newly constructed garden terraces, and a hog barn was converted into a quaint guest house. Visitors said the estate had a country club look to it.

Mrs. Warner named the grounds Wahkeena after admiring Wahkeena Falls in the Columbia River Gorge in Oregon.

Dr. Warner, a noted surgeon and instructor in Columbus, passed away at age 88 in 1943. Carmen Warner died in 1956, and bequeathed the estate to the Ohio Historical Society "for nature study and as a preserve for birds and other wildlife."

In the early 1960s, the historical society and the Ohio Association of Garden Clubs, whose many members made pilgrimages to Wahkeena, set up a trust fund for nature education programs. The association also advises the owner on preservation matters.

Journal

Spring 1993. To me, the female frog has the profile only a mother—or a male frog—could love. On warm spring days in these shallow pools, the females become "wah-keena" to the males. The amphibians stage wild, X-rated orgies, complete with splashing and high-pitched croaking, a sort of "Animal House," amphibian style. Parents with young children might want to visit the wetlands this time of year for this very reason. It's a perfect introduction to their instruction on the birds and the bees . . . and the frogs. Have your lesson plan ready.

CENTRAL OHIO

Sycamore tree

BLACKHAND GORGE STATE NATURE PRESERVE

The Licking River has scoured a "lick" through dense layers of ancient sandstone creating a steep-walled gorge that's been a landmark for prehistoric Indians as well as canalboat, trolley, and railroad passengers.

Location

Eastern Licking County, Hanover Township.

Start in Newark and go east on State Route 16 to its intersection with State Route 146 (about eight miles). Travel southeast on SR 146 just 1/4 mile then turn right on County Road 273, heading south. CR 273 dead ends at Township Road 275 (Rockhaven Road) near the village of Toboso.

Here you have a choice. Turn right (northwest) on TR 275 and park in the lot a half mile away to explore the foot path on the north side of the Licking River. Or, turn left, cross the river, and pull into the main parking lot. Bicyclists and wheelchair visitors use the latter entrance.

Reaching the preserve from I-70 is complicated. Westbound travelers exit at Gratiot, cross U.S. Route 40 and head north on Poplar Forks Road (Township 339). Turn right (east) on Flint Ridge Road, then shortly go left (north) on Township 278. Where T278 joins Township 277 bear left on T277, but then take your next right, continuing north on T278. In Toboso, turn left on T275 and park in the lot at the left.

Eastbound I-70 travelers exit at Brownsville and go north on State Route 668, right (east) on Flint Ridge Road, left on Township 291, right on T277, and finally left on T278 to Toboso.

Ownership

Ohio Department of Natural Resources, Division of Natural Areas and Preserves.

Size & Designation

Blackhand Gorge became an interpretive nature preserve on September 20, 1975. It comprises 980.8 acres.

Nearby Natural Attractions

Licking Country also is the home of Flint Ridge State Memorial, The Dawes Arboretum, Morris Woods State Nature Preserve, and Buckeye Lake State Park.

Access

Blackhand Gorge has seven hiking trails and is one of only a few nature preserves with a bicycle and wheelchair trail. Five trails stem from the main parking lot, where you also will find latrines, picnic tables, information board, and a log cabin. The main trail is the North Central Bikeway, a four-mile, paved path that clings to the south shore of the Licking River. It used to be the bed of a railroad track. At one point the path goes through a man-made gorge called the "Deep Cut," a path blasted through sandstone for the railroad. At this spot follow the short path to your right that leads to the river. The rock wall on the north bank (not actually in the preserve) once held the "black hand." More on that later.

About a quarter mile down the bikeway look for a sign pointing left to the Quarry Rim Trail, which wanders through a buttonbush swamp and passes a recovering quarry. This trail, measuring 1.25 miles, rejoins the bikeway.

Farther along the bikeway, a trail appears at the left. This is the 2.5-mile Chestnut Trail, a ridgetop path which parallels the bikeway and merges with it farther upstream. The Owl Hollow Trail is a mile-long offshoot loop, beginning and ending at the same point on the Chestnut Trail.

The Canal Lock Trail is on the north bank of the river, just 3/4 of a mile long. You'll find it off CR 273 by the bridge that crosses the river.

The less-traveled, two-mile Marie Hickey Trail, named for one of the previous landowners, leads from the north parking lot off Rockhaven Road. Basically, it traces the perimeter of a meadow (once a cultivated farm field) and visits a waterfall, cool hemlock ravine, a pine plantation, the north bank of the river (no decent overlook once the forest has "leafed"), a railroad bridge (stay off of it), and a young forest.

The Oak Knob Trail is a one half mile offshoot on the eastern side of the Marie Hickey loop. It features some giant specimens of oak and hemlock, and a view of a ravine.

The trails are easy to follow, but expect brief, steep climbs up a few ridges. Being a former railroad grade, the paved bikeway is flat. Bikers are asked not to race or speed down the bikeway, nor ride their cycles on other trails. Rock climbing is forbidden. Again, stay off the railroad trestle.

Like all state preserves, Blackhand Gorge is open daily from dawn to dusk. Naturalist programs are held here. For information call the Ohio Department of Natural Resources, Division of Natural Areas and Preserves, Fountain Square, Building F-1, Columbus, Ohio 43224-1331; phone (614) 265-6543.

Geology

The exposed rock walls reveal the timeless tread of the river, and the temporary toil of man.

A vast inland, shallow ocean, called the Waverly Sea, covered much of Ohio around 325 million years ago (late Mississippian Period). It was refreshed by fast-running rivers and streams descending from heights today known as the Appalachian Mountains. These waterways deposited coarse sand and finer sediments into this sea in huge, interlocking deltas roughly stretching from Wayne County to the Ohio River. It some places, these layers of sand were 250 feet thick. Strata more pebbly than others (indicating they were closer to the base of the highlands) are called conglomerates.

Overlaying layers of mud and sediment compressed the sand, and water enriched with iron oxide cemented the grains into rock called Blackhand sandstone.

Like the rest of Eastern North America, the land gently rose, or uplifted, probably during the Permian geological period some 285–225 million years ago. The sea also may have shrunk. During the ensuing millions of years rain, wind and sun feasted on the softer strata above the sandstone, and then the sandstone itself, creating the rocky knobs, gorges, cascades, caves, outcrops, and rock bridges characteristic of eastern and southeastern Ohio.

As they have for many millennia the Licking River and its tributaries continue to cut a path through this sandstone. The river started as a meltwater stream tumbling from the Wisconsinan glacier which left this area about 15,000 years ago.

The slow work of the river cannot compare with the pace of humans, who, armed with explosives and rock-breaking tools, removed tons and tons of this ancient beach for canal locks, railroad trestles, glassworks, and gravestones during the last two centuries. Slowly, though, nature is covering up the human disturbances.

Wildlife

Follow the succession of tree species from the heights to the river. On the formerly deforested ridgetops, Virginia pine, oaks, hickories, and mountain laurel grow in dry soil. Various hardwoods (oaks, maples, beech) and an extravagance of wildflowers carpet the slopes, but in the floodplain, sycamores, willow, box elders, and cottonwoods hold sway.

The Licking River forms the boundary between two major types of forest, though only a trained eye can detect the differences. The north bank favors what scientists call the mixed mesophytic forest species—a melting pot, or stew, of oaks, hickory, chestnut, tulip tree, beech, maple, even hemlock. Trees characteristic of a mixed oak forest—white, black, and chestnut oaks with sourgum, dogwood, Virginia pine, and others—prevail on the southern slopes.

Various surveys show that the preserve harbors 73 different trees and shrubs, 150 kinds of wildflowers, and 15 varieties of ferns. Mosses (including the rare rock club moss) and liverworts wrap many boulders and rock walls.

Animals common in these parts—deer, raccoons, squirrels—live in the gorge. Red-tailed hawks and vultures often hover above the valley. Sixty-four bird species have been counted here, as well as nine species of toads and frogs, and six categories of salamanders.

History

Long ago, a large petroglyph (a carving, etching, or painting on rock) shaped like a hand, and black in color, appeared prominently on a gorge wall above the river. Pioneers who saw it claimed it was twice the size of a man's hand.

The origin of the "black hand" inspired many legends. Some say it pointed to the valuable nearby flint quarries where native people manufactured arrowheads, axe heads, and other essential tools. The symbol also may have been an early "peace" sign, marking the boundary of sacred grounds (like contemporary neutral or demilitarized zones). The tribal leaders of various nations may have sanctified the area so that nobody controlled the strategically important quarries upstream.

Other tales claim the hand was the blood-stained hand of a murder victim, or that it marked a lover's leap. Floods failed to erase the blackened stain.

Unfortunately, the black hand was blasted away by dynamite during the construction of the Ohio-Erie Canal. The current flowing through the "Licking Narrows," at first too skinny and shallow for canal boats, was fattened by a dam downstream. Quarries on the south side of the river provided stone for canal structures still visible on the Canal Lock Trail.

The completion of the Central Ohio Railroad through the gorge in the 1850s signaled the end of the canal era. The railroads built tracks through the narrows and a trestle across the river. Later, an electric, interurban trolley line running between Newark and Zanesville blasted a tunnel through the sandstone on the north side. The last interurban steamed through the narrows in1929. Relics of the bygone transportation systems can be seen in the preserve.

The former Rock Haven Park resort, located on Rockhaven Road east of the Marie Hickey and Oak Knob trails, became a popular destination. When trolley service ceased, autos carried tourists to the park on the old interurban right-of-way, but even this pleasure ended with the advent of bigger cars, paved highways, and new pastimes.

COLUMBUS METROPARKS

In the 1930s, the members of the Wheaton Club, avid birdwatchers and naturalists, surveyed Franklin County and compiled a list of precious sites worth preserving. On August 14, 1945, the Columbus and Franklin County Metropolitan Park District was formed. The sites researched by the Wheaton Club served as the park district's acquisitions list. They included the metroparks known as Highbanks, Sharon Woods, Blacklick Woods, Blendon Woods, and Battelle-Darby Creek. Like similar metropark systems, the Columbus district dedicates 80 percent of the park land as a natural area. Nine of the district's 12 holdings are described in this book. For more information, contact the Metropolitan Park District of Columbus and Franklin County, P.O. Box 29169, Columbus, Ohio 43229; phone (614) 891-0700.

- **Battelle Darby Creek Metropark**
- **Blacklick Woods Metropark (Walter A. Tucker State Nature Preserve)**
- **Blendon Woods Metropark**
- **Chestnut Ridge Metropark**
- **Highbanks Metropark**
- **Inniswood Gardens Metropark**
- **Pickerington Ponds Metropark**
- **Sharon Woods Metropark (Edward S. Thomas State Nature Preserve)**
- **Slate Run Metropark**

BATTELLE-DARBY CREEK METROPARK

The trails in this wooded metropark take you to a stream considered to be the most vital and diverse aquatic ecosystem of its dimension in the Midwest—bar none.

Painted turtle

If that is not impressive enough, then consider the thick oak-hickory woods and the tallgrass prairie meadows that cover the creek banks, the half- dozen ancient Indian burial mounds hidden in the forest, and the thousands of migratory birds who either bed down here, or, like their ancestors, get their north-south bearings from the creek.

Location

Southwestern Franklin County, Pleasant Township.

From Interstate 70 (west of Columbus and I-270), travel south on Rome-Hilliard Road, then west (right) on U.S. Route 40 (National Road). Turn south (left) on Darby Creek Road. The Cedar Ridge entrance to the park will appear on the right in about three miles. The Indian Ridge entrance, also on the right, occurs in four miles.

Ownership

Metropolitan Park District of Columbus and Franklin County.

Size & Designation

At 3,114 acres, Battelle-Darby Creek Metropark is the largest park in the Columbus metropark system. Little and Big Darby creeks, which converge in the park, are national scenic rivers. The U.S. Department of the Interior designated the creeks national scenic rivers in March 1994.

Nearby Nature Attractions

Battelle-Darby Creek is one of nine Columbus metroparks. The others are Highbanks (Highbanks State Nature Preserve), Sharon Woods (Edward S. Thomas State Nature Preserve), Inniswood, Blendon Woods, Blacklick (Walter A. Tucker State Natural Preserve), Pickerington Ponds (also a state preserve), Slate Run (Pickaway County), and Chestnut Ridge (Fairfield County). Big Darby Public Hunting Area borders the park to the south.

Access

The route described below begins at the Cedar Ridge picnic area, but it also can be picked up at the Indian Ridge picnic area. Two other paths lead to Big Darby Creek from the Cedar Ridge picnic area. Another goes to the Cedar Bluff Overlook, a wooden deck offering a pleasant view of Big Darby Creek (best in winter).

I prefer the route just to the right (north) of the ranger station. The path enters the woods and descends via steps to a wide gravel trail along the creek. Walk downstream. The Indian Ridge Trail (3 miles) starts where the last of the side paths from the picnic area joins the main trail.

Indian Ridge Trail continues south through woods, climbs the east creek bank, then angles across an open hillside often slippery due to trickling springs above. After crossing Alkire Road, walk to the canoe launch site (toilets and water available here) for a look at the confluence of Big and Little Darby (left) creeks. Recent construction realigned the road and replaced two ornate steel truss bridges (1910s) with the uninspired (though safer) concrete structures you see ahead. Pity the old bridges could not be restored.

The trail goes on beneath a towering railroad bridge and into the Indian Ridge section of the park. Shortly, you will reach an intersection and a sign indicating the beginning of the two-mile loop. Go left (east), up an old farm lane. Ahead, you will notice a path leading to the Indian Ridge Picnic at the right. Folks seeking a shorter walk can park at this picnic area and enter the trail here.

At this point the trail spans a creek and heads southeasterly up a ridge of hardwood trees. It crosses the park driveway, snakes through a wet forest, and traces the edge of a farm field (look for the rusty, abandoned pickup truck). Soon it turns northwest into taller woods and descends a ridge to a wet meadow. Here, for several hundred feet, a boardwalk keeps your feet dry. The trail crosses this large meadow (Darby Creek at your left) and returns to the start of the loop, near the railroad bridge. Retrace your steps to the starting point. This walk covers about 3½–4 miles.

The park is open from 7 a.m. to dark every day. Park brochures (with trail maps) can be found at the ranger station (Cedar Ridge). Restrooms and drinking water are located at Cedar Ridge, Indian Ridge, and the canoe access. Vault toilets are found at the fishing site on Gardner Road. Cedar Ridge and Indian Ridge have plenty of picnic areas, playgrounds, and open space.

Park naturalists conduct programs here all the time. The program schedule is posted on bulletin boards in the parking lots.

Geology

For all of its natural gifts, the metropark does not possess any geological splendors, except for a steep 50–70-foot bluff on which the Cedar Bluff Overlook sits.

The creeks are outwashes of the Wisconsinan glacier, which scoured this terrain about 12,000–15,000 years ago and spread a layer of till, a mixture of gravel, sand, and cobble. This till strata varies in thickness and composition in the Darby Creek watershed. For most of their journey, the creeks flow over and carry away this till. In the park, tributaries have carved steep slopes into the east bank.

In spring, the Darbies cannot hold their water. This frequent flooding has been a blessing because it has discouraged human development. The high water often overwhelms the creekside trails, and inundates portions of the floodplain in the park.

Wildlife

The Darby Creek watershed is a paradise for small fish. Eighty-nine varieties of darters have been recorded in the park's waters. These tiny fish spawn in the shallow, cobbly riffles of the stream.

Twenty-eight species of minnows thrive in these currents, alongside a long list of mollusks and shiners, notably the silver and rose-faced. Oddly, the streamline chub and verigoot darter, uncommon residents elsewhere, are familiar faces in the Darby.

These critters, of course, attract herons—great blue and green—and kingfishers and osprey, occasionally. Ducks also ply the waters. All totaled, 80 species of birds have been observed in the park. Some of these are the pileated woodpecker, yellow-throated warbler, rose-breasted grosbeak, barred owl, and several brands of hawk. Look for the eastern meadowlark, bobolink, and Henslow's sparrow in the meadows. The last bird is listed a "special interest" by the Ohio Division of Wildlife, roughly a designation equal to "potentially threatened."

The usual assemblage of quadrupeds are present—deer, raccoons, squirrels, fox. Recently, beaver and coyote have moved in. Visitors and park neighbors have seen the feisty badger.

In July and August the park's tallgrass prairies brighten the landscape. The park district began cultivating prairie species here in the late 1970s. The seeds came from other pockets of prairie lands in the Darby Plains. (See the Darby Plains prairies.)

The entrance to the Indian Ridge section of the park is lined with prairie dock, prairie coneflower, bergamot, purple coneflower, and others. Elsewhere, royal catchfly (a potentially threatened species), tall larkspur, and blazing stars compete with grasses called little and big bluestem.

Forest wildflowers are abundant, especially in the Cedar Ridge section. Keen observers may find yellow lady slipper, showy orchis, and pale jewelweed (touch-me-not).

Nine kinds of oak (among them white, pin, chinkapin, bur) and five types of hickory dwell here. Some mammoth white oaks preside over the main trail in the Cedar Ridge area. You will also discover red, sugar, and silver maple, pawpaw, aspen, blue ash, sycamore, and osage orange, whose wood made the stoutest bows and arrows on the Great Plains. This tree from Texas may have been planted here as a fencerow thicket. Altogether, some 50 species of trees and shrubs grow in the park.

History

The ancient Indians favored the banks of Darby Creek. Six of their burial mounds have been discovered in the park (though they are off limits to the public). Stories are told of local farmers filling barrels with arrowheads, pottery, pipes, and other artifacts which they collected after plowing the fields. The bones of wolves, bears, and sandhill cranes, animals now extirpated in Ohio, also have been unearthed.

The Shawnee nation used this land before white settlers pushed them out in the late 18th century. Because Columbus has expanded fastest north and east, the Darby watershed (west of Columbus) has avoided the natural degradation associated with unchecked urban development. When farmers began to employ intensive farming techniques in the 1970s, water quality in the currents began to decline due to greater amounts of chemicals and silt. Still, it is an area of small towns, small farms, and clean water—relatively speaking.

In the 1960s, the U.S. Army Corps of Engineers planned to dam Darby Creek near SR 665. The reservoir was to quench the thirst of burgeoning Columbus. The Corps bought the land marked for flooding, and evacuated people. Fortunately, that is as far as the project progressed.

The dam stalled following the discovery of numerous endangered species in the water and the ancient Indian earthworks in the floodplain. Seizing the chance, the park district bought the Cedar Ridge section from the Corps for $2 million. The Corps of Engineers still holds title to several hundred acres north of SR 665 (the public hunting area).

In spite of all the protection for the Darbies the "dam" project keeps popping up. Because of low-head dams, a portion of Big Darby Creek from US 40 to the confluence in the metropark is not designated scenic. A dam could be built there, and that was discussed during a drought in Central Ohio in the early 1990s. Conservation groups rallied public sentiment and again squelched the dam.

In 1993, the National Park Service was considering a national scenic river designation for the streams.

Beech tree

BLACKLICK WOODS METROPARK (WALTER A. TUCKER STATE NATURE PRESERVE)

Though encircled and threatened by the vagaries of development, this quiet forest preserve of huge beeches and maples, a National Natural Landmark, remains a peaceful place amidst urban sprawl. ♿

Location

Northwestern Fairfield County, Violet Township, near the Franklin County border.

From Interstate 70 (east of Columbus) head north on Brice Road, then east on Livingston Avenue to the entrance of Blacklick Woods Metropark (not the golf course). The state nature preserve has four entrances. Park at the Beech-Maple Lodge, Ash Grove, or The Meadows picnic areas, or the metropark nature center.

Ownership

Metropolitan Park District of Columbus and Franklin County.

Size & Designation

On April 27, 1973, this 55-acre beech-maple, swamp forest was designated a state scenic nature preserve. Blacklick Woods, encompassing the same boundaries as the state preserve, was declared a National Natural Landmark in December 1974. Blacklick Woods Metropark totals 632 acres.

Nearby Natural Attractions

The Tucker preserve lies in Blacklick Metropark, whose cousins are Chestnut Ridge, Sharon Woods, Blendon Woods, Inniswood Gardens, Battelle-Darby Creek, Slate Run, Pickerington Ponds, and Highbanks, all Columbus metroparks. Gahanna Woods State Nature Preserve is nearby.

Also visit Shallenberger State Nature Preserve and Wahkeena Nature Preserve in Fairfield County.

Access

Two trails, both starting in the metropark, visit Blacklick Woods. A half-mile, self-guided boardwalk, the Buttonbush Trail, begins and ends at the park's nature center. This wheelchair and baby stroller trail loops through the swampy southeast corner of the site, but does not connect to other trails. The nature center has exhibits, books, and a wildlife viewing window which overlooks Ashton Pond and a meadow.

From Beech-Maple Lodge follow the eastbound trail which turns south (left at the first fork) into the preserve then loops north. A path on the west side of this loop trail goes to The Meadows and reservable picnic grounds. The trail returns to the Beech-Maple Lodge Trail. Go right to return to the lodge, or head left to the Ash Grove Picnic Area.

From the Ash Grove Picnic Area follow the trail behind the ranger station into the woods. Turn right at the first intersection to enter the preserve. Follow this trail south. Ignore the side path at the right to The Meadows Picnic Area. The path circles north and returns to the Beech-Maple Lodge Trail. Go left to return to the Ash Grove Picnic Ground, or go right to the lodge. A short stem from the lodge parking lot leads to a deck that overlooks a pond.

Look for maps at the lodge, nature center, or the ranger station at the Ash Grove Picnic Area. Blacklick Metropark is open every day from 7 a.m. to dusk.

Nature education programs are held at the lodge and nature center. The lodge is available for group activities. Restrooms and drinking water are located throughout the park, but none are located within the preserve. Playgrounds and a bicycle-jogging trail are found in the park.

Geology

Two factors saved Blacklick Woods from the axe and plow—flat terrain, and clay. The area is covered by a thin loamy topsoil atop a subsoil of firm clay which stops water from seeping deeper into the ground. Because of the level topography and clay, the topsoil becomes waterlogged. Excess water collects in shallow pools in the forest. Consequently, the location was unsuitable for farming, barring extensive draining.

Bedford shale of the Mississippian geologic period (330 million years ago) is exposed in Blacklick Creek which serves as the southeast border of the metropark. (The creek does not pass through the preserve.) The formation, however, is visible only if one wanders from the bike trail.

Wildlife

Blacklick Woods has some of biggest beech trees in Central Ohio. (In fact, many giants in this forest are believed to be more than 200 years old.) They have spread their roots in the shallow soil on the ground above the swamp, often sharing it with sugar maple. They are identified by their smooth, gray bark, which, unfortunately, is easy to scar with a pocketknife. Beech trees growing beside trails carry the initials of humans far too often.

The extinct passenger pigeon favored beechnuts. Storytellers claim that roosting pigeons once were so numerous at Blacklick Woods that their weight bent beech branches to the ground. Turkeys and grazing hogs also like to fatten themselves on beechnuts.

The slow-growing beech does not produce edible fruit until it is about 40 years old. The nuts ripen in the fall. Beech is a masting tree, meaning it produces a bumper crop every 2–3 years. The bumper crop is timed to occur among all beeches in a region, not among individual trees. Fewer nuts ripen between peak years. Oaks, hickories, white pine, firs, and spruces also are masting trees.

The beech is thin-skinned, making it susceptible to fire, frost, fungi, and human-carved initials.

Look closely around a big beech. Notice the many young sprouts that have climbed above the surface from roots. Sprouts also will rise from stumps and the depressions created by uprooted trees. Black bears, once prevalent in these woods, often chose the hollows and root cavities of toppled beech trees for dens.

Sugar maples and beeches seem to be inseparable, mostly because they enjoy the same habitat. They nurture each other. Beech seedlings grow best under the shade of the sugar maple, and vice versa.

Trees which do not mind "wet feet"—white ash, swamp white oak, red maple, silver maple, pin oak—thrive in the swamp forest. You will also find elms (slippery and American), American hornbeam, wild black cherry, shagbark and pignut hickory, ironwood (also called musclewood), honey locust, other oaks (burr, northern red), tulip tree, Ohio buckeye, dogwood, sassafras, black walnut, black gum (black tupelo), sweet gum, black willow, box elder, and redbud. Along the creek the sycamore and eastern cottonwood preside. Pawpaw, whose buds deer refuse to eat, is increasing in number.

Due to overbrowsing by deer, a problem in other Columbus metroparks (see Sharon Woods Metropark), the varieties of wildflowers has decreased in recent years. Trillium and Dutchman's breeches, once abundant, have nearly disappeared. Still, about 100 kinds can be observed in the preserve and park, such as cardinal flower, corn salad, spring beauties, Miami-mist, wild sweet William, Star of Bethlehem, hooked crowfoot (buttercup), lizard's tail, and pasture rose. Ferns are represented by Christmas, sensitive, rattlesnake, and oblique grape.

The woodland ponds and swamps (scarce habitats in Ohio) attract a large assemblage of life, much of it tiny and inconspicuous. The waters in the park contain catfish, smallmouth bass, bullhead, bluegill, fairy shrimp, fingernail clams, snails, crustaceans, frogs, salamanders, and crayfish.

Snakes like the black rat, blue racer, garter, DeKay's, and the water snake are free to slither. Both terrestrial (eastern box) and aquatic (midland painted) turtles dwell here.

Ducks (mallard and wood ducks are common), great blue herons, swallows, and Canada geese visit the ponds. Try spotting the common flicker (listen for "klee-yer" call in the hardwoods), cedar waxwing, cuckoo (occasional), flycatchers (several types), rufous-sided towhee, pine siskin (winter), and these warblers—American redstart, yellow-rumped, cerulean, black-and-white, and prothonotary. The black-crowned night heron, indigo bunting, and oriole have been seen near Blacklick Creek. Cooper's hawk, barred owl, great horned owl, and the screech owl find homes here.

Mammals include the usual collection for this type of woodland: deer (too many actually), bats, opossum, squirrels (gray, red, flying, fox), muskrat, jumping mouse, weasel, mink, red fox, mole, vole, and shrew.

History

White settlers arrived after an 1801 congressional act set aside more than 100,000 acres in this area, the so-called Refugee Tract, for Canadians dispossessed of their land during the American Revolutionary War. In 1823, pioneers organized a wolf hunt (a massacre, really) to exterminate predators from the woods. They shot one black bear, three wolves, 49 deer, 60–70 turkeys, and one owl.

William Ashton bought 160 acres from a "refugee" settler and took up farming. He operated a steam-powered sawmill near the pond behind the nature center, and allowed his live stock to graze except in the forbidding swamp forest that is Blacklick Woods. The property was handed down to family members until 1948 when much of it was sold to the park district. Some of Ashton's descendants still live nearby.

The preserve's namesake, Walter A. Tucker, was the park district's first director.

Wood duck

BLENDON WOODS METROPARK

This bucolic setting at the edge of sprawling Columbus offers a variety of natural attractions for humans and wildlife—a waterfowl refuge, hardwood forest, brooks, and ravines.

Location

Northeast Franklin County, Blendon Township.

Leave Interstate 270 (the beltway surrounding Columbus) at State Route 161 (Dublin-Granville Road) and travel east 1.3 miles to the park entrance. Stay on the main road through the park, following signs to the nature center. You will find parking beside the new nature interpretation center, the best place to begin your visit.

Ownership

Metropolitan Park District of Columbus and Franklin County.

Size & Designation

Blendon Woods totals 646 acres, much of it designated by the park district as a natural area. The park includes Thoreau Lake and Walden Waterfowl Refuge (118 acres).

Nearby Natural Attractions

Blendon Woods is one of nine metroparks rimming Columbus. The others are Inniswood, Sharon Woods, Highbanks, Battelle-Darby Creek, Slate Run, Chestnut Ridge, Pickerington Ponds, and Blacklick. Highbanks, Sharon Woods, and Blacklick enclose Highbanks, Edward S. Thomas, and Walter A. Tucker state nature preserves, respectively. Gahanna Woods State Nature Preserve also lies within Franklin County.

Access

Begin by visiting Thoreau Lake in the Walden Waterfowl Refuge via the Pond Trail. This paved and flat path begins next to the nature center and heads northeast through a hardwood forest and a meadow to a pair of observation decks, a distance of less than a half mile.

Wheelchair drivers can manage this blacktopped trail. Choose this path if you have limited time, or if you are pushing kids in strollers. Bicycles are prohibited. Naturalists or volunteers may be on duty at the blinds to help visitors identify birds. Binoculars or small telescopes are sometimes available. Of course, children will want to explore both blinds.

Return to the nature center. Now, proceed to the nature trail which starts across the road. At the first intersection (about 100 yards) turn right on the Ripple Rock Trail which crosses the road and enters a forest of deciduous trees. (Deciduous trees lose their leaves in the autumn.) Several tall specimens of oak, hickory, and beech stand here. The trail circles and follows a small ravine where you will find examples of ripple rock next to an interpretive sign.

The Ripple Rock Trail crosses the road and merges with the Overlook and Hickory Ridge trails. Go straight on the Overlook Trail, which rides a ridge and overlooks two small hollows before descending to a bridge. Here the trail becomes the Cherry Ridge Trail, after the wild cherry trees growing on the ridge.

Cherry Ridge Trail ends at the next crossroads. Bear left and follow the Brookside Trail. (Avoid the offshoots branching to picnic areas.) The Brookside Trail follows a stream and heads back toward the nature center. At a footbridge, it becomes the Hickory Ridge Trail (same trail, different name). This path goes to the trail that returns to the nature center.

Walk all these trails for a 2–2.5-mile hike. The paths are wide and smooth. Interpretive nature signs add to your understanding of the woods.

The new, modern nature center is the departure point for the many scheduled nature programs. Drinking water and toilets are found here too. The center is usually staffed by a naturalist who is ready to answer questions. The center has a small bookshop, and natural artifacts (deer antlers, turtle shells, skulls, etc.) for children.

Take your first right after entering the park to reach the open picnic areas, ranger station, and disc golf course. The nature trails also can be reached from the picnic areas. Groups can reserve picnic areas in other parts of the park. Look for trail maps at the nature center and ranger station.

The park opens at 7 a.m. and closes at dusk. Swimming and fishing in Thoreau Lake are prohibited. Blendon Woods is a popular weekend destination during the spring, summer, and autumn. Folks who do not want to fight the crowd should visit during the week.

Geology and Wildlife

The forest grows above what once was a relatively flat and thick layer of till, that wonderful mixture of gravel, sand and clay deposited by the last glacier (the Wisconsinan) some 15,000 years ago. It has taken centuries for the many small seasonal streams that meander in the park to wear away the till and form hollows.

In some places (Ripple Rock Trail), the streams have reached the bedrock of shale (composed of compressed mud or clay). The "ripples" in the rock were shaped by water currents (or waves) that once flowed over this deposit.

All of the brooks flow southwesterly into Big Walnut Creek, creating ridges with slopes facing north and south. Consequently, you will see more beech and maple trees on the north slopes because these plants prefer shadier, cooler and moister sites. On the other hand, oaks and hickory, which prefer sunnier and drier soil, will dominate the southern slopes.

The Hickory Ridge Trail passes through a small and unique swamp forest. (It is located about 100 yards in a straight line from the nature center.) Water which has been unable to penetrate a stratum of impervious shale close to the surface has created a woodland swamp in this flat location. Many trees have toppled here from their own weight because the wet soil and shale prevented them from sinking deep roots.

Thoreau Lake is a man-made pond, freshened somewhat by tiny rills. Thousands of waterfowl and other birds may gather in these waters during the spring and autumn migrations. Bring your bird guides and binoculars. Ask a naturalist for a bird checklist at the nature center.

In the spring of 1993 some owls hatched their young in baskets placed by naturalists in a hollow tree beside the lake. Hawks often circle overhead, and perch in trees overlooking the pond.

During my visit that spring I twice spotted a wood duck flying in the woods along the Ripple Rock Trail. I suspect the bird was darting back and forth between its hidden tree nest and Thoreau Lake. Farther along this trail, a trio of pileated woodpeckers flushed in a crisscross pattern from the ground to the safe heights of nearby shagbark hickories. They clung to the bark long enough for me to fix them in my field glasses.

More than 160 kinds of wildflowers carpet the grounds. Pick up a checklist and blooming schedule for 50 cents at the nature center. Monkey flower, beard-tongue, small skullcap, mouse-ear chickweed, heal-all, clammy ground cherry, and naked-flowered tick-trefoil (say that one fast three times) are some of the little miracles you can see at Blendon Woods.

Journal

Memorial Day 1993. The volunteer naturalist at the observation blind said the lithesome, long-necked, white bird swimming in Thoreau Lake was a mute swan. The bird is rarely seen in these parts—an accidental tourist. Sure enough, the mute swan was not listed on the checklist given to me at the nature center.

This Eurasian import lives along the northeastern coast of the U.S.. However, my trusty Peterson's field guide reports that the bird has established colonies in the Great Lakes region.

This is the swan I remember in fairy tales. The graceful S-curved neck, the distinctive black lobe at the base of an orange bill, an effortless, buoyant swimmer.

Chestnut tree

CHESTNUT RIDGE METROPARK

"Chestnut Ridge is a place that doesn't fit easily into human plans and categories," wrote David Rains Wallace, who lived in a cabin below the ridge in the late 1970s. His observations that year led to his nationally acclaimed book *Idle Weeds: The Life of an Ohio Sandstone Ridge*, which briefly placed Chestnut Ridge in a pantheon of special places alongside Walden Pond and Sand County.

Location

Northwestern Fairfield County, Bloom Township.

Drive northwest from Lancaster about eight miles on State Route 33 (or southeast 15 miles on SR 33 from Columbus) and turn right onto Winchester Road at the traffic light in Carroll. In three miles, bear right at the "Y" intersection to stay on Winchester Road (Old Route 33). Go another half mile to the entrance on the left.

Ownership

Metropolitan Park District of Columbus and Franklin County.

Size & Designation

Total acreage of the park is 486 acres. The park opened on December 17, 1988.

Nearby Natural Attractions

The Walter A. Tucker (Blacklick Metropark) and Shallenberger State Nature

Preserves and Wahkeena Nature Preserve are located in Fairfield County, as well as Buckeye Lake State Park.

Access

A two-mile loop trail takes visitors through mature woodlots, a large meadow, a tiny bog, and along a creek. From the trailhead in the parking lot bear right, paralleling the road. The trail becomes steep as it ascends the ridge but it levels off when you reach a boardwalk. At the end of the boardwalk the trail hooks southward along the top of the ridge through an old orchard, woods, and some open areas.

Eventually, you will emerge from the woods into a large meadow. The trail descends to a creek which runs through the southeast part of the site, traces the eastern boundary, and returns to the forest and the starting point. A recently completed shortcut wanders through an old orchard and beyond the residence of a former owner.

The terrain is hilly, and the trail can be steep in places. The parking area offers picnic tables, drinking water, a small playground, and toilets. The man-made pond is a new addition to the park.

Nature programs are held at the park regularly.

Geology

Chestnut Ridge lies at the edge or the boundary between the region of Ohio influenced by the Wisconsinan glacier and the region that missed the ice pack.

Blackhand sandstone above beds of shale forms the shell of the ridge. These strata were made during a span of time called the Mississippian Period, 350-325 million years ago. Here's what happened.

Ohio, at that time, was covered by an ocean. However, to the east, the continental plates of Europe and North America collided head on. This tremendous clash caused the bedrock layers in North America to fold up like an accordion. You can simulate this action by spreading a tablecloth across the dining room table. Put books on one edge of the table to secure the cloth, then slide the cloth across the table from the other side. The long wrinkles represent the Appalachian Mountains (though they were more like the Alps 350 million years ago).

Rain water eroded these new mountains. Streams transported the sediment westward and dumped them in a delta (or beach) that stretched across Eastern Ohio. These sediments later dried and compressed to form the shale and sandstone of the Appalachian Plateau, also known as the Allegheny Escarpment.

The shales beneath the Blackhand sandstone are made from the finer, lighter sediments, such as mud and silt, which the mountain streams carried farthest offshore. The coarser, pebbly, and heavier sediments landed on the beach and became the Blackhand sandstone. (See Blackhand Gorge State Nature Preserve.)

Over tens of millions of years, weathering and erosion sculpted the sandstone into the knobs, gorges, bony ridges, and shelter caves characteristic of eastern and southeastern Ohio.

Now comes the Ice Age (Pleistocene Epoch) which began about two million years ago. At least three and maybe four different glaciers swept across Ohio. The last and most recent one, the Wisconsinan, covered about two-thirds of the state from 18,000-12,000 years ago.

The Wisconsinan glacier stopped near Lancaster. Scientists think the ice mass surrounded Chestnut Ridge to its neck, but did not swallow it. The ridge's height—1,110 feet—may have been too much for the thin vanguard of the glacier. In similar fashion, the glacier may have wrapped around the bases of the knobs at Shallenberger State Nature Preserve, just south of Lancaster. From a satellite these knobs would have looked like stepping stones in a stream.

The glacier heaped soil, gravel, and pebbles—collectively called glacial till—on the west slope of the ridge. The east slope is steeper because less till was left behind when ice released Chestnut Ridge from its grip. A pair of moraines—long rolls of till—running across Bloom Township mark the advance of the glacier.

Wildlife

Chestnut Ridge owes its name to the American chestnut trees that attracted nut gatherers at harvest time from as far away as Columbus. The trees are gone now, victims of the blight in the 1930s. Occasionally, though, a sprout emerges from the roots of a stump, a slim reminder of its giant ancestors.

The chestnuts probably attracted thousands of passenger pigeons to the ridge. Like the tree, this bird, is gone. Passenger pigeon flocks once were dense enough to blacken the sky. Bears and bobcats also lived here before 1900.

The chestnuts and their oak kin grew best on the steep, acidic, east side of the ridge, while beech and maple dominated where the glacial till covered the sandstone. These boundaries continue today, though there has been mixing. You will find black cherry, hickory, and other trees and shrubs typical of the forests in this region. Mature pines, surrounding a home in the center of the park, were planted by previous landowners.

An especially luxuriant forest (look for the grove of sugar maples) lies to the east of the nature trail, just before it comes into a big meadow. Willows, sycamores, and some poplars and walnuts thrive along two intermittent rills which feed Little Walnut Creek. Multiflora rose and berry patches have invaded the open spaces in the forest.

White-tailed deer, once scarce in the area, browse the ridge, and wild turkey recently were spotted here for the first time in this century. A pair of red salamanders, typical in the Appalachians but uncommon in Central Ohio, were sighted in 1989.

The flowers and birds typical of the area's forests and meadows can be counted. The park district manages the growth of the open areas to protect the species who thrive in this varied habitat.

History

Did the ancient people come here for chestnuts too? Early woodlands Indians (Adena culture, 1500–100 B.C.) did settle here and build five mounds, but they look like all the other little forested knolls and without a map or guide you won't find them. One of them, Old Maid's Orchard Mound, is conical, with a diameter of 60 feet. It is listed on the National Registry of Historic Places.

Early pioneers built cabins and barns near the springs that trickle from the base of the ridge. Sandstone quarried from the ridge became the foundations of local structures and perhaps canals in the 19th century, but nature has covered these scars too with hardwoods.

After decades of dormancy, the ridge was bought in 1918 by an Army veteran who cleared it, and planted apple trees. People drove many miles to buy fruit at the family's farm market (known as the Smith Sisters' Market). Homes rose along the dirt roads that bordered the ridge.

From an opening on the ridgetop, the concrete mountains of downtown Columbus appear as faint apparitions on the horizon.

A developer had a different view from the ridge—a subdivision of country estates. Little by little neighbors who worried about the encroaching city began selling tracts to the metropark district. By 1970 the park district had bought all the land.

In the late 1970s, nature writer David Rains Wallace lived in a cabin at the base of Chestnut Ridge and wrote *Idle Weeds*. He saw more skyscrapers on the horizon and wrote, "Even if the ridge becomes the only green spot in a hundred square miles of skyscrapers its fundamental value will not be in rarity, in diversion from the human world, but in commonness, in union with the biosphere on which the human world depends."

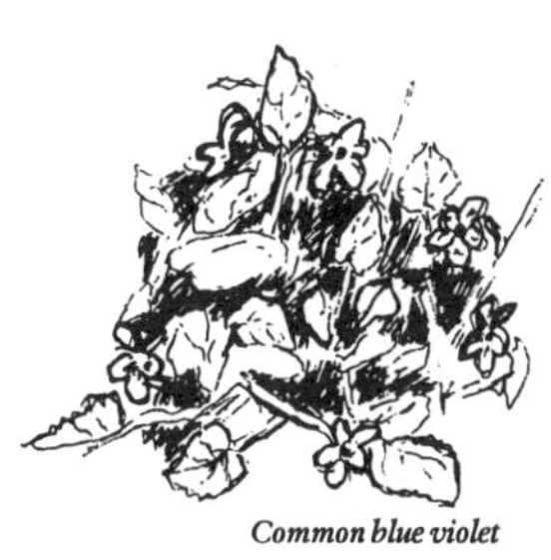
Common blue violet

HIGHBANKS METROPARK

It has taken the Olentangy River eons to slice through the bedrock shale which formed the "high banks" in this preserve. From these strategic bluffs Adena Indian warriors guarded a slumbering village, smoked "kinnikinnick," stargazed, and watched for the silhouettes of canoes moving like dark shadows against the silver moonlight that glistened on the Olentangy below.

Today, their spirit soars on the wings of the red-tailed hawks. The echo of their chants and prayers still swirls in the hollows and cliffs.

Location

Northern Franklin County, Sharon Township, and Delaware County, Orange Township.

The nature preserve comprises the southwest section of Highbanks Metropark. Exit Interstate 270 at U.S. 23 and travel north about four miles. The entrance will be on the left. Park in the Oak Coves Picnic Area.

Ownership

Metropolitan Park District of Columbus and Franklin County.

Size & Designation

The U.S. Department of the Interior designated the site a National Natural Landmark in February 1980. The park also protects two ancient Indian earthworks which are National Historic Landmarks.

Highbanks became a state scenic preserve on April 27, 1983. The preserve comprises 206.5 acres; the metropark is 1,050 acres. The Olentangy River, a state designated scenic river, flows on the western border of the sanctuary.

Nearby Natural Attractions

In Franklin County, explore Blendon Woods Metropark, Gahanna Woods State Nature Preserve, Pickerington Ponds Metropark and State Nature Preserve, Edward S. Thomas State Nature Preserve (Sharon Woods Metropark), Walter A. Tucker State Nature Preserve (Blacklick Metropark, also in

Fairfield County), and Battelle-Darby Creek Metropark.

Access

The wooded preserve can be reached by a trail that begins in Highbanks Metropark. Pick up a map at the nature center in the Oak Coves Picnic Area, then park in the westernmost lot in that picnic area. A 2.5-mile foot trail begins here. Head southerly (or left as you face the woods) and bear right at each fork, following the Overlook Trail. Just after the first fork, the wooded path passes through a meadow favored by bird-watchers. Most trail intersections display a "You Are Here" map. At the southernmost spot on the trail (near the Indian earthworks) an arrow points to a path to the observation deck.

Please don't wander off the viewing deck. Exploring the bluffs tramples the fragile plants growing there, and climbing is prohibited. Loose turf on the edge of the 100-foot tall cliffs makes them dangerous.

The observation deck offers a decent view of the valley, but photographers may be disappointed if they are expecting a panorama free of obstructions and human intrusions. Unfortunately, development on the west bank of the Olentangy River is spoiling the view.

To exit, retrace the path, or try another trail that explores other parts of the metropark. *The trails are easy to follow, but caution is advised for children while crossing bridges that span deep hollows.* You will encounter some moderate slopes.

For a closer look at the Olentangy River, go to the Big Meadows Picnic Area on the west side of the park and hike the nature trail along the river. Licensed anglers can try their luck here.

Nature programs and special events are held in the park all the time. One is the "Hike to the Giants," a journey to a secret place where a pair of sycamore trees believed to be more than 500 years old hide from humans. Each of the giants is 23–24 feet in circumference!

A new nature center is expected to open soon. You will find restrooms, picnic areas, playgrounds, and open areas for ball playing and kite flying in the park.

Geology

The "high banks" are actually cliffs of Devonian era shale formed about 350 million years ago when a shallow, murky ocean covered most of Ohio. Later, the land swelled and this former mud-clay sea floor hardened into bedrock. The shale that you see in the bluffs, known as Ohio black shale (so-called because of its charcoal gray color) sits above lighter-colored Olentangy shale, and a bed of limestone. Rotting plants which washed and settled into the Devonian sea account for the dark hue of Ohio shale.

The glaciers that scrubbed the land many millennia ago piled till (a mixture of gravel, sand, silt, and rocks) on top of the shale. The Powell end moraine, a roll of till that stretches east-west into Indiana, goes through the park. The moraine is hard to detect in the park, but travelers driving north from Columbus on U.S. Route 23 might notice the gentle undulation of this feature before reaching the park.

Water running off the last ice mass, the Wisconsinan glacier some 15,000 years ago, created the Olentangy River which has washed away the till and cut through the Ohio shale.

At Highbanks, the river now scours Olentangy shale and in places limestone (Columbus limestone), the compressed remains of an even older sea floor. In midsummer, when the water level is low, the limestone layer is exposed.

Southwesterly moving tributaries, fed by rain and snow, have roughed up the terrain by gouging ravines into the bluffs. These hollows run perpendicular to the river, and give a "whaleback" (or hogback) look to the relief.

Though it is hard to see them from the overlook, the "high bank" is shot full of round rocks, some the size of wrecking balls, oddly stuck among the horizontal layers of shale. These are concretions. From the river it looks like some giant creature long ago threw mud balls into the cliff, or that some army from the Middle Ages catapulted them randomly into a mud dome.

Scientists believe concretions began as pieces of organic matter (a tree branch perhaps) which secreted minerals, such as iron, and attracted sediment. The concretions grew in concentric layers, like pearls or onions. You might see smashed ones at the bottom of deep ravines, or in the river during low water.

Wildlife

It has been said life at the top is tough. That is true at the top of the "high banks" where it is thin-soiled and dry due to constant pounding by westerly winds and long sun exposure. Nevertheless, this environment is good enough for lichens and mosses, and shrubs such as viburnum and blackhaw. This fragile spot harbors some plants uncommon in Central Ohio, such as star toadflax, butterfly weed, smooth aster, and nodding wild onion.

Not far from the edge a forest takes over with hickories, oaks, maples, and beeches stretching skyward. Walnuts, Ohio buckeyes, and hackberries like the moist soils near the ravine mouths. Cottonwoods and sycamores prefer the river's edge. Dogwoods, redbuds, pawpaws, and hornbeams spread out in the understory soaking up whatever sunlight penetrates the canopy.

Winter's dreariness ends when the wildflowers blossom. Overbrowsing by deer has trimmed the wildflower patches, but you will still find large-flowered trillium, ragworts, phlox, violets, Dutchman's breeches, and bloodroot.

A reclusive reptile called the Jefferson salamander resides at the Indian earthworks. The creature is named after President Thomas Jefferson, an amateur naturalist. When the early spring rains fall these tiny lizards emerge from their tunnels and begin a 2–3 week breeding spree. Then they return to their burrows and pray for rain next spring.

The surrounding metropark offers wooded and open natural areas worth exploring. These former farm fields and orchards, which are in various stages of succession, yield milkweed (the host plant of monarch butterflies), grasses, goldenrod, briar patches, and pioneer trees like sumac, hawthorn, crabapple, and ash. If left undisturbed, these fields will eventually give way to the woodland.

Birds are abundant. As many as 150 species have been tallied. Bald eagles and osprey have loitered here, though none have been seen recently. More promising for birders are red-tailed hawks or owls (barred, great horned, and screech) who perch in trees at the edge of meadows hunting prey. Sometimes Cooper's, broad-winged, and kestrel hawks are observed. At night, swarms of swallows dart in the fields. Look for bluebirds at one of the 71 nesting boxes standing in the meadows.

A specially built garden behind the nature center attracts butterflies and hummingbirds when deer don't devour the flowers. Quiet walkers may see these deer (abundant), and perhaps a red fox.

The Olentangy sponsors aquatic creatures such as the eastern softshell turtle, water and queen snakes, crayfish (a favorite prey of queen snakes), many insect larvae, and small fish called darters, notably the blue-breasted darter, considered a rarity. The park also supports black, ring-necked, and milk snakes.

History

Humans have been fond of the "high banks" and the Olentangy for hundreds of years.

Archeologists continue to wonder about a horseshoe-shaped, 1,500-foot earthen mound and moat built by the so-called "late woodlands" Indians of the Cole Culture about 1,000 years ago. It is hard to detect it near the overlook because erosion has worn it down and vegetation conceals it.

Most believe it was a U-shaped fortification protecting a settlement. The open end of the horseshoe ends at the "high bank," and deep ravines border the sides. The moat bolstered the defensive position at the bottom of the "U." The site also may have served as a ceremonial plaza. Two burial mounds of the Adena culture, located elsewhere in the park, indicate that the area also was sacred to our forebears. The earthworks are listed on the National Registry of Historic Landmarks.

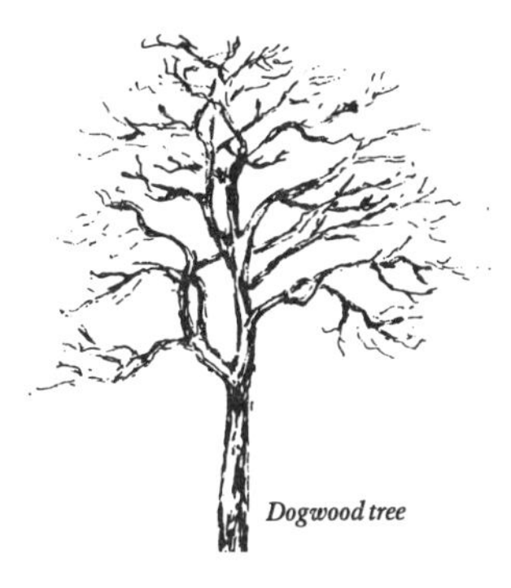
Dogwood tree

INNISWOOD GARDENS METROPARK

Although the main attractions of this metropark are its cultivated gardens, a half-mile boardwalk trail loops through two distinct forests and offers a glimpse into nature's wilder side. Gardeners, landscapers, and nature lovers should make Inniswood Gardens a destination.

Location

Northeast Franklin County, City of Westerville.

Leave Interstate 270 at the Westerville exit and travel north a half mile on State Route 3 (State Street), then turn right (east) on to Schrock Road. Follow Schrock Road to its end (about 1.4 miles), then turn right (south) on Hempstead Road. The entrance is on the left in 3/10 mile.

Ownership

Metropolitan Park District of Columbus and Franklin County.

Size & Designation

Inniswood comprises 92.3 acres. It is called a botanical garden and nature preserve.

Nearby Natural Attractions

Inniswood Gardens is one of nine metroparks in the area. Several metroparks are in the vicinity—Sharon Woods (Edward S. Thomas State Nature Preserve), Highbanks (Highbanks State Nature Preserve), Blendon Woods, and Blacklick (Walter A. Tucker State Nature Preserve). Gahanna Woods State Nature Preserve also is just a few miles away. Swimmers and boaters should visit Hoover Dam Reservoir, a Columbus city park, just northeast of Inniswood.

Access

Visitors can tour the gardens and natural area daily from 7 a.m. until dark. Innis House, a former estate, is open from 8 a.m.– 4:30 p.m. Tuesday–Friday, and on weekends for scheduled gardening, nature, and art programs. Maps of the grounds can be found at a small reception area by the parking lot or at Innis House.

The half-mile nature trail begins at the edge of the woods to your right as you walk from the parking lot to the gardens and Innis House. The boardwalk trail is flat and accessible to visitors in wheelchairs. Benches along the trail provide rest and views of the wet woods. The trail concludes at the north lawn. Just follow the sidewalk to the gardens.

The grounds feature a herb garden, rock garden, rose garden, and a memorial garden. Beds of irises and peonies are located west of the rock garden (bottom of the hill). The park brochure has a blooming schedule for the many flowers that add color to the park. Obviously, the best time to visit are the warm months.

A multipurpose room in Innis House seats up to 100 people for lectures and meetings. Art exhibits and horticultural programs are also held in this air-conditioned building. Dining facilities are available too. Tours led by staff naturalists or volunteers begin at Innis House.

Restrooms and drinking water are located at the east end of the parking lot and at Innis House (handicapped accessible).

Unlike other metroparks, Inniswood does not have picnicking or recreational facilities. Activities such as jogging, kite flying, and ball playing are not allowed—and leave your radio at home.

Geology & Wildlife

The Wisconsinan ice mass that swept across the state 15,000 years ago left the terrain here relatively flat. Nevertheless, there are subtle and important changes in elevation. For instance, the divide separating the watersheds of Big Walnut and Alum creeks runs through the gardens. The water on the east side of park ends up in Big Walnut Creek, but water on the west side slowly flows into Alum Creek.

Divide aside, water hardly drains quickly to either stream, so the wooded natural area remains swampy year-round (another reason for the boardwalk). You will notice several intermittent (seasonal) rills in the woods, but the main brook winds through the west side of the park. Innis House lies above the floodplain of this picturesque brook.

Notice, as you negotiate the boardwalk, that buxom beech and maples dominated the south side of the natural area, but that oaks, hickory, and their kin rule on the north side. An almost imperceptible change in topography allowed the oak-hickory community to claim the higher ground, leaving the beech-maple group on the lower ground.

You also will see a smattering of wild black cherry, American hornbeam, dogwood, and ash in this wet forest.

People come to Inniswood mostly to see the gardens. Here the planted flowers and herbs are identified by small plaques. In the woods, however, the blossoms emerge without the advantage of brass plates. Look for bloodroot, blue phlox, cutleaf toothwort, jack-in-the-pulpit, trillium, purple bittercress, rue anemone, violets, Virginia bluebell, wild geranium, wild ginger, and white baneberry. A small cattail pond on your left at the end of the nature trail teems with colorful dragonflies in the spring and summer. Walk to the shore and watch them dip and climb for mosquitoes. Dragonflies, also known as darning needles and stingers, are not at all harmful to humans. Their elongated bodies are designed for flight, not for piercing skin.

The pond grew out of a mistake during park development. An errantly excavated hole filled with water and was neglected. It developed into a pond that attracted frogs, snakes, and other wildlife. People liked it, so the pool stayed.

These woods are thick with squirrels and chipmunks, perhaps too many for the habitat. I suspect the surrounding residential developments have forced these critters into the park. They appear smaller and much more tame than their brethren in oak forests of southeast Ohio. These animals, and the rabbits, are chased by the foxes who reside in the woods, perhaps in the hollows of fallen beech trees.

Inniswoods lures the usual collection of birds in Central Ohio. The challenge for birders will be spotting the owls (barred and great horned), Cooper's hawk, red-tailed hawk, eastern bluebird, and pileated woodpecker, whose shrill song does not match its beauty.

Hungry deer fleeing suburban development raid the gardens. In 1993, they wiped out the day lilies (400 varieties) and all of the hostas.

History

Inniswood reflects the lifelong interests of Grace and Mary Innis, whose 37-acre garden estate forms the nucleus of this metropark. Grace Innis was an avid horticulturist, Mary an ornithologist.

Grace Innis, the surviving sister, donated the estate to the park district in 1972 and during the next decade worked with officials to develop a master plan for the grounds. She died in 1982.

The remaining 54 acres, the wooded natural area, was purchased with grant money from the Innis sisters, metropark funds, and matching grants from the U.S. Land and Water Conservation Fund of the U.S. Department of the Interior.

The herb garden was completed in 1987 with funds from the Columbus Foundation, Lancaster Colony, individual benefactors, and the Inniswood Society, a support and fund-raising group created to improve the grounds and boost interest in gardening and horticulture. The group holds a flower sale in the spring to raise money for the gardens.

The park district will be adding gardens and other facilities to fulfill the master plan of the Innis sisters.

Journal

June 13, 1993 (Sunday). Dozens of people in their Sunday best are milling around Innis House. Unknown to me, it is the Inniswood Society's annual meeting and garden party. Inside the Innis House, a horticulturist is talking about Japanese gardens. Outside, a string quartet seated in the shade of an oak tunes up; golf carts arrive laden with punch bowls.

As usual I am dressed for the woods—khaki pants, boots, T-shirt, wrinkled Aussy hat, camera gear vest, and tripod. Add a quart of sweat to my apparel, and my seven-year-old son who dressed himself that day and—you get the picture. Not the day to pick the brain of staffers and volunteers. They are up to their necks in fruit punch, napkins, and pressed clothes.

Indeed, a certain natty decorum reigns at Inniswood. Shoes and shirts must be worn at all times. Keep that in mind, all of you bare-chested, barefooted, haltertopped, cutoff jeans, radio-blasting, and Frisbee throwers, when visiting Inniswood.

Muskrat

PICKERINGTON PONDS METROPARK

The calamitous and chaotic honking of thousands of waterfowl can be downright rapturous when they converge at the glacier-formed ponds. The cacophony climaxes in the spring and again in the fall during the height their cross-country migration.

Here you have a front row seat for aerial performances. Observe the tight flying formations and graceful landings of incoming Canada geese. Over there, ducks bob and dive for food.

Location

Southeastern Franklin County, Madison Township, and northwestern Fairfield County, Violet Township.

From Columbus take State Route 33 southeast to Gender Road. Head north on Gender Road for two miles, then east on Wright Road. Bowen Road, which connects with Wright Road, also passes through the preserve.

Ownership

The Metropolitan Park District of Columbus and Franklin County owns and manages the wetlands.

Size & Designation

Pickerington Ponds, covering 356.8 acres, was designated a state scenic nature preserve on December 31, 1985. The park district describes the site as a wetlands wildlife refuge.

Nearby Natural Attractions

In Franklin County, see Blendon Woods, Battelle-Darby Creek, and Inniswood Gardens metroparks, as well as these state nature preserves: Highbanks (Highbanks Metropark), Edward S. Thomas (Sharon Woods Metropark), Walter A. Tucker (Blacklick Metropark, also in Fairfield County), and Gahanna Woods. In Fairfield County, visit Shallenberger State Nature Preserve and Chestnut Ridge Metropark.

Access

There are no parking lots, no observation decks, nor trails (the park district plans to build them in the future). Visitors can observe wildlife from their cars parked on the berms of Bowen or Wright roads. Feel free to walk along the roadside, but do not climb fences for a better look. Don't enter private property. The refuge is open everyday during daylight hours.

Geology

Most lakes in Ohio are manmade, but not the Pickerington Ponds. These are ancient kettle lakes created when enormous blocks of ice split from the withdrawing Wisconsinan glacier some 15,000 years ago. The weight of these chunks caused depressions which filled with water when the ice melted. The marsh in the preserve also is a kettle that has filled in with vegetation.

Long ago, there were hundreds of kettle ponds in glaciated Ohio, providing habitat for migratory waterfowl and other animals. The birds still follow this ancient trail of teardrops left behind by the glacier. All but a few kettles have vanished, the victims of draining.

The knolls surrounding the ponds are kames formed when gravel, sand, and clay washing across the top of the glacier fell through a hole in the ice. The kames serve as a watershed for the ponds.

Wildlife

Birdwatching is the big (and only) attraction here. Some 212 different species have been sighted, including rarities like the sandhill crane (just stopping for a visit) and the marsh wren, an endangered species. At the height of the spring and fall migrations 2,000–4,000 birds stop for rests and refills.

On any day, birders are apt to observe any of the waterfowl known to Ohio waters, such as teals, mergansers, and pintail and ring-necked ducks. Shorebirds (sandpipers, woodcock, killdeer), rails, and gulls visit the ponds. Hawks might be seen perched on trees at the edge of the ponds and marsh.

The marsh sponsors muskrats, those painted turtles and other shelled species, frogs (just listen to the croakers on a summer evening), northern water snakes (hunting frogs), and even fox and deer on its edges. You might see herons and bitterns hanging out here.

History

In the early 1970s, developers eyed these ponds. That prompted William W. Ellis, Jr., a Columbus attorney, to organize the Pickerington Ponds Committee under the leadership of the Ohio Chapter of The Nature Conservancy. The groups raised money and bought the ponds, marsh, and surrounding higher ground. Major contributors were The Columbus Foundation, the Jeffrey family, the Schumacher Foundation, Wolfe Associates, and the Columbus Audubon Society.

The park district has bankrolled about half the project, relying on tax dollars and matching funds from the Federal Land and Conservation Fund which were obtained by the Ohio Department of Natural Resources. The conservancy has deeded the land to the metroparks as a wildlife refuge. Improvements like observation shelters will be built when money becomes available.

Journal

October 1992. Every preserve has its challenge. Here, it's goose feces the size of small Tootsie Rolls. It litters Bowen Road and produces a mild, but persistent stench. Hard not to step in it. Hard not to gag. How fast can you roll up the car windows?

Hundreds, maybe thousands, of geese collected here recently. Hard to criticize that. The stink and manure they left behind is what you expect when any large number of animals gathers in any location.

At another collecting point just 15 miles away—Downtown Columbus—hundreds of thousands of humans sweat, rev their engines, and add to the waste stream everyday. Don't see any geese with binoculars at Broad and High streets.

Of course, the nauseous odor makes geese feel right at home at Pickerington Ponds. It is their place, and we humans will just have to live with their litter.

White-tailed deer

SHARON WOODS METROPARK (Edward S. Thomas State Nature Preserve)

Curious white-tailed deer may tiptoe within an arm's length of you in this sanctuary of meadows and hardwood trees in suburban Columbus. You can hike or bike to the state-dedicated nature preserve. ♿

Location

Northern Franklin County, Sharon Township.

The Edward S. Thomas State Nature Preserve occupies the western third of Sharon Woods Metropark, which is wedged into the northeast corner of the junction of interstates 71 and 270. From I-71 drive east on I-270 about a mile and take the Cleveland Avenue (Westerville) northbound exit. Go north on Cleveland Avenue about a mile to the park entrance (traffic signal) on the left. Park at the Maple Grove Picnic Area for the bicycle path (also a foot trail); or at the Schrock Lake Picnic Area for the mile-long nature trail.

Ownership

Metropolitan Park District of Columbus and Franklin County.

Size & Designation

The metropark totals 762 acres. The 319.8-acre preserve became a state-dedicated natural area on September 25, 1975.

Nearby Natural Attractions

In Franklin County, visit the Big and Little Darby Creek, national and state scenic streams at Battelle-Darby Creek Metropark; Olentangy River, a state scenic river, at Highbanks Metropark; Gahanna Woods State Nature Preserve; and Blendon Woods, Pickerington Ponds, Blacklick Woods, and Inniswoods Gardens metroparks.

Access

The Edward S. Thomas Nature Trail, a flat, wooded, one-mile loop, starts and ends at the Schrock Lake Picnic Area. About half of the trail meanders through the preserve. A wildlife observation deck at the boundary of the preserve and metropark offers a magnificent view of a long meadow, the evening gathering point for the park's deer herd.

The paved bicycle trail, measuring 3.8 miles, wanders deeper into the preserve from the Maple Grove Picnic Area. Folks in wheelchairs or pushing strollers can use this trail, but expect several steep slopes when the trail crosses ravines. Bikers must follow the arrow and stay in their designated lane. All other visitors should travel in the pedestrian lane. Benches are conveniently spaced along the trail, and there is a water fountain midway. Trail maps are located at the ranger station and information boards.

Metropark naturalists and local conservation groups hold meetings, workshops, and programs at the Spring Hollow Outdoor Education Center, reached from the entrance to the park district headquarters on West Main Street, Westerville. Natural history programs are held in various locations within the park throughout the year.

Youngsters 15 years and under can fish for bass, bluegill, and catfish at 11-acre Schrock Lake. The park offers three picnic areas (with toilets), playgrounds, shelters, sledding hill, ice skating, and open spaces.

Geology

The general terrain is flat, though some gentle knolls and ravines exist. Till, a mixture of sand, gravel, rocks, clay, and silt, deposited here by the Wisconsinan glacier some 15,000 years ago rests upon shale of the Devonian geological period (roughly 375 million years ago). Intermittent streams and forest wetlands can be viewed from trails. Many of the boulders in the preserve are refugees from Canada, some of the debris left behind by the receding glacier. Geologists call these rocks erratics, though none of them show much erratic behavior.

Wildlife

Sharon Woods Metropark is famous for its abundance of white-tailed deer. It is easy to spot them roaming through the woods and across the meadows. Come July, stately bucks browse in the fields, their formidable racks still sheathed by velvet. Cautious does, at the edge of the woods, guard curious, spotted fawns. In the autumn bucks who wandered from the park return to mate (a season called rut). Lucky visitors may see the bucks fighting for supremacy by clashing their antlers. Enjoy the scenes. What you don't see, however, is a small ecological disaster.

Study the vegetation carefully. Notice the "browse line" among the trees and shrubs, marking the reach of the deer. The white-tails, in fact, have been overbrowsing, eating everything in their reach. Several hundred varieties of wildflowers once grew in the park, but overbrowsing by an ever-growing herd of deer has drastically reduced the number of species.

The deer, of course, cannot be blamed for the decline in wildflowers. Rapid residential and commercial growth that destroyed their habitat has packed them into Sharon Woods. The metropark is just not big enough to sustain the wildflowers and all those deer. Overbrowsing also is blamed for the drop in the rabbit and ground hog populations, and for diminishing the habitat of ground nesting birds, such as the woodcock. The herd also did not look healthy. Many deer, especially young ones, looked malnourished, undersized, and deformed.

After years of study, park administrators decided that the deer herd had to be trimmed to reinvigorate the wildflowers and the deer. Park officials opted to relocate some deer in 1993 rather than shoot them. There are mixed reviews as to whether this has worked.

In spite of the overbrowsing, some bloomers persist, notably trillium, violets, daisy, thistle, fleabane, chicory, and

Queen Anne's lace. Swampy hollows show off skunk cabbage, marsh marigold, and turtlehead. Higher on the ridge live showy orchis and twin leaf.

In the bottom of ravines look for sycamore and black walnut growing alongside Ohio buckeye, pawpaw, and red elm trees. The pawpaw is abundant here because the deer find its sprouts and buds distasteful. Higher ground supports beech, white oak, swamp white oak, red oak, chinkapin oak, bur oak, and white ash. Several huge oaks (bur and chinkapin), believed to be 250 years old, preside along the Thomas Trail in the nature preserve. Other trees include hickories (shagbark and pignut), elm, ash, silver maple, locust (black and honey), dogwood, hawthorn, and crabapple, a remnant of the orchard that once flourished here.

Schrock Lake attracts Canada geese and other waterfowl. At dusk, watch bats and swallows gobble insects. The usual cast of birds resides here. Keep your eyes open for bluebirds, killdeer, woodcocks (dusk), and barred owl.

History

The preserve is named after Edward S.Thomas, a park board commissioner until the late 1960s and former curator of natural history at the Ohio Archeological and Historical Society. Land purchases in the 1960s culminated in the opening of the park in 1968. More than a third of the land was set aside for nature preservation. In September 1975 the Ohio Department of Natural Resources, Division of Natural Areas and Preserves, designated the undisturbed parcel a scenic nature preserve.

Journal

July 1993. Some folks snicker at slogans like "Think Planet First," thinking them banal or self-righteous. But the "deer problem" at Sharon Woods (and other Columbus metroparks) illustrates the conflict underlying the slogan. Metropark officials wrestled with the "deer problem" for several years. The solutions boiled down to shooting the animals (the fast, cheap plan, but the one arousing public protest) or relocating them (the slow, expensive plan). The debate focused on the fate of the animals. The "real" problem—controlling human development—was not publicly addressed. Land developers still see wildlife as an obstacle; and few elected officials are willing to stop suburban spread to protect critters.

Scarlet tanager

SLATE RUN METROPARK

Easterners settling here mistook the black shale beside the creek for slate, hence the name. Nevertheless, the beauty of the oak-covered ravines and the "slate" run are still unmistakable.

Location

Northeast Pickaway County, Madison Township.

From U.S. Rte 23, running south from Columbus, turn left (east) on Duvall Road (two miles south of the Franklin County line) and go about eight miles to State Route 674. Turn right (south) to the entrance a half mile away on the right. From State Route 33 exit at Canal Winchester and head south on State Route 674, about 7.5 miles, to the park.

Size & Designation

Slate Run Metropark is part of a 1,707.8-acre park which includes the adjacent Slate Run Living Historical Farm.

Ownership

The Metropolitan Park District of Columbus and Franklin County.

Access

A visit to the Slate Run complex, combining a tour of the living historical farm and the natural area, is an ideal family outing. The natural area has picnic areas, toilets, drinking water, and an outdoor classroom for nature programs.

The double-loop nature trail starts at the west end of the parking lot and journeys through various habitats—an oak-hickory forest, meadows, successional growth, and creeks. The inner loop measures 1.6 miles, while the outer loop, or perimeter trail, takes 2.3 miles. Study the map at the trailhead before departing.

The path begins by following the crest of an oak-hickory ridge which overlooks the scenic ravine of Slate Run to the right. Notice the young trees to the left and mature trees to the right, indicating that farming and grazing once took place up to the edge of the ravine and stream. This demarcation between new, successional growth and mature trees is evident throughout the trail.

I turned right at the first fork and descended into a small valley. The path crosses

Slate Run, climbs the north bank, and heads west through a meadow (look for deer), and along a vegetation line separating old and new growth.

Eventually, the outer trail turns left (south), crosses the ravine, climbs to the south ridge, and goes east to the trailhead. You can cut the walk in half by taking a shortcut across the ravine.

The trails are wide, smooth, and well-marked. A couple of climbs up and down the ravine are a little steep, but brief. Interpretive signs explain some of the natural history of the woods.

The park is open daily during daylight hours. Naturalist-led programs on natural history topics are held almost weekly. Program schedules can be found at the information board near the drinking fountain.

Nearby Natural Attractions

Other places to visit in Pickaway County are Stage's Pond State Nature Preserve, and A.W. Marion State Park. Slate Run is one of nine local metroparks. The others are Chestnut Ridge, Pickerington Ponds, Blacklick, Blendon Woods, Sharon Woods, Highbanks, Inniswood and Battelle-Darby Creek.

Geology

The shale wrongly identified as slate is actually Ohio shale which formed at the bottom of a shallow, murky ocean about 350 million years ago during the Devonian geologic period. Unfortunately, very little of this formation, whatever you call it, can be seen on the nature trail. The best examples lie upstream from the trailhead. (Winter offers a better view from ridgetops.)

It is easy for amateurs to confuse these rocks. Both are dark gray in color and composed of clay and tiny quartz crystals. Shale is a sedimentary rock created from bits (or sediments) of ancient rock that broke off due to erosion or weathering. Slate, a metamorphic rock, is shale whose mineral composition or texture has been changed, or metamorphosed, because of higher temperature or pressure in the earth.

During the mountain-building period many millions of years ago, extreme pressure transformed particles in shale into mica and drew foliations (waves or cleavages) in the layer, sometimes perpendicular to the direction of the rock bed. Slate slabs sliced from these cleavages have been used for roof tiles.

So, Slate Run has really been washing away shale, sandstone, and glacial till all these years. Younger Bedford shale, also dark gray, and Berea sandstone of the Mississippian geologic era (a mere 325 million years old), are above the Ohio shale. Above all of this sedimentary bedrock is till (sand, gravel, clay) left behind by the Wisconsinan glacier 15,000 years ago.

The Slate Run you see is a meandering brook which empties into Little Walnut Creek, then Walnut Creek, and the Scioto River.

Wildlife

The woods here is the typical Central Ohio blend of oaks, hickories, maples, and beech, called a mixed mesophytic forest. You will also find slippery elm, whose inner bark was used by Indians and early settlers as a fever and cold remedy. The extinct passenger pigeon once favored the tree's wafer-shaped fruit.

An interpretive sign on the trail pointing to a pignut hickory explains that white settlers give the tree its derisive name because its bitter nuts were fit only for pigs. The nuts of the shagbark hickory are edible.

Several mighty specimens of northern red oak grow on the ridgetop near the trailhead. This hardwood was prized for its sturdiness and was used to prop up coal mines and for railroad ties. Many years ago, 300 acres of northern reds would be cut annually to make the charcoal needed to feed an iron furnace.

A board at the trailhead listed the warblers nesting in the woods. I spotted several species in the valley but they moved too fast to identify. A scarlet tanager greeted me near the entrance. We studied each other for 2–3 minutes until the next group of hikers disturbed him. A solitary killdeer stood in grass near the entrance when I arrived.

Listen for the hooting of the barred owls, and the shrill cries of the flicker and pileated woodpecker.

History

The land here has been settled and farmed since the early 1800s. The living historical farm recreates farm life in Central Ohio in the 1880s when Samuel Oman owned this acreage.

A former metroparks commissioner, Walter A. Tucker, foresaw the ecological value of the farm and woods.

Journal

It's easy for the untrained eye to confuse slate and shale. Both are usually thinly layered and break off in plates. When heated, pressured, stretched and baked (which occurs when continental plates collide) shale turns into metamorphic rock called slate.

Royal catchfly

THE DARBY PLAINS PRAIRIES

- **Bigelow Cemetery**
- **Smith Cemetery**
- **Milford Center Prairie**

In seed-sized patches of land, the survivors of the great tallgrass prairie grow over the first prairie settlers. So when you visit the Darby Plains prairie in the summer, you're enchanted by the exploding hues of flowers. But in the winter, you're bewitched by the ghosts of Lucinda Smith and Lucy Bigelow. ★

Location

These three preserves are located a few miles apart in Madison and Union counties.

To reach Smith Cemetery (Northern Madison County, Darby Township) head west from Plain City on State Route 161. In about two miles, go south (left) on Kramer Road, then west (right) on Boyd Road. Look for a patch of oak trees and tall grass 100 feet off the road to the right. Park alongside the road or off to the side of the small farm lane leading to the cemetery. Do not block the potholed lane nor drive to the site.

Bigelow Cemetery is in Pike Township, Madison County. Continue west on SR 161 about five more miles, then go south one mile on Rosedale (formerly Weaver) Road. Again, look for trees surrounding a cemetery. You will have to park your car on the berm.

Milford Center Prairie is in southwestern Union County (Union Township), just north of the intersections of State Route 4 and State Route 36. From Bigelow Cemetery, return to SR 161 and travel west to the hamlet of Irwin, nearly five miles, then go north (right) on State Route 4. About two miles up SR 4, a little north of SR 36, you cannot miss seeing the broad-shouldered towers of an electric power line intersecting with the road. Park the car in the grassy area on the west (left) side of SR 4. Walk north (toward Milford Center) on this former railroad grade.

A small gravel parking lot designated for utility company vehicles is located off Connor Road. You can park in the vicinity. Walk south from here. The railroad grade north of Connor Road is not mowed.

Departing from Marysville, take SR 4 to the Milford Center preserve; or SR 38 to SR 161 to reach the Smith and Bigelow cemeteries.

Ownership

The respective township trustees own the Bigelow and Smith preserves. Dayton Power & Light owns the Milford Center site. All three locations are managed by the Ohio Department of Natural Resources, Division of Natural Areas and Preserves.

Size & Designation

The pioneer graveyards, each measuring about a half acre, have been designated as interpretive nature preserves. Bigelow was dedicated on October 3, 1978; Smith on December 6, 1982.

Milford Center Prairie, also an interpretive preserve open to the public, stretches for 1.3 miles along the right-of-way of a former rail line. It joined the state preserve system in 1986.

Nearby Natural Attractions

Madison Lake State Park and Deer Creek Wildlife Area are found in Madison County. Close by are Battelle-Darby

Creek Metropark in Franklin County, and Little and Big Darby Creek National and State Scenic Rivers, wandering through Union, Madison, Franklin, and Pickaway counties.

Access

These sanctuaries are at their natural best when the prairie blooms in July and August. However, folks who like to visit old bone yards should come in the winter, when the stones and the ghosts are easier to see.

Bigelow Cemetery lies right beside the road—you cannot miss it. Smith Cemetery is 100 feet off the road but is reachable by a path. Mowed paths serve as trails in these preserve. The trail at Milford Center, also a mowed path, follows the power line.

You will have to park on the side of the road at all three locations, so don't bring the RV. Consider turning on your flashing emergency lights if your car partially juts into the road, especially at dusk.

Keep in mind that some of the gravestones are nearly 180 years old and fragile. The preserves are open every day from dawn to dusk.

For more information contact the Ohio Department of Nature Resources, Division of Natural Areas and Preserves, Fountain Square, Building F-1, Columbus, Ohio 43224-1331; phone (614) 265-6453.

Geology

Though prairies may have existed in Ohio before the Ice Age, scientists are rather certain that about 4,000–6,000 years ago (long after the last glacier) the land experienced a long warm and dry spell called the Xerothermic Period. The heat wave triggered the eastward migration of the Great Plains tallgrass prairie. A finger, or peninsula, of the western prairie overwhelmed the forest and probed as far east as Pennsylvania and north into Michigan.

Scientists suspect that the climate cooled again, and drove back the frontier of the prairie (the French word for meadow) to the Illinois-Indiana border. Some 300 prairie islands, however, withstood the reemergence of the forest. These patches of prairie ranged in size from a few acres to several square miles. One of these outposts was the Darby Plains of Central Ohio.

The Darby Plains is located between Big and Little Darby creeks. Though a slight summit, or divide, separates the watersheds of these creeks, the flat terrain drains slowly. Consequently, the grassland stays swampy in the spring and early summer, deterring the sprouting of tree seedlings.

By late August or early September, however, the soil becomes parched and cracked. Any tree seedlings that survived the soggy spring would be wiped out by summer drought or fires ignited by lightning or Native Americans. Likewise, sprouts that make it through the summer drown next spring. The Darby Plains would remain a prairie as long as this wet and dry cycle continued.

Fires are essential for the survival of the prairie. While the infernos wreak havoc on the encroaching hardwoods, they did little harm to the fire-tolerant prairie plants whose underground life processes avoid the flames. The fires, then, help the prairie in its turf fight by suppressing the forest.

The blaze also destroys the thick mat of dead grass on the surface, and returns nutrients (ash) to the soil. With the suffocating mat gone, the spring's rain and warm sun reach the seedbeds faster, and trigger rapid growth.

Cinders spewing from passing railroad engines set the Milford Center Prairie (and nearby fields) ablaze. During dry months farmers feared for their crops every time a train roared through the countryside. Few of them realized the fires they extinguished abetted the prairie they had suppressed.

The plains Indians called the fires "red buffalos." They torched the tallgrass following an ancient hunting strategy of stampeding game to awaiting marksmen. They also knew the fires opened the grassland for the grazing bison they hunted.

Following nature's cue, naturalists revive prairie remnants and new meadows with periodic burnings, which are said to be good for the prairie's soul as well as for its seed.

Wildlife

Who can resist their names? Ox-eye, whorled rosinweed, flowering spurge, black-eyed Susan, royal catchfly. Some 30 types of flowers and grasses have been counted at Smith Cemetery, a fewer number at Bigelow Cemetery.

In July and August, the "rainbow" blooms. Bring your field guides, but remember that prairie flowers often go by several names. Keep in mind that the plants you see represent only a portion of the varieties that once flourished on the Darby Plains.

You are likely to find big bluestem ("big" because it soars to 10 feet), Indian grass, flowering spurge, Canada anemone, wild bergamot, purple and gray-headed coneflowers, black-eyed Susan, and stiff goldenrod at both sites.

Little bluestem grass, wild garlic, smooth aster, New Jersey tea, gray dogwood, gray willow, guara, ox-eye, prairie false indigo, Virginia mountain-mint, prairie cord grasses, skunk meadow-rue, and golden Alexanders nearly conceal the gravestones in Smith Cemetery.

At Bigelow Cemetery look for the potentially threatened royal catchfly (once thought to be the only colony in Ohio), plus hazelnut, wax-leaved meadow-rue, wild petunia, sainfoin (also called scurf pea), tall coreopsis, pale-leaved sunflower, and prairie dock (sometimes reaching 10 feet).

Milford Center has the greatest variety of plants (57 different species in the last count). Its cache of royal catchfly is the largest in the state, and its small community of vetchling, or veiny pea, a rare legume, may be the only one left in Ohio.

Here butterflies and dragonflies collide and bounce about in reckless flights. Bees dive for nectar. These insects are the pollinators and propagators of the prairie. Birds and bugs make up part of the day watch at a prairie cemetery. At sunrise in the summer, hundreds of spider webs glisten like diamond necklaces.

Bison, elk, and the prairie chicken (grouse) once lived on Ohio's prairies. Their departure, however, benefited the cow, the groundhog, and the meadowlark, the residents of more cultivated landscapes. Early morning visitors may see matted grass where a deer had slept.

The wood bison that once roamed here was larger than its cousin on the Great Plains. It carried the "wood" prefix because it could graze in the forest and in grassy openings. Indian and white hunters preyed on the beast. The last one in Ohio was killed in Lawrence County in 1803. Only a couple thousand of them survive in Canada.

History

Native Americans harvested prairie plants for food, medicines, and fibers. The white pioneers, however, came here to plant corn and wheat. Their plows, more than any other factor, destroyed the prairie.

The first shipment of settlers arrived between 1810 and 1820, mostly from New England and Pennsylvania. They traveled down the old "post road" (State Route 161 today), to an area they called the "barrens," paying from 40¢ to $2 an acre.

The prairie proved formidable at first, being either too wet, too thick, or too dry for the plow. Swarms of mosquitoes sometimes darkened the sky. Some pioneers gave up and went home. Benjamin Hough bought 172 acres of the barrens on Oct. 21, 1815, but a year later he sold the tract (cemetery and all) to Russell and Lucy Bigelow who toiled there for at least six years. Lucy and four of her children are buried in the cemetery. The land has had many owners, but the cemetery always carried the name of these early settlers. Bigelow Cemetery received its last body in 1892, for a total of 78 markers. It became a state preserve in 1978.

Samuel Smith, a Methodist minister and a Revolutionary War veteran, brought his family from Vermont to the area in 1818. In 1824 his son, Samuel Smith Jr., married a 14-year-old orphan named Lucinda Andrews, whose sister and parents were among the first occupants of what became known as Smith Cemetery. Samuel Jr. bought the land containing the graveyard shortly after Lucinda died at age 22 on February 11, 1832.

Two years later, Samuel Jr. and his second wife deeded the cemetery to the Darby Township trustees and said good riddance to the Darby Plains. A century and a half after Lucinda Smith's death, the graveyard holding her bones became a sanctuary.

It is remarkable, given the historical record, that these tiny botanical jewel boxes survived at all. During the last two centuries, the prairie has been drained and cultivated, its fertility unlocked to feed a hungry nation. Weed killers, insecticides, and chemical fertilizers shrunk the prairie even more.

Amazingly, specks of the original prairie held on—as oversights, in neglected, overgrown pioneer cemeteries, along untidy fencerows, and beside abandoned railroad tracks.

Journal

July 1993. As I walked through these little gardens I recalled an observation by William Least Heat-Moon, author of PrairyErth. *Heat-Moon recommended visiting old prairie graveyards to rediscover what the Indians called the "flower nation." He wrote, "But if you stay in a white man's old burial ground long enough, this darkness must come to you: his way of life is the land's death and his way of death is the land's life."*

Like short-lived pioneer plants, pioneer people usually died young. One exception was Solon Harrington, now a resident in Smith Cemetery. His survivors noted on his stone that he died on May 15, 1855, having lived 99 years, four months, and 19 days.

hicles, are marked by their leaf designs.

Visit the log cabin and pioneer cemetery along the way. The cabin and surrounding woods present a picture of what Ohio looked like around the time of statehood. This route passes through Holly Hill, where more than 100 different kinds of holly grow, a prairie, forestry test lots (7,000 trees planted in 1930 are studied for growth and survival), and back to the visitors center.

Ambitious hikers can stay on the Oak Trail for a 2.5-mile journey to the many nooks and crannies of the grounds.

Small parking lots off the auto route allow visitors to see plant collection and special features. Children will insist on climbing the observation tower at the southeast corner of the grounds to look at the nearly half-mile long arborvitae hedge spelling out Dawes Arboretum.

The auto route also visits:

- The Famous 17, a grove of Ohio buckeye trees planted to form the number 17. The design symbolizes Ohio's admission to the United States as the 17th state;
- Dawes Memorial, a Grecian-style mausoleum in the northeast corner of the property where Beman and Bertie Dawes, the former owners, are buried;
- Daweswood House, the former home of Beman and Bertie Dawes, serves as a museum, and exhibit hall for the arboretum shovel collection (see History section); and
- Education Center, a renovated barn used for classrooms, meetings, and workshops.

The Henry Dawes Visitor Center has a nature center (a favorite place for kids), gift shop, information desk, Bonsai collection, library, classrooms, restrooms, drinking water, and administrative offices.

American holly leaves

THE DAWES ARBORETUM

Folks searching for a pastoral, manicured setting to study nature will discover it on this cultivated landscape, more a series of exquisite gardens than a wild natural area. Still, you can easily spend a day wandering around this living horticultural museum.

Location

Southern Licking County, about six miles south of Newark on State Route 13.

From Interstate 70, exit at SR 13 and head north. From the interstate to the entrance is about 2.5 miles.

Ownership

The Dawes Arboretum.

Size & Designation

The arboretum encompasses 1,149 acres, but only 1/3 of the property is open to the public. One third is farmland, the other third is a forest plantation and natural area.

The owners define arboretum as "a place where trees, shrubs, and other woody plants are grown, exhibited and labeled for scientific and educational purposes."

Nearby Natural Attractions

A tour of Dawes Arboretum may complement a visit to Blackhand Gorge and Morris Woods state nature preserves, Flint Ridge State Memorial, and Buckeye Lake State Park, all in Licking County.

Access

To familiarize yourself with the grounds stop at the visitors center for a guide and map, then drive the two-mile auto tour. Return to the visitors center and begin your hike.

To explore the Deep Woods, a hardwood forest of oak, maple, beech, black cherry, and hickory trees, follow the Maple and Oak trails, and return via the Holly Trail. It's about 1.5 miles. Pick up brochures on the Maple and Holly trails at the visitors center (though both are written for elementary school students). The trails, wide and smooth enough for small ve-

The natural area located across the highway can be explored with written permission. Inquire at the visitor center. A tunnel safely carries visitors to the area.

The grounds of the arboretum are open every day from dawn to dusk, except on Thanksgiving, Christmas, New Year's Day, or when threatening weather strikes. There is no admission charge. The visitor center is open from 8 a.m.–11:30 a.m. and 12:30 p.m.–5 p.m. Monday–Friday; 9 a.m.–11:30 p.m. and 12:30 p.m.–5 p.m. on Saturday; 1–5 p.m. on Sunday and holidays. The center is closed on Sunday during January and February.

Ball playing and other recreational games are prohibited. Pets must be kept on a leash. Swimming, wading, boating, and ice skating are forbidden at Dawes Lake. (Members of the arboretum can fish there, however.)

For more information contact The Dawes Arboretum, 7770 Jacksontown Road S.E., Newark, OH 43056-9380; phone (614) 323-2355 or 1-800-44-DAWES.

Wildlife

As you would expect, the arboretum exhibits fine examples of exotic and native plant communities. Collections of maples, oaks, crab apple, pines, apples, and holly grow in special groves. Scientists study their growth, adaptability, and resistance to diseases. Elsewhere on the property, the Ohio Department of Natural Resources manages plots of test trees for future seed production.

Rare trees, such as the Japanese stewartia, lacebark pine, and paperbark maple, thrive in special areas at the edge of the Deep Woods. A recently renovated Japanese garden is just a stone's throw away from an Ohio prairie garden.

A unique cypress swamp, accessible by a boardwalk, gives visitors a feel for this tropical ecosystem. In the winter and spring, murky water reaches the knobby "knees" of the cypress, but by July the water has vanished. The arboretum sponsors one of the northernmost plantings of this tree.

Birdwatchers might spot 173 species of birds on the grounds. Get a checklist at the nature center before eyeing the sky.

Count the sharp-shinned hawk (special interest), northern harrier (endangered), northern bobwhite, American kestrel, red-headed woodpecker, bluebird, cedar waxwing, and brown-headed cowbird among the year-round residents. These beauties also have been seen—pine siskin (winter), northern oriole, northern parula, bobolink, summer tanager, whip-poorwill, and ruby-throated hummingbird.

Migratory waterfowl visit Dawes Lake and Tripp Higgins Pond in the spring and fall. Warblers, 31 different kinds, arrive in the spring and summer, even the yellow-breasted chat and the blackpoll warbler.

History

Beman Gates Dawes and Bertie O. Burr, both descendants of Revolutionary War era personalities, made their mark in history by founding The Dawes Arboretum in 1929 with hefty oil company profits.

Dawes, born in Marietta in 1870, is a descendant of William Dawes who shouted "The British Are Coming!" on that midnight ride with Paul Revere. In his lifetime, Beman succeeded as an engineer, businessman, and as a politician.

Bertie O. Burr, born in Lincoln, Nebraska, in 1872, could trace her line to Aaron Burr, Thomas Jefferson's vice president. (Burr is better known as the duelist who killed Alexander Hamilton, and as a political schemer linked to a western secessionist plot.) At age 20, Bertie received a gold medal from the U.S. Treasury for her bravery in saving two girls from drowning in a flooded Nebraska river.

Dawes was toiling in the coal and coke business in Lincoln when he met Bertie Burr. The couple married in Lincoln in 1894.

Beman brought his bride to Central Ohio in 1896 and began making a fortune in the oil and natural gas business. They also raised five children—four boys and a girl. He served in the Ohio House of Representatives from 1905–1909, and bought 140 acres and a large brick house (Daweswood House) south of Newark in 1918. (The couple lived in Columbus but used the Licking County home as a weekend and summer residence. In fact, at one time, they had five homes, but Daweswood was his preference.) Dawes established the Pure Oil Company in 1920. They founded the arboretum on June 1, 1929.

An endowment for the arboretum was created from the oil company's profits. Over time the arboretum grew in size and reputation.

Beman's well-known brother, Charles Gates Dawes, also contributed generously to the endowment. Charles Dawes, a brigadier general, won the Nobel Peace Prize in 1925 for the so-called Dawes Plan, establishing the framework for German reparations after World War I. He served as vice president of the United States from 1925–29.

The tree dedications began after Dawes saw a ceremony in England. Almost 100 famous people have dedicated trees at the arbo-

return. His first plantings were gifts of Admiral Byrd, Orville Wright, General Pershing, Red Grange, Gene Tunney, Jesse Owens and over sixty others.

Pershing Avenue, flanked by two long, straight rows of trees representing the typical species planted alongside U.S. streets, marked the visit of "Black Jack" Pershing in 1929. It is located in the southern section of the property, west of Dawes Lake.

It is said that among its peers, Dawes Arboretum is know for its innovative use of computerized plant records, one of the best local educational resources available.

Too, Dawes has a wonderful variety of programs for the amateur and the professional, and maintains a 3,000 volume library.

The Dawes died in the 1950's.

Journal

June 1993. I reached an intersection on the trail. To my left a trail led to a pioneer cemetery in a trimmed clearing. Here lie the bones of the Beard and Green families, descendants of John Beard and Benjamin Green, the first permanent white settlers in the area.

Dawes and his wife are buried in the arboretum, too, and, as a local writer once wrote, "while we have no first-hand knowledge of the view, he left the rest of us with a notable one."

The thought occurs to me that it would be pleasant to be buried on ones own property—a little family plot in the corner of the backyard, perhaps close to the pet gerbil and the family cat. Alas. It will not be. I should begin thinking of cremation. Ashes scattered on a favorite preserve?

Flint blade

FLINT RIDGE STATE MEMORIAL

Prehistoric Indians converged at this spot to gather flint, a stone more valuable to them than gold. The Great Spirit required all who entered the sacred region to pledge peace and harmony, a pact apparently respected for centuries. A hardwood forest has buried the quarries, leaving us to ponder the peace and serenity that still prevails. ★

Location

Southeast Licking County, Hopewell Township.

Eastbound travelers leave Interstate 70 at the Brownsville exit and take State Route 668 north about four miles. The site is at the intersection of SR 668 and Flint Ridge Road.

Westbound visitors must exit I-70 at Gratiot, go north (right) a quarter mile to U.S. Route 40 (National Trail), then west (left) on US 40 to Brownsville. Turn right on SR 668, and right on Flint Ridge Road.

Ownership

Ohio Historical Society.

Size & Designation

Flint Ridge is a state memorial totaling 525 acres.

Nearby Natural Attractions

Licking County also boasts Blackhand Gorge and Morris Woods state nature preserves, Dawes Arboretum, and Buckeye Lake State Park.

Access

Several trails snake through the hardwood forests of this nature preserve. All trails, except the Overlook Trail, begin in the picnic area. Handicapped explorers can take the 1/4-mile paved trail with handrails and Braille interpretive signs from the picnic area to the museum.

The half-mile Upper Trail leads to former quarries. From the picnic area, it winds south (behind the museum), around a pond (really a former flint quarry filled with water), and northward to the museum and parking lot. A shortcut, called the Wagon Road, heading to the right just before the pond, shortens this walk.

The two-mile Lower Trail branches off the Upper Trail, wanders downhill gradually to the southeastern corner of the preserve, crosses a couple of small creeks, and returns to the Upper Trail near the pond.

These three paths also begin at the museum, where you will find a map of the Upper and Lower trails.

The 1.5-mile, lasso-shaped Overlook Trail starts across

Flint Ridge Road and heads north to an open ravine of flint outcrops. This is the overlook. There, the trail loops around a ridge. Retrace your steps to return.

The depressions or small black pools you see along the trails are the ancient flint quarries. Soil eroding off the sides closed the abandoned mines. Some have become permanent ponds, filling up with water that runs off the slopes.

Colorful blue-gray flint boulders and chips can be seen everywhere along the trails. Please examine the chips, but leave them in the preserve. Don't dislodge or move flint boulders or chip them. These are historical artifacts! The ridges were sacred grounds.

Although the memorial is open daily during daylight hours, the museum operates on the following schedule: 9:30 a.m.–5 p.m., Wednesday–Saturday, and noon–5 p.m. on Sunday between Memorial Day and Labor Day; 9:30 a.m.–5 p.m. Saturday and noon–5 p.m. on Sunday during the fall.

The museum, built above a quarry, features a diorama of Indians mining and shaping flint. Rockhounds can buy flint and other souvenirs in the gift store. Restrooms and drinking water also are located in the museum. You will find picnic tables and latrines in the picnic grounds.

Geology

This area is one of the few places in the country where flint is so bountifully seen on the surface. This deposit, known as Vanport flint, sits on top of ridges covering an area of six square miles. The thickness of the layer varies from one to 12 feet.

Though many flint deposits date back to Silurian times (440 million years), the rock at Flint Ridge is younger, a mere 300 million years old, formed during the Pennsylvanian geologic period. Though it resembles limestone, flint is a type of quartz, mainly composed of silica (silicon dioxide).

Back in the Pennsylvanian times, a warm, shallow sea covered this part of Ohio. The ocean was tropical because Pangea, the huge land mass that later would split and separate into the continents we know today, rested at the Equator. The marine life that died fell to the ocean floor, creating a soft, limey soup. The silica needed to make flint probably came from the skeletons of sponges, specifically their spiny spicules. The sponges must have been abundant in this particular spot. The silica was compressed into flint by the weight of several layers of clay and other sediments that fell on top of it.

Chemical impurities trapped in the soggy stew gave flint its shades and streaks of red, green, yellow, pink, blue, black, and white. About 200 million years ago the land rose, or uplifted. Erosion carried away the soft surface layers and exposed the flint bedrock.

Though heavy and hard, flint is brittle enough to crack and chip. The flint that Indians found on the surface sometimes flaked, weakened by the weathering of rain, sun, and wind. They also discarded an inferior form of flint, called chert. The good stuff was found in seams beneath the surface.

Mining flint with primitive tools was backbreaking work. After removing surface obstacles like dirt and trees, the ancient people split open the flint by pounding wooden wedges into natural cracks with granite or quartzite rocks weighing 25 pounds or more. These heavy hammering stones were brought here from Canada by the glaciers.

Large chunks of flint were carried to worksites and cut into smaller pieces roughly matching the size of the desired implement. Some implements were manufactured at the mine, but most intricate toolmaking was done at locations beyond the ridges.

Today, flint is collected for its beauty, not its utility. Its hardness, color, and glossy polish make it a favorite gemstone of jewelers and collectors.

Wildlife

The flint ridges may have been one of the few places in prehistoric Ohio that showed the wear and tear of constant human habitation. The ancient people who assembled here probably blazed a network of trails. The tread of miners beat down the grounds around the quarries. The surrounding woods must have been vigorously hunted, and trees were felled to support mining activities as well as for shelter and fires. But their impact on land was comparatively minor compared to that of those who lived here for the last two centuries.

Though white settlers cleared the ridges for farming, a mature, mixed hardwood forest has grown back during the 60 years that the land has been protected. Even the ancient quarries have filled in with natural debris. In the spring they become black pools sponsoring aquatic life and quenching the thirst of animals. By autumn most have dried up.

Tracks on the shore of one "black pool" revealed the presence of deer and raccoons. Streaks of yellow in the forest canopy revealed the beauty of warblers.

History

The Ancient People, called Palaeo-Indians, arrived here

about 10,000 years ago, near the end of the Pleistocene Era or Ice Age. Maybe they noticed the colorful rocks while hunting for mastodon or bison, and quite by chance discovered that the rock could be chipped into durable tools and arrowheads.

Soon a prehistoric version of a gold rush ensued. Indians from faraway lands showed up for flint. To avoid territorial disputes and bloodshed, the flint ridges were declared sanctified grounds, or neutral zones. The Great Spirit, tribal leaders decided, made the flint for all the people.

A few miles east of the flint ridges, a "black hand" once appeared in a sandstone cliff above the Licking River. Many believe the black hand marked the eastern boundary of this demilitarized zone. (See Blackhand Gorge State Natural Preserve.)

Smaller flint deposits also were mined by Indians in Vinton, Jackson, Coshocton, Hocking, and Perry counties.

Indian traders distributed the gem widely. Artifacts carved from the local flint have been uncovered in Kansas City, Louisiana, and on the Atlantic coast.

Flint lost its luster when European explorers brought iron tools and weapons into the continent. White settlers utilized a lesser grade of flint for buhrstones to hone tools or grind grain. The sparks produced by striking flint started fires. The famous rifle of the frontier, the flintlock, got its name from the flint used to detonate the gunpowder.

Flint chips gathered from the ridges formed part of the roadbed of the National Road (U.S. 40) through Licking and Muskingum counties.

The Ohio Historical Society purchased the historic and geologically unique ridges in 1933. The museum opened in 1968.

Spring peeper

GAHANNA WOODS STATE NATURE PRESERVE

If you block out the roar of jets at the nearby Columbus airport, you will hear the plaintive song of spring peepers, or the ominous creaking of old trees swaying in the wind.

Location

Northeastern Franklin County, Jefferson Township.

Exit Interstate 270 at State Route 16, go east 1/4 mile and turn left (north) on Taylor Station Road for about three miles.

Ownership

Ohio Department of Natural Resources, Division of Natural Areas and Preserves.

Size & Designation

Gahanna Woods, comprising 50.7 acres, was dedicated an interpretive nature preserve on January 10, 1974.

Nearby Natural Attractions

In Franklin County, visit Highbanks State Nature Preserve (Highbanks Metropark), Battelle-Darby Creek Metropark, Edward S. Thomas State Nature Preserve (Sharon Woods Metropark), Walter A. Tucker State Nature Preserve (Blacklick Metropark), Pickerington Ponds Metropark and State Nature Preserve, Inniswood Gardens Metropark, Blendon Woods Metropark, and Olentangy and Big and Little Darby National and State Scenic Rivers.

Access

This preserve, open every day from sunrise to sunset, is next to a city park which has a parking lot, picnic area, a short nature trail, and a small playground. Look for the sign pointing to the nature preserve trails on the south side of the parking lot. Stop at the information board for a brochure which contains a trail map and a list of all the plants found in the preserve.

The Beechwood Trail heads south across a meadow and into the swamp forest (pond at left). Skip the Woodland Trail (unless you want a short walk) which branches to the right. The Beechwood Trail then arches west and north, passes a pair of small ponds on the left, and merges with the Woodland Trail in the middle of the forest. At this point you will be standing on a boardwalk surrounded by a swamp forest.

A right turn here on the Woodland Trail goes southwest back to the Beechwood Trail. To the left the path follows the edge of a pond to the northern property line and back to the start. The trails measure 1.5 miles on flat terrain.

Gahanna Woods is a swamp forest, so remember that the trails may be wet year-round. Boardwalks have been built over soggy areas. Also protect your body against insect attacks.

Nature education programs are held here during the year. For more information contact the Ohio Department of Natural Resources, Division of Natural Areas and Preserves, Fountain Square, Building F-1, Columbus, Ohio 43224-1331; phone (614) 265-6453.

Geology

The large boulders you see in the woods are chunks of granite from Canada left behind by the Wisconsinan glacier that swept across central Ohio some 15,000 years ago. The ice mass also deposited a layer of unsorted soil composed of sand, gravel, clay, boulders, and silt, a mixture called glacial till.

Now imagine that this layer of till is chunky peanut butter unevenly spread across a slice of bread. The bread represents the bedrock and the chunks in the peanut butter (till) are the blocks of granite (known as erratics). In some spots the layer of till will be thin, sunken, or pitted. The rain that filled these shallow depressions and potholes formed ponds and made the land ready for the plants and animals you see in the preserve.

Wildlife

In the glacier-made ponds at Gahanna Woods plants quickly took root. Grasses and shrubs appeared along the edge. The remains of these plants accumulated in the ponds and shrunk them. That enabled trees fit for wet soil to invade, dump more debris (leaves, dead trees), and begin taking over the area.

So, in the soggy shallows of the swamp forest at Gahanna Woods pin oak, swamp white oak, silver maple, black cherry, elm, and ash have sunk their roots. On higher and drier ground (and here it is only a few feet) beech and sugar maple muscle each other for space.

The old farm fields that make up much of the preserve are in various stages of succession—a naturalists' term referring to the slow transformation of open areas to forests. In that transitional area between the forest and the field, trees such as hornbeam, sassafras, hawthorn, honey locust, as well as impenetrable thickets of black raspberry and multiflora rose, are common. A stand of prickly ash grows here too. It offers its branches to caterpillars that change into the striking swallowtail butterflies.

All totaled some 40 woody species can be found here, and about 160 different varieties of herbaceous plants (get out your field guides), even characters such as bedstraw, rattlesnake fern, hog peanut, skunk cabbage, maddog skullcap, Philadelphia fleabane, tick-trefoil, heal-all, and Indian tobacco.

Some of the pastures here remain quite grassy and open because they have been cleared by ODNR. The mowing controls succession and maintains the preserve's diverse habitat for the numerous birds, insects, and mammals who prosper in a mixed environment.

Though you may never see them, it is still worth knowing that four rare moth species reside here. One of them—the winter moth—owes its existence to the controlled habitat of the meadow.

The uncommon and reclusive four-toed salamander, an amphibian designated "special interest" (or potentially threatened), lives in the rotting logs on the forest floor, and an endangered sedge called Cypress-knee sedge may sprout beneath the lowest limb of the buttonbush. False-hop sedge, a threatened plant, may be growing nearby.

According to a 1987 bird survey, woodcocks, belted kingfishers, wood ducks, Acadian flycatchers, ruby-throated hummingbirds, blue-gray gnatcatchers, scarlet tanagers, downy woodpeckers, and the great horned and barred owls were some of the birds nesting in the preserve. Visiting birds included the dark-eyed junco (an endangered species), ruby-crowned kinglet, great blue and green-backed herons, veery, Eastern meadowlark, and the Canada (endangered), hooded, Nashville, Tennessee, black-throated green, bay-breasted, and prothonotary warblers.

Focus on the forest in the spring when wildflowers and bird song are abundant, then switch to the fields in the summer and fall for the butterflies, bugs, birds, and bloomers common in this habitat. The ponds will be their fullest in the spring, but by July some will dry up.

Mosquitoes can be bothersome in the swampy forest in the summer; less so in the fields but mosquito-eating dragonflies are abundant by the ponds. Those who like to watch nature's details will enjoy this preserve more than the recreational hiker and seeker of sensational scenery.

History

The Ohio Chapter of The Nature Conservancy bought 101.5 acres in 1972 with private funds matched by federal dollars from the U.S. Department of the Interior, Land and Water Conservation Fund. Some of the purchase was given to the Ohio Department of Natural Resources and City of Gahanna. ODNR designated 50.7 acres as an interpretive nature area on January 10, 1974.

Tulip Tree

KNOX WOODS STATE NATURE PRESERVE

Two people hugging the same ancient tree in this woodlot will never touch their fingers. This is how the forest must have looked when white settlers arrived. The woods has towering sugar maples, beeches, black oaks, shagbark hickories, red oaks, and black walnuts with a forest floor free of thickets, briars, and vines. Knox Woods is rare and one of the last healthy and undisturbed small forests in Ohio. zzz

Location

Knox County, Monroe Township.

Knox Woods is just a mile northeast of the Mt. Vernon city limits on State Route 36. Park behind the Knox County Opportunity Center.

Ownership

The Knox County Commissioners own the site, but it is managed by the Ohio Department of Natural Resources, Division of Natural Areas and Preserves.

Size & Designation

This 30-acre woodlot was dedicated a scenic nature preserve on October 11, 1973.

Access

A grassed-over lane lined by stately walnut, oak, and hickory trees leads to an information board at the edge of the woods. Study the trail map and description of the preserve before starting.

Two loop trails totaling 1.5 miles—the Shawnee and Mingo trails—make a complete circuit of the preserve and snake along ridges and creek beds. The Shawnee Trail wanders through the northern two-thirds of the property, while the Mingo Trail covers the southern third. The trail names pay tribute to the first Ohioans who saw this forest.

A T-shaped ravine lies in the middle of the preserve, but the trails winding up and down this feature remain gentle. Knox Woods is open daily during daylight hours.

Nearby Natural Attractions

Try Mohican State Park and Clear Fork Gorge in bordering Ashland County, Mount Gilead State Park in Morrow County, and Morris Woods State Nature Preserve in Licking County.

Geology

Glacial till (gravel, sand, rocks and other sediments) left here by the Illinioan ice mass, which invaded Ohio about 125,000 years ago, rests above sandstone 325–345 million years old. The woods are just six miles east of the reach of the Wisconsinan glacier, the last ice mass passing over Ohio some 15,000 years ago.

Intermittent streams have washed away some of the glacial drift to form ravines, but this erosion has not reached the bedrock so don't look for outcrops and ledges here.

Wildlife

Knox Woods is a good place to study the life cycle of a forest.

During the spring you are apt to find a tiny, pale sprout uncurling in a scrape (a patch of ground recently scraped by browsing deer). A deer searching for acorns tossed off the leaves above this sprout, giving it an advantage, perhaps, over others struggling through the mat.

Wildflowers common in a mixed hardwood forest thrive on this forest floor, notably trillium, violets, bloodroot, hepatica, and toothwort. However, by mid-June the forest's canopy closes and little sunlight strikes the ground. That explains the absence of multiflora rose and wild grape vines, plants that seem to choke trees in the woods. There isn't enough light for these invaders. A 1990 survey, however, found 34 herbaceous plants (species whose stems wither every year) growing in the preserve.

Also, notice the colorful fungi and mosses growing on the fallen trees. These breakdown the old trees, and speed up the return of the nutrients back into the soil for the young ones.

Besides the varieties mentioned above, this strip of forest, surrounded by cornfields, harbors huge specimens of tulip tree, black gum, black cherry, sugar maple, various oaks, and white ash.

History

Many years ago, Knox County commissioners had a farm and woodlot at its children's home. The tree-lined path to the preserve once was a farm lane that led from the barn to the pasture and woods. Eventually, the children's home was converted to the county social services office. Though the woods remained undisturbed, they were also unprotected.

The county still leases the cornfields straddling the preserve, and from time to time somebody suggests thinning out the woods. But the commissioners are just going to let nature take its course in Knox Woods.

Cardinal flower

MORRIS WOODS STATE NATURE PRESERVE

Birders, raise your binoculars. The former owners converted this farm into a wildlife sanctuary, then gave it to the state for everybody to enjoy.

Location

Northwest Licking County, Liberty Township. From Johnstown take State Route 62 northeast, then east on Dutch Lane Road for a half mile. Leave Newark west on State Route 16, then north on State Route 37 to Alexandria. Just beyond this village turn right (north) on Northridge Road for about 5.5 miles, then left on Dutch Lane Road.

Ownership

Ohio Department of Natural Resources, Division of Natural Areas and Preserves.

Size & Designation

This 104-acre site became a scenic nature preserve on February 5 1980.

Nearby Natural Attractions

Elsewhere in Licking County, visit Blackhand Gorge State Nature Preserve, Flint Ridge State Memorial, The Dawes Arboretum, and Buckeye Lake State Park.

Access

Four trails traipse for about four miles past a couple of ponds, through a luxuriant forest, and across an open meadow. Review the trail map on the information board before departing. Two trails start at the parking lot.

I began on the Cardinal Flower Trail, a grass and moss-covered path that heads east (parallel to Dutch Lane Road) to a small clearing rimmed with cedar bushes.

The path hugs the bank of L-shaped Lake Helen, then enters the woods. Cardinal Flower Trail ends at the intersection of the mile-long Woodland Trail and the Silver Bark Trail, a shortcut to Abbott's Pond Trail.

The Woodland Trail wanders through a rich beech-maple forest where various oaks also grow alongside hickory, black cherry, and other typical hardwoods. This trail explores the southeastern part of the property before circling north to its junction with the Silver Bark and Abbott's Pond trails.

The curious will turn right here and follow the Silver Bark Trail (about a quarter mile) back to the confluence of the Woodland and Cardinal Flower trails. Completing that journey, backtrack and resume the walk on Abbott's Pond Trail (3/4 mile). This path goes through a grove of pines, a thicket of young trees, shrubs, and briars, then along the edge of the first of two meadows. Abbott's Pond, a small water hole, appears on the left. The trail spans a rill that feeds Lake Helen, then crosses a field to the parking lot.

The driveway leads to the home of the previous landowner. This area is off limits, though. ODNR nature programs are occasionally staged there. Check the information board for a schedule of these programs, or contact the Ohio Department of Natural Resources, Division of Natural Areas and Preserves, Fountain Square, Building F-1, Columbus, Ohio 43224-1331; phone (614) 265-6543. The preserve remains open daily from sunup to sundown.

Geology

The terrain around here is generally flat, thanks to the bulldozing action of several glaciers. The last ice mass (Wisconsinan glacier) left behind till, or unsorted gravel, rocks, sand, and other sediments. The till and the flat landscape sponsored the growth of the enormous beech-maple forest that dominated the land in presettlement days. The gentle slopes posed no obstacle to the pioneers who cleared the forest for farming.

Wildlife

Wildlife surveys done in the mid-1980s counted 42 species of birds, including rose-breasted grosbeaks, Kentucky warblers, redstarts, veery, pileated woodpeckers, and barred owls. The ponds attract waterfowl common to Ohio.

Moth and butterfly types numbered 300, and 85 kinds of wildflowers have been observed. American ginseng, a rare plant, grows here. Harvesting the plant in the preserve is illegal.

A mature beech and maple forest, interspersed with oaks, cherry and hickories, rules the forest. Elsewhere, saplings compete in thickets, and briar patches provide habitat for birds and rabbits. Abbott's Pond Trail cuts through a grove of planted pines and across a grassy meadow kept trim by ODNR.

History

James Abbott, owner of a Columbus auto parts store and a passionate birdwatcher, bought this old livestock farm in the 1950s and transformed it into a wildlife sanctuary. He planted trees, dug a pair of ponds, installed birdhouses, and built trails and a home. He invited school groups and nature clubs to the sanctuary. Abbott called the estate Morris Woods, a tribute to his father Morris Abbott

James Abbott died in 1979. The Ohio Department of Natural Resources received the property as a gift in 1979, and designated it a scenic preserve on February 5, 1980.

Journal

April 4, 1993. Three turkey vultures circle overhead. Their pterodactyl-sized shadows run across the forest floor and up tree trunks, adding menace to the primordial mood of the woods.

Ominous as they appear, buzzards do not do their own killing. They are scavengers who rip the flesh from dead animals. Nature's clean up crew.

Humans have given vultures a bad rap, viewing them with distaste or as comic and clumsy creatures. Our disgust for buzzards stems from their unsightly looks (a face that only a mother could love), and their eating habits. We shudder to think of them mistakenly pecking out our eyeballs while we nap under a tree. To us, they represent doom and avarice, working in league with body snatchers.

If nature has been partial in this matter (which it has not, of course) then perhaps it is the migratory vulture, more abundant and adaptable than buteos, harriers, and owls, who has won its favor. Maybe the vulture's face is the one nature loves.

Merganser duck

STAGE'S POND STATE NATURE PRESERVE

Binoculars and telephoto lens are a must because the observation deck is one the best spots in Central Ohio for viewing the antics of migratory birds.

Location

Pickaway County, Walnut Township.

From Circleville, head north on U.S. Route 23 about five miles, then go east two miles on Haggerty Road (also known as Red Bridge Road). Look for the parking lot on the north (left) side, just east of Ward Road.

Ownership

Ohio Department of Natural Resources, Division of Natural Areas and Preserves.

Size & Designation

Stage's Pond, totaling 178 acres, has been a state interpretive nature preserve since August 23, 1974.

Nearby Natural Attractions

In Pickaway County, try out A.W. Marion and Deer Creek state parks, Deer Creek Reservoir State Wildlife Area, Slate Run Metropark, and Big and Little Darby Creek National and State Scenic River.

Access

Stage's Pond, the larger of two ponds on the premises, is ideal for a quick glimpse of birds, and for a longer walk. If you are coming here for a fast gander at the geese, an observation blind is just a couple of hundred yards from the parking lot. Your approach to the lookout is concealed by white pines bordering the path.

The unhurried will find the Moraine Trail worthwhile. It starts at the information board (trail maps may be available here) and heads north (a sign points the way). The Moraine Trail crosses a field and enters a wooded area where the Kettle Lake and Multiflora trails branch off to the left. Ignore these for now and continue ahead of the Moraine Trail. This path ends where the White Oak Trail begins. The White Oak Trail, a thinner and less defined path, loops through the northeastern section of the preserve. It returns to the Moraine Trail.

On the way back, follow the Multiflora Trail, named for the multiflora rose thicket the path cuts through, to the Kettle Lake Trail. (A bench on the Multiflora Trail offers a peak of both ponds during the "leafless" months.)

The Kettle Trail goes downhill from the woods into the meadows. Resist the temptation to run down this hill because you will spook the critters on the ponds, and those living at the edge of the forest. This trail runs between the ponds, up a knoll, then traces the wooded southwestern shore of Stage's Pond. The trail ends at the northwestern corner of the property, at Ward Road. (Bicyclists and hikers will find an entrance here, but its use is discouraged by ODNR.)

The terrain is relatively flat, with a few gentle knolls. The trails are usually wet year-round, and some spots hold ankle-deep water. Boardwalks have been constructed across rills and swampy places, and benches along the trail serve as rest spots and observation points.

The preserve is open from sunrise to sunset every day. For more information contact the Ohio Department of Nature Resources, Division of Natural Areas and Preserves, Fountain Square, Building F-1, Columbus, Ohio 43224-1331; phone (614) 265-6543.

Geology

Stand on a knoll overlooking the ponds and try to imagine the size of the ice chunk that formed the 64-acre depression below. That's what happened about 15,000 years ago when the Wisconsinan glacier covered the area. Geologists believe a huge block of ice broke off from the glacier and parked here. Water melting from the receding glacier piled sediments like sand and gravel around the ice block. The knoll you are standing on is made of that glacial debris. Eventually, the ice melted into the pit and formed what geologists call a kettle lake.

At one time the water level may have been much higher, so that one large pond flooded the lowland. The ponds swell and shrink depending on the rainfall. After heavy spring rains, the two ponds may briefly merge, but by summer they have shrunk to separate bodies of water.

Water from the shallow and smaller pool, the one beneath the observation blind, flows toward the larger and deeper pond.

A drought in 1988 reduced the ponds to muddy puddles. Such an event, of course, requires all species to survive on less of this vital resource, and some animals may abandon the site altogether in search of water.

Wildlife

The waterfowl poster on the back wall of the observation blind helps you identify the various migratory birds that visit the preserve. Common tenants include the great blue heron, pintail, mallard, green and blue-winged teal, merganser, canvasback, and red-billed grebe. A great blue heron swept away when I emerged from the woods on the Kettle Lake Trail, followed by a hawk which had been perched atop a lifeless tree a couple hundred yards away. Less skittish was a pair of red-winged blackbirds, guarding their territory from the branches of saplings.

The meadows host many songbirds (eastern meadowlark included), plus pheasant, quail, and rabbits. ODNR manages a habitat for woodcock near the parking lot. Robins and cardinals were abundant during my March visit. Deer and fox tracks crisscrossed through the uplands woods in the White Oak Trail section.

The forested areas, once heavily lumbered and grazed, sponsor the wildflowers common among oak, hickory, walnut, and maple. You'll find multiflora rose suffocating the understory in some areas, and raspberry patches along the trail. Meadow flowers bloom in the summer and attract butterflies.

Specimens of an endangered aquatic plant called featherfoil, resembling a cluster of floating upright stalks 3–8 inches tall, were planted here in 1981 from a colony in Scioto County. Their survival, however, is suspect because they are abundant one year then disappear for 6–7 years before reappearing again.

History

A Scot named Richard Stage originally settled on this land, payment for his service in the Revolutionary War. At first, Stage was given land in Adams County, but he sold that parcel and staked his family's future on the Pickaway Plains.

When the Stage family sold their holdings in 1970, stories circulated that a housing development was on the way. Though Stage's Pond showed the scars of grazing and the plow, the Pickaway County Garden Club believed the land was worth rescuing and began its "Save the Stage's Pond" campaign in the early 1970s. In 1973, the club raised $20,204 (the amount needed to reserve $62,000 in matching state and federal funds) with the help of the Columbus Regional Council of the Garden Club of Ohio, other conservation and garden clubs, news media, school groups, and businesses. The Ohio Chapter of The Nature Conservancy negotiated the 123-acre sale and transferred the property to the Ohio Department of Natural Resources when federal matching funds were approved.

Surveys taken in 1973–74 concluded that 60 percent of the property had been cultivated in row farming, 25 percent was classified as grazed woodlot, while 15 percent was open pasture. Seventy wildflower species, and 20 different kinds of trees and shrubs were counted.

Stage's Pond was the first preserve established by a grassroots money-raising effort. You'll find a tribute to that conservation work stamped on a granite boulder near the parking lot. The Pickaway County Garden Club also has contributed money for construction of the bird blind and for more land. An additional 54.7 acres were purchased in 1980 by ODNR.

There is still work to be done. The northern half of Stage's Pond belongs to a property owner who allows hunting and fishing. The state agency hopes to acquire this property someday to fully protect this valuable kettle lake.

Journal

***March 28.** As I started up the White Oak Trail, I was certain I would spot deer. The woods here provided food and cover for them and was surrounded by fields. Hunters' blinds on the property line, and fresh tracks raised my expectations.*

Sure enough, I startled a pair of white-tails from their bed behind the branches of a fallen tree near the northernmost turn in the trail. They snapped branches and tossed leaves as they fled. They were frightened, not I, but my heart went racing along with them.

SOUTHWESTERN OHIO

Yarrow

ADAMS LAKE PRAIRIE STATE NATURE PRESERVE

It is said that Dr. Emma Lucy Braun, Ohio's foremost botanist-ecologist, knew every flower and tree in Adams County–and that they knew her. She believed that the short-grass prairie growing on the thin soil of her native county was much older than the tallgrass prairie of Central Ohio. Adams Lake Prairie is a remnant of that early prairie invasion.

Location

Central Adams County, Tiffin Township.

Enter the preserve from Adams Lake State Park, located a mile north of West Union on State Route 41.

Ownership

Ohio Department of Natural Resources, Division of Natural Areas and Preserves.

Size & Designation

This 25.8-acre prairie became an interpretive nature preserve on May 16, 1973.

Nearby Natural Attractions

Adams Lake State Park surrounds the preserve. The Edge of Appalachia nature preserves are just a few miles away. Tranquility Wildlife Area is in northern Adams County.

Access

The double-loop trail begins across the street from the parking lot. In a few places the Post Oak Trail splits. Take the left fork, heading east into the forest. After crossing several small creek beds, the path swings south and up a hill. At the summit the path veers west and comes to a clearing–the prairie opening.

Here, on a boardwalk, the path forks. Turn left onto the Prairie Dock Trail which traces the periphery of the prairie and rejoins the Post Oak Trail. Go left at this junction to return to the parking lot.

This 1-1.5-mile walk can be shortened by a half mile by bearing right on Post Oak Trail (near the entrance), and walking the Prairie Dock Trail. The latter route bypasses the forest on the eastern half of the preserve.

The preserve is open every day from the crack of dawn to sundown. The best time to view the prairie blossoms is mid-July through Labor Day. You will find toilets, drinking water, swimming beach, and picnicking at the state park.

Geology

The prairies in Adams County are older and different than their counterparts in the Darby Plains, which grew on moist flatlands 4,000-6,000 years ago, a span of time called the Xerothermic Period. (See the chapter on the Darby Plains Prairies.) The shortgrass prairie here is a leftover of an earlier western prairie invasion, perhaps predating the Illinoian glacier which came within a stone's throw of this site 125,000 years ago.

The tallgrass prairie on the Darby Plains has flourished on thick beds of glacial till deposited by the Wisconsinian glacier roughly 12,000 years ago. In contrast, the prairies in unglaciated Adams County struggle on dry and thin soil derived from bedrock.

Beneath Adams Lake Prairie lies a layer of Crab Orchard shale. It is made of mud and silt that settled to the bottom of an ocean more than 455 million years ago (Ordovician geological period). When the sea retreated this goo, now exposed, turned into shale.

Once exposed, Crab Orchard shale does not stay shale for long. Rain, sun, and wind cause it to disintegrate into a cream-colored mud filled with bits of dolomite, giving it a calcareous flavor. When moist it once again becomes sticky, and easily erodes away. When baked it becomes hard as a brick. Trees have difficulty sinking roots in this kind of soil, but not the members of the shortgrass prairie. They arrived during some other long-term heat wave, either before or after the Illinoian glacier. Nobody knows for sure.

Eventually, though, the climate changed and the forest took over much of the land. By the time white settlers reached Central Adams County, the shortgrass prairie had been reduced to isolated islands on rocky promontories, gullies, and eroded conical-shaped hillsides called "bald hills" and "buffalo beats." These treeless places did not favor the farmer's plow so livestock grazed on these meager fields.

Adams Lake Prairie appears to be an offspring of a remnant patch of prairie. Prairie vegetation (shortgrasses, red cedar, wildflowers) often spreads into abandoned farm fields (former forests). That is what happened here sometime in the 1920s, according to the Ohio Department of Natural Resources. The prairie continues to struggle against the surrounding oak-hickory forest which also has taken back some this hillside too.

Wildlife

In his journal, Dr. John Locke wrote that the "buffalo beats" of Adams County were "a paradise for the botanist." Locke, then assistant state geologist, had been commissioned to prepare a geological survey of Adams County in the mid-1830s. His description of the prairie still rings true.

Folks who have visited a lush, thick-matted tallgrass prairie are going to see a different kind of prairie at Adams Lake. The vegetation here is sparse, clumped together, and shorter. Some of slopes in gullies are barren, and erosion continues its dirty work. Observe the details. Look how the vegetation is thicker at the base of the handful of trees that have managed to sink their roots. The roots of these trees grow on clumps, or little earthen islands, a foot or so higher than the surrounding turf. Grasses and wildflowers also flourish on these mounds because the tree roots have trapped the moisture and soil needed for their survival. The herbaceous clump-dwellers, in turn, retard erosion and add nutrients to the soil.

There are plenty of the familiar prairie flowers. Prairie dock, nodding onion, pale-spiked lobelia, flowering spurge, golden Alexanders, and long-leaved bluets survive better than others on the barren spots. The endangered Sampson's snakeroot, little bluestem (a grass), shooting-star, prairie rose, downy wood mint, stiff gentian, three-lobed violet, and green milkweed (potentially threatened) grow on more fertile sections.

Almost 100 wildflowers and grasses are listed in ODNR's preserve brochure. Downy skullcap, prostrate tick-trefoil, madder, king devil, self-heal, featherfleece, and gall-of-the-earth are some.

The preserve sponsors 27 shrubs (shrubby St. John's-wort) and trees (notably red cedar and juniper) that grow slowly in shallow soils. Other trees, usually on the fringe of the prairie opening, have established themselves, including shingle oak, post oak, white oak, sassafras, black locust, flowering dogwood, and redbud.

The shade of these trees inhibits the spread of the sun-hungry prairie and prepares the land for the return of the trees of the deep forest. In the preserve these latter species are represented by white, red, and black oaks, and shagbark and pignut hickories.

Critters are not fond of this hostile habitat. The one that stands out, or rather crawls out, is the notorious red mound builder ant, or Allegheny mountain ant, said to be the most aggressive of its clan east of the Mississippi River.

As their name suggests, these busy bugs build mounds, perhaps 12–18 inches high, composed of unearthed dirt with a sprinkling of twigs, bark, and leaf scales. Beneath the mound is a maze of tunnels (think of a bowl of spaghetti) that may house 100,000 laborers.

These fearless ants will attack almost anything with their pinching mandibles. Humans are safe unless they stand beside an anthill too long. They secrete formic acid when they bite.

The mounds are scattered throughout the preserve. Leave the anthills alone. Disturbing an ant nest is just as harmful and disrespectful as teasing a caged tiger to hear it growl.

History

As noted above, the beauty of this prairie was first reported by Dr. Locke in the 19th century.

In 1947, Adams Lake was created when the Lick Branch of Ohio Brush Creek was dammed. The water in the 47-acre lake quenched the thirst of nearby West Union. In 1950 the lake became the centerpiece of Adams Lake State Park.

Later, Dr. Braun, who knew the flora and fauna of the region better than the back of her hand, brought the Adams Lake prairie to the attention of her colleague at the University of Cincinnati, Dr. Richard H. Durrell.

In 1971, Durrell, then a member of the newly formed Ohio Natural Areas Council, raised the idea of protecting this prairie. ODNR purchased the site in 1972, and dedicated it as an interpretive preserve on May 16, 1973.

Journal

September 1993. Just wish Lucy Braun was alive to show me around this place. I picture her dressed in khaki pants, cotton blouse rolled up to the elbows, floppy hat shading her tawny, bespectacled face. With a pencil, she lifts petals with her pinky, then jots down a note on a clipboard. She moves about the prairie randomly, instinctively, flower to flower, a course not unlike a butterfly's. Not especially scenic, this preserve. I have come too late for the peak floral performance, though a few tall prairie dock retain their wrinkled yellow petals. Best to come here in mid-July to early August. I don't recommend snoozing against a tree in this arid preserve because the ants will soon be crawling on your skin. They number in the millions here.

Thirteen-lined ground squirrel

AULLWOOD AUDUBON CENTER

Thoughtful stewardship has transformed this once-tired land into a wildlife sanctuary teeming with life. Children and grown-ups find this hands-on, living nature lab an exhilarating experience.

Location

Montgomery County, Randolph Township.

Leaving Dayton, take Interstate 75 north, then Interstate 70 west one stop. Exit northbound on State Route 48. Travel a mile and turn right (east) on SR 40 and cross Englewood Dam. Just past the dam, take the first right onto Aullwood Road and bear right as you round a bend. Park in the lot on your left.

The entrance to the Aullwood Farm is on Frederick Road. Stay on SR 40 after crossing the dam. Turn right to Frederick Road.

Ownership

National Audubon Society.

Size & Designation

The grounds at the Aullwood Center comprise 70 acres.

Nearby Natural Attractions

Englewood Reserve, including Aullwood Garden, is next door. Try these other reserves in the Dayton-Montgomery Park District: Taylorsville, Sugarcreek, and Germantown. Also, Sycamore State Park.

Access

The center is open Monday through Saturday from 9 a.m.-5 p.m., and Sunday from 1 p.m.-5 p.m. The facility is closed on some holidays. Admission for adults (over age 18) is $3; for students (ages 2-18) $2. Admission is free to the members of the National Audubon Society and Friends of Aullwood.

A web of interconnecting trails threads through the sanctuary. Pick up a trail map when you pay your admission charge at the center.

Specialty trails such as the Wildflower Trail, Geology Trail, and Discovery Trail travel to particular areas in the refuge. The Center-Farm Trail links the nature preserve with the adjacent farm. I walked the perimeter of the property which took me through a variety of habitats. Starting at the center, I followed Aullwood Brook downstream along the edge of Honeybee Meadow to Bluegill Pond, then through a pine stand and the Wet Woods (a swamp forest). After the forest, the path traces the edge of a prairie. A climb to the top of the tower overlooking the prairie is a must.

The trail continues along the eastern property line

through a brushy area and into the tall trees of the North Woods. Return via the Muskrat Marsh and past an oak tree that must be 200 years old.

Side trails lead to a woodcock meadow (across the street from the center) to the Big Swamp section of bordering Englewood Preserve, and to a fossil bed on the Stillwater River.

Natural history exhibits fill the nature center. You will discover poisonous snakes and animal skulls and other exhibits. A must-see place for kids. A gift shop and restrooms are located here. Naturalist-led tours begin here.

For information contact the Aullwood Audubon Center and Farm, 1000 Aullwood Road, Dayton, Ohio 45414-1129; phone (513) 890-7360.

Geology

What Aullwood lacks in grand geological landmarks, it makes up for in fossils. Unlike other preserves, Aullwood allows, indeed encourages, visitors to collect specimens at its fossil bed (although you are limited to one of each kind).

Fossils are pictures in rocks, the remains of plants and animals that sank to an ocean floor and became encased in the rock. Study the large stones beside Aullwood Brook and find the fossils. A magnifying glass might be helpful.

The plants and animals frozen in these rocks tell us that this part of Ohio once was covered by a warm, shallow ocean because their relatives live in that type of environment today.

About a half mile from the center, on the west side of the spillway at the base of the Englewood dam, lies a pile of 450 million-year-old (Ordovician Period) limestone rocks with fossils in them.

You can walk to the fossil bed, about 20 minutes, or drive. Turn left from the center, then take your first right to the river parking lot. Climb around the spillway to the other side of Stillwater River.

You can purchase a guide at the center ($1) that describes these ancient and extinct animals—brachiopods (fanlike shells), bryozoans (spotted twigs), crinoids (mop head), pelecypod (clam shell), horn corals (ice cream cone), cephalopod (ringed cylinder), gastropods (snail-shaped tube), and trilobites (beetle, or crab-shaped), the official state fossil.

The center provides fossil-hunting gear for organized groups. Don't take too many fossils. Let others enjoy the thrill of finding prehistoric critters.

Wildlife

Being an Audubon-owned refuge, Aullwood is a birder's paradise, attracting numerous species, especially warblers, thrushes, woodpeckers, woodcocks, and owls.

In 1959–60 the Aullwood staff planted a 2.5-acre tallgrass prairie, using seeds collected from an Adams County prairie. Supposedly, it was the first prairie restoration project in Ohio. Now more than 74 various prairie residents thrive here, notably big bluestem, Canada wild rye (both grasses), and flowers like foxglove beard tongue, blazing star, bergamot, prairie and purple coneflower, compass plant, and tall tickweed. July and August are the peak months for prairie viewing. You will also find this meadow swarming with bees, birds, and butterflies.

Prairie plants are perennials, meaning their roots stay alive after the above-ground stems wither away in the fall. Because most of a prairie plant lives underground it is able to survive harsh winters, ground fires, and temperature and water extremes.

In its first year of life, a prairie plant may sink roots a foot deep but grow only an inch above ground. An eight-foot tall plant, like prairie dock, may have a root system equally deep in the earth. Early farmers found it nearly impossible to plow prairies because the roots would entangle their wooden plows. However, the steel plow, invented in 1840 by John Deere, ripped through the prairie sod and led to the demise of the prairie that for a while stretched from Pennsylvania to the foothills of the Rocky Mountains.

The Aullwood Center manages its prairie by burning it every so often. Burning allows spring rain and sun to nourish new shoots without killing the forbs and underground root system.

Most of the common woodland and meadow animals live in the Aullwood sanctuary. Astute observers might see a meadow jumping mouse, foxes, a bog lemming (like a vole), muskrat, mink (a rarity), a thirteen-lined ground squirrel, and the endangered Indiana bat.

At Muskrat Marsh, look for the snapping turtle and common musk turtle, sometimes called a stinkpot turtle because it sprays a foul odor when pestered. The eastern box turtle crawls in fields and wooded areas. The map turtle, with whorled and striped patterns on its shell, lives at Bluegill Pond.

Queen snakes may be curled around tree limbs over Aullwood Brook looking for frogs, crayfish, and salamanders. Blue racers and black rat snakes, both can be five feet long, lurk in the woodlands. These two constrict, or squeeze, their victims (mice, shrews, birds) before swallowing them.

Turning over a rock or log may reveal a red-backed salamander (the most common type at Aullwood), or the colorful spotted salamander, introduced to Muskrat Marsh in 1965. Various kinds of frogs raise their voices in the spring and summer. During the spring breeding season you will see their frenzied splashing and jumping in the shallows.

History

A plaque in the parking lot of the nature center and farm reminds visitors that the preserve and adjacent farm is a gift from John and Marie Aull. John Aull, a businessman, bought this former farmland in the early 1900s. Over the years he and his wife, Marie, transformed it into their country residence, a nature preserve, and landscaped gardens.

Mrs. Aull, who still lives in her home at Aullwood Gardens (see Englewood Preserve), gave the land to the National Audubon Society and established a fund for an outdoor education complex. The center was dedicated in 1957, and claims to be the Midwest's first community nature center.

Journal

Here's a nice balance to Dayton's juvenile crime statistics. Aullwood overflows with children whose energy and curiousity are consumed with the out-of-doors. The naturalists here excel at getting youngsters interested in nature. The schoolchildren I watched were not shy about putting their hands in pond muck in search of acquatic critters. Joy was finding fossils in limestone. In spite of such exhuberance, I found myself hiking in the opposite direction...

Red-tailed hawk

BRUKNER NATURE CENTER

Trails wander through wooded floodplains, ravines, pine groves, and ridgetops in a preserve created by an aviation pioneer and continued by an enthusiastic membership. When you tire of hiking, you can browse through the nature center, a 190-year-old restored log house, and a wild animal hospital that treats 1,500 patients a year.

Location

Southwestern Miami County, Concord Township.

From Troy, the county seat, travel west on State Route 55. Turn right (west) on Horseshoe Bend Road (roughly three miles from the SR 55 and SR 718 split), then right (north) onto the preserve's driveway. Park at the nature center. Horseshoe Bend Road also joins State Route 48 just north of Ludlow Falls. Head east from that point to reach the center.

Ownership

The Brukner Nature Center is a nonprofit environmental and nature study center chiefly supported by its members.

Size & Designation

The grounds total 165 acres. The Stillwater River, which borders the preserve, is a state scenic river. Iddings Log House, a refurbished pioneer home, is listed on the National Registry of Historic Places.

Nearby Natural Attractions

Miami County boasts Greenville Falls State Nature Preserve, the Stillwater Scenic River, plus Charleston Falls Preserve, Stillwater Prairie Reserve, and Big Woods Reserve, the latter three sites owned by the Miami County Park District.

Access

Ten well-marked trails measuring nearly seven miles entice hikers to every habitat in the preserve. They are open (and free) year-round during daylight hours. Pick up a map and trail guide at the nature center, the starting point.

The connector trail behind the nature center descends into the floodplain of the Stillwater River and leads to a number of paths. One of them, the Stillwater Loop (3/4 mile) traces the edge of the creek and the bottom of Bluebell Hill, so named for the showy April display of mertensia, or Virginia bluebells or Virginia cowslip. A bluebell by any other name is still a bluebell.

Another path, the half-mile Swamp Boardwalk Trail, zigzags across a marsh to an observation tower. This soggy trail can be impassable during spring floods.

The Buckeye Valley-Wilderness Ridge Trail (1.4 miles) is the longest and most rugged in the preserve. This lasso-shaped path stems from the Wren Run Trail (north of the observation deck) and visits the ravines and ridges in the north section.

Folks who prefer flat terrain and the scent of conifers should follow the half-mile Pinelands Trail, starting at the totem pole on the east side of the parking lot. The Trillium Valley Trail (3/10 mile) branches north from the Pinelands Trail, then swings west and joins the connector trail at the confluence of two intermittent brooks. As the name suggests, trillium abound along this trail.

The Interpretive Center features nature exhibits, a wildlife viewing room, an auditorium, classrooms, 1,000-volume natural history library, gift shop, restrooms, and one of only a few wildlife rehabilitation centers in the state. The center runs programs for adults and for schoolchildren. Special interest clubs—birdwatchers, beekeepers, quilters, photographers, astronomers, carvers, etc.—also convene at the center. Kids love the holidays, and seasonal events such as Maple Sugaring Days and Honey Harvest are scheduled throughout the year.

The Interpretive Center is open Monday through Saturday from 9 a.m.–5 p.m. and Sunday from 12:30 p.m.–5 p.m. An admission fee is charged to non-members only on Sunday. The charge is $1 for adults, 50¢ for children, or $2 for a family. The center stays closed on holidays. (Remember the trails stay open year-round during daylight hours.)

Please respect some rules. No plant picking, picnicking, and pets. Trails are for foot travelers, not for horses and vehicles, including trail bikes.

For more information contact the Brukner Nature Center, 5995 Horseshoe Bend Road, Troy, Ohio 45373; phone (513) 698-6493.

Geology

In high water, the Stillwater River cannot decide which way to flow around the oxbow, or horseshoe-shaped bend in this preserve. When I visited one autumn day, this swollen riverbend masqueraded as a delta, with a maze of tangled currents flowing helter-skelter.

On gentler days the meandering creek stays on course as it sweeps the banks and trickles around shifting sandbars. This leaner current, now easier to follow with the human eye, continues to reshape its path but at a much slower pace.

Stillwater Creek and its dissecting tributaries still wash away glacial till deposited by the Wisconsinan ice mass around 12,000 years ago. Some day, perhaps, they will reach rock bottom here.

Clayton Brukner, the center's founder, dammed a couple of small brooks with a bulldozer to make Cat Face Pond and Cattail Pond, both located along trails south of the Interpretive Center.

Wildlife

This natural area protects the habitats of 360 kinds of wildflowers. (The staff and members conduct an annual blooming count.) Look for skunk cabbage and squirrel corn along the Swamp Boardwalk Trail. Try to find false hellbore, rose gentian and Crane's orchid (both rarities), showy orchid, butterfly weed (meadows), snow trillium, marsh marigold (also called cowslip), and large bellflower.

Thirty-five species of trees and shrubs have been counted, such as white and red oak, sassafras, tulip tree, sugar maple, witch hazel, black walnut, shagbark hickory, and wild black cherry. The softwoods are represented by non-native white and red pines, planted in the 1950s.

The center publishes an annual bird list and conducts a census at Christmas time. So far, 170 varieties have been sighted. Red and white-winged crossbills (uncommon), pine siskins, and red-breasted nuthatches favor the pines. Owls (great horned, barred, and screech) and pileated woodpeckers prefer the deep hardwood stands.

Evening and rose-breasted grosbeaks, ruby-throated hummingbirds, and little green herons (creek) are regular visitors.

Countless species of warblers brighten the forest canopy in the spring with their colorful feathers and rich songs.

The northern harrier, an endangered species in Ohio, and the saw-whet owl and sharp-shinned hawk, both potentially threatened birds, have been spotted here.

More common are the red-tailed and Cooper's hawks.

The regular cast of four-legged furry beasts appears—deer, red and gray fox, mink, muskrat, ground hog, musk-rat, and others. Amphibians are represented by the two-lined, red-backed, and tiger salamanders; reptiles by the painted box turtles, black rat, northern water, and northern ring-necked snakes.

The emergency room of the wild animal hospital attends to as many as 1,500 patients a year. Veterinarians try to patch them up and return them to their natural habitat. Some orphaned or injured critters become traveling actors for nature programs in the center or at schools. The center also offers loaner pets, or companions, for people recovering from strokes, and other ailments.

History

Clayton J. Brukner, a bachelor known to be a bit ornery, was a self-taught aviation designer and manufacturer in Troy. He is remembered as the innovative builder of the WACO airplane in the 1920s.

Brukner bought this farmland in 1933, the darkest year of the Great Depression, and simply let nature take its course. The 50,000 red and white pines planted in the 1950s have grown into the lush evergreen forest east of the Interpretive Center.

In 1967, Brukner and a small group of followers began building trails, ponds, and facilities for a nature center. They completed their work in the spring of 1974, and opened the center in May. Brukner died in 1978.

The restored log house, built in 1804 by the Iddings family, sits in its original location on a bluff overlooking the Stillwater River.

Banded darter

CAESAR CREEK GORGE STATE NATURE PRESERVE

First, a torrent of water gushing from the last glacier widens a crack in 440–500 million-year-old limestone and sculpts this gorge. Then, two centuries ago, a former black slave adopted by the Shawnees names the creek after himself—Cizar. And just two decades ago, nature persuades new human arrivals to preserve this splendid place as Ohio's third state natural area. How lucky can you get?

Location

Northwestern Warren County, Wayne Township.

Exit Interstate 71 at State Route 73 and go west toward Corwin. Just before SR 73 crosses the Little Miami River, turn right on Smith Road, which bends left and empties into Corwin Road. Turn left on Corwin Road and travel south for about two miles. The parking lot for the hiking trails will be on the left after crossing Caesar Creek bridge.

From Waynesville, where U.S. Route 42 and SR 73 meet, travel east on SR 73 across the Little Miami River (a half mile), turn left on Smith Road and left on Corwin Road.

Ownership

Ohio Department of Natural Resources, Division of Natural Areas and Preserves.

Size & Designation

Dedicated as a scenic nature preserve on January 2, 1975, this preserve encompasses 483.4 acres. The Little Miami River, which forms the west border of the preserve, is a state and national scenic river.

Nearby Natural Attractions

Caesar Creek State Park, Little Miami State Park and Scenic River, Caesar Creek Lake, and Spring Valley State Wildlife Areas are just a few miles away from the preserve.

Access

The trail network in the preserve is known as Caesar's Trace. The eastbound trail emerging from the parking lot briefly ascends an old farm lane before dropping into the floodplain of Caesar Creek. (The end of the loop route described below continues up the lane.)

The path heads upstream, following the south bank of the creek beneath the rim of the gorge. The creekside trail is the most scenic part of the journey, and you will not be branded a slacker if you backtrack to the car when the trail swings away from the stream.

A little more than a half mile along the creek, the path turns inland, across the floodplain, through a small meadow, to an old lane that climbs to the top of the gorge. Here the trail snakes through fields, roughly heading west, along what appear to be abandoned farm roads. First- time visitors should stick to the main trail and ignore the smaller branching paths. Eventually, the trail returns to the start of the loop and the parking lot.

The Little Miami Scenic Park Trail cuts through the preserve, hugging Corwin Road. After the hike, drive north on Corwin Road, take your first left, and visit the new covered bridge (the Corwin M. Nixon Covered Bridge) stretching across the Little Miami River. You also can view the river up close by parking in the lot for canoe access on the right before the bridge.

Vegetation hides the gorge walls in the summer. To see them, come back in the winter. The trail along the creek and floodplain is often soggy and slippery. Restrooms are found at the parking lot, which is large enough for school buses and recreational vehicles.

Interpretive nature programs are conducted here throughout the year by naturalists. For more information contact the Ohio Department of Natural Resources, Division of Natural Areas and Preserves, Fountain Square, Building F-1, Columbus, Ohio 43224-1331; phone (614) 265-6453.

Geology

Raging torrents of water gushing from the melting Wisconsinan glacier some 12,000 years ago created this picturesque gorge and stream. Meltwater from the glacier's brow cut a path through the loose glacial till, composed of gravel, clay, sand, and boulders. Then it scoured limestone and shale bedrocks dating back to the Ordovician geological period, roughly 470 million years ago.

These fossil-rich ancient rocks reveal the creatures who lived in the broad shallow sea that inundated Ohio at that time—brachiopods, bryozoans (corals), trilobites, crinoids. Their remains made the limey soup which became limestone. Look, but do not collect the fossils. (Author Edward Abbey called these precious stones "leavemrites," or leave-em-right where you found them.)

Caesar Creek runs into the Little Miami River which forms the western boundary of the preserve. Come here in the winter when the trees have dropped their leaves to see the geological features. The gorge wall reaches a height of 180 feet.

Wildlife

Several varieties of bass, plus suckers, bullheads, sunfish, carp, catfish, black crappie, and rare brook pimpernel swim in Caesar Creek. The creek's abundance of darters, minnows, shiners, frogs, and crayfish attract great blue herons and kingfishers.

In the floodplain forest, flickers screeched at me while other woodpeckers, less alarmed, continued their excavations. Driving in, I noticed two hawks (species unknown) flying separate routes up the Little Miami River.

I know the preserve has a healthy red fox. I saw it jogging up the old farm lane. Its bushy tail stiffened and its eyes bulged in panic when it saw me. Judging by tracks along the trail and shore, white-tailed deer and raccoons reside here.

More than 110 kinds of wildflowers blossom in the preserve. Notables include rarities like shooting star, large summer bluets, plus Miami mist, wild ginger (roots taste like ginger), and cleavers, golden ragwort, among many. Prairie species and pokeweed (with its distinctive black berry clusters) grow conspicuously in the recovering meadows.

A late 1970s, inventory found 63 woody species in this mixed deciduous forest—sycamore, cottonwood, walnut, beech, several oaks, sugar maple, hickory, flowering dogwood, box elder, black maple, tulip tree, burning bush, American elm, etc.

Except for the steep gorge wall, the entire preserve has been subjected to farming, lumbering, or grazing. Now natural succession, nature's slow process of changing the meadows back into hardwood forests, is reworking its wonders on this land.

History

Humans have been visiting this gorge for 8,000 years. The first group of ancient people, conveniently classified by archeologists as the Paleo Indians, gave way to the Mound Builders, and then the so-called Fort Ancient Indians by 1200 A.D. These latter hunters and gatherers supposedly built several villages near here. They grew corn, beans, and squash in the floodplain to supplement a diet of animals killed by a bow and arrow. Later, the Wyandot, Miami, and Shawnee people used this area.

In 1776, Shawnee warriors defending their territory attacked a flatboat on the Ohio and captured a black slave named Cizar. Some might say the Shawnees freed Cizar. Anyway, Cizar enjoyed hunting near this stream, and named it after himself, so the story goes. It could be that the Shawnees referred to the stream as Cizar's because he had chosen it as his hunting ground.

Supposedly, Cizar advised Simon Kenton, Ohio's Daniel Boone, to follow Caesar Creek to the east bank of the Little Miami River when he escaped from the Shawnee village at Oldtown. A major Indian trail followed the west bank of the river. A lesser Indian trail on the Caesar Creek side of the river was dubbed Bullskin Trace by white settlers. Runaway slaves followed this branch of the Underground Railroad to safe houses owned by Quakers.

In spite of its designation as a state nature preserve in January 1975, the U.S. Army Corps of Engineers dammed Caesar Creek a mile upstream in 1978. The corps' action (supposedly to control flooding in the Little Miami Valley) flooded a hamlet called Henpeck, the entire town of New Burlington, and several ancient Indian sites. Caesar Creek State Park and State Wildlife Area were the byproducts of the impoundment too.

Journal

Summer, 1993. Rain had soaked my clothes and boots, but I didn't care. It was just water and it would dry in a few hours. I could wear the soggy clothes as long as I wanted—hurrah! I could never understand my mother's panic at seeing her drenched kids at the doorstep. My wife never gets upset—not since I began doing the laundry.

Edward's hairstreak

CHAPARRAL PRAIRIE STATE NATURE PRESERVE

It is a wonder anything grows at all in this dry, skinny soil, which, until 1984, had cows tearing out its grass. But Chaparral Prairie's rehabilitation has been remarkable during its decade under state protection. It looks like a shortgrass prairie opening again. Come here in the middle of summer and see attractions like rattlesnake master (a non-poisonous prairie plant), and a butterfly named Edward's hairstreak.

Location

Central Adams County, Tiffin Township.

Starting in West Union, take State Route 247 north about 2.5 miles, then go west (left) on Chaparral Road. In 5-6 miles Chaparral Road bends sharply left. However, you bear right on Hawk Hill Road. The entrance will be on the left in about 200 yards. The small parking lot only handles a few autos.

Ownership

Ohio Department of Natural Resources, Division of Natural Areas and Preserves.

Size & Designation

Chaparral Prairie is an interpretive preserve protecting 66.7 acres.

Nearby Natural Attractions

Just a stone's throw away are Adams Lake Prairie State Nature Preserve and Adams Lake State Park. The Edge of Appalachia nature preserve complex also is located in Adams County. Also visit Tranquility State Wildlife Area and Serpent Mound State Memorial.

Access

The preserve is open every day from dawn to dusk. Follow the mowed Hawk Hill Trail which begins just to the left of the stout barn at the end of the lane. The trail heads straight to the back of the meadows, curves left through a grove of cedars, ascends an oak ridge, then returns to the starting point for a .75-mile hike. The other paths that stem from this main trail are firebreaks.

Interpretive nature programs held during the year point out the highlights of this area. Visit from mid-July until Labor Day when the prairie flowers bloom in their full majesty. For more information contact Ohio Department of Natural Resources, Division of Natural Areas and Preserves, Fountain Square, Building F-1, Columbus, Ohio 43224-1331; phone (614) 265-6453.

Geology

One of the world's top ecologists, the late Dr. Emma Lucy Braun, believed that the dry, shortgrass prairies in her beloved Adams County were much older than the lush, tallgrass of Central and Northern Ohio.

The latter prairies (see Darby Plains Prairies) arrived during a warm spell 4,000–6,000 years ago and sprouted in a fertile soil deposited some 12,000 years ago by the Wisconsinan glacier.

That ice mass never reached into central Adams County. Dr. Braun concluded that the Adams County prairies came during an earlier warm or Xerothermic Period, perhaps even before the Illinoian glacier which covered most of Ohio and the northwestern corner of Adams County 125,000 years ago.

Another authority on Ohio prairies, K. Roger Trautman, believes 300 prairie openings, perhaps covering 1,000 square miles, broke the endless carpet of Ohio's hardwood forest at the time of European settlement of the New World.

Lacking the repeated dumpings of glacial topsoil, the soil at the dry Chaparral prairie is thin, less fertile, and it washes away easily. These factors make a difficult environment for wildlife.

Wildlife

Technically, this preserve is a "shortgrass blackjack/post oak-red cedar shale glade prairie." Though a mouthful to say, the description reveals some of the trees you will find here.

The blackjack oak, growing here at the northern edge of its range, is a potentially threatened species in Ohio. The leaves of both the post oak and the blackjack oak feel leathery with hairy undersides. These adaptations enable the trees to retain water during hot days in this scrubby landscape.

Eastern red cedar is a typical tree in abandoned fields (so is post oak). Since it prefers calcium-rich soil, its presence usually indicates limestone or shale. Earthworms also like calcareous soil, and their numbers swell in red cedar meadows.

The major attractions at Chaparral Prairie, of course, are the flowers and grasses of the shortgrass prairie. Rattlesnake master, a potentially threatened plant in Ohio, grows abundantly here. Its thistle-like burry head produces tiny greenish-white florets in mid-July.

Prairie dock is the tall, yellow flower that seems to be watching your movements in the field. It is well-represented on this site, as is pinkish-blue spiked blazing star. An uncommon white variety of the latter species lives alongside the trail.

The endangered Carolina leaf-flower finds refuge here along with prairie false indigo and pink milkwort (both threatened), Carolina buckthorn, hairy wingstem, and narrow-leaved summer bluets. All potentially face extinction in Ohio.

Fifty-nine kinds of butterflies and moths (lepidoptera) have been observed here, including the rare Edward's hairstreak (listed as a "special interest" insect). Try to spot beauties called confused cloudy wing (more common in southern states), banded hairstreak, cross line skipper, northern broken dash, and imperial moth, among others.

As you might suspect, the cedar trees attract cedar waxwings and robins, the latter gobbling up the earthworms in the cedar soil. At the start of my walk a dozen goldfinches exploded from the shrubs and briars behind the barn. They scattered widely and dove into the meadow flora until I passed. They must have reunited because they all flushed again when I reached trail's end.

History

This land was heavily farmed and grazed until 1984. Philip and Margarite Hahn sold the land to the Ohio Department of Natural Resources which designated it an interpretive preserve on December 19, 1986.

Journal

September, 1993. Chapparal comes from the Spanish word chaparra, meaning "scrub oak," and refers to lands in the American Southwest, especially southern California, dominated by scrub oak, smalled-leaved evergreens like cedar, and shrubs like manzanita and chamiso. A chaparral, like a prairie, depends on fire to remove "decadent" growth, eliminate vegetative litter, and restore nutrients. Though manzanita and chamiso are absent, this arid preserve can be characterized a chaparral.

Regal fritillary

CHARLESTON FALLS RESERVE

The petite Charleston Creek emerges from a subterranean source and flows several miles west before dropping 37 feet over a precipice made of the same ancient bedrock that trips the Niagara River 350 miles northeast of here. Except for this quirky geological link, the so-called "Miniature Niagara" of Miami County hardly compares with the thunderous Niagara. No matter. It has a charm of its own, though showering is no longer allowed.

Location

Southeast Miami County.

Leave Interstate 70 at the exit for State Route 202 and drive north on SR 202 about 3 miles. Turn left (west) on Ross Road for about a mile to the entrance on the right. Follow the driveway to the parking lot.

Ownership

Miami County Park District.

Size & Designation

Charleston Falls Preserve protects 169 acres. The park is a nature sanctuary.

Nearby Natural Attractions

Charleston Falls is one of four sites managed by the county park district. The other county-owned sites (described briefly below) are Garbry's Big Woods Sanctuary and Stillwater Prairie Reserve. Greenville Falls State Nature Preserve is in northwest Miami County. The Stillwater & Greenville Creek Scenic River flows through the county. Decker Lake State Wildlife Area also is located in Miami County.

Access

Charleston Falls Preserve has 2.5 miles of foot trails which travel along rock escarpments and brooks, and visiting hardwood forests, meadows, and prairies. Pick up a preserve brochure/trail map at the bulletin board in the parking lot.

The waterfall, of course, is the big attraction. The .3-mile trail from the parking lot heads east for a few paces then joins the main trail. A right turn at this junction goes to a picnic area. Turn left for the trail to the falls, and bear right at the first fork.

At the falls I recommend the trail at the left, marked "lower viewing platform," which descends a moss-covered limestone escarpment into the gorge and amphitheater at the base of the waterfall. Here you can best observe the size and depth of the cascade, the forces of erosion, as well as the geological storybook expressed in the rocks. On a hot summer day the fine, powdery mist of the falls, combined with the canopy of the forest, provide cool relief.

Unfortunately, showering under the cascade is no longer allowed. Climbing the cliffs is unlawful and foolhardy. Thousands of humans before you bathed and climbed, and in doing so trampled the plants and mosses living around the falls. Such frolicking aided erosion, and caused numerous injuries.

The trail continues up a steep cliff highlighted by a deep, columnar cave which, if I did not know better, was carved by a giant burrowing worm. One man leading a family down the trail told preschoolers, eager to explore the dark depth, that a nocturnal snake lay coiled inside. The children doubted his story, but none dared to test its validity. (Actually, water squirting through a seam in the limestone formed the cave.)

At the top of the cliff the trail splits. A right turn loops back to the top of the falls and parking lot, and to the

Thorny Badlands Trail which explores a pine plantation in the northeast corner of the preserve. (An observation tower on this trail overlooks a meadow.) But I like creeks, so I followed the Redbud Valley Trail through a small field guarded by some cedars, and along the north bank of Charleston Creek. I soaked my feet in the brook where the Redbud Valley Trail ends and meets the Thorny Badlands Trail from the right and the Creek Trail going left.

The Creek Trail follows the stream into the northwest corner of the preserve, crosses the creek, and enters a planted prairie meadow. At the next fork, I strayed left, preferring to peek at Cedar Pond than walk along Locust Grove Trail. These paths converge again in the woods and return to the main trail and the parking lot.

Picnickers can head for the picnic area (no fires). You will find drinking water (Baker pump) and toilets in the 32-car parking lot. Motorcyclists should park in a designated lot. The preserve is open daily from 8 a.m. to sunset. (Charleston Falls is the only site I visited that posts the time of sunset to the minute.) For more information, contact the Miami County Park District, 2535 East Ross Road, Tipp City, Ohio 45371; phone (513) 667-1086.

Geology

Charleston Falls performs daily, and continually, in a natural amphitheater of its own creation, built upon some of the oldest uncovered rock in Ohio.

The story began 440–500 million years ago (Ordovician geologic period) when Ohio was covered by a shallow, muddy sea. Eventually the ocean receded, allowing the mud to dry into a flaky sedimentary rock called shale, specifically the Elkhorn variety of Cincinnatian shale.

Another ocean washed over the bedrock of shale. This one teemed with sea creatures—crustaceans, jellyfish, sponges, trilobites, brachiopods. Their skeletal remains fell to the sea floor in calcium-rich beds. Many skeletons became embedded in the sediment, and became fossils.

When this ocean withdrew, the limey soup hardened into limestone. The brand of limestone at both Charleston and Niagara Falls is called Brassfield limestone. It is chunky (scientists call it blockular), resistant to erosion, and rich in fossils.

More oceans came and went, and each dumped a layer of sediment atop the limestone. When the last sea retreated, the erosive power of rain, wind, and sun slowly ate away the strata until it reached the limestone.

Water is predictable. It always goes to the lowest place, and takes the path of least resistance. Here, it seeped into the fissures (cracks) of the limestone blocks. Over millennia, erosion widened the cracks and formed caves. Rain water ran to low spots on the surface, then carved troughs that became streams and gorges.

Then, mile-high glaciers pushing south from the polar cap arrived. The ice mass slid across the earth on melted water produced by the friction of its own enormous weight. When the planet's temperature rose, the shrinking glacier sent roaring torrents of meltwater down channels like Charleston Creek and the Great Miami River. The currents carved deeper gorges and wider paths. Underground caverns literally burst and collapsed. Where limestone had been removed, the mad torrents attacked the softer shale "as easily as we tear pages out of a loose-leaf notebook," said one writer. That left limestone outcrops hanging over the valley.

The last glacier (Wisconsinan ice mass) scoured this part of Ohio about 12,000–15,000 years ago. It deposited mounds of glacial till (sand, gravel, rocks, etc.) in its wake. The demise of the glacier forced the Great Miami River to feed itself with tributaries like Charleston Creek.

At the falls, stream water has eroded the shale layers beneath the limestone, forming a recess cave. Limestone overhangs which lose their shale foundation eventually fall into the creek.

Diversions in the current can change the location of the spout on the precipice. The drape of the falls may be in a different location each year. Notice too, that Charleston Creek has fashioned a charming little gorge before it enters the floodplain and the Great Miami River a mile downstream.

Wildlife

Charleston Falls is the centerpiece of the preserve. The limestone walls surrounding the cool, shady glen support some uncommon plants, notably wild columbine, walking fern, purple cliffbreak, and rock honeysuckle. The boardwalk and platform at the falls protects these plants from human trampling.

The preserve is largely wooded, containing trees common in Ohio—oaks, beech, maples, hickory, tulip tree, etc. In an abandoned farmlot, redbud, black-haw, and cedar have moved in. Redbud Valley Trail gets its name from the tree that blossoms there every spring.

Black and honey locust grow here in healthy groves. Locust Grove Trail passes through a community of this hardwood. Park staff used black locust found in the preserve for the split-rail fences you see.

A special place is Cedar Pond and the adjacent planted tallgrass prairie. The spot looks still and passive enough, but it actually overflows with life. In summer, dragonflies diving for mosquitoes may be swallowed by a rough-winged swallow. Butterflies intoxicate themselves on the nectar of the prairie blossoms. On a hot summer day, I watched a group of regal fritillaries feast on a single milkweed plant for 20 minutes. One of them landed briefly on my shoulder.

The preserve's brochure says the pond, built in 1977, will be a marsh in 100 years, and a forest two centuries hence. Until then, it will be a collecting point for frogs, turtles, crustaceans, raccoons, as well as humans. If you sit on a bench at dusk, silent and still, a deer might tiptoe to the shore for a drink.

Elsewhere, mink and fox hunt for mice and rabbits in the bushes. Purple finches and pine warblers hide in the pines. Listen for the sonorous hoot of the barred owl, "who cooks for you, who cooks for you all."

You are apt to look twice at the sign in the pond. The writing makes no sense until you study its reflection in the pool. Only in the reflection can you read, "Cedar Pond."

On the ride home, parents can get the kids to write their name upside-down and reversed so that it reads correctly in a mirror.

Sinewy, young trees growing in dense groves tell us that the land had been cleared for human use not too long ago.

History

The Indians who gathered here for centuries undoubtedly skinny-dipped under the falls without fear of provoking a ranger, and without harming the wildlife. They left behind fire pits, artifacts, and burial mounds to prove that they visited the site.

White landowners enjoyed the falls for its peace and beauty too. Though much of the land surrounding the cascade was cleared for agriculture, park officials say they left the falls itself "relatively undisturbed."

The Ohio Chapter of The Nature Conservancy, aided by the George Gund Foundation, purchased the site in 1975. The next year the park district acquired the preserve from the conservation group with tax levy money and a matching federal grant. Charleston Falls was the county park district's first acquisition.

Try these other Miami County parks:

Garbry's Big Woods Sanctuary

A boardwalk trail measuring just .75 miles loops through the "big woods" which the Garbry family protected for 130 years. This sanctuary guards the largest and nearly the last mature upland woods in Miami County.

The "big woods," a wet beech-maple forest, encompasses 150 acres and is part of the 272-acre Big Woods Reserve. In spring, the "peepers" raise their voices and wildflowers blossom above the forest floor. The Garbry family of Piqua gave its enduring woods to the park district in 1981.

Location

Northeast Miami County, Spring Creek Township.

From State Route 36 east of Piqua, travel south on Union-Shelby Road, then east (left) on Statler Road. The boardwalk accommodates wheelchairs and strollers. Restrooms, drinking water, picnic tables, and a fishing pond are available here.

Stillwater Prairie Reserve

The Stillwater River, a state scenic river, passes peacefully through this 217-acre preserve. Wild columbine, harebell (a threatened species), and shadbush thrive on fern-covered cliffs, but the main attraction is the tallgrass prairie which grows on both sides of the river.

A 1,600-foot boardwalk along the river wanders through half the prairie. You will have to wade across the stream to see the rest of it. The main trail also passes through woods, fields, shrubland, and marshy areas. Look for the deer and buzzards, both in abundance here.

Early white settlers built mills on the banks of the river. A brick home, vintage 1846, can be seen from the trail. The reserve was opened in October 1979.

Location

Northwest Miami County, Newberry Township.

The entrance is on State Route 185, a half mile west of Range Line Road. Facilities include restrooms, picnic area, drinking water, and two fishing ponds.

Journal

June 15, 1993. I have arrived in time to see the last wild columbine blossom on the cliff, and to feel the soft spray of spring water which has fallen two-score feet over the lip of this limestone bowl. The mist offsets the mid-June heat and recharges body and soul.

Dogwood flower

CINCINNATI NATURE CENTER

Just beyond the eastern reach of Cincinnati's suburban sprawl lies this place of softness, tranquility and peace. Here, the seasons unfold undisturbed, and the word, "collaboration" describes Nature's behavior. We owe this to a 17-year-old boy, Carl Krippendorf, who, a century ago, spent all his earnings to save a beech forest that was about to be felled for tobacco.

Location

Western Clermont County, Union Township.

From Interstate 275 travel east on State Route 50 (one of the Milford exits). At the traffic light in the small village of Perintown turn right on Round Bottom Road. Follow the signs. A mile up the road go left on Tealtown Road. The entrance will appear on the right. After paying a $3 entrance fee (non-members), drive to the parking lot.

From Batavia, the county seat, head north on State Route 222, west on State Route 50, then left at the light in Perintown.

Ownership

The Cincinnati Nature Center is a private, nonprofit, environmental, education organization.

Size & Designation

The center protects 1,425 acres set aside for nature.

Nearby Natural Attractions

Three state parks—East Fork, Stonelick, and Little Miami River—are located in Clermont County.

Access

Wanderers have their pick of 15 trails, totaling almost 15 miles. Pick up a trail guide at the Rowe Building (visitors' center) and take a few minutes to familiarize yourself with the detailed map and legend. The map even highlights the location of benches. Because of the complexity of the trail system, I recommend that you trace your path and check off each numbered intersection as you reach them.

During my visit, I combined routes, visiting a lake, a stream with petite waterfalls, groves of tall hardwoods, hilltops and hollows, a meadow, pond, and the sprawling, big-porch estate of the Krippendorfs.

Leave the Rowe Building from its east door and follow the boardwalk that hugs the shore of Powell Crosley Lake. This is the Edge Trail. Returning to land, bear left, heading easterly along the lakeshore. At the intersection marked by Signpost 5, turn right on the Geology Trail and descend the steps into the valley of the East Branch of Avey's Run. At the bottom (Signpost 6), note the tiny cascade at the left. Cross the bridge and follow the Fox Rock Trail up a ridge.

At Signpost 33, take the left fork, rambling now on the Deep Woods Trail. The loop of the Deep Woods Trail begins at Signpost 34. Here, I went right, crossed a pair of bridges, and admired the mixed collection of hardy, mature hardwoods. Ignore the path going right at Signpost 35, turn right at Signpost 34, and return to the Fox Rock Trail at Signpost 33. Now go left (westerly), following the spine of a long, steep ridge which overlooks the creek to the right. A small gazebo at the prow of the ridge invites you view the vista. This is Fox Rock, an unusual conglomerate formation (explained below) named by Ohio Wildlife photographer Karl Maslowski for the red foxes who once lived in a den here.

Descend the steep stairway to the right to Avey's Run, a good place to observe fossils in the limestone plates. Stepping stones act as a ford (though these may be flooded after heavy rains). On the north bank of the creek go right on the Geology Trail for a few paces, then left on the Wildflower Trail at Signpost 9. This path follows the edge of a meadow then climbs a steep hill filled with giant-sized trees.

Near the summit, at Signpost 12, lean to the right, and cross a bridge. You now tread on the Buckeye Trail. Just ahead, at Signpost 15, go right to visit a pond and the Krippendorf Lodge. Turn left at Signpost 2 and take the Krippendorf Trail back to the Rowe Building.

This three-mile ramble gives you a sample of the natural treats at the preserve. It journeys over heights and hollows and is moderately challenging. The paths are easy enough to follow with the trail map—the best map of its kind among all the large preserves I have visited.

Folks with physical limitations can enjoy the preserve on the paved "all-persons" trail. Children will especially enjoy viewing wildlife from the boardwalks that rim the edge of ponds, most a short walk from the Rowe Building.

The public can visit the grounds Monday-Friday from sunrise to sunset. Everybody can visit the Rowe Interpretive Building from 9 a.m.-5 p.m., Monday-Friday. However, the center remains open for members only on Saturday (9 a.m.-5 p.m.), Sunday (1-5 p.m.), and holidays. Only members can visit on weekends.

The nature center (Rowe Building) offers exhibits, a gift shop, library, restrooms, drinking water, meeting rooms, and a cozy fireplace on cold days. The center schedules numerous educational programs for children and adults during the year—even safaris (North American and overseas nature trips).

For information about programs and membership contact the Cincinnati Nature Center, 4949 Tealtown Road, Milford, Ohio 45150; phone (513) 831-1711.

Geology

Imagine entering a time capsule that goes back 450 million years, to the Ordovician geological period. Back then Ohio was located near the Equator and covered by a shallow sea that teemed with creatures on the ocean floor.

Eventually, the sea withdrew and the remains of the animals became entombed in exposed layers of bedrock we call limestone and shale, the former ocean floors. Other sediments then probably buried the rock.

Later, the land that is now called Southwestern Ohio swelled, or arched, probably when the Earth wrinkled and formed the Appalachian Mountains, roughly 250 million years ago. Think of Cincinnati sitting on the peak of the arch, and the nature center on the eastern slope. The shrug also brought the ancient limestone and shale to the surface again.

Nobody knows for sure what happened during the next 249 million years. Maybe the sediments that topped the bedrock got washed away by erosion. Maybe the arch was a lonely, torpedo-shaped island, or an archipelago of islands, surrounded by another sea. Perhaps a primeval forest stretched out across area. Maybe dinosaurs browsed here.

The story resumes about a million years ago, when the second of four glaciers, this one the Kansan glacier, put down a layer of till (sand, gravel, boulders, clay, silt) over the Ordovician rock. Milky-colored meltwater laden with silt and pebbles rushed from nostrils in the snout of the glacier. Later, this coarse deposit compacted and cemented forming the conglomerate rock visible at Fox Rock.

The next glacier, the Illinoian, spread a blanket of till over Clermont County about 400,000 years ago, but the Wisconsinan ice sheet, the most recent glacier dating back just 12,000-15,000 years, did not extend into the area.

After many millennia of gentle brushstrokes, Avey's Run has removed hills of glacial dirt and uncovered the alternating layers of Ordovician limestone and shale. The creatures who lived in that long ago marine environment—brachiopods, bryozoans, gastropods, trilobites, crinoids, cephalopods, and the like—are imbedded in the rock. The best place to see this slice of ancient life is along the half-mile Geology Trail (see numbered trail landmarks 6-9 on the trail map).

In spots, the fossils are so abundant that I was reminded of modern shell-crowded beaches, like those on Sanibel Island in Florida. By straining your imagination these locked-in-rock bottom feeders will wiggle a little or jettison into Avey's Run.

Fossil observing is certainly encouraged, but digging and collecting them is not allowed. Consider these finds "leavemrites," or "leave them right there" for the next beachcomber.

Avey's Run tumbles over a trio of petite waterfalls along the Geology Trail. Notice that the strata of limestone and shale alternate. When, long ago, water began flowing across these exposed layers, the softer (less resistant) shale washed away faster than the harder (resistant) limestone, creating steps. The current and backsplash at these cascades gnaws small caves into the shale, a process called undercutting. Eventually, the unsupported limestone layer, whether it is a precipice jutting from the bank or a protruding lip of the waterfall, collapses into the stream.

Wildlife

The founder's beloved beeches share this second-growth (previously logged) forest with maples (especially sugar maple), seven varieties of oak, hickories, sycamore, tulip tree, ashes, and an occasional black cherry, walnut, and elm. In ravines, some individual trees boast enormous girths and heights.

Dogwood, hackberry, Ohio buckeye, staghorn sumac, catalpa, pawpaw, persimmon, ironwood, hornbeam, black locust, basswood, Kentucky coffee-tree, magnolia, pines, red cedar, and cottonwood round out the tree list.

A checklist and blooming schedule printed by the center lists 237 different flowers, an extraordinary number, growing on the grounds. The blooming period lasts nine months.

Christmas rose and snowdrops, appropriately named, appear in January followed by bloomers called spring snowflake and windflower in February. These winter species represent a group of 39 plants introduced on the property by the Krippendorfs.

In March, the forest floor explodes in color with 35 plants emerging including toothwort, yellow adder's tongue, twinleaf, and wild stonecrop. April brings 35 more flowers into view, such as blue-eyed Mary, butterbur, henbit, dame's rocket, and jack-in-the-pulpit.

Green dragon, common speedwell, thimbleweed, and lily-leaved twayblade are among the 31 plants that blossom in May. Look for yellow goat's-beard, king devil, birdfoot trefoil, and foxglove beard-tongue (containing digitalis) in June.

You can count 41 flowers in July—ragged fringed orchids, moonweed, bouncing bet, and American lotus among them. August introduces 39 beauties, like sharp-winged monkeyflower, virgin's bower (a clematis-type vine), flower-of-an-hour, and dodder, followed by five in September—knapweed, asters, and goldenrods.

The diversity of birds (153 sightings) almost matches the flower list. (Birders can get a checklist at the Rowe Building.) Six endangered birds—yellow-bellied sapsucker, winter wren, hermit thrush, northern waterthrush, Canada warbler, and dark-eyed junco—have been observed here. Seven birds designated "special interest" (potentially threatened) have caught the eye of astute watchers. These include the sharp-shinned and red-shouldered hawks, saw-whet and long-eared owls, sora, purple martin, Henslow's sparrow.

All totaled, 32 species of warblers and 11 kinds of sparrows might be seen.

The preserve offers sanctuary to the Indiana bat, an endangered animal and one of five bat species found in the area. Another endangered critter, the blue-spotted salamander, succeeds along with seven others from the salamander clan. Nine types of toads and frogs (Fowler's, gray treefrog, etc.) find habitats on the grounds.

Snakes are represented by nine species, notably the rough green snake, designated special interest (potentially threatened). Five kinds of turtle, and two brands of skunk are found here.

Badger, a rarity nowadays and designated a special interest animal, and coyote enjoy the safety of the refuge along with weasels, fox, mink, flying squirrel, and others.

History

Carl Krippendorf, the son of a shoe manufacturer, was a sickly child. But his long summers of fresh air at the Clermont County home of Dr. Colin Spence restored his health and emboldened his heart.

When he learned that the beloved beech forest that he tramped through as a boy was going to be flattened for a tobacco farm, Krippendorf, just 17 years old, swiftly bought the parcel with the cash he earned at his father's factory. He added tracts to his domain when he could, and with his father's help built a stately lodge, a wedding gift for his bride.

Krippendorf and his wife, Mary, lived at "Lob's Wood" from Easter to Thanksgiving for 64 years. In the early years, Carl commuted to Cincinnati every day, an exertion that required Mary to shuttle him to train stations by buggy. Over the years, the Krippendorfs planted trees and flowers (39 varieties mostly around the lodge) and built a pond, a pumping station, and Clermont County's first swimming pool. They farmed some, too. They died within a month of each other in 1964.

Rosan Krippendorf Adams, the daughter, told friends that her parents had no intention of ever developing the estate. That prompted Stanley Rowe, a businessman and arboretum founder, and Karl Maslowski, an outdoors photographer, to revive their idea of establishing a nature center. The pair had been unable to acquire a neighboring property, now an outdoor education center called Wildwood.

National Audubon Society planners reported that the Krippendorf site was ideal for a nature center. The 175-acre preserve was purchased by the newly formed Cincinnati Nature Center Association on January 17, 1966. The Interpretive Center, named for Rowe, opened in the early 1970s, and improvements have been added since then.

More land has been acquired too—Long Branch Farm in 1973, Fox Rock in the mid-1970s. The property now totals 1,425 acres. The center has more than 5,000 members, and more than 6,000 school children attend nature programs here.

Journal

October 27, 1993. Standing on the heights above Avey's Run and Fox Rock, a jet of cool polar air, the first of the season, enters my nose. It is sweet, refreshing, tinged with the nectar of ice crystals.

Leaves that last week clung to the uppermost, frayed branches of the canopy—here being oaks ,tulips, and maples—have since been liberated by the recent winds and bone-chilling rains. Autumn is past its prime here. Nature requires tiny icy tempests, working like wild sabers, to loosen the tenacious grip of the leaves from the understory. These sudden, cold blasts stir the litter on the forest floor. The gusts die as quickly as they spring up.

In still air, I watch leaves randomly float. Most reach the ground, but some become impaled or entangled by twigs, and others rest softly on ferns, shrubs, and rocks.

Each flake delivers a message to the earth. By late October the forest floor has a winter's worth of information to digest. I wonder—does the maple sapling who spears the topmost autumn leaf from an ancient red oak learn the secret of longevity?

Arborvitae foliage

CLIFTON GORGE STATE NATURE PRESERVE

The Little Miami River, boiling through a narrow chasm of steep dolomite walls, makes Clifton Gorge State Nature Preserve one of the most impressive natural areas in Ohio. It's famous for spectacular geological formations, diversity of plant life, and the charm of local legends. ★

Location

Northern Greene County, Miami Township.

Located just a quarter mile west of the Village of Clifton on State Route 343, the preserve is the easternmost link of a three-mile-long chain protecting the canyon of the Little Miami River. To the west are John Bryan State Park and Glen Helen Nature Preserve in Yellow Springs. From Interstate 70 go south on State Route 72 eight miles to Clifton, then west a half mile on State Route 343.

Ownership

Ohio Department of Natural Resources, Division of Natural Areas and Preserves.

Size & Designation

The preserve comprises 269 acres. The portion north and west of the Little Miami River was designated an interpretive preserve on October 2, 1973. It is open to the public daily from sunrise to sunset. The biologically unique southern section (75percent of the preserve) is reserved for scientific study, and written permission must be obtained to explore it.

Clifton Gorge also is a National Natural Landmark. The Little Miami River is a national and a state scenic river.

Nearby Natural Attractions

John Bryan State Park borders the preserve. Drive west on SR 343 to the park entrance. SR 343 also goes to Yellow Springs where you find Glen Helen Nature Preserve. Also visit these Green County Metroparks: Indian Mound Reserve near Cedarville and The Narrow Reserve near Beaver-creek. Little Miami State Park and Spring Valley

State Wildlife Area lie in the southwest corner of the county.

Access

From a roomy parking lot, a clearly marked trail leading from the parking lot splits into three paths at the edge of the gorge. The most popular is the John L. Rich Trail which descends from the rim to the bottom of the gorge where it winds around boulders once attached to the cliff, and trees that reach to the top of the gorge. The path hugs the Little Miami River whose abrasive action and fresh mist are best experienced from this vantage.

Heading west (downstream) you pass features like Steamboat Rock, the squared boulders of an old dam and paper mill, a calm pool called Blue Hole, and a plaque commemorating the site as a National Natural Landmark.

At the western border of the preserve you can retrace your path to the starting point; continue west (straight ahead) into John Bryan State Park (following the old Pittsburgh-Cincinnati stagecoach trail); turn right and climb out of gorge (tracing a stagecoach switchback) to walk the North Rim or Orton trails; or cross the river and hike the state park trail on the south side of the river.

The North Rim Trail offers several scary views into the chasm (scary for parents with adventurous kids). It returns to the starting point (east) with branches leading to a parking lot in the state park and to the Orton Memorial.

Back at the start, I recommend heading east (upstream) along The Narrows Trail, which follows SR 343. Along the way mark the spot of Darnell's Leap, the falls of the Little Miami, and the ruins of several mills. Observation platforms peek into the chasms. This path empties into a parking lot at the end of Jackson Street in the village. Another plaque commemorates this national landmark at this spot.

A small picnic area and latrines are located in the parking lot. A water well is found here too, but it is not always in service.

Attend one of the nature programs to learn more about the gorge. The programs usually begin at The Bear's Den, a small amphitheater at the trailhead. Look for a trail map at the spot. For more information phone the preserve manager at (513) 964-8794 or the Ohio Department of Natural Resources, Division of Natural Areas and Preserves, Fountain Square, Building F-1, Columbus, Ohio 43224-1387; phone (614) 265-6453.

The portions of the trail that climb the gorge wall are somewhat challenging, though aided by sturdy stairs. Boardwalks and decks have been built over rocky sections of the rich trail. Several interpretive signs add spice to the visit.

Stay on the trails! Hiking on the rim, especially The Narrows, can be dangerous if you leave the trail. *Keep an eye on small children.* Don't let teenagers test their invincibility and immortality by reenacting Darnell's Leap. And stay out of places marked as restoration areas where rare and fragile plants are protected. Rock climbing and swimming are not permitted.

Geology

The cliffs that you see are made of thick layers of dolomite (60 feet or more) lying above a vein of shale (Massie shale). Their formation began more than 400 million years ago (Silurian Period) when Ohio was flooded by a shallow, murky inland sea. Successive blankets of sediment, including marine life, fell to the bottom of this sea. Eventually the land lifted above the water surface and the latest layers of rock eroded away leaving the bedrock exposed.

In the more recent Pleistocene times, the last two million years or so, a series of continental glaciers sculpted the land. The last glacier, the Wisconsinan, left its deep mark in Clifton Gorge, carving the 80-foot high cliffs 16,000 years ago. Meltwater from the retreating ice mass poured into the newly formed Little Miami River Valley and began cutting through cracks in the bedrock.

In this part of Ohio, Cedarville dolomite (35 feet thick) lies above Springfield dolomite (in thin layers about seven feet thick in the gorge). Cedarville dolomite resists erosion more than Springfield dolomite. Consequently, the Springfield stratus which you see at the level of the river or just above it has worn away faster than the Cedarville strata, creating recesses (undercuts), overhangs, and eventually gorges.

The house-sized chunks of rocks in the riverbed, like Steamboat Rock, once loomed as precipices of Cedarville dolomite. They fell into the valley when the Springfield dolomite beneath them eroded away.

The conical-shaped formations in the cliffs are giant potholes formed by swirling water during the glacial period. Notice how the turbulence has formed a pothole at the base of the Falls of the Little Miami along The Narrows Trail.

The cutting of the Little Miami River continues today. Downstream in the gorge, and into John Bryan State Park, the river has carved into deeper layers of bedrock, revealing more shale, another dolomite layer (Euphemia) and limestone (Brassfield formation). These strata look like benches on the sides of the river. Springs bubble out from between the shale and dolomite.

Wildlife

The 80-foot-high gorge and preserve boasts an extraordinary assemblage of plant life—some 343 kinds off wildflowers, 105 species of trees and shrubs, and 16 types of ferns.

The hemlocks, ferns, Canadian yew, and arborvitae clinging to the dolomite walls remind us of those long- ago years of glaciation. These plants from the northern woods survive here, along with mountain maple and red-berried elder, on the cool, shaded south wall. Clifton Gorge also is one of the last refuges in Ohio for the red baneberry bush.

Various micro-habitats have emerged on the darker south bank of the gorge. Life in these fragile communities depends on the intensity of sunlight, soil moisture, and steepness of the cliff. Some of the flora here is "disjunct," or separated from its natural range, which partly explains why this section of the preserve is designated scientific and closed to the public. Several groups grow on slump rocks (boulders), which partly explains why rock climbing is prohibited.

Chinkapin oaks flourish on the steeper slopes enriched by calcareous (calcium enriched) soils, while other oaks and sugar maples grip the gentler grades beneath cliffs. Along the river grow sycamore, cottonwood, willow, silver maple, box elder, and elm. Species typical of prairies can be found in clearings and outcroppings at the top of the gorge, an area once heavily farmed.

Ten species of snakes and five types of turtle represent the reptile collection in the preserve. Salamanders (eight species) and frogs and toads (seven kinds) reside here.

The preserve shelters many common mammals, but the most reclusive are mink, weasel, skunk, short-tail shrew, and red fox.

History

Clifton Gorge is famous for its lovers and leapers. The Indians knew the Blue Hole as the Spirit Pool in honor of an Indian maiden who drowned there after a warrior rejected her love. Legend says the girl's spirit mingles with the mist on a midsummer's night and moans sorrowfully. Later, the pool became a favorite spot for artists.

In 1799, Daniel Boone and a party of white frontiersmen were captured for trespassing by the Shawnee chief Black Fish and taken to the Shawnee village near Old Town. One of the men in Boone's party, Cornelius Darnell, escaped by outrunning his captors and leaping across the chasm at The Narrows, a death-defying, 22-foot jump, ill-advised today.

The river and gorge were prized for their water power in the 19th century. The evidence of several dams and mills can be seen along the trails. The overgrown, faint ruins of a stagecoach inn lie beside the Orton Trail (named for pioneering geologist Edward Orton, past president of Antioch College and Ohio State University). Travelers, of course, could not resist peeking into the gorge.

In December 1924, the state finally accepted a 500-acre parcel bequeathed by John Bryan, an inventor and conservationist. Three governors had rejected the gift because Bryan had placed a ban on the land's use for public religious worship. Much of this land became the state park.

Hugh Taylor Birch, who gave Antioch College land for nearby Glen Helen Nature Preserve, also left 161 acres around the gorge to the state.

The Ohio Chapter of The Nature Conservancy purchased a portion of the upper gorge in 1963 with an anonymous gift in memory of Dr. John L. Rich, a geology professor at the University of Cincinnati and member of the Ohio Natural Resources Commission from 1952 until his death in 1956. The parcel was managed by the Dayton Museum of Natural History. In 1968, the conservancy raised $38,000, and transferred its holding for inclusion in the state park. Cincinnati garden clubs held fund-raisers to help the state buy more land. The purchases stopped residential and recreational developments planned for the gorge.

The gorge also was designated a National Natural Landmark in 1968 by the U.S. Department of Interior. A year later the Little Miami River became a state scenic river, followed in April 1973 by national scenic river designation. Clifton Gorge was further protected as a state nature preserve in October 1973.

Journal

I shudder standing at the spot Cornelius Darnell leaped across the gorge. He must have been in great shape. Of course, being pursued by Shawnees who had visions of death by torture might have given him the extra edge. If Darnell could perform that feat today (and I'm not suggesting that it be duplicated) surely he'd have Olympic possibilities. And perhaps a Shawnee coach wouldn't be a bad idea, either.

DAYTON METROPARKS

The Dayton Metroparks (Park District of Dayton-Montgomery County) owes its existence to a terrible flood on Easter Sunday, 1913, that swallowed Dayton and other communities along the Great Miami River and its tributaries. By the end of the decade the Miami Conservancy District, the first watershed management program of its kind in the U.S., had constructed five flood-control dams in the area. The land surrounding the impounded lakes became parkland managed by the conservancy district. The park district, established in 1963, has more than tripled its holdings since it began leasing reserves from the Miami Conservancy District. The district now manages nine sites and more than 8,000 acres, including Cox Arboretum, Possum Creek Reserve, Eastwood Reserve, and Huffman Reserve not mentioned below. For more information, contact the Park District of Dayton-Montgomery County, 1375 East Siebenthaler Avenue, Dayton, Ohio 45414; phone (513) 275-PARK (7275).

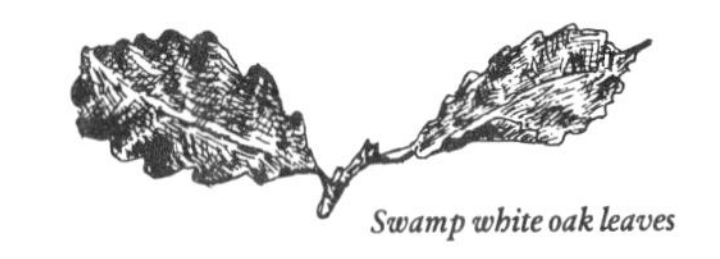

Swamp white oak leaves

- **Englewood Reserve**
- **Germantown Reserve**
- **Sugarcreek Reserve**
- **Taylorsville Reserve**

ENGLEWOOD RESERVE

The trails through the natural area in this metropolitan park visit waterfalls, natural springs, a state natural landmark, and a state scenic river. The floral scent in the air reminds visitors of gardens that surround the Aull estate in the southeast section of this park.

Location

Northern Montgomery County, Randolph Township, near Englewood.

From Dayton travel north (about six miles) on Interstate 75, west a few miles on Interstate 70, and exit northbound State Route 48. Less than a mile on SR 48 turn right (east) on State Route 40, and turn left into the reserve just after crossing the Englewood Dam. To reach the trails described below, drive beyond the lake at your left to the end of the road, turn right (Patty's Road) and pull into the parking lot on the right. The trail begins across the street.

To reach Aullwood Garden, bear right after crossing the dam, and turn right on to Aullwood Road. Just beyond the Aullwood Audubon Center, pull into the drive on the right which goes to a parking lot beside Stillwater River.

Ownership

The Park District of Dayton-Montgomery County leases the land from the Miami Conservancy District.

Size & Designation

Englewood Reserve encompasses 1,500 acres (including all areas). Aullwood Garden is 32 acres.

Nearby Natural Attractions

The Aullwood Audubon Center and Farm are just across the road. Also visit the Taylorsville, Germantown, and Sugarcreek reserves, and Sycamore State Park.

Access

Twelve miles of trails wander through the reserve. Maps are usually available at the trailheads. Here are my favorites.

The trail to Martindale Falls, round trip 1.5 miles, begins across the street from the parking lot designated for the picnic area and shelter house on the left side of Patty's Road (not the riding center). You will find restrooms at this location. The path goes north, on the side of a ridge. Halfway to the falls, the River Trail joins from the left. You continue north (straight) to the falls. (The River Trail hugs the east bank of the Stillwater River and returns to Patty's Road.)

At the falls, the trail climbs the steep cliff and returns south, now on the top of the cliff. Midway back, I recommend a left turn at the first intersection. This trail goes to the Pumpkin Ash Swamp Forest, a state natural landmark. Hereafter, bear left at each junction to Patty Falls. Continue south on the trail to Patty's Road, turn right to your car.

The trails are gently sloped, though briefly steep in places, and well-marked. Stairs and boardwalks assist your walk in places. Please stay on the trails. Climbing the cliffs near Martindale and Patty Falls can be dangerous. The path near Martindale Falls gets close to the edge of a limestone ledge, so watch your step.

Several paths loop through the Big Spring section of the reserve bordered by Meeker and Aullwood roads. Trailheads are at the Aullwood Audubon Center.

The reserve is open daily from 8 a.m. to dusk. It is closed Christmas and New Year's Day. You also will find restrooms, picnic areas, bicycle paths, fishing areas, and horse riding trails in the preserve.

Aullwood Garden is open Tuesday–Saturday, 8 a.m.–7 p.m. It remains closed on Sunday and Monday, and January–February.

Geology

At Martindale Falls and Patty's Falls, notice the alternating layers of limestone and shale. These strata date back more than 450 million years ago to the Ordovician geologic period when Ohio was covered by a shallow, warm inland sea.

When the creatures living in this ancient ocean died their shells and skeletons floated to the bottom and mixed with other sediment. Eventually, this limey soup hardened into limestone.

The waterfalls show a process called undercutting at work. The limestone layer on the top is resistant rock, meaning it bears up to or "resists" erosion more than shale, a less-resistant rock. The water falling over the resistant limestone erodes the shale layer beneath creating ledges and recess caves. The limestone overhangs break off into the ravines when their support rock, the shale, disappears. The Stillwater River and its tributaries have been eroding, or undercutting, these limestone and shale walls for centuries.

The creeks that tumble over Patty Falls and snake through Aullwood Garden emerge from underground water sources. The Patty family, once owners of the land, tapped this spring for its water.

Wildlife

A rare pumpkin ash community, population 80 and growing, thrives in a swamp forest just off the trail connecting Martindale and Patty Falls. This tree was believed to be extinct in Ohio. The spot is a state natural landmark.

Just a few hundred yards away is a pine plantation planted nearly 60 years ago by the Civilian Conservation Corps. Three white-tailed deer tiptoed within 50 feet of me. The May breeze, brisk in my face, never carried my odor to them. Either that, or they, like me, lingered to inhale the pine vapors.

Much of land here has been farmed and grazed, and much of the vegetation is in various stages of succession growth. Birds and other critters common in Ohio reside here. Look for waterfowl in Englewood Lake.

Though not a wild, natural area, take a peak at luxuriant Aullwood Garden, especially if you are a devoted gardener and landscaper. A plaque on the trail from the parking lot to the garden reminds you that some of trees along the river have been there for 300 years. Swarms of butterflies as well as bees float like confetti above the blossoms in the summer.

History

After a devastating flood in 1913 dams and other flood control projects were constructed under the management of the Miami Conservancy District (MCD). In spite of pressure from developers, the agency wisely left most of the land surrounding the impoundments for park and recreation land. One of these dams blocked the Stillwater River at Englewood.

1963 marked the creation of the Dayton-Montgomery Park District which began leasing land around the MCD for parks and natural areas. One of these projects became the Englewood Preserve. Quite by accident the preserve's size grew in the early 1970s when 100 acres along Meeker Road was acquired through eminent domain to block construction of a housing development and waste treatment plant.

In 1907 John Aull, a businessman, bought 150 acres along the Stillwater River as a refuge. He built a modest home on the site and reconfigured Wiles Creek after the 1913 flood. In the ensuing years, he and his wife, Marie, developed a garden that maintains a natural look.

To revive the woodland floor cover that had been beaten down by grazing, the Aulls planted native wildflowers, such as the thousands of Virginia bluebells which cover the hillsides and the blue-eyed Marys rescued from a nearby farm. Each week of each season has a different look in the garden.

In 1977, Marie Aull donated her home and garden to the park district. Mrs. Aull lives in her estate atop a rocky knoll, and occasionally strolls into the garden to greet visitors.

Eastern red cedar

GERMANTOWN RESERVATION

Twin Creek has lacerated this land right down to the bone, in this case the bone being 450 million-year-old limestone packed with fossils of creatures that lived on Earth long before the dinosaurs.

Nature bandaged the wound with a forest.

Later, farmers removed the woods for crops and allowed livestock to graze on the gentler slopes. But they just could not extract the ornery trees hiding in the rugged places—sycamores and cottonwoods mostly, and a few maples, red oaks, and beech. These giants have reseeded the area with hardwoods. Former croplands and pastures have evolved into meadows teeming with plants and wild animals.

Location

Southwestern Montgomery County, German Township.

From Germantown, travel west on State Route 725 roughly four miles, then turn right (north) on Boomershine Road. The entrance is a mile up the road on the right. Park at the nature center, located on the west bank of Twin Creek. The east side of the reserve is accessible from Conservancy Road running between SR 725 and Manning Road.

Ownership

Park District of Dayton-Montgomery County.

Size & Designation

The metropark comprises 1,400 acres.

Nearby Natural Attractions

Germantown Reserve is one of nine nature reserves managed by the park district. The others reviewed in this book are the Englewood, Taylorsville, and Sugarcreek (in Greene County) reserves. Also journey to Aullwood Audubon Center next door to Englewood Reserve. Sycamore State Park is located in Montgomery County.

Access

Hikers can take pleasure in 10 miles of trails which visit forests, steep ravines, meadows, streams, and ponds. The well-marked, color-coded trails are open daily from 8 a.m. to dusk (closed Christmas and New Year's Day) but during spring floods the paths along Twin Creek may be impassable.

Get a trail map at the modern nature center and study the color-coded trail sign before departing. I recommend the following route (basically the yellow blazes) for starters.

The path begins to the right of the parking lot (Signpost T) and descends through a cedar glade. Turn left at the first intersection (Signpost N) just before a creek where you will find fossil-rich Ordovician-era bedrock and a waterfall.

Bear left at the next junction (Signpost J) and drop into the floodplain of Twin Creek. The path traces the edge of the stream for a while, then hooks back into the floodplain (look for the huge cottonwood tree) and climbs a slope. At the next intersection (point J on the map) go right, continuing a gentle ascent.

The trail bends to the right when it reaches a meadow. I saw a pair of deer here. Ignore the trail branching left to the Oak Ridge Campground. Ahead, at point L, bear left if you want to ramble through a cedar meadow and traipse by a tiny pond en route to the nature center (beyond Signposts M, N, and T). Or, take the right fork if you desire more woods, then turn left at Signpost J and retrace your entry route.

Hiking trails on the north side of Twin Creek, accessible from the Conservancy Road entrance, lead to the Broad-Winged Prairie, a colony of red cedars, Sunfish Pond, and the Valley Overlook, which presents a scenic view of the Twin Creek valley.

The underground, energy-efficient nature center features one of the best wildlife windows in the state. Speakers amplify the songs of the birds that flock to the outdoors feeders. There are plenty of exhibits in the nature center, even some live critters. The naturalist on duty wants to answer your questions. Restrooms and drinking water are available here.

The reserve also has picnic areas (some reservable), and two group campgrounds. Fishing is allowed in Twin Creek (south of the Germantown Dam, Creek Road entrance) and at Sunfish Pond (off the Conservancy Road entrance). Canoeing is permitted below the dam (use the Creek Road entrance). Fossils are reportedly abundant in the vicinity of the dam.

For more information contact the Park District of Dayton-Montgomery County, 1375 East Siebenthaler Avenue, Dayton, Ohio 45414; phone (513) 275-PARK (7275).

Geology

The fossils embedded in rock are the remains of extinct creatures that clung to the floor of an ocean around 450 million years ago. Their remains, largely made of calcium, mixed with other sediments to make a limey stew at the bottom of the sea. When the ocean receded, the sediment hardened into limestone. The rock is sprinkled with fossils.

A wall at the entrance of the nature center describes the ancient sea critters. The most common fossil is the bryozoan which grew in colonies like moss. They look like small bones or twigs. Brachiopods, or lamp shades, had tiny, symmetrical fan-shaped shells. Snail-like gastropods preyed upon brachiopods. Horn corals have radiating lines inside their cups and striations around their horn-shaped bodies. Cephalopods, identified by coiled shells, are related to modern squids.

An uncommon discovery here was a predatory trilobite, now the official state fossil. Finding a whole specimen is a prize, fragments are common. All types had two grooves running from head to toe, and a body split into three sections. One variety reached a length of two feet.

The last continental ice mass, known as the Wisconsinan glacier, deposited thick layers of dirt called till, an unsorted blend of sand, gravel, boulders, clay, and other debris. As the glacier withdrew, roughly 12,000 years ago, its meltwater rushed down newly created streams, like Twin Creek. These post-glacial currents washed away till, right down to bedrock in some cases, and formed steep valleys. Tributaries running off the valley slopes now fatten the creek and carve their own hollows. Twin Creek flows into the Little Miami Valley, another post-glacial waterway.

The flood control impoundment known as Germantown Dam (built in the late 1910s) has slowed the pace and increased the depth of the creek.

Wildlife

Germantown Reserve protects land on the mend, and southwestern Montgomery County's largest mature forest. Evidence of the land's agricultural past—patches of grass in the forest, ground hogs, fencerows, barbed wire scars on tree trunks—still faintly exist, but these reminders eventually will disappear.

Though white settlers deforested the upland and gentle slopes for farms in the first half of the 19th century, many trees avoided the axe. These lucky ones live in rugged nooks and crannies, or steep slopes, or soggy bottomland, places loggers simply ignored.

Some mammoth beeches are thought to be more than 200 years old, and there are maples and oaks just as old, and just as big. And some of the grandfather cottonwoods near the creek must be older. The reserve also boasts buxom tulip trees, shagbark hickories, and wild black cherries.

Red cedar groves dot the landscape. This pioneer tree (one of the first to populate a played-out field) likes open areas with alkaline soil. Some 50 species of birds consume the tree's berries, including bobwhite quail, pheasant, grouse, and mourning dove. Opossum have been seen eating the fruit too.

The tree also appeals to two rare birds—the saw-whet and long-eared owls. The Ohio Division of Wildlife has declared both of them "special interest" birds, a designation roughly equal to potentially threatened. Quiet walkers hiking through the cedars in the winter might catch a glimpse of the diminutive saw-whet, the smallest owl in Ohio. Great-horned, screech, and barred owls are also present.

Broad-winged hawks supposedly nest near a prairie patch discovered in 1982, hence the name Broad-winged Prairie. The Cooper's, red-tailed, red-shouldered (special interest), and kestrel hawks often glide above the valley.

Look for these colorful birds—indigo bunting, scarlet tanager, cerulean warbler, ruby-throated hummingbird, and slate-colored junco. The northern waterthrush, an endangered species, has been spotted here, along with the cedar waxwing, eastern meadowlark, pileated woodpecker, redstart, and evening grosbeak. Waterfowl residents include mallard and wood ducks. Great blue herons and kingfishers occupy the creek habitat.

Wildflowers, hundreds of varieties, brighten the landscape from the dawning of the skunk cabbage in late February to the waning of the New England aster in late October. For kicks, try to find the spring larkspur, yellow goatsbeard, dewberry, wild columbine, Greek valerian, toadshade (one of the trillium family), deptford pink, jack-in-the-pulpit, white beard-tongue, and firepink.

The prairie, a relict of the sweeping grassland that thrived here just 4,000 years ago, sponsors little bluestem (a grass), wild bergamot, purple coneflower, oxeye daisy, sunflower, and prairie coneflower.

Insects named great-spangled fritillary, pink-edged sulfur, and clear wing sphinx moth represent the butterfly kingdom.

Bass (smallmouth, large-mouth, and rock), bluegill, and crappie swim in Twin Creek, a good spot to look for the two-lined, red-backed, smallmouth, and long-tailed salamanders.

Germantown Reserve is the only known habitat in Montgomery County for the eastern hognose snake, a reptile becoming rare in Ohio. More common are the black race, water, and queen snakes. Five kinds of turtle get old here—the box, painted, softshell, map, and snapping.

History

People of the Miami and Shawnee nations moved into the region in first half of the 18th century, but by the time white settlers arrived only a small band of Shawnees survived south of Germantown.

Most of the land comprising the reserve was cleared by farmers in the first half of the 19th century. One cash crop, tobacco, rapidly depleted the soil.

The terrible flood that swamped Dayton on Easter Sunday, 1913 inspired the creation of the Miami Conservancy District two years later. The MCD was the first major watershed district established in the U.S., according to historian George W. Knepper. The Germantown dam was one of a six earthen impoundments built by the MCD in the late 1910s.

Arthur Morgan, the MCD's hired engineer, recommended that the land surrounding the dams be used for recreation. The suggestion was adopted, enabling Twin Creek valley above the dam to return to its natural state.

The newly formed Park District of Dayton-Montgomery County began leasing four MCD park sites, including Germantown, in the early 1960s. The park district has been improving the reserve since then.

The Three Sisters

SUGARCREEK RESERVE

The Three Sisters, a hoary and revered triumvirate of white oaks, have presided over their redoubtable slope for more than 550 years. They have seen the forest reduced to cornfields, and the cropland reverting back to forest.

In spite of their many years they look fit enough to carry on for another five centuries. It is said that the secrets of eternity rise from the sweet water of Sugar Creek to their roots, then spread, like gossip, into their brittle, intertwining branches.

Location

Southwestern Greene County, Sugarcreek Township.

From Xenia, go southwest on U.S. Route 42 to Spring Valley, then turn right (west) on State Route 725 to Bellbrook. Go left (south) on Waynesville Road in downtown Bellbrook. Just south of the village turn right on Ferry Road, and right on Conference Road which takes you to the entrance on the right.

Ownership

Park District of DaytonMontgomery County.

Size & Designation

The reserve, featuring woodlands, meadows, ravines, and prairies, encompasses 596 acres.

Nearby Natural Attractions

Sugarcreek is one of nine metroparks managed by the park district. Englewood, Taylorsville, and Germantown, all in Montgomery County, are included in these pages.

Greene County also boasts Indian Mound and The Narrows reserves (Greene County parks), Clifton Gorge State Nature Preserve, Glen Helen Nature Preserve, John Bryan State Park, and Spring Valley State Wildlife Area.

Access

Five miles of trails are open daily (except Christmas and New Year's Day) from 8 a.m. to dusk. Trails are color-coded with lettered signposts at intersections. Study the trail map, available at the trailhead, before departing. A separate brochure on the Three Sisters Trail is available too. The route described below visits a planted prairie, the Three Sisters, an osage orange grove, Sugar Creek, and an oddly placed community of sycamore trees.

A northbound trail from the parking lot leads to a picnic area and the trailhead. Follow along with trail map in hand. Take the path at the right (east) which traces the edge of a prairie meadow (green blazes). At Point E on the map bear right on the green trail, which continues along the edge of woods (not the right turn that loops through the prairie). This path goes to Point G located beneath electric power lines. Go straight across the meadow (green arrows) and into woods (ignoring a connector trail branching to the left).

Intersection O lies at the top of a steep ridge. Go left here to Point N, then right (following orange arrows) to Point M. The Three Sisters will be to the right. Traipse passed these beauties, then turn left (north, orange arrows) at the intersection marked Point H on the map.

Go left at Point I and walk between rows of intertwining osage orange trees. At the end of the osage "tunnel" take the right fork to Point K, then bear left and go upstream (westerly) along the bank of Sugar Creek. Follow this scenic creekside path for the next 3/4 miles to the junction marked Point C. (You can shorten the walk by turning left at Point D and climbing the steep ridge via stairs to F, then continue straight to Point E and backtrack to the picnic area.)

Continue forward at Point C. The path soon bends left, visits Sycamore Ridge, and returns to the picnic area. Retrace your steps to the car. This ramble measures about three miles. It is an easy to moderately strenuous walk (hard to follow without a map) with a couple of steep grades when you descend and ascend from Sugar Creek.

The reserve also boasts 6.5 miles of bridle trails, accessible from the Riding Center at the Wilmington Pike entrance, although horseback riding is not allowed on the footpaths described above. Rental horses are available.

Archers can test their aim at the free, 50-target archery range located off Ferry Road. The Sugarcreek Archers maintain the site. Archers must bring their own equipment.

A primitive campground for groups is located next to the picnic area. Restrooms are found at the picnic area, riding center, and archery range. Anglers can fish at Spring Lakes Park, a Greene County park, located off Ferry Road, just before the archery range.

The regular rules are enforced. Stay on trails. Don't pick wildflowers or damage trees. Fossil looking is permitted, but not collecting.

Naturalist-led educational programs usually begin at the trailhead. For more information contact the Park District of Dayton-Montgomery County, 1375 East Siebenthaler Avenue, Dayton, Ohio 45414; phone (513) 275-PARK (7275).

Geology

The last of three or four continental glaciers affecting the area, the Wisconsinan glacier, left behind a dense layer of sand, gravel, boulders, and clay (called till) about 12,000 years ago. A cigar-shaped deposit of the glacier called an esker, formed by sediments carried in a stream beneath the ice mass, rises near the Three Sisters at Point H on the map.

Though nobody knows for certain, this land may lie above a buried tributary of the ancient Teays River, which coursed northwest toward Indiana about a million years ago. The Wisconsinan glacier and its predecessors covered this vast river system under tons of sediment.

The swift streams of water rushing off the melting Wisconsinan glacier carved valleys in the till. Sugar Creek is one of these post-glacial streams. In the reserve, Sugar Creek has gnawed down to bedrock Ordovician-aged limestone dating back 450 million years. The rock is filled with the fossils of sea creatures that lived on the sea floor. The remains of these ancient animals mixed with other sediments to form the limestone (see Germantown Reserve).

White settlers found the water sweet tasting, hence the name Sugar Creek. Later, when sewage flowed into the stream, the water was everything but sweet. Waste treatment facilities have cleansed the water considerably, but nobody is advised to drink it.

Wildlife

At Sugarcreek Reserve, the best is yet to come. In the two decades or so that it has been a nature park, this former farmland has begun to change back to forest land.

Look closely. Notice how hundreds of small trees, many the same size and age, have migrated into the fields.

According to early land surveys a forest of sugar maples, beech, oak, and hickory stood where the grasses and flowers of the prairie meadow now brush the sky.

Just before you reach Point O on the map, look for the stand of wild black cherry trees (on the right). In 1968, corn grew on that spot. These youngsters are probably the offspring of the mammoth grandfather cherry who presides a few paces north (near Point N on the map).

Somehow the Three Sisters missed the axe, lightning bolts, forest fires, and diseases. Test bores suggest they were already 50 years old when Christopher Columbus landed on Hispanola in 1492.

Indeed, these ancient ones inspire veneration and curiosity. White oaks that rise in a mature forest sport tall, straight trunks and narrow crowns; and their branches appear 40–50 feet above the ground. But the Three Sisters have stocky, squat trunks and wide-spreading crowns, suggesting that they grew in a clearing rather than a forest. Seeing the burly scars on the trunk (the former location of lower branches) loggers may have concluded the trunks were too knotty for timber. Later, farmers saw the advantage of letting them flourish because their sprawling limbs shaded livestock in summer.

American beech dominates the southeast corner of the reserve. Elsewhere, the forest supports a mix of oak, maple, hickory, walnut, and other hardwoods. Even tulip trees are returning in numbers. White settlers favored these straight trees for log homes and barns.

Osage orange is not a native Ohio tree. Farmers planted it in rows in the mid-1800s because its gnarly, intermingling branches created a hedgerow that livestock could not penetrate. The practice declined after the invention of barbed wire in 1874. The Osage Indians, who lived where Texas, Oklahoma, and Arkansas meet today, prized the wood for bows. (The fruit resembles a round, orange brain the size of a grapefruit.)

Sycamore trees love moist soil which explains their presence in floodplains and along stream banks. Sugarcreek Reserve protects a stand of sycamores that strangely thrives on the top of a ridge west of the picnic area. Park officials suspect the trees are fed by water that percolates beneath the ridge.

Wildflowers have rebounded, especially hepatica, bloodroot, large-flowered trillium, phlox, twinleaf, spring (purple) larkspur, and firepink. White snakeroot (white fuzzy flower heads) grows here. The milk from cows that eat snakeroot can be fatal. Abraham Lincoln's mother supposedly died after drinking "snakeroot" milk.

The prairie planted in an old cornfield blooms from mid-July–Labor Day. Grasses called big bluestem, Indian switchgrass, and nodding rye live here, alongside flowers named royal catchfly (potentially threatened in Ohio), purple coneflower, compass plant, prairie dock, and tall coreopsis, to recall a few.

Birders will find the forest canopy teeming with warblers in the spring, including the yellow-rumped (myrtle) and yellow-throated varieties. Trained eyes will find these tiny triumphs—the golden-crowned kinglet, red-eyed vireo, fox sparrow, Louisiana waterthrush, and yellow-breasted chat. You also might see an indigo bunting, kingfisher, pileated woodpecker, red-tailed hawk, bobolink, great horned owl, and yellow-crowned night heron, an endangered critter in Ohio.

Coyotes have been seen in the preserve, but they will not disturb you. The biggest four-legged animal found in these woods is the white-tailed deer.

Bass, sunfish, daces, and minnows swim in Sugar Creek. Common snakes are the black rat, black racer, and water snakes.

History

Sugarcreek Reserve was the second property purchased (late 1960s) by the newly created park district.

Local archers manage a 50-target range in one section of the reserve, an uncommon but creative recreational activity in a metropark. Recent neighborhood developments, Spring Lakes Park and a new 18-hole golf course, have increased the traffic and could intrude on the solitude of Sugarcreek Reserve.

Virginia bluebell

TAYLORSVILLE RESERVE

As it passes through this reserve, the Great Miami River, born 15,000 years ago from a shrinking glacier, is refreshed by spring-fed rivulets which emerge from ruptured layers of 450-million-year-old bedrock. The rock is limestone, composed of the shells and skeletons of extinct sea creatures all churned with other sediments. Now water oozes from the depths of the Earth. Is it the nectar of that venerable sea? A liquid remnant of the glacier?

Location

Northeastern Montgomery County, Wayne Township.

Leave Interstate 70 at the exit for State Route 202. Drive south on SR 202 for a half mile and turn right (west) on Taylorsville Road. Drive north (right turn) on Bridgewater Road (crossing over I-70) to its end at U.S. Route 40. Turn right on US 40, then left 1/2 mile to the reserve entrance, marked by a wooden park sign. A sign says you have arrived at Location TR-5 in the reserve. Park here.

Ownership

The Park District of Dayton-Montgomery County leases the land from the Miami Conservancy District.

Size & Designation

The reserve protects 865 acres, most of it wooded.

Nearby Natural Attractions

Taylorsville Reserve is one of nine nature sites managed by the park district. The other reserves described in the book are Englewood, Germantown, and Sugarcreek. Sycamore State Park also is located in Montgomery County.

Access

The reserve is open daily from 8 a.m. to dusk, except on Christmas and New Year's Day when the grounds are closed.

The 3.5-mile trail described below is moderately rugged by Ohio standards (piece of cake for Adirondackers), but easy to follow. The trail becomes rocky, narrow, and steep in ravines. Benches appear every so often to rest weary legs. A half dozen connecting trails shorten the walk. Pick up a guide to the reserve (found in the parking area or shelter house) before setting out.

From the stone shelterhouse built by the Civilian Conservation Corps in 1936 head northeast to a geological feature called the Rock Outcrop. The trail continues north, parallel to U.S. 40, which sits atop the limestone escarpment at your right. After passing through a picnic area, the first of seven connecting trails appears on the left. Ignore all of these shortcuts. Continue north until you reach an open area serving a powerline. However, before reaching this landmark you will cross several creek beds, pass by two more picnic areas, a stand of pines, and three shortcut trails.

At the powerline the path turns left (west), but dips into the woods to an overlook—a not-so-scenic view of utility poles crossing the river. The village of Tadmor, now a ghost town, once thrived on the far river bank. Now the trail goes south and descends into the flat floodplain. Eventually, it reaches the river and follows it downstream, or south. Again, ignore the connecting trails, unless the trail becomes flooded or you become fatigued.

The trail visits a platform overlooking the river (best viewed when the foliage has fallen from overhanging trees). Here you can return to the shelter house via a trail to the left, or finish the journey by following the river (past several small islands). Before reaching the dam, the trail curls north, through a small pine stand, to the parking lot.

The famous Buckeye Trail passes through the reserve (see map). From I-70 the "blue-blazed" foot trail traces the east bank of the river, crosses the dam, then splits. One trail heads straight north beside the old Miami-Erie Canal; the other goes east to the river then north along the west bank of the river. The trails converge again near the powerline on the west bank of the river.

Folks seeking a quick walk can hike the Forest Ridge Trail, a one-third-mile loop trail which starts at the shelterhouse, travels to the Rock Outcrop, to the overlook, and back to the start. Look for the trail guide at the shelterhouse.

Picnic areas are located throughout the reserve. The departure site has drinking water (Baker pump) and restrooms near the shelterhouse. Sledding hills are found at the TR-1 site off Brown School Road. Fishing (license required) is permitted south of the dam. The Taylorsville Dam is a favorite canoeing destination, and a canoe pick-up road west of the dam (Cassel Road) is open April through October. Canoes are not allowed through the dam. Swimming is not allowed either.

Reserve naturalists hold a variety of nature programs in the park throughout the year. A schedule of events usually hangs in the bulletin board near the shelterhouse.

For more information contact the Park District of Dayton-Montgomery County, 1375 East Siebenthaler Avenue, Dayton, Ohio 45414; phone (513) 278-8231. Taylorsville Reserve phone (513) 898-1254.

Geology

The landmark called "rock outcrop" near the shelterhouse reveals the geological history of the reserve. Some 450 million years ago (Ordovician geological period) this limestone was an ocean floor, a calcareous stew of dead sea creatures, mud, and other soggy sediments. When the ocean disappeared this limey soup, now on the surface, hardened into rock. The layer is jam-packed with fossils, but removing them is illegal.

Over time, other layers of rock and soil buried the limestone, but these were washed away by centuries of erosion and the most formidable shaper of the land in recent geological times—the glaciers.

The Great Miami River started as a storm sewer of the Wisconsinan glacier, the last ice mass to bulldoze over Ohio (18,000–12,000 years ago). The outwash of the glacier eventually formed a river which knifed through the limestone and underlying layers. The rim of the limestone escarpment once served as the river bank.

Notice that a spring gushes from the base of the outcrop. It is one of many tiny springs in the reserve which recharge the river. Look for these fountains on the hiking trail. (Although the water looks pure, drinking it is not advised because many springs are refilled by surface water which may be contaminated.) Their streams have sculpted the ravines that you must trudge across on the trail.

At this spot in 1984, when nobody was watching, 375 tons of overhanging limestone slid off the cliff and piled up at the base of the wall. The boulders crushed a trail bridge. Park officials blame the rock slide on a combination of factors: Seeping water erosion, freezing and thawing of water in cracks, tree roots wedging into cracks, and the vibrations of traffic on US 40. If left undisturbed, these factors will someday, perhaps thousands of years from now, swallow the highway.

Wildlife

Trees that typically grow in an Ohio hardwood forest can be appreciated here—oaks, beech, maples, hickory, tulip tree, black walnut, ash, and the like. "Wet feet" trees like sycamore, cottonwood, and willow grace the river banks.

Clusters of planted pine and spruce struggle to hold their ground against encroaching hardwoods.

From mid-March to mid-May wildflowers such as skunk cabbage, bloodroot, trillium, hepatica, spring beauty, Virginia bluebell, and mayapple brighten the forest floor. By June, most of these little miracles have vanished because "leafed out" trees have stolen the sunlight and darkened the ground. Animals like deer become invisible in all that summer green camouflage. Color returns in autumn, and falling leaves open the canopy.

The Great Miami River is a corridor for migrating birds—waterfowl and warblers. Adept observers may count as many as 60 different species moving through the preserve during the spring and autumn migrations. The river, in fact, may be an ancient skyway, a path these nomadic birds have followed for millennia.

During the summer, woodland birds are hard to find amidst all the greenery. On very hot days, as is the case with all wise animals, they stay hidden in shade and motionless as much as possible. Birders will have better luck along the river where they might spot a great blue heron quietly fishing, or flush a noisy kingfisher.

The reserve has the usual year-round residents—chickadees, nuthatches, blue jays, and cardinals. You might hear the barred owl's emphatic eight-hoot toot (who cooks for you who cooks for youaall) more often in winter. Deer are easier to see in the colder months.

History

For centuries, the Great Miami River was an important waterway for the Native American tribes who lived here. Early white settlers also plied the waters in canoes, but as commerce increased the canoe was replaced by the canal boat.

A remnant of the Miami-Erie Canal, completed in 1845, runs through the west side of the preserve. It took 20 years to hand-dig the channel that linked Cincinnati, Dayton, and Toledo. The Buckeye Trail follows the old canal route. The foundations of a canal aqueduct still stand a couple hundred yards north of the dam.

The canal brought prosperity to the village of Tadmor, located at the intersection of the canal, National Road (U.S. 40), the Great Miami River, and the Dayton-Michigan Railroad. Tadmor vanished after the canal and railroad died, and the National Road lost its traffic to the interstate highway.

The Taylorsville Dam was one of five flood control projects built in the early 1920s by the Miami Conservancy District. (The Easter Sunday flooding of Dayton in 1913 inspired the dam projects.) The land around the dam was managed as a recreational area by the Civilian Conservation Corps. When the CCC disbanded, the conservancy resumed management.

The park district, formed in 1964, began leasing the Taylorsville Dam acreage from the conservancy in the mid-1960s. The district has developed portions of the land for recreation but most of it has been set aside as a natural area. The conservancy still manages much of the land on the west bank of the river.

Journal

July 5, 1993. I have visited six natural areas today in 90° heat, and Taylorsville is the last. Except for matted grass seen at Smith Cemetery in the early morning, I have seen no evidence of white-tailed deer, and few squirrels and chipmunks. That is not surprising. Animals reduce their activity in extreme heat, plus the overwhelming greenery of the woods lets them hide easily, and escape unseen. Deer will simply freeze in their tracks and let hikers pass them undetected. In summer they survive by hiding; in leafless months they flee for their lives.

Turkey vulture

EDGE OF APPALACHIA PRESERVE

Here, in the rugged hills of Adams County, ecosystems influenced by several geological epochs present a botanist's paradise, as well as some of the most prodigious topography in the state. One stout incisor, ominously called Buzzardsroost Rock, stands sentry over one of the state's best natural panoramic views.The Edge of Appalachia Preserve System protects about 100 rare or endangered plants and animals which cling to life at the "edge" of the Appalachian Plateau.

Location

This group of 12 preserves lies about 10 miles east of West Union, near the village of Lynx. It roughly forms a 12-mile long corridor on the east bank of Ohio Brush Creek from the Ohio River to north of State Route 125.

Ownership

Cincinnati Museum of Natural History and Ohio Chapter of The Nature Conservancy.

Size & Designation

More than 10,500 acres are protected, making the Edge of Appalachia the second largest preserve in Ohio. Lynx Prairie (53 acres) is a National Natural Landmark registered by the U.S. Department of the Interior. Two other preserves in the system—Buzzardsroost Rock (465 acres) and The Wilderness—carry the same distinction.

Completing the system are Cave Hollow, The Rieveschl, Hanging Prairie, Cedar Falls, Ohio Brush Creek Swirl, Abner Hollow, Red Rock, and the Ray and Margaret Kenney preserves. Only Lynx Prairie and Buzzardsroost Rock are open to the public.

Nearby Natural Attractions

In Adams County visit Adams Lake State Park, Adams Lake Prairie and Chaparral Prairie state nature preserves, and Tranquility State Wildlife Area.

Access

The climb to Buzzardsroost Rock begins at the parking lot on the south side of Weaver Road, off State Route 125, and east of Ohio Brush Creek. Weaver Road is a staple-shaped loop road that begins and ends at SR 125.

The trail heads south, crosses SR 125, and enters the woods. After crossing the footbridge that spans Easter Run (look for the small waterfall at the right) the path zigzags through a thick, new growth forest and a cedar grove. Just beyond a group of house-sized dolomite boulders, the trail turns left and begins a steep and strenuous climb to the promontory.

An oak forest crowns the top of the ridge. The trail dips into a hollow, bends right, then proceeds along the edge of ridge. Finally you reach the prow of this rock formation. A boardwalk on the summit leads to an observation deck where the beauty of Adams County unfolds below.

I rate this one of the best overlooks in the state. Besides the wonderful view, you experience the harsh environment, especially the brisk wind, on the rock. In spite of their ungainly appearance and undeserved notoriety, the turkey vultures (or buzzards) are a joy to watch soaring on thermals. This spot also served as a lookout for Indians.

Simply backtrack to reach the starting point. The round trip is about 3 miles. The path is easy enough to follow. It is narrower than many paths and blocked in places by fallen trees, but these features add to the excitement and challenge of the journey. Small children easily bound over obstacles for adults.

To reach Lynx Prairie, travel to Lynx on SR 125, then south on Tulip Road for a half mile to East Liberty Church.

Park by the white fence at the end of the driveway. The trail begins at the southeast corner (to the right) of the church cemetery. Here you will find a plaque commemorating Lynx Prairie and Buzzardsroost Rock as National Natural Landmarks.

The double-loop trail is flat, narrow, and wet in spots. Visit in July, August, and September when the prairie blooms.

The red and white blazed trails stem from the main path. The trails visit 10 disconnected prairie islands surrounded by cedars, shrubs, and hardwoods.

Contact the Cincinnati Museum of Natural History, Union Terminal, 1301 Western Avenue, Cincinnati, Ohio 45203; phone (513) 287-7020; or the preserve director at Edge of Appalachia Preserves, 19 Abner Hollow Road, Lynx, Ohio 45650; phone (513) 544-2880 for a schedule of educational programs, information on group outings, or permission to visit the other preserves. Facilities like restrooms, picnic tables, drinking water, etc. are not available in these preserves.

Geology

The secrets of the rich diversity of plants here are locked in the rocks below. Three dramatic geological events have made the "Edge" a remarkable place.

As its name implies, the preserves straddle the boundary of the Appalachian Plateau (or Appalachian Escarpment) east of Ohio Brush Creek, and the Interior Low Plateau to the west. This geological border, which runs diagonally through Ohio from northeast to southwest, and as far south as Alabama, also acts as a biological demarcation. In the eastern third of Adams County, the "edge," or brink, of the plateau travels north-south facing Ohio Brush Creek. This is the only place in Ohio where the escarpment is dramatically exposed.

Now board a time capsule and go back 410–440 million years ago to the Silurian geological period. During this time forces in the Earth's crust created a fold, or roll, known as the Cincinnati Arch. Imagine that Cincinnati sits on the crest of this arch with the rock sloping gently west and east (also northward).

Erosion over many millennia washed away much of the crest, exposing ancient limestone and shale of the Ordovician Period (450 million years ago) as well as formations of Silurian and younger Devonian (350–410 million years ago) rock. The Edge of Appalachia preserves sit on the eastern "edge" of this erosion.

So, in this compact area, you will find the plants that grow in soils derived from Ordovician, Silurian, and Devonian rocks. An educated observer can trace the borders of these soil-rock types by reading the vegetation lines.

Another influence, the ancient Teays River, explains why some plants have been orphaned from their relatives in the southwestern Appalachians. The Teays River flowed through Ohio from southeast to the northwest. Tributaries feeding this preglacial river drained the area. An endangered plant like cliff-green, also called Canby's mountain lover, migrated up the tributaries. This rare evergreen grows at the Edge.

Successive glaciers bulldozed everything in their path, even the great Teays River. However, the ice sheets stopped about 10 miles north of the preserves, and cut off the southern plants from their kin.

Buzzardsroost Rock, separated from the main wall by a 50-foot cleft (hence its other name, Split Rock), boasts the steepest topographical relief in Ohio. This tarnished rock molar from the Siluran geologic period (420 million years ago) measures 81 x 75 x 36 feet. The slump rocks you pass on the trail, and Buzzardsroost Rock itself, are composed of Peebles dolomite (whitish color). This stratum lies above a thinner layer of Bisher dolomite (yellowish), Crab Orchard shale, Brassfield limestone (exposed at Easter Run Falls), and Richmond formation (beds of limestone and shale). Ohio Brush Creek (at the right from the overlook) flows over this latter formation in this area.

The rock creating the whale-back, or swelling, behind the promontory is Ohio black shale, a younger, Devonian-aged formation. The roots of toppled trees grip shards of this shale.

Wildlife

As noted above, the preserves support plants growing at the outer limits of their range. You will also find odd plant communities competing in the same locale—the eastern deciduous (hardwood) forest, the prairie, the north woods or boreal forest.

At Lynx Prairie, for example, red cedars ring one prairie opening and mark the border between soils derived from Devonian black shale (for the cedars) and Silurian dolomite (for the prairie). Pines and other "acid-tolerant" plants (blueberry, huckleberry) also appear in the "sour" soil derived from shale, both at Lynx Prairie and Buzzardsroost Rock. False aloe, an agave plant common in the Southwest, grows in the prairie too.

Note the prairie grasses—big and little bluestem, Indian grass and side-oat grama—as well as the wildflowers like purple coneflower, blazing star, rattlesnake master (potentially threatened), obedient plant, lobelia, prairie dock, and others.

There may be as many 100 patches of prairie in the preserves, allowing 250 plant varieties to bloom. These prairies are remnants of a larger prairie that swept into Ohio long ago. Exactly when the Adams County prairies arrived, and what areas they occupied, are still being debated.

Dr. Emma Lucy Braun thought the prairie patches in Adams County were relicts of early prairie invasions, perhaps 100,000 years old. Lynx Prairie and nearby Adams Lake and Chaparral prairies are examples of the ancient prairie. (Also see the Darby Plains for a discussion on younger prairies.)

The prairies in the Edge may have stretched to SR 125 in the 1910s, according to Dr. Braun. The extensive farming being practiced then kept the forest at bay and actually may have helped the prairie survive. Red cedars also dotted the prairie landscape 80 years ago.

Dr. Braun named each of the 10 prairies in the preserve. The names describe the wildlife you will see and three describe shape and location. One site is Annette's Prairie, named after her sister, a zoologist who helped in all field work. Another is called Elizabeth's Prairie.

Buzzardsroost Rock also harbors a small prairie of roughly 20 species. Trees have not taken root because of severe exposure to sun, heavy winds, and lack of water.

Elsewhere, a rare saxifrage and wall rue spleenwort (a threatened fern) cling to some cliffs. Northern white cedars (arbor vitae), stowaways on the last (Wisconsinan) glacier, have migrated into the preserves. This potentially threatened species is found in only two other places in Ohio—Cedar Bog and Clifton Gorge nature preserves.

The cliff-dwelling sullivantia, a potentially threatened plant in Ohio, thrives in a few cool gorges, and in the dolomite cracks. Tiny rock gardens grow in the pocked Peebles dolomite (a good reason for not climbing the slump rocks beside the trail). Here struggles wild columine, purple-stemmed cliffbrake (a rare fern), and rock cresses (four species are endangered in Ohio). The potentially threatened Carolina buckthorn encroaches on the edges of the prairies, along with redbud and dogwoood.

The endangered green salamander and the Allegheny wood rat reside here. In mature forests look for the pileated woodpecker, several kinds of hawks, warblers, and vireos. Turkey and black vultures, or buzzards, soar above the cliffs, inspiring the name for Buzzardsroost Rock. The black vulture carries the "special interest" designation, meaning it is a potentially threatened bird. Bluegrosbeaks, Hens-low's sparrows, and indigo buntings have been spotted, too.

History

In 1959, the Ohio Chapter of The Nature Conservancy purchased its first land in Ohio, the 53 acres comprising Lynx Prairie. Officially, this preserve is the E. Lucy Braun Preserve, honoring the University of Cincinnati botanist, author, ecologist, and conservationist whose studies brought national attention to this unique natural area.

Buzzardsroost Rock, also known as the Christian and Emma Goetz Nature Preserve,was acquired by the conservancy using contributions from three Cincinnati garden clubs.

Due to Dr. Braun's work, Lynx Prairie was dedicated a National Natural Landmark by the U.S. Department of Interior in April 1967. That distinction also is held by Buzzardsroost Rock and The Wilderness preserves (December 1974).

Richard and Lucille Durrell, whose names appear in the title of the preserve system, have been long-time champions, organizers, and benefactors of this "ark" in southern Ohio. Both are retired geologists from the University of Cincinnati.The Kenney Preserve is a gift from Ray and Margaret Kenney, the latter a student of the renowned Dr. Braun.

Edge of Appalachia may be the largest museum land holding in the United States.

Journal

September 2, 1993. *A biker I meet on the trail tells me I will not be disappointed by the view at Buzzardsroost Rock. A half dozen buzzards swirled above the cliff, he said.*

When I arrived, the buzzards were not flying (my luck) but the view was splendid. The tops of oaks and tulip trees, rooted in the valley below, almost reached the brow of the rock.

Then I saw a shadow paint a black line across the canopy. A pair of buzzards hovered above, appearing on cue for the latest visitor. Altogether, five vultures winged around the cliff—soaring, dipping, circulating. They performed for 20 minutes, then vanished—my cue to leave.

Walking fern

FORT HILL STATE MEMORIAL

We can imagine what inspired the Hopewell people to build the astonishing earthworks on this lofty site. Its elevation offered protection and the extravagant forest and creek provided nourishment. Perhaps, though, they were just struck by its simple, natural beauty, and saw it as a sacred place.

Location

Southeastern Highland County, Brush Creek Township.

From Hillsboro, the county seat, travel east 10 miles on U.S. Route 50, then south (right) seven miles on State Route 753. Go right (south) on SR 41. The entrance will appear on the right in a half mile. From Chillicothe travel west on US 50.

Ownership

Ohio Historical Society.

Size & Designation

This state memorial encompasses 1,200 acres.

Nearby Natural Attractions

Rocky Fork and Paint Creek state parks, both in Highland County, are just minutes away from Fort Hill. The county boasts Fallsville and Oldaker state wildlife areas.

Another archeological wonder, Serpent Mound State Memorial, is in northeastern Adams County, a 20-minute drive from Fort Hill.

Access

Drive past the museum, cross the narrow bridge, and park at the right of the loop-shaped parking lot. Look for wooden signs to the trailheads. Picnic tables ring the parking lot. You also will find restrooms, a shelter house, and a soda pop machine. Check out the information board and trail map before departing. Brochures might reside in the mailbox at the board.

Decisions. There are 10 miles of nature trails at Fort Hill. If your primary interest is the Indian embankment then you will want to walk the two-mile Fort Trail which begins at the information board, ascends the steep hill, and loops around the ridge before returning to the parking lot. The hike up the hill certainly makes you appreciate the effort required to build the earthworks. The overlook at the top (best viewed in the winter when the vegetation is gone) is a small reward for your strain.

The Fort Trail is recommended for folks with limited time and endurance, or with small kids in tow. A steep climb greets the hiker but once you reach the summit, the trail flattens, topographically speaking.

The 4.5-mile path described below is for adventurous hikers seeking a challenging and rugged journey featuring quietude, solitude, and hidden geological wonders. The terrain is hilly, steep in places, rocky, rooty, and slippery. The path gets thin in places, and blocked by fallen trees. The color-coded trails and signposts keep you on the right track.

This trail visits Baker Fork Gorge and the earthworks. Four trails depart from the northeast corner of the parking lot—the Gorge Trail (yellow metal blazes), the American Discovery Trail, the Deer Trail (blue metal blazes), and a section of the Buckeye Trail (blue-painted markers).

This combined trail swings west into the Baker Fork valley where you will march around outcroppings of dolomite, hike under cliffs of dolomite, and climb to perchs of dolomite overlooking the creek. Another decision:

The Deer and Buckeye trails split from the Gorge Trail about a mile into the adventure and head west (right) across Baker Fork. They strain up to Reed's Hill (in half a mile you ascend 350 feet), then turn south into a hollow and up to Jarnigan's Knob, elevation 1,273 feet. From here they descend to Baker Fork and rejoin the Gorge Trail.

The Gorge Trail continues south along Baker Fork. Just beyond the trail split you will come to a clearing with a log cabin. (It is okay to walk inside, but do not add graffiti to the walls.) Ahead, look for the natural bridges on the opposite bank of Baker Fork. The second and most spectacular natural arch yawns above the creek. The rill that sculpted this little masterpiece still drools through the pore and down a waterfall.

The merger of the Gorge, Deer and Buckeye trails is just south of this dolomite gem. You are about halfway through the journey.

The trail follows the creek for a while before turning east (left) up a steep slope. Another natural bridge, smaller than the others, appears on the right. Soon an old road joins from the right, and the trail becomes wider and smoother. Folks hiking the Buckeye Trail want to go right (south) on this lane.

A few hundred feet ahead the Deer Trail heads off to the right and returns to the parking lot. However, I recommend staying on the Gorge Trail which climbs to the summit of Fort Hill.

Next, turn left on the Fort Trail (red blazes) which visits the Indian earthworks atop Fort Hill, elevation 1,255 feet. (The Gorge Trail goes straight to the parking lot.) The embankments will be on your left.

Though recognizable year-round, the mounds and surrounding countryside are best seen during the winter. Stop at the overlook at the north end of the "fortress" before dropping off the ridge and returning to the parking lot.

I hiked this trail on a hot, muggy day in early September and found it strenuous, but exhilarating. Located far from the rat race, the only human sounds were my footfalls. Go ahead and snooze beneath a tree by the natural bridge.

Protect yourself with insect repellent if you come here in the summer. Winter hikes will offer better views of the geological features and rugged terrain.

The trails are open from 8 a.m.-8 p.m. daily. The Fort Hill museum, boasting exhibits on the archeological and natural features in the preserve, has irregular hours and was not open when I visited. Only one person manages the entire property.

For more information contact the Ohio Historical Society, 1982 Velma Avenue, Columbus, Ohio 43211; phone (614)-297-2300; or Fort Hill State Memorial at (513) 588-3221.

Geology

Like the Edge of Appalachia Preserve to the south, Fort Hill lies on the "edge" or boundary of different geological regions. It stands as one of the westernmost outliers of the Appalachian Plateau which rises to the east. The Central Lowland spreads out to the west. The preserve also marks the border between glaciated and unglaciated Ohio. The Wisconsinan glacier flattened the lowlands to the north and west, but never touched the highlands (hence the county name) here.

A finger of the glacier did probe into an area known as the Beech Flats, northeast of Fort Hill. The ice dammed the Paint Creek valley and created a new divide. Two new streams, fed by the melting glacier, drained into different systems. Heads Branch entered Rocky Fork Creek while Bakers Fork cut through a gap west of Fort Hill and refreshed Ohio Brush Creek.

The cliffs above Bakers Fork and along the Gorge Trail consist of Peebles dolomite, whose origin dates back about 410 million years ago to the Silurian geological period. Similar to limestone, dolomite contains large amounts of calcium derived from marine life whose remains fell to the floor of an ocean that covered Ohio. This ocean bed later hardened into bedrock.

Ohio shale of the Devonian era (375 million years ago) rests above the dolomite and comprises the thickest layer on the hill. This is topped by thinner layers of Bedford shale and Berea sandstone, both products of the Mississippian geologic period (320-345 million years ago). The shales and sandstone represent the floors of later oceans, only these were much shallower seas. The forest mat covers these younger bedrocks, so few outcrops appear.

Three natural rock bridges can be seen from the Gorge Trail on the west wall of Baker Fork. Two of them may be hard to spot behind vegetation in the summer, but only the most self-absorbed hiker would fail to be impressed by the formation found near the intersection of the Gorge and Deer trails. A recluse named David Davis lived in one of the recess caves on the west wall in the mid-19th century.

Be ready for rugged terrain. The summit of Fort Hill stands more than 420 feet above the water level of Baker Fork, and reaches an elevation of 1,280 feet.

Wildlife

Because of its unique geographic position, geological history, and difficult terrain, the state memorial protects one of the most botanically diverse areas in southwestern Ohio.

The soils derived from the various bedrocks support their favorite plants. The flora thriving on the cool, moist north and east hillsides differs from the plants rooted on the warm, drier south and west facing slopes.

Several plants and animals listed as rarities in Ohio find refuge here. One of these is Canby's mountain lover, or cliff-green, an endangered plant in Ohio, which clings to life on the edge of the dolomite cliffs. This creeping survivor entered Ohio from the south along the ancient and abandoned Teays River valley. It lives in only one other location in the state, the Edge of Appalachia preserve in neighboring Adams County. Fort Hill's remnant community lies at the northwestern frontier of this plant's range.

Sullivantia (potentially threatened) and the rare Canada yew, both plants from northern climates, came here in the vanguard of the glacier and found a habitat in the gorge. Sullivantia was collected and studied for the first time in 1839 by William Starling Sullivant, an early Ohio botanist whose father, Lucas Sullivant, happened to have founded Columbus.

This unusual walking fern, sullivantia's other name (though it is not actually a fern), rises from the moss on rocks then spreads its slender stems along the surface. The tips take root when it finds a suitable habitat. Purple cliff-brake, another uncommon plant and a real fern, grows in crevices on the sunny side of the rocks.

Some treasures struggle at the top of the dolomite cliffs. Here the overlying shale pans out creating a narrow, harsh, and thin-soiled environment. But that's where you will find Walter's violet, an endangered wildflower which went undiscovered north of Kentucky until the 1960s. And here survives the potentially threatened dwarf hackberry, so-named because it rarely exceeds eight feet in height; and plantain-leaf pussytoes and moss phlox, somewhat rare, both of them, but unprotected.

On the sun-baked acidic upper slopes look for rock chestnut oak (at its western limit in Ohio), with purple wood-sorrel growing beneath it. Chinkapin oaks thrive in the alkaline soil of these exposed areas. Other familiar plateau species sink roots here, such as huckleberry, round-leaf greenbrier, low blueberry, and veined hawkweed.

Elsewhere, the forest boasts large specimens of tulip tree, sugar maples, and red and white oak, among others. Many American chestnut trees filled out to diameters of five feet before they were felled by disease.

Other flowers begging for your glance include wild geranium, wood-poppy, black cohosh, Solomon's plume, zigzag goldenrod, and purple spring-cress. Bulblet fern is tucked away in the nooks and crannies of the cliffs.

With so many different habitats colliding, the state memorial sponsors a rich assemblage of birds. Scan the treetops for scarlet tanager, red-bellied and hairy woodpeckers, crested flycatcher, wood pewee, tufted titmouse, white-breasted nuthatch, blue-gray gnatcatcher, yellow-throated vireo, and cerulean warbler.

In the tree canopy look for warblers (14 kinds such as the Kentucky, black-and-white, worm-eating, redstart, and hooded), red-eyed vireo, ovenbird, wood thrush, Acadian flycatcher, and the downy woodpecker.

Near streams see if you can glimpse the Carolina wren (the largest of Ohio's wren and one of its most memorable singers), the yellow, parula, and so-called sycamore warblers, and phoebes and rough-winged swallow (tucked in the dolomite cliffs along Baker Fork). Clearings in the forest attract the yellow-billed cuckoo, flicker, and ruby-throated hummingbird.

The thickets of saplings at the edge of the forest and field conceal towhees, yellow-breasted chat, indigo bunting, goldfinches, and the omnipresent cardinal.

Hikers might flush ruffed grouse or whippoorwill. Great horned and barred owls, red-tailed hawk, and turkey and black vultures cruise the airways above the forest. The rare black vulture (listed as a special interest bird in Ohio), here at the northern edge of its range, is distinguished from its commonly seen cousin, the turkey vulture, by a splash of white on the wing tips.

Butterflies are plentiful. Test your powers of observation by seeking rarities named brown elfin (feeding on redbud trees), olive hairstreak (red cedar eater), and the extremely rare early hairstreak, seen by the historical society's natural history curator in April 1947.

Daring nature lovers can find the rare wood-eating cockroach in the caverns of rotting logs. These peculiar critters care for their offspring, one of only a handful of insects who do. The preserve is the northwesternmost limit of its habitat.

Another miracle, Sanborn's crawfish, reaches its westernmost influence in the waters of Baker Fork.

History

The stone and earthen embankment on the top of Fort Hill was constructed by the Ancient People (probably the Hopewell Indians) long before Europeans migrated to North America. Excavations did not turn up artifacts to identify the builders. Nevertheless, scholars figure the "fort" was erected by the same people who constructed nearby circular earthworks, namely the Hopewell Indians whose heydey ranged from 300 B.C.–600 A.D.

"Fort" implies an earthwork for military defense. Earlier witnesses concluded it must have been a defensive structure because of its location on high ground near known villages. More likely, the enclosure was a ceremonial site, perhaps a place for crowded religious gatherings, though this is an educated guess. Nobody can explain the absence of artifacts, nor the actual goings-on atop this knob.

The embankment is an amazing accomplishment, considering the primitive tools used back then. The earthwork encloses 40 acres. Three borrow pits, where dirt for the mounds was excavated, become intermittent ponds.

The wall measures a little more than 1.5 miles, and has 33 irregularly spaced gateways, or gaps. The reason for the gaps remains a mystery to archeologists. The height (perhaps uniform long ago) ranges from 6–15 feet, and the width at the base is about 40 feet.

The embankment lies just below the actual summit level of the hill. In some places it descends more steeply than the natural slope of the hill. Slabs of Berea sandstone mined from the summit serve as a foundation.

A cross-section of the wall indicates the builders had an elaborate blueprint, proof of their skill as planners and organizers. First, they raised the natural slope slightly with dirt and topped it with flat stones. Then they piled on more soil and capped it with more rock. The slabs retarded erosion, strengthened the walls, and gave builders solid stepping stones.

It is not known if the native civilizations succeeding the Hopewell Indians knew the significance of the earthworks. When white settlers arrived in the late 18th century an ancient forest of towering trees concealed the embankment. John Locke, an early naturalist, estimated in 1838 that one chestnut standing on the wall and a tulip tree beside it were 600 years old.

The area was part of the Virginia Military District, land set aside between the Scioto and Little Miami rivers for veterans of the Revolutionary War. John Wilcoxson established a settlement in 1795 near Sinking Spring (though he did not stay long), and Jacob Hiestand owned a nearby tavern in 1807.

Settlers usually traveled along Limestone Road (now State Route 41) which joined Wheeling, West Virginia, and Limestone (today's Maysville), Kentucky. This rugged road, following the Zane Trace laid out in 1797, supposedly was one of the earliest stage routes in the Northwest Territory.

Sawmills and gristmills appeared on Baker Fork in the early 1800s. Reed's Mill (actually built by Henry Countryman in 1802) operated on the north side of the grounds, hence the name of Reed's Hill. The sawmills, of course, had ample supples of virgin timber. A 1860 tannery, in Lincolnville, used the bark of chestnut oaks in the tanning process.

Baker Fork sheltered a hermit named David Davis in the mid-19th century. Davis reportedly made a paint from a rose-colored mineral and sold it in the area.

The state established the preserve in 1932 with the help of local citizens. More land has been acquired over the years, bringing the total to 1,200 acres. Trails and facilities have been constructed with the help of the Civilian Conservation Corps and National Park Service. A museum featuring archeological and natural history exhibits was constructed in 1968.

Journal

Sitting on a log and studying the slender, snaking mound, I am tempted to write my own story about the builders of the Fort Hill earthworks. I suspect the Hopewell Indians moved to a better site before completing the enclosure. That could explain the gaps in the wall and the absence of artifacts.

The gateways are simply unfilled openings in the wall, perhaps paths for workers treading between the interior and exterior slopes. It certainly is easier to carry tools, rock, and dirt through level gaps than over mounds, even slight elevations. Though erosion has randomly worn down the earthwork to odd heights, one could argue the original height of the embankment also was irregular because it was not finished.

Because of its unfinished state, no group ceremonies had been held and no permanent settlements were established on the summit, so the debris of large-scale human gatherings would not have been uncovered. Vital building tools were removed to a more promising site, or left to rot and hide in the humus.

I cannot picture why they abandoned the site. Perhaps they found a better hilltop with more earth and rocks that broke easily from their solid foundations? Who knows?

Yellow Spring

GLEN HELEN NATURE PRESERVE

Glen Helen has it all—babbling brooks, a scenic river, fountains of golden spring water, glens, caves, moving rock pillars, summer nature camps, a hospital for hawks, covered bridges, a school forest, a pine forest and prairie, a butterfly preserve, a swinging cable bridge, historic sites, cool cascades, a forest, an Indian mound, an abundance of birdsong and wildflowers, a handsome visitors center and museum, cliffs, trails going every which way, a national following, a cadre of protectors, a quarterly newsletter, plenty of land and money, and so many shrines that the place has a mythical life of its own. ★

Location

Greene County, Yellow Springs.

Central Ohio travelers take Interstate 70 west, then south 6.5 miles on State Route 68 to Yellow Springs. Turn left at the first traffic light onto Corry Street. The parking lot to the main entrance will be a half mile away on your left. Dayton and Cincinnati area travelers take Interstate 675 to the Dayton-Yellow Springs Road exit. Go east six miles to Yellow Springs. Turn right on Corry Street, beyond SR 68, to the parking lot.

Ownership

Antioch College, Yellow Springs.

Size & Designation

Glen Helen is a privately owned 1,000-acre nature preserve and outdoor education center. The U.S. Department of the Interior designated the preserve a National Natural Landmark in October 1965. The Little Miami River is a national and a state scenic river.

Nearby Natural Attractions

Next door is John Bryan State Park and Clifton Gorge State Nature Preserve. Little Miami State Park and Spring Valley State Wildlife Area are located in southwestern Greene County. Also visit Indian Mound Reserve and The Narrows Reserve (Greene County parks), and Sugarcreek Reservation, a Dayton Metropark.

Access

Glen Helen offers a complex web of interconnecting nature trails, adding up to 20 miles. They are open during daylight hours. The paths briefly described below will whet your appetite, but I recommend just letting your eyes and curiosity be your guide. Trail maps are found at the Glen Helen Building (visitors center) and the Trailside Museum.

Folks interested in geology might trace the path outlined in booklet entitled "Teaching Geology in Glen Helen," available at the visitors center. Starting at the preserve's Outdoor Education Center (off State Route 343), the geology trail visits features in the western portion of the glen, such the Cascades on Birch Creek, Helen's Stone, the Yellow Springs, Bone Cave, a travertine mound, Pompey's Pillar, and the Blue Hole.

The most challenging walk might be a 10-miler established by local Boy Scouts. This one starts at the visitors center, descends into the ravine, and follows Yellow Springs Creek downstream to its confluence with the Little Miami River. Here you cross to the south shore of the river and hike into the south glen. Turn around at Jacoby Road, bear right at the next fork, and climb a ravine. The trail returns to the North Glen, passing Grinnell Mill (a national historical landmark), and memorials to Horace Mann, founder of Antioch College, and Erastus Birch, one of the first college trustees. Turning north the trail marches through a pine forest, passes the Cascades of Birch Creek, and returns to the starting point.

Numbered signposts on the trails designate locations along the historical trail. Pick up a "Guide to Historical Spots in Glen Helen" at the visitors center. Consult your trail map as you proceed, and mark your progress and location as you walk.

Children usually hurry to the Swinging Bridge, an elevated cable footbridge across Yellow Springs which recalls those scary rope bridge scenes in Tarzan or Indiana Jones movies.

The Glen Helen Building, 405 Corry Street, has restrooms, gift shop, meeting rooms, and exhibits. The Trailside Museum, a favorite children's hangout, has natural history exhibits and hands-on curiosities. A blind for observing wildlife is located on the trail between the buildings. The museum and Glen Helen building are open Tuesday-Saturday, 9:30 a.m.- 4:30 p.m., and Sunday 1-4:30 p.m.

Since 1956, the Glen Helen Outdoor Education Center has held summer camps and weekend nature programs for groups of people of every age. Injured and sick birds of prey repair at the OEC's Raptor Center, open for visitors.

Fishing is allowed in the preserve only in the Little Miami River south of Grinnell Road. Additional parking is located in the Yellow Springs lot off SR 343.

Geology

The creeks that have gouged ever-deepening ravines in the glen expose rock created about 500 million years ago. To see all the layers, go to the crossing on Birch Creek known as the Stepping Stones and walk upstream. You start off standing on bedrock called Dayton limestone. Rising from the creek the west bank shows alternating layers of shale (Osgood), limestone (Laurel), shale, three types of dolomite (Euphemia, Springfield and Cedarville), topped by glacial till (a blend of clay, sand, and gravel that serves as the foundation for soil).

The dolomite and limestone deposits signal the presence of marine animals. The remains of these ancient creatures sank to the bottom of oceans that inundated the continents. Shale is essentially compressed mud (clay and fine-grained quartz) also deposited in sea floors.

The youngest strata, the dolomites, were formed a mere 400 million years ago. But not all dolomites are alike. Notice that the top layer, Cedarville, appears dense and chunky, while the ones below it are thinner and brick-like. It also is important to know that Cedarville dolomite resists erosion more than the other dolomites. (See Clifton Gorge State Nature Preserve.) And of all the strata here, shale is the least resistant to erosion, meaning it wears away faster than limestone and dolomite.

Knowing this gives you insight into the formation of the cascades and the Blue Hole below the falls. The turbulence and spray behind the cascade erodes the less resistant Euphemia and Springfield dolomites, creating stairs and ledges beneath the lip of resistant Cedarville dolomite. This undercutting action eventually weakens the support beneath the cap, causing it to fall into the stream.

A short distance downstream is the Blue Hole, where Birch Creek tumbles over a small ledge of Euphemia dolomite into a round pool. The creek has washed away the shale beneath the dolomite creating the crescent-shaped falls.

The village derived its name from the "yellow springs" found in the glen between Yellow Springs Creek and Birch Creek. The spring bubbles from a dolomite outcrop and flows at the brisk pace of 68-80 gallons a minute. The water temperature is always around 55ºF.

The "yellow" (actually rust-color) in the water comes from iron pyrite (also known as fool's gold) deposits in the rock. The water is much clearer than the orange-colored rocks let you think; nevertheless, don't drink from the spring.

Nearby is an unusual travertine mound some 75 feet high and 500 feet across. It began growing as the continental Wisconsinan glacier retreated from Ohio about 15,000 years ago. Water flowing from the Yellow Spring has given the soil on the mound its orange tint. The mound is mostly composed of calcium carbonate (85 percent), iron oxide (6 percent) and organic material.

Pompey's Pillar looks like a lonely chess piece awaiting nature's next move. It split from the wall long ago and has been sliding downhill ever since. Geologists call this slow slide "creeping." During a freeze the earth expands and lifts up the pillar, but during a thaw gravity takes over and pushes it ever so slightly down the slope.

Careful observers will find cavities in the cliffs. These lead to small caves in limestone formations. Water which became acidic when it seaped through the dead vegetation of the hardwood forest dissolves through cracks in the limestone. As erosion occurs these slits grow into crevices and holes in the bedrock. These subterranean water vessels dry up when the water, for any number of reasons, stops flowing. Passages that open at the ground are called caves. The most famous one in the preserve is Bone Cave. Supposedly, a dozen fourth graders can be stuffed into this hole. But don't try it!

Boulders of igneous rock, called erratics, dumped here from Canada by the glaciers, are strewn throughout the grounds. An example is Helen's Stone, located near the Yellow Springs parking lot.

Wildlife

Few places are more blessed and enriched with wildflowers and birds. Seventy-four varieties of blossoms have been counted in the late winter and spring, and 76 species during the summer.

Mayapples and trilliums are easy enough to spot in spring but can you find squirrel corn, stonecrop, golden Alexander, corn salad, dwarf larkspur, showy orchis, or jack-in-the-pulpit? This summer look for flora named enchanter's nightshade, dogbane, boneset, beggar's ticks, flower-of-an-hour, moneywort, selfheal, bouncing bet, and sweet flag. Pick up checklists at the visitors center before exploring.

The Glen Helen Association Birding Group keeps track of the feathered animals in the preserve. The group has recorded sightings of 145 different species in the glen. Some of them are rare or occasional visitors. Year-round residents include the red-tailed hawk, belted kingfisher, pileated woodpecker, cedar waxwing, and American goldfinch. The gift shop has a checklist.

In the summer, butterflies rise in flocks at the Ralph Ramey Butterfly Preserve in the south glen. Ramey, director of Glen Helen from 1973–1990, is the former head of the Division of Natural Areas and Preserves at the Ohio Department of Natural Resources.

History

Native Americans enjoyed the cool waters in the glen for centuries. A mound built by the Hopewell people is located between the cascades and spring. The glen fell within the stomping grounds of the Miami and Shawnee nations. The latter tribe built its central village on the banks of the Little Miami River just six miles away at Oldtown. The Indians considered the water from the yellow spring a health potion and a major trail passed near this landmark.

The first white settlement in the early 19th century was a stagecoach tavern. Later, came water, mills, Antioch College, and railroad tracks. The yellow spring also attracted tourists seeking scenery and medicinal water. By the second half of the 19th century, the glen had become a vacation resort.

The glen's popularity as a tourist destination faded by the turn of the century. It now was sought as a nature sanctuary. Antioch College's president, Arthur Morgan, started the trend by purchasing some of it for the college in the 1920s. But it was a Chicago attorney and Antioch alumnus, Hugh Tayor Birch, who bought many parcels and gave them all to the college in 1929.

He called the place Glen Helen, in honor of his daughter. A commemorative plaque embedded in a glacial erratic, called Helen's Stone, rests near the Yellow Spring parking lot. Birch Creek remembers the benefactor, not the tree.

Over the years, more land has been acquired, and facilities such as an outdoor education center (1956), visitors center, museum, and raptor center have been added.

The pine forest in north glen was planted by the Ohio Department of Natural Resources, in the 1920s. For many years, local high school students have been growing and selling Christmas trees for the preserve's school forest.

The preserve was designation as a National Natural Landmark in October 1965.

Journal

May 7, 1993. Near the yellow spring a large boulder orphaned from its northern origin lies beneath a mammoth white oak. Locals call this shrine Helen's Stone because a plaque bearing a poem written by Helen Birch Bartlett, the preserve's namesake, is stamped to the rock. The rock and tree speak her words.

"The earth smells old and warm and mellow,

And all things lie at peace.

I, too, serenely lie here under the white oak tree,

And know the splendid flight of hours,

All blue and gay, sun-drenched and still."

The verse echoes through the glen. Her father's name—Hugh Taylor Birch. I've heard that name before. The Rolodex in my brain spins—Hugh Taylor Birch State Park. The same man donated oceanfront property for a state park in the Sunshine State.

Gray-headed coneflower

GREENVILLE FALLS STATE NATURE PRESERVE

Think of a stream scouring a slightly tilted washboard—a pocked inclination of 425-million-year-old rock. That is Greenville Falls. Here, Greenville Creek, a state scenic river, tumbles like a Slinky over dolomite and limestone rocks. Rather than plummeting over the lip of a ledge, the creek roils over an elongated 28-foot descent. Though Greenville Falls may not satisfy your traditional vision of a waterfall, it is worth a peek, especially near dusk in October when the puddles in the potholes reflect the crimson glow of autumn leaves.

Location

Northwest Miami County, near Covington.

From the intersection of State Routes 48 and 36 in Covington, travel west on SR 36 one mile, then left (south) .7 mile on Range Line Road, and right (west) on Covington-Gettysburg Road just one-tenth mile to a small gravel parking lot for 2–3 cars.

Ownership

Ohio Department of Natural Resources, Division of Natural Areas and Preserves.

Size & Designation

Greenville Falls State Nature Preserve is a 79.4-acre scenic river preserve open to the public.

Nearby Natural Attractions

Waterfalls aficionados can spend a day touring Miami County's natural downspouts. Brush Creek takes several spills—one in Ludlow Falls, another behind the West Milton Inn, a privately-owned landmark at the crossroads of State Routes 48 and 571. A couple of blocks upstream you can view Overlook Park Falls, also privately owned. Kindly ask the owners for permission to peek at these cascades.

The granddaddy of them all is Charleston Falls, protected in a preserve near West Charleston. Charleston Falls, reviewed in this book, is one of four preserves managed by the Miami County Park District. The others are Big Woods Reserve, Stillwater Prairie Reserve, and F.L. Blankenship Riverside Sanctuary.

Greenville Creek joins the Stillwater River in Covington. Both currents share state scenic river designation.

Access

You will want to make a beeline to the falls. The mowed path across the field will take you to a ledge that overlooks the falls. The rocks and footing at the edge can be slippery, so be careful.

After gawking at the falls, take the riverside trail at the left, heading downstream toward the bridge. Find the natural bridge dug out by erosion. The trail concludes near the bridge on Range Line Road. Reverse the route to reach the starting point.

Officially, this is the only footpath for hikers. Please avoid the many side paths so that the land can recover from past degradation. Many local residents view the falls as an extention of their backyards and have blazed numerous paths along the banks. In the past, Greenville Falls was a popular place for "partying," swimming, fishing, and all-terrain vehicle use. Litter from these activities was a problem. Swimming, picnicking, and ATVs are no longer permitted here.

Fishing and canoeing are allowed. Anglers can wade into the river, or drop lines from the bridge or south bank, near the old electric power station. Smallmouth bass is the favorite catch.

Canoeists and rafters should not "shoot" over the cascade. It is more dangerous than it looks. Instead, leave the creek above the falls, and portage to a safe downstream location for reentry.

Like all state interpretive preserves, Greenville Falls opens at sunrise and closes at sunset. For more information contact the Ohio Department of Natural Resources, Division of Natural Areas and Preserves, Fountain Square, Building F-1, Columbus, Ohio 43224-1331; phone (614) 265-6453.

Geology

The bedrocks seen in the preserve are dolomite (specifically Dayton dolomite) and Brassfield limestone, the latter being the same rock found at nearby Charleston Falls and faraway Niagara Falls. These layers trace their origins to the Silurian geological period, some 425 million years ago.

These sedimentary rocks are composed of the remains of ancient sea creatures. After the ocean receded, the muddy ocean floor that entombed these plants and animals hardened into rock. The product contains high concentrations of calcium carbonate, or lime, hence the name limestone. You might find the fossils of these critters in the limestone.

A specialty of the falls are its potholes, best seen during low water periods in autumn and winter. Pebbles tumbled by the fast currents gouged these tiny pots in the limestone.

Along the river trail, notice the natural rock bridge, a result of erosion. Surface and spring water seeping through seams and cracks behind the edge of the cliff caused the rock to collapse. The activity left a slab, or bridge, spanning a recess cave.

Wildlife

Greenville Falls protects several precious and rare plants, the best reason for restricting visitors to trails. These plants are the threatened harebell and the limestone savory, wand lily, tufted hairgrass, and rock sandwort, all potentially threatened.

The trees of a mixed floodplain forest—sycamore, ash, box elder, cottonwood, and elm—are here. The striking orange blaze of sugar maples splashes the area with color in autumn. A few oaks grow on the bluff.

The Division of Natural Areas and Preserves has planted prairie grasses and flowers in the field that you cross en route to the falls. These blossoms, notable gray-headed coneflower, butterfly weed, wild nodding onion, goldenrods, and asters, explode with color under the hot midsummer sun.

History

The remnants of an old woolen and flour mill stand on the south bank of the river. Mill races and dams constructed by these industries can still be seen.

Dayton Power & Light once operated an electricity relay station at the site. The utility still owns the brick building on the south side.

The Ohio Department of Natural Resources purchased the land from the City of Covington in 1989. It was designated a state scenic preserve in 1989.

Journal

May, 1993. I caught a bare-breasted, barrel - chested man in shorts sneaking along an "unofficial" path on the south shore of the creek. But who am I to "catch" someone where they are not supposed to be? I am not, technically, supposed to be here either.

I found out he lived nearby with other refugees who had fled town life for country living. He had just "barreled" down the falls, an annual test of his manhood, which has left him scarred from his chest to his belly, but, at age fifty or so, probably salves a delicate ego. He invited me to his house, just a beer can's throw from the creek, where he had plenty of the latter stacked in neat rows in his refrigerator. He removed two cans and ruined the symmetry. The man and I talked about the creek, golf, and good books.

Finally, I had to leave, though it dawned on me as I drove away that the fellow could likely use a friend—perhaps a drinking friend, a "falls shooting" friend. Gee, I wonder where I can find him one?

Ten miles upstream from the falls, Greenville Creek flows through the city of Greenville and through the Greenville City Park. Thick with civilization, it nevertheless provides great entertainment for canoeists as they wind through the park, under the swinging bridge exiting the city to the west. I hear this creek has been the place of many adventures for young boys testing their *manhood. What is it about manhood that it always needs testing? I, for one, don't think of it as testing manhood. It's more play than anything. Testing for me means checking the car battery, my cholestoral level, and renewing my driver's license. Heavens. I'm sounding ancient. Perhaps I'd better test my pulse.*

HAMILTON COUNTY PARK DISTRICT

Nature lovers near Cincinnati can satisfy their open-air vigor at one of the 16 sites (12,000 acres) owned by the Hamilton County Park District. Since 80 percent of the parkland is reserved for wildlife, Hamilton County does not boast a maze of footpaths. Not that this is bad. Much of the parkland remains trackless and consequently, undisturbed by humans. Seven favorite sites are reviewed. You can hike with your dog provided he's on a leash no longer than six feet. (You're responsible for scoop-ups.) Purchase the annual $3 permit through the mail by writing the Hamilton County Park District, 10245 Winton Road, Cincinnati, Ohio 45231; phone (513) 521-7275. The parks are open every day from dawn to dusk.

Pileated woodpecker

- **Miami Whitewater Forest**
- **Mitchell Memorial Forest**
- **Sharon Woods Park**
- **Shawnee Lookout Park**
- **Winton Woods Park**
- **Withrow Nature Preserve**
- **Woodland Mound Park**

MIAMI WHITEWATER FOREST

The heads of four deer, all does, raised in unison to face me on an oak-covered ridge. They took turns watching me while they browsed for acorns, which rained from the trees. Through the binoculars I could see that their breath, like mine, steamed in the frosty autumn morning.

Suddenly, the most skittish in the bunch sprang to another ridge, adding 70 yards to her distance from me. The others, following their leader, bounded away in a wedge formation. They disappeared the way fog melts into clouds. Saplings, twigs, bark, leaves, and a ridge hid them though an occasional flick of a white tail. My soft footfall revealed their presence.

Later, I would surprise them in the "badlands," a woods of mounds, sinkholes, and gullies where these clever browsers can frustrate any hunter.

Location

Northwestern Hamilton County, Crosby and Whitewater townships.

From Exit 3 on Interstate 74, travel north on Dry Fork Road for a mile, then turn right on West Road. At the park's tollgate turn left and follow the driveway (Timberlakes Drive) to the parking lot (on the left) for the Badlands and Oakleaf hiking trails. A nature center is located beside the parking lot.

Ownership

Hamilton County Park District.

Size & Designation

Miami Whitewater Forest encompasses 3,639 acres.

Nearby Natural Attractions

This site is the largest of 16 parks owned by the park district. The others reviewed in these pages are Mitchell Memorial Forest (the closest one to Miami Whitewater), Shawnee Lookout, Winton Woods, Sharon Woods, Woodland Mound, and Withrow Nature Preserve.

Access

Nature hikers can choose among three foot-paths, totaling about 3.6 miles. The Oakleaf and Badlands trails depart from the same location. To reach the tallgrass Prairie Trail turn right at the park entrance on West Road, or enter from Harrison Road.

From the parking lot, the 1.25-mile Oakleaf Trail descends an oak ridge to a short causeway that passes between two woodland ponds (man-made). The loop begins at the end of the causeway. Turn right and follow the boardwalk along the edge of the upper pond. Overhanging beech limbs may cause you to duck. This spot is especially scenic in spring and autumn.

At the end of the pond, the trail swings left and climbs and loops around a knob. Note that oaks and hickories take over the top of the hill, while beech and maple dominate the slopes. The path passes near the lower lake and returns to the causeway where you can backtrack to the parking lot. The Oakleaf Trail is moderately hilly and easy to follow.

The 1.75-mile Badlands Trail begins across the street from the parking lot. This is a challenging, winding, and hilly loop trail. It also is a narrower and more rugged trail than the Oakleaf Trail.

Go left at the split for the loop. Soon you enter the "badlands," so named for the group of mounds and sinkholes, and poor soil, that made this land a "bad land" to farm. The skinny trail climbs and winds around the mounds and cedar groves of the badlands.

Ahead, the trail crosses a few ravines, traces the side of a ridge, and winds through a mature hardwood forest back to the start of the loop, and the parking lot. The Badlands Trail is the most rugged footpath in the park, a pleasant walk every season. Choose this one for a "deep woods" experience.

The Tallgrass Prairie Trail, a 2/3-mile loop path over easy terrain, visits the only prairie in Hamilton County (five acres planted in 1980), plus a mature woods, meadows, and a young woodlot. Bear right at the fork, signaling the beginning of the loop, if you are in a hurry to view the prairie (best seen when the flowers bloom from mid-July to early September). The path wanders through forest and field before completing its journey.

Another trail (not a nature trail) is the 7.8-mile outer loop of the paved Shaker Trace Multipurpose Trail, which is shared by joggers, bicyclists, and roller skaters, as well as pedestrians. An inner loop is 1.2 miles. Both loops depart from the recently renovated visitor center, which boasts the Nature's Niche gift and book shop, snack bar, restrooms and drinking water, and exhibits.

The park also has horseback riding trails, a boathouse, fishing (boat only), picnic areas, fitness trail, campground, Frisbee golf course (the first in Ohio), golf course, and playgrounds.

(Note: The Hamilton County Park District owns four state-designated nature preserves—Greenbelt and Spring Beauty Dell (within Winton Woods), Trillium Trails, and Newberry Wildlife Sanctuary—which can only be visited on appointment. The same limited visitation policy exists for Richardson Forest Preserve and Kroger Hills, both designated conservation and wildlife areas by the park district. These restricted areas are not included in this book.)

These metroparks are not free! Visitors must pay a fee, called a motor vehicle permit, upon entering a park. The annual charge is $3 (the best option if you plan to visit often); the daily fee, $1. Buy the permits at any park facility (visitor or nature centers, golf courses, marinas, ranger stations, gift shops, etc.) or from rangers and technicians.

Geology

The "badlands" in Miami Whiterwater Forest hardly resemble the Badlands in North Dakota. Still, they do fit the common definition of badlands—an odd-shaped terrain with soil unsuitable for farming.

Sinkholes give this spot its "badlands" look. These are the numerous cup-shaped depressions, or sinks, surrounded by hillocks. Sinkholes form when acidic water dissolves the underlying limestone bedrock. A cave-in occurs when the limestone (a rock containing the alkaline mineral calcite) weakens and can no longer support the soil above.

The limestone is 450 million years old (Ordovician geological period) and composed of the sediment that spread across the floor of an ancient ocean. The alkalinity of the rock derives from the remains of the marine animals that fell to the bottom of the sea. The fossils of these ancient creatures, much older than the dinosaurs, appear in the limestone.

About 20,000 years ago the vanguard of the Wisconsinan glacier stopped just north of the park. When the climate warmed huge volumes of water poured from the melting glacier and created streams like Dry Fork Creek and Whitewater River. The two currents, stems of the Great Miami River watershed, have been eroding the land ever since.

Dry Fork Creek meanders through the park before emptying into the Whitewater River. One of the creek's tributaries was dammed in 1971 to create Miami Whitewater Forest Lake.

Wildlife

Exhibits inside the nature center at the trailheads of the Oakleaf and Bandlands trails explain the animals and plants you might see in the park's various habitats.

In the mature forest, for example, look for beech and sugar maple, oaks (white, red, bur), ash, shagbark and pignut hickory, tulip tree, and wild black cherry, among others. Here live birds like the barred owl, pileated woodpecker, scarlet tanager, tufted titmouse, red-eyed vireo, wood pewee, ovenbird; mammals—gray squirrel, short-tailed shrew, white-footed mouse; mourning cloak (butterfly) and luna moth; or reptiles and amphibians, such as black rat snake, two-lined salamander, and fence lizard.

Areas of successional growth (usually a young woodlot or thicket meadow en route to becoming a mature forest) include trees like elm, black cherry, box elder, dogwood, yellow buckeye, honey locust, black gum; birds—blue-winged warbler, woodcock, goldfinch, indigo bunting, catbird; mammals—deer, woodchuck, skunk, pine vole; bugs—cicada, bald-faced hornet, walking stick; rough green snake and box turtle.

Plants such as bluegrass, broom sedge, goldenrod, and milkweed prevail in open meadows and grasslands. Here lives the red fox, rabbit, meadow vole, weasel, least shrew; birds—eastern meadowlark, dickcissel, grasshopper sparrow, bluebird; insects—monarch butterfly, bumblebees, praying mantis; reptiles and amphibians—black racer snake and toad.

In wetland habitats (ponds, streams, swamps) observe cattail, willow, water lily, skunk cabbage, swamp white oak (swamp forest), or critters like raccoon, mink, muskrat; birds—kingfisher, marsh wren, red-winged blackbird, least bittern, great blue heron; bugs—dragonfly, mayfly, mosquito; reptiles and amphibians—leopard frog, bullfrog, snapping turtle, and banded watersnake.

The Badlands Trail wanders through groves of eastern red cedar which can survive on rocky and impoverished soil. The tree provides excellent cover for many birds and usually indicates the presence of limestone in the soil, which is certainly the case in this forest. Cedars prefer open areas, but here encroaching hardwoods may someday "shade" them to death.

The Tallgrass Prairie Trail journeys to a five-acre planted prairie where beauties such as blazing star, rattlesnake master, prairie dock, purple coneflower, mountain mint, and gray coneflower rise alongside grasses called switchgrass, little bluestem, big bluestem and Indian grass.

Elsewhere, feast your eyes on wildflowers such as mayapple, rockcress, Joe-pye weed, jack-in-the-pulpit, whitetop, wild quinine, field pussytoes, Venus' looking-glass, stickseed, and monkey flower, among others.

Miami Whitewater Forest is noted for its fungi, both the nonpoisonous and the poisonous kinds. Eating wild mushrooms is risky, and picking them is prohibited. Here are some of the ones you could see (Oakleaf Trail)—earthstars, scarlet cup, stinkhorns, mycena, birds nest, emetic russula, and morels.

The park boasts 33 species of reptiles and salamanders, the greatest variety among the metroparks. One member of this community is the rare and endangered cave salamander, a colorful creature which lives near the entrance of limestone caves only in Hamilton and Adams counties.

Birdwatchers spotted 77 sandhill cranes (visiting migrants) and 32 dark-eyed (or northern) juncos in the park during an annual winter bird count in 1993. Both birds are endangered species in Ohio.

History

Miami Whitewater Forest encircles an old Shaker village, founded at New Haven in 1824. It was one of three Shaker villages in southwestern Ohio.

The sect formed in Manchester, England in 1747 after splitting from the English Quaker church. They called themselves the United Society of Believers in Christ's Second Appearing. Outsiders knew them as Shakers because of their "shakings" (gyrations and spins) during worship services.

Many Shakers moved to New York and New England after 1774 to escape religious persecution in England. Later, some moved to Ohio and established Union Village near Lebanon and Watervliet Village near Kettering, both in 1806. Next came North Union Village near Cleveland (1822) and Whitewater Village (1824), near New Haven, an offshoot of Union Village.

The Shakers lived a celibate, communal, and agriculture life. The Whitewater Village grew from 18 members on 40 acres in 1824 to 200 members on 1,700 acres in Hamilton and Butler counties in 1857. The colonies began to decline after 1870 and by 1916 Whitewater Village had ended.

The park district has acquired several Shaker buildings and is restoring them for later public visitation. One of them is the only brick meeting house (1827) in the country. Shaker meeting houses elsewhere were made of wood. Other local Shaker buildings are privately owned.

The park opened in 1949 following the purchase of

709 acres for $141.18 per acre. It has grown to 3,639 acres, making it the largest in the district. In 1978, Ohio's first Frisbee golf course was constructed here.

Cooper's hawk

MITCHELL MEMORIAL FOREST

A quotation from William Shakespeare is posted at the trailhead. "This, our life away from public haunt, finds tongues in the trees, books in the running brooks, sermons in stories, and good in everything."

The din of urban progress vanishes in this hill preserve. The pervading susurrus is sung by a chorus of rustling leaves, scurrying creatures, croaking old trees, rapturous birdsong, and the drumming of a woodpecker. Alert deer, fleeing at my footfall, seem to be the only animals frightened by my presence. The rest take no notice of me.

Location

Western Hamilton County, Miami Township.

Leave Interstate 74 at Exit 7 and head north on State Route 128 into the Village of Miamitown. At the traffic light, turn right (eastbound) on Harrison Road. About 1.5 miles, turn right (south) on Wesselman Road, then right on Buffalo Ridge Road (County Road 177), and left on Zion Road (County Road 186). The entrance is a few hundred feet ahead on the right. Park at the lot for the Wood Duck Trail on your left.

Ownership

Hamilton County Park District.

Size & Designation

The forest preserve protects 1,329 acres.

Nearby Natural Attractions

Mitchell Memorial Forest is the third largest metropark in the park system. Visit the other parks portrayed in the book—Miami Whitewater Forest, Shawnee Lookout, Winton Woods, Sharon Woods, Withrow Nature Preserve, and Woodland Mound.

Access

The Wood Duck Trail is a 1.5 mile lasso-shaped path that visits forest, brook, pond, and former field.

The path begins a gentle descent south from the parking lot down an old farm lane. Sugar maples turn this section of the trail into a kaleidoscope of golden hues in the autumn. Note, on the right, the hardwoods slowly reclaiming their turf from planted pines.

The loop trail starts near the bottom of the slope, just as the trail bends a little left after passing a sugar maple. Bear left at the fork and follow the brook. Stop alongside the rill for a spell and examine the fossils in the rock plates. Nature writer Edward Abbey called these rocks "leavemrites," short for "leave 'em right there."

The trail turns right at a gate, crosses the brook, and swings up a slope on the west side of a man-made duck pond. The dam is located at the south end of the pond. The path continues its route up the slope and curves northward along a fencerow. It goes down the ridge to the creek. Turn left, and return to the trailhead along the familiar farm lane. The moderately strenuous walk wanders for about 1.25 miles. The terrain in the rest of the forest preserve is much more rugged.

Most of Mitchell Memorial Forest is a heavily wooded nature preserve and off limits to the public. Don't come expecting to play golf, Frisbee golf, softball, or to pursue other recreational activities. However, you will find picnic areas, a playground, restrooms and drinking water, and a fishing pond.

Geology

As Shakespeare foresaw, there is a book in this running brook, and sermons in its stones. The fossil-rich limestone slabs lay scattered in the creek bed. From the fragments we assemble a picture of life on earth during the Ordovician Period, some 450 million years ago, but we are far from knowing the whole story.

The fossils embedded in the rock are the remains of extinct creatures who flourished near the bottom of an ancient tropical ocean. When they died, their bodies settled to the sea floor and mixed with other sediments. Most dissolved, but many became encased, entombed in the soup. Later, the sea floor solidified into limestone and was lifted to the surface.

Much later, the rock was buried beneath the rubble and debris left behind by the continental glaciers that swept across Ohio during the Ice Age (within the last million years). Streams born from the glaciers have cut through the debris to reveal the template of the Ordovician Period.

I lifted one fragment from the water and saw a congealed colony of fossilized snails (gastropods) piled atop one another as if they had been the victims of a mass execution. A larger plate beside it revealed a community of brachiopods, their fan-shaped, symmetrical shells widely and evenly spaced like cemetery gravestones. Lying side-by-side, the pieces did not seem to come from the same jigsaw puzzle. This discovery provokes a sermon, a possible rule of geological exploration: even leaving no stone unturned can still leave mysteries unsolved.

Wildlife

Though heavily wooded, much of Mitchell Memorial Forest is a young second growth forest, meaning that it was previous logged (perhaps several times), cleared for cultivation, grazed, or all three. Now this old farmland is being allowed to grow back.

Notice the numerous small sugar maples, the wild grape vines and berry patches, multiflora rose, redbud and dogwood trees, and wildflowers such as white snakeroot, bedstraw, and hog peanut (weeds to some people). These are some of the "indicators" of a young woods.

You will see a number of large sugar maples, sycamores, some oaks and hickories on higher, drier ground, pines (planted), and beeches too. Box elder thrives in moist spots. Eastern red cedar, which prefers open areas and limestone soils, reminds us of the land's agricultural and Ordovician past.

Birders can test their skill here searching for the wood duck (namesake of the trail), green heron, brown thrasher, wood thrush, Acadian flycatcher, rufous-sided towhee, Cooper's hawk, and warblers (blue-winged, Kentucky, pine, myrtle), brown creeper, red-breasted nuthatch, golden-crowned kinglet, and red-eyed vireo.

Several rare and protected birds have been spotted in the park, including the dark-eyed junco, yellow-bellied sapsucker, barn owl, and sandhill crane (11 sighted in December 1993)—all endangered species in Ohio. Other beauties seen here are the sharp-shinned and red-shouldered hawks, and long-eared owl, all designated "special interest," or potentially threatened.

History

Mitchell Memorial Forest became the 12th local metropark in 1977, thanks to a 617-acre gift by the late William Morris Mitchell. The donation honors his parents, William Henry and Lucile Morris Mitchell. Acquisitions have brought the total to 1,329 acres. Roughly 80 percent of the land will be retained in its natural state.

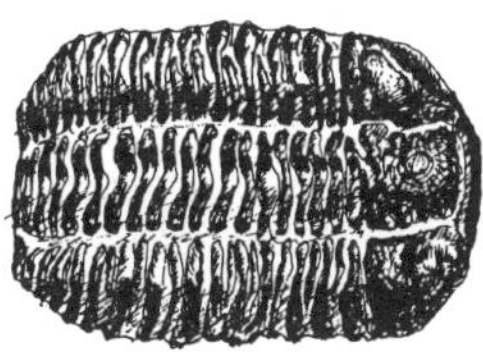

Trilobite

SHARON WOODS PARK

The fossils of extinct animals who lived in an ocean 450 million years ago rise like ghosts from the rocks in this spooky gorge. Every so often the current of Sharon Creek washes these "signatures in rock" off the steep banks.

The creek, however, is no longer unruly. The current, now just a trickle, lacks the power, and perhaps the will, to remove the rubble that hides other ghosts on the stream bank. Few striking fossils turn up anymore.

Some say it is best to keep the ancient creatures locked in their tombs. Though hidden from eyes, their haunting presence can be felt by sensitive wanderers who stop for a moment at the waterfall overlook. ♿

Location

Northeastern Hamilton County, Sycamore Township.

From Interstate 275 drive south .8 mile on U.S. Route 42, then turn left at the entrance. The driveway crosses Sharon Creek, bends left past the visitor/nature center and historical village, crosses the creek again, and curves to the right. Ignore the left turn to Sharon Harbor. Just after you travel over the bridge which spans the gorge, turn into the parking lot on the right. The lake appears across the street.

Ownership

Hamilton County Park District.

Size & Designation

Sharon Woods Gorge, just 20.8 acres, was designated a state scenic nature preserve on January 31, 1977. The metropark comprises 737 acres.

Nearby Natural Attractions

Try out these other Hamilton County Park District sites: Winton Woods, Miami Whitewater Forest, Withrow Nature Preserve, Shawnee Lookout Park, Woodland Mound Park, Richardson Forest Preserve, and Mitchell Memorial Forest.

Access

First, pick up a free park brochure and a guide for the gorge trail at the nature center before departing. The grounds open daily at dawn and close at sunset.

The Gorge Trail explores both sides of Sharon Creek. Officially, the path is called the Richard H. Durrell Gorge

Trail, named after a former park board member and geology professor at the University of Cincinnati.

The trip begins on the west side of the bridge and travels downstream. Notice the small waterfalls on the left. A little more than half a mile into the valley the trail crosses Sharon Creek over a footbridge then swings along the eastern bank of the stream. An 18-hole golf course borders the preserve on the right. Stop at the observation deck overlooking another cascade before concluding the hike on the east side of the bridge.

The walk measures about 1.25 miles. The gravel path is wide and easy to follow with a few moderate slopes to climb.

The park also features a hiking trail around the lake, a transplanted late 19th century small town called Sharon Woods Village, a boathouse and snack bar at Sharon Harbor, a fitness trail, ball fields, and numerous picnic areas. Restrooms are located at these attractions. The historical village opens to the public (admission charge) from May–October on Wednesday, Thursday, and Friday, 10 a.m.–4 p.m.; Saturday and Sunday, 1–5 p.m. Phone: (513) 563-9484.

For information on nature programs at the park, contact the Hamilton County Park District, 10245 Winton Road, Cincinnati, Ohio 45231; phone (513) 521-7275.

Geology

Sharon Creek tumbles over limestone and shale beds, the oldest exposed bedrock in Ohio. The fossils frozen in the stone show the abundant life forms that swam in an ocean 450 million years ago, during the Ordovician geologic period.

The names of these alien creatures sound otherworldly: brachiopods, bryozoans, crinoids, trilobites (the official state fossil).

These were the earthly beings who lived in the ancient tropical sea, long before mammals and dinosaurs. Their remains sank to the depths and mixed with all the other sediment on the ocean floor. When the water disappeared the deposits dried, compacted, and solidified into limestone or shale. The ecoskeletons of many creatures became embedded, or fossilized, in the rock layers.

Illustrations of these fossils appear in the trail guide. The park's small nature center has some examples, but better specimens can be viewed at the Cincinnati Museum of Natural History and similar facilities in Ohio.

Long ago Sharon Creek excavated a channel nearly 100 feet deep through layers of limestone and shale. Now, the channel is a thin brook. Several large boulders in the creek suggest that the tip of a glacier reached this spot during the last million years or so. The boulders are called "erratics," or "foreigners," chunks of igneous rocks brought here from Canada by the glaciers.

Wildlife

There is more to Sharon Woods gorge than fossils—a forest of tall timbers, a kaleidoscope of wildflowers, and a bustling community of birds.

Mature maples (sugar and silver mostly), oaks (white, red, bur), beech, sycamore, ash, tulip tree, walnut, hickories, and basswood form the canopy in this deep valley. (The flower of the basswood, or linden, supposedly produces tasty honey.) Beneath the canopy, in the understory, pawpaw, dogwoods, and ironwood (blue beech) flourish.

Closer to the ground look for these blossoms in the spring and early summer—jack-in-the-pulpit, green dragon, lady's thumb, wild comfrey, salt and pepper, white baneberry, and wild ginger, or heart's ease, used as a medicine by Indians and as a seasoning by white pioneers.

Late summer and autumn flowers include false foxglove, clammy ground cherry, Indian plantain, yellow wood sorrel, and touch-me-not (jewelweed), said to stop the itch of poison ivy, athlete's feet, and nettle. See if you can identify the Christmas, spinulose wood, and rattlesnake ferns.

Sixteen species of reptiles and amphibians, such as the red-backed salamander and ring-necked snake, were counted in the park in 1992.

During a winter count in 1992, birdwatchers recorded 32 species of birds. Around Sharon Lake, 103 mallards and 90 Canada geese floated on the water while 142 Carolina chickadees, 34 tufted titmice, and 18 nuthatches climbed trees in the woodlands searching for meals. Eighty-two robins scattered leaves on the forest floor to expose bugs and other eatables. Twenty downy and 10 red-bellied woodpeckers tapped into trees for burrowing insects. The cardinal, Ohio's state bird and a permanent resident, numbered 43. All totaled, 1,012 birds were counted.

Spring, of course, is a different story. Other birds arrive in waves, like the warblers who build nests in the canopy and raise their voices in song. The ominous-looking turkey vulture also returns, as well as some hawks, waterfowl, the scarlet tanager, hummingbird, and others. The bird population in late spring swells to many thousands.

History

Sharon Woods, originally called the Reading Tract, opened to hikers and picnickers in 1932, the first in the Hamilton County Park District. By 1938, most of the remaining parkland had been acquired.

During the years of the Great Depression, park developments were funded by the federal government, and built by workers employed by the Civilian Conservation Corps, Works Progress Administration, and Hamilton County Welfare Department.

Kreis Dam, the impoundment you see on the Gorge Trail, was finished in 1937. The dam created 35-acre Sharon Lake, but flooded a section of Sharon Gorge.

Recreational facilities have been added over the years, with an 18-hole golf course christened by the legendary golfer Bobby Jones. A two-year lake restoration project returned 50-year-old Sharon Lake to its original state. A modern Sharon Harbor opened in 1990.

The Ohio Department of Natural Resources, Division of Natural Areas and Preserves, designated Sharon Woods Gorge a state scenic nature preserve on January 31, 1977.

Hackberry leaves

SHAWNEE LOOKOUT PARK

Two centuries ago the Shawnees stood on this sacred hilltop and admired the majestic view above the confluence of the Great Miami and Ohio rivers. Back then, the wind, just before sunset, would be susurrous and light with birdsong.

Today, this natural fortress and important historical site is clouded by fumes, and crowded by steel bridges, railroads, smokestacks, and interstate highways. Birds still sing loudly and earnestly, but their cheer is drowned by the steady, monotonous whine coming from a looming electric power plant.

Location

Southwestern Hamilton County, Miami Township.

From U.S. Route 50, at a traffic light in the Village of Cleves, turn westerly on Mt. Nebo Road. After crossing railroad tracks, turn right on River Road. This road follows the Great Miami River and becomes Lawrenceburg Road.

The park entrance (about four miles from the turnoff on River Road) will be on your left just past Dugan Gap Road (which appears on your left). Go to the parking lot at end of the driveway to hike the Miami Fort Trail.

Ownership

Hamilton County Park District.

Size & Designation

The park comprises 1,027 acres. Miami Fort has been listed on the National Registry of Historic Places.

Nearby Natural Attractions

Shawnee Lookout is one of 16 parks owned by the Hamilton County Park District. The others included in this book are Mitchell Memorial Forest (the nearest to Shawnee Lookout), Miami-Whitewater Forest, Winton Woods, Sharon Woods, Withrow Nature Preserve, and Woodland Mound.

Access

The Miami Fort, Blue Jacket and Little Turtle trails take you on a time voyage through thousands of years of Indian history.

Let's begins the voyage at Miami Fort, found at the western tip of the park. The "fort" refers to the mounds, resembling fortifications, that encircle a strategic ridge overlooking the confluence of the Great Miami and Ohio rivers.

The 1.5-mile Miami Fort Trail begins at the parking lot and zigzags to the top of the ridge where the earthworks and loop trail begin. Go straight (west) at the split for the loop. Notice the rolling earthworks on the right. Ahead, pause at an opening in the trees to view the Great Miami River.

The trail forks again where the ridge narrows. Ignore, for now, the path that branches left, the south leg of the loop. Instead, go straight to the lookout at the tip of this finger-shaped ridge. Backtrack to the last trail intersection after viewing this ho-hum scene of bridges, interstates, industries, and railroad tracks that scar the joining of the Ohio and Great Miami rivers.

At the trail junction, go right on the south leg of the loop trail. Another overlook peers upon the Ohio River and a power plant. Note the commemorative plaque to Boy Scouts founder Daniel Carter Beard (1850–1941), a Cincinnati native. Turn right at the next intersection and descend the ridge to the car.

Just down the road, consider stopping at the archeological museum (open May–September from 1–5 p.m. on Saturday, Sunday, and holidays), and the restored log cabin and Springhouse School (Sundays only, May–September).

Driving from the Miami Fort Trail, the parking lot for the Little Turtle and Blue

Jacket trails is located on the left just beyond the historic log cabin. Restrooms and drinking are found nearby.

The Blue Jacket Trail (1.25 miles) starts on north side of the road just to the right of an Indian burial mound. The trail honors Blue Jacket, a chief of the Maykujay Shawnees.

This lasso-shaped, relatively flat trail traipses through fields and woods (and under powerlines) to a scenic view of the Great Miami Valley, the best overlook, I think, in the park. Benches at the overlook and at the start of the loop ease the feet. Interpretive nature signs ease the mind.

The two-mile Little Turtle Trail, a longer and more difficult walk than the Blue Jacket Trail, meanders across shallow ravines and streams to panoramic views of the Kentucky hillsides and Ohio River Valley. You will also visit an Indian burial ground. Little Turtle, or Michikiniqua, was a chief in the Miami nation. More on Little Turtle and Blue Jacket below.

As you enter, pick up a park brochure, as well as guides for each trail.

The park, open daily from dawn to dusk, has a golf course, picnic areas, a playground, and a boat ramp near the park entrance on the Great Miami River. The Uhlmansiek Wildlife Sanctuary, bordering the Great Miami River, lies within the metropark but remains off limits to the public.

Geology

The ancient people could not have picked a better place to stage ceremonies, build villages, or simply to enjoy the scenery. The earthworks encircle the summit of a four-sided ridge which rises 300 feet above the Ohio and Great Miami rivers. A narrower ridge extends toward to the west from the main hilltop.

The tip of the skinny ridge presents a commanding lookout over the merger of two major rivers, the hillsides and bluffs to the south (Kentucky), and the gentler landscape west and north (Indiana). A dip, or trough, separates the ridges.

Notice the steep upper slopes of the ridges. If you peeled back the vegetation you would see that these slopes are composed of limestone layers, specifically Fairview (Maysville) limestone. The gentler slopes have alternating layers of shale and limestone. Geologically speaking, they are members of the Lower Kope or Eden formation. All of the bedrocks began as sea floors back in the Ordovician Period, some 450 million years ago.

A cross-section of the ridge would reveal a dividing line between the upper and lower formations at the 650 foot elevation. The earthworks are 80–100 feet above the dividing line.

A five-foot layer of windblown silt (loess) spreads across the ridgetop and may have been an important reason for putting the mounds on this particular hill. This soil, which originated from the meltwater outwash of Ice Age glaciers, is much easier to dig, haul, and dump than the heavy, sticky clay soil found at other sites.

The ancient builders also used slabs of the local rock in the earthworks and burial mound. A quarry below the fort may have been established by the Indians. Nobody knows with certainty.

On a clear day, from the lookout, you can see in the distance the abandoned valley of a tributary that flowed into the ancient Teays River, the major river system in Ohio before the Ice Age. Look downstream along the Ohio River. Opposite Lawrenceburg, Indiana, on the Kentucky side, find the shelf-like terrace about 100 feet above the river, and 150 feet from the top of the bluff. That is the floodplain of the ancient tributary called the Kentucky River.

The Teays River roughly flowed from West Virginia and across the southern third of Ohio and into Indiana. The former Kentucky River flowed north into the Teays River. The Great Miami and Whitewater rivers flow in the opposite direction—south into the Ohio River.

The Great Miami River makes a couple of sweeping, and scenic S-shaped curves called oxbows before spilling into the Ohio River. You can see the oxbow from an overlook on the north leg of the Miami Fort Trail.

These river brushstrokes beg us to look far ahead. Someday, perhaps, the river will wash over the base of the curves and straighten the current. The event, if it happens at all, could be thousands of years away. The relicts of the abandoned channels would form crescent-shaped ponds, which over more time become marshes. What will humans see from this vantage a millennium from today?

Wildlife

Artifacts found here suggest humans have occupied the ridge at various times during the last 14,000 years. The ancestors of some of the plants and animals that you will see have lived on the ridge a good deal longer.

The abundance and diversity of life in the forest would have been an important factor to the Woodland Indians who were scouting sites for villages and "forts." The lush primeval forest that greeted their arrival is gone.

Most of the trees who are retaking this hill are newcomers. These include a new crop of oaks (white, red, bur), maple, tulip tree, hickory, wild black cherry, slippery elm, ash, black locust, beech, basswood, and a few sycamore who occupy the canopy. Beneath them grow box elder, hackberry, dogwood, sassafras, pawpaw, staghorn sumac, ironwood (blue beech), and Ohio buckeye, among others.

Hawthorn is especially prevalent along the Blue Jacket and Little Turtle trails. Deer and other animals enjoy its fruit which resembles tiny apples. Apple and pear trees appear along the Little Turtle Trail, the remnants of the land's agricultural past.

The wildflower collection includes jack-in-the-pulpit (Indian turnip), wild delphinium, bindweed, jewelweed (touch-me-not), pokeberry, mouse-eared chickweed, asters (several kinds), squirrel corn, larkspur, fire pink, Joe-pye weed, and Miami mist, a waterleaf thickly populated in the park. According to the park district, this little blossom finds its beauty only in the Great Miami and Little Miami valleys, hence its name.

During the spring and fall migrations, the overlooks above the oxbows become hunting lodges for observing hawks, ospreys, bald eagles (endangered), comorants (designated special interest), and an occasional peregrine falcon (endangered). In 1971, a pair of black vultures, rare in Ohio, nested at Shawnee Lookout. When the bottomland floods, look for great blue herons, egrets, and wood ducks.

Warblers also flock to the area, including the prothonotary warbler and American redstart, as well as the rose-breasted grosbeak, considered a rarity in southwestern Ohio. Quiet walkers might catch a glimpse of a wild turkey on the Little Turtle Trail.

Winter can be rewarding for the birdwatcher. Participants in the park district's annual December bird survey counted 2,283 individual birds from 40 species. Sixty-eight bluebirds, 151 killdeers, 57 red-bellied woodpeckers, and 40 downy woodpeckers were seen, the most sightings of each of these birds in all the metroparks. Birders spotted several endangered birds—the dark-eyed junco (4), winter wren (3), and yellow-bellied sapsucker (4).

Shawnee Lookout may have the largest deer herd among the local metroparks, largely because it offers the animal a prime habitat. Twenty-six kinds of reptiles and amphibians flourish here, such as the hognosed snake (a rarity), eastern spiny softshell turtle, Fowler's toad, Blanchard's cricket frog, and the Jefferson salamander.

History

Two years before he was elected the ninth president of the U.S., William Henry Harrison visited and studied the many of the ancient Indian earthworks in Ohio, including the "fort" situated within a cannon's blast of his homestead on the north bank of the Ohio River.

This famous frontier general, then 65 years old, imagined that the brave mound-builders chose this spot to make their last stand against invading tribes.

It was a natural conclusion. Harrison knew about military fortifications. Earlier in his career he fought in the Indian wars with General Anthony Wayne, and commanded the American troops against the Indians and British in the War of 1812. His homestead was just a short walk from the ruins of Fort Finney, a stockade built by the British in the mid-1780s. It was this general-politician who would make his homestead near such an important military and political position—Miami Fort and Fort Finney being, in his mind, the outposts of two former empires that dominated North America.

Harrison's physical description of the site in 1838 still fits. "It occupies the summit of a steep insulated hill and consists of a wall carried along its brow, composed of earth, thrown from the interior; the wall conforms strictly to the outline of the hill, except at the west where there is a considerable promontory which is left unenclosed." The knoll on this promontory served as a lookout, according to Harrison. It is really a prehistoric Indian burial mound.

Relying on research unavailable to Harrison, scholars now believe Miami Fort, a 12-acre enclosure, primarily served as a ceremonial site.

Archeological digs in and around Shawnee Lookout in this century have uncovered artifacts indicating that the so-called Paleo Indians who lived in Ohio from 14,000–8,000 B.C. utilized this area. Their successors, categorized as the Archaic (8,000–1,500 B.C.), Woodland (1,000 B.C.–800 A.D.), and Ft. Ancient Indians (800–1650) also left their marks.

The Adena people (early Woodland period) established villages on the ridgetop, around 900–400 B.C., but they did not build the impressive earthworks. Those were built by the Hopewell people a century or two later. After the Hopewell people, the Fort Ancient people came here, followed by the Miamis, Shawnees, and Europeans.

Michikiniqua, or Little Turtle (1752–1812), a chief among the Miamis, was a fearless warrior and able tactician in battle. He ruined the military campaigns of Generals Josiah Harmar and Arthur

St. Clair. He often fought alongside a Shawnee chief known as Blue Jacket. After signing the Treaty of Greene Ville in 1794, supposedly ending the Indian wars, Little Turtle met President George Washington. He died in Indiana in 1812.

As a white child, Blue Jacket was named Marmaduke van Swearingen. The Shawnees who adopted him in 1771 called him Wehyehpihehr-sehnwah. His white enemies and admirers called him Blue Jacket. As a Shawnee warrior he captured the legendary frontiersmen Daniel Boone and Simon Kenton. He became a Maykyjay Shawnee chief in 1784, fought with the British during the Revolutionary War, signed the Treaty of Green Ville in 1794, and died of a fever in 1810.

The first white military expedition to this spot was led by French explorer Pierre Joseph Celoron, who buried a lead tablet at the confluence in 1749 and proclaimed Louis XV ruler of the land. The claim did not stick, of course, and the tablet has never been found.

During the last two centuries the forest has been cleared for farms, cities, industries, and housing developments. Many local Indian ruins, and they were numerous, have been bulldozed or looted. It is a wonder Miami Fort survived at all.

Though the park district discussed creating a park at this location in the early 1930s, action did not begin until University of Cincinnati scientists started poking through the ruins in the mid-1960s. In 1966, a citizens' committee raised $91,000 to buy 177 acres on Shawnee Lookout. The following year the park district received as gifts 684 acres from Cincinnati Gas & Electric, owner of the adjacent power plant, and 114 acres from the Cincinnati Park Board.

The Miami Purchase Association funded a major archeological survey of the site in 1968. In 1971 Shawnee Lookout was listed on the National Registry of Historical Places. The restored cabin arrived at the park in 1973, and the golf course opened in 1979. Miami Fort Trail was built in 1979–80.

Journal

October 1993. At Shawnee Lookout we remember lost civilizations, and the struggles of our ancestors, Indian and white. Those days have vanished, but the forest seen by our ancestors, if left undisturbed, will return.

Northern red oak leaf

WINTON WOODS PARK

Hamilton County's busiest and most crowded metropark for humans has plenty of amenities for wildlife too.

Location

North-central Hamilton County, Village of Greenhills.

Leave Interstate 275 at Exit 39 and travel south on Winton Road to the entrance on the right. From Interstate 75 take Sharon Avenue west, then Winton Road south (left turn). Park in the lot at the Kingfisher Picnic Area, also serving the hiking trail.

Ownership

Hamilton County Park District.

Size & Designation

Winton Woods totals 2,549 acres. Two state-designated nature preserves—Greenbelt and Spring Beauty Dell—are located within the park, but they can be visited only with permission from the park district.

Nearby Natural Attractions

Winton Woods is the area's most popular metropark. It is one of 16 sites owned by the park district. The others described in the book are Sharon Woods, Miami Whitewater Forest, Mitchell Memorial Forest, Shawnee Lookout, Withrow Nature Preserve, and Woodland Mound. Trillium Trails, another state-designated nature preserve in the park system, can be visited by appointment.

Access

The park only has two footpaths for hikers—the Kingfisher and Great Oaks trails. Each traces a ridge overlooking a cattail pond called Kingfisher Lake.

From the parking lot at the Kingfisher Picnic Area proceed into the woods on the designated trail. Kingfisher Lake will be on the left. Bear left at the fork marking the start of the loop. Notice, as you walk, that the lake tapers to a brook which in the summer is shallow indeed. The path follows this rill.

Just before the Kingfisher Trail bends to the right (at its northwestern limit), you will notice a couple of improvised trails crossing the creek and climbing yonder ridge. You might see a stone structure (a trail bridge) on the far ridge. If you investigate the stream and the short uncharted trail (as I shamefully did) you will discover the path leads to the Great Oaks Trail.

Folks who live by the letter of the law (count me out) will ignore the connecting trail and finish the loop of the Kingfisher Trail. But if curiosity compels you to wander across the stream, then turn right upon reaching the Great Oaks Trail and follow this path around the north-facing bank of Kingfisher Lake.

After making the turn, ignore the westbound path (heading right) which goes to the Great Oaks trailhead at the Walnut Ridge Picnic Area. Instead, proceed ahead and make another left turn which brings you to the bank of the lake/stream. Just beyond a pair of mammoth oaks (200 years or older), recross the stream to the Kingfisher Trail on the connecting trail. Finish the Kingfisher Trail (stopping to study a sinkhole) and return to the car, completing a walk of a little less than two miles.

Park district rules urge hikers to stay on trails. Those who want to walk the Great Oaks Trail separately will find the trailhead near the Walnut Ridge Picnic Area. Do not cross the creek during periods of high or swift water and flooding.

The metropark also has a three-mile paved hike-bike trail, a bridle trail and riding center on the south side of Winton Lake, a public campground, a visitor center (Winton Centre) with nature exhibits, more than a dozen picnic areas and nine reservable shelters, an 18-hole golf course, an 18-hole Frisbee golf course, a mile-long parcourse fitness trail, ballfields, and a boathouse (rentals, scenic rides available). Fishing is permitted in the lake, but check the restrictions published in the park brochure.

The park district's administration building also is located in Winton Woods.

Geology

On old trail maps, Kingfisher Lake looks bigger and deeper than its present size. Indeed, this pond and Lake Winton have shrunk due to the settling of excessive amounts of silt, tiny bits of clay or mud.

Silt is a common particle suspended in Ohio streams. The sediment travels like wind-borne pollen or dust and gives many streams their muddy appearance. Swift streams can carry silt great distances and distribute it all along its banks. Obstacles which slow down the current, such as logs or dams, can become silt collecting points.

The currents of the Mill Creek watershed carry silt to the lakes. Water running off from surrounding hills also contains silt. When the silt reaches the peaceful lake water behind West Fork Dam it settles and accumulates. The bottom of the lake rises with sediment and water inches up the shoreline.

Since its construction in 1952, Lake Winton has lost half its volume to siltation, and about a third of the lake is no longer navigable by small boats.

The silting of a lake is a natural process. Barring a catastrophic event, it usually takes hundreds or thousands of years for sediment to fill a lake bed.

Humans, as we know, can make Nature's clock tick faster. Intense development around the park over the last four decades is responsible for the high silt content in Lake Winton and Kingfisher Lake. Precipitation runoff transports silt from construction sites into the Mill Creek watershed, and into the lakes.

Excessive silt affects the aquatic life of a lake or pond. Though some life forms benefit, others may suffer, especially critters higher up the food chain such as fish, frogs, crayfish, snakes, and some birds (see below). Silt from development sites also may be charged with contaminants that can harm wildlife. For example, black-crowned night herons, and the red-shouldered and sharp-shinned hawks (the latter two designated special interest birds by the Ohio Division of Wildlife) may have abandoned the lake because of pollution and silting.

Wildlife

In spite of silting, Kingfisher Lake remains a vital habitat for carp, catfish, and bass when the water level is suitable. Gizzard shad, bluegill, and bullhead also swim in Lake Winton, as well as stocked crappie, trout, and perch.

The Kingfisher Trail derives its name from the belted kingfisher which feasts on the small fish in streams and ponds. Sometimes it hovers before diving on its victim. Greater yellowlegs, great blue heron, various flycatchers and woodpeckers, killdeer, and ducks have been observed here.

Kingfisher Lake, really more a marsh, occasionally attracts a muskrat or a mink. Footprints on a sand bank revealed the presence of raccoon and skunk.

The red-eared and snapping turtles, queen snake, and bullfrog may reside in this wetland too. The park, in fact, protects 19 species of reptiles and amphibians, especially the endangered cave salamander, known to exist in Ohio only in Hamilton and Adams counties.

The long-beaked arrowhead (a potentially threatened plant in Ohio) and the rare water speedwell survive on the banks of the pond. Wildflowers like trout lily, wild delphinium, salt and pepper, Japanese honeysuckle, tall bellflower, jewelweed (touch-me-not), and lobelia will brighten your hike on Kingfisher Trail from spring to autumn.

As its name implies, the Great Oak Trail protects giant oaks. One stand of red oaks rises 75–100 feet, and probably have grasped the ridge for two centuries. An interpretive sign next to set of twin oaks points out that each tree drinks 100 tons of water a year.

Besides the oaks, sugar maple, shagbark hickory, black walnut, sycamore, and tulip tree occupy the canopy while blackgum (tupelo), pawpaw, sassafras, and honey locust thrive in the understory. The honey locust, by the way, is the tree that bristles with spikes which Indians used for fish hooks.

The park as a whole provided a refuge to 2,747 birds representing 47 species, according to a December 11, 1993 winter bird count. That compares to 601 individuals from 37 species tallied in a 1984 winter survey. Either Winton Woods is attracting more birds, or bird watchers are becoming better counters.

Birders recorded a group of 44 dark-eyed juncos (an endangered bird in Ohio) in the December 1993 count, plus 31 golden-crowned kinglets, 542 robins, 257 chickadees, and 191 mallards (the most in any metropark), and two yellow-bellied sapsuckers, another endangered bird.

History

Winton Woods opened in 1939 when the U.S. Department of Agriculture agreed to lease 902 acres to the park district. Known at the time of its purchase as Greenhills Park, the park district considered calling its new site Simon Kenton Forest, Springfield Forest, and West Branch Forest. It settled on Winton Woods, derived from a pioneer named Mathew Winton who settled along the road that later carried his name. Winton Woods is the second oldest facility in the park district.

Additional land purchases over the years have raised the total holdings to 2,375 acres, making it the second largest park in the district. Recreational facilities have been added as the park grew. Golfers started swinging on the park's 18-hole golf course in April 1951.

To control flooding in the industrialized Mill Creek Valley, the U.S. Army Corps of Engineers constructed West Fork Dam, completed in 1952. A year earlier the park district signed an agreement to lease 529 acres in Winton Woods from the corps.

The dam also created Winton Lake, whose surface size can increase from 188 acres to 557 acres when Mill Creek is fully restrained. Besides encouraging boating and fishing, the lake provides a habitat for aquatic wildlife.

Two sections of the metropark became state nature preserves on November 15, 1976. The Ohio Department of Natural Resources, Division of Natural Areas and Preserves made the designations. The Kingfisher Trail goes near Greenbelt State Nature Preserve, a 97-acre tract known for its mature beech-maple forest and expanding sinkholes. Spring Beauty Dell State Nature Preserve (41 acres), another beech-maple forest, is an excellent birding woods. Permission is required to visit these preserves.

Round-lobed hepatica

WITHROW NATURE PRESERVE

This secluded spot, once the estate of Adelaide and Andrew Withrow, lays on a bluff some 300 feet above the Ohio River. In spring, the rugged woodland slopes are softened with wildflowers, and the song of newly arrived warblers.

Location

Southeastern Hamilton County, Anderson Township.

Exit I-275 at Five Mile Road. Head west on Five Mile Road to the preserve entrance on the left. From Kellogg Avenue on the bank of the Ohio River, turn north on Five Mile Road to the entrance on the right. The parking lot is at the end of the driveway.

Ownership

Hamilton County Park District.

Size & Designation

Withrow Nature Preserve encompasses 270 acres.

Nearby Natural Attractions

Withrow Nature Preserve is one of 16 sites owned by the Hamilton County Park District. The other parks described in this book are Woodland Mound (the one nearest to the preserve), Sharon Woods, Winton Woods, Miami Whitewater Forest, Mitchell Memorial

Forest, and Shawnee Lookout. Also visit the Cincinnati Nature Preserve just east of nearby Milford in Clermont County.

Access

Two footpaths wander through this rugged terrain, but none is especially strenuous. You will have to climb several sets of stairs on the trail as you traverse ridges. As you face Highwood Lodge at the end of the parking lot, both trails begin to the left, at the edge of the woods. Consult the trail map near the parking lot before departing.

Shortly after entering the woods you will reach a fork marking the start of the Hepatica and Trout Lily trails. Go left on the Trout Lily Trail, cross a bridge, descend some stairs, and proceed ahead through woods. A picturesque ravine of tall hardwoods will be at the right, the parking lot and driveway at the left. Ignore the path entering from the left, an old jeep road.

Near the entrance to an overgrown meadow, the trail splits for its loop. The path to the right goes through young vegetation and a maturing forest to a patch of open space advertised as an overlook.

The overlook, however, has become too overgrown to see the Ohio River. Still, it is a great place to rest for a while. Sit beneath the branches of the spreading oak that guards the spot. Some folks backtrack from here, but I recommend pushing ahead along the path to the left.

Trout Lily Trail (1.75 miles) now proceeds to a radio transmission tower. (To shorten your walk a little take the shortcut stemming left just before you reach the tower.) At the tower, the trail bends left, and after a while it swings left again and goes through a meadow of wildflowers, berry patches, vines and small trees—a good birding trail if you are looking for meadow dwellers.

Upon completing the loop, retrace your steps back to the first trail fork, near the trailhead. At this point turn left on the Hepatica Hill Trail (3/4 mile) which circles the ridge below the lodge. A bench midway around the ridge offers rest and a view of the steep ravine on the left. A tall set of stairs and an observation deck (built by the Youth Conservation Corps administered by the Ohio Department of Natural Resources) appears near the end of the walk. The trail empties into the lawn behind Highwood Lodge.

Folks looking for solitude and quiet should find it here (though the distant echo of traffic on I-275 sometimes intrudes upon the silence). The preserve lacks picnic areas, restrooms and drinking water (except when Highwood Lodge is open), and the recreation facilities familiar in other county metroparks.

Geology

The small brook that has carved the deep ravine in this preserve empties into Five Mile Creek and the Ohio River. It has washed away soil dumped here by the Illinoian glacier, roughly 125 million years ago.

Wildlife

The mature forest that you see is a beech-maple climax forest, meaning that the land has reached the last stage of successional growth (from field to forest) and has become self-perpetuating with beech and sugar maples being the dominate trees in the woods. Mixing with the beech-maple giants are healthy examples of red and white oak, shagbark hickory, black cherry, and ash.

Aside from the mature wooded areas in the ravine and river slope, much of the preserve shows various stages of successional habitats from open fields packed with grasses, wildflowers and fencerow plants like bittersweet, to young forests of rising maples, cherry, and beech. Thickets of shrubs, sumac, briars, and wild grape vines are also present.

The trails honor two spring wildflowers abundant in the preserve. The hepatica (meaning liver) has small, dainty white to lavender flowers. Its leaves supposedly are shaped like a human liver. Early white settlers believed the plant cured liver ailments.

The nodding yellow blossom of the trout lily appears from late March through early June. It is sometimes called the dogtooth violet because of the toothlike shape of its subsurface bulb. This delicate lily (not a violet) got its name from its mottled leaves which resemble the markings of a brook or brown trout.

Also search for flowers called sessile trillium, salt and pepper, twinleaf, shooting star, and ferns named Christmas and maidenhead.

In the field, find the round, brown, tumorous balls growing on goldenrod stems. It looks like the plant tried to swallow a large marble. These are goldenrod galls.

In the summer, gall flies lay eggs on the stem. A chemical secreted by the flies swells the galls. The balls become cozy winter homes for larvae (maggots) which hatch in the spring and eat their way through the gall to the surface. They complete their development inside the gall and later emerge as adult gall flies.

Elliptical shaped goldenrod galls house moth larvae, instead of maggots. Sometimes an ichneumon wasp emerges from these elliptical galls. This predator injects its eggs into the gall next to the moth larvae. The wasp larva eats the moth larva, then beds down in a cocoon and comes out in late summer.

The preserve attracts birds of many varieties. Woodpeckers are abundant judging from the constant rapping on trees. During the park district's December 1993 winter bird count, 10 red-bellied, 8 downy, and 3 hairy woodpeckers, plus 3 yellow-bellied sapsuckers, endangered in Ohio, were counted. Birders also sighted 10 golden-crowned kinglets.

History

Adelaide and Andrew Withrow bought this piece of paradise in the 1930s. The hilltop offered a remarkable view of the Ohio River, Kentucky hillside, and Five Mile Creek valley. Though the couple landscaped around the home and planted some exotic trees, like ginko, they largely left the land alone.

In the 1970s the Withrows approached the park district about buying the land for a nature preserve. The first purchase, 145 acres, was completed in 1977 with the help of the Ohio Chapter of The Nature Conservancy. In 1979, Adelaide Withrow Farny and Eugene Farny donated an adjoining 126 acres to the park district.

The nature preserve opened to the public in 1983. It is a favorite site for outdoor weddings and nature programs.

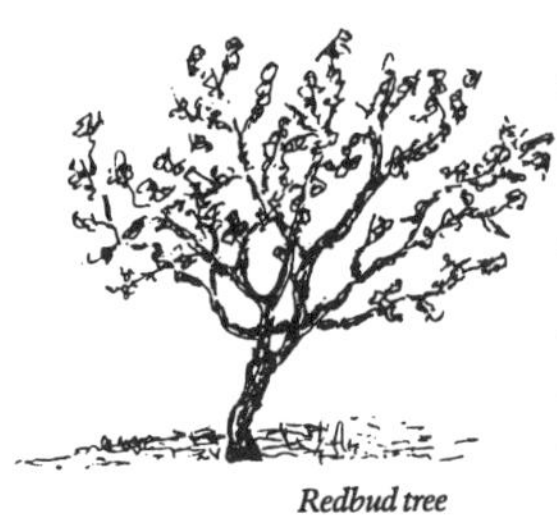

Redbud tree

WOODLAND MOUND PARK

Humans have been surveying the Ohio River valley from this hilltop for 14,000 years. For centuries, perhaps for millennia, hawks and vultures have floated on the thermals rushing up the steep slope. Early morning visitors might catch the fog floating above the river. Soon sunlight bakes the fog and it dissolves into the air.

Location

Southeastern Hamilton County, Anderson Township.

Going eastbound on U.S. Route 52, turn left (north) on Eight Mile Road, then make an immediate right on Old Kellogg Avenue. The entrance is ahead on the left. Park at the Seasongood Nature Center.

Ownership

Hamilton County Park District.

Size & Designation

The park land totals 926 acres.

Nearby Natural Attractions

Woodland Mound is one of 16 metroparks owned by the park district. The other parks described in this book are Miami Whitewater Forest, Winton Woods, Shawnee Lookout, Withrow Nature Preserve (right next door to Woodland Mound), Sharon Woods, and Mitchell Forest Reserve. Just east of nearby Milford (Clermont County) is the privately owned Cincinnati Nature Center.

Access

Two footpaths leave the hilltop. First, though, enjoy the best county view of the Ohio River valley.

The half-mile Seasongood Trail goes from the rear of the nature center into the woods. The loop circles a ridge of hardwood trees and returns to the nature center. This relatively young woods is a second-growth forest, meaning its has been logged at least once.

This noisy trail was disappointing, even when I visited it in the middle of the week. The hiker never escapes the simple building sounds of the nature center. That's unfortunate because the urban clamor of Cincinnati, some 18 miles away, cannot be heard here. Instead, the growls, wheezings, and whines of machines that power the Seasongood building disturb the peace. Adding a mile to this path would make it a "feel good" trail.

The mile-long Hedgeapple Trail is quieter and a little more strenuous. It departs from the parking lot for the Weston Amphitheater to the right of the parcourse fitness trail.

The trail forks shortly after leaving the parking lot. This is the beginning of a loop. Take the left leg of the loop which hikes to a vernal pond. Vernal means water only appears in the spring. Ahead, the path meets the other leg of the loop. Go left to see a woodland pond and a cattail pond.

The trail deadends at the cattail pond. Retrace your steps to the last intersection and take the other leg of the loop back to the trailhead. The Hedgeapple Trail also visits woods, meadows, stands of osage orange (also known as hedgeapple), and vines of various plants.

Pick up a map for this trail at the nature center. The numbered stops will give you insights on the natural habitats you will observe.

The modern Seasongood Nature Center features interactive nature exhibits, interior overlooks, outdoors decks, wildlife viewing windows, an auditorium, restrooms and drinking water, and Nature's Niche Gift and Bookshop. A gift from the estate of Murray and Agnes Seasongood paid for the construction of the attractive building. Murray Seasongood advocated for the creation of a metropark district when he was mayor of Cincinnati, 1926–30.

The park also has a top-rated golf course, The Vineyard, and the Weston Amphitheater, a 10,000-seat outdoor concert hall. Picnic areas, Frisbee golf course, ballfields, snack bar, and playground are found in the park.

Geology

Limestone and shale created back in the Ordovician geological period, some 450 million years ago, provide the foundation for steep hills overlooking the Ohio River. These bedrocks started as soupy sea floors enriched with the remains of the era's marine life. The fossils of the ancient sea creatures are found in the exposed Ordovician rocks.

Recently, say within the last 500,000 years, continental glaciers, notably the Illinoian, laid blankets of sand, silt, gravel, rocks, and boulders—a deposit called till—atop these bedrock formations. The soil on the ridgetop of this park is made of glacial till.

Some streams running off the steep hills have washed away the till and brought the old rocks and sea creatures back into the sunlight. None of the hiking trails mentioned above visits one of these streams.

Wildlife

The wrinkled yellowish-green "brains" found along the Hedgeapple Trail in autumn are the softball-sized fruits of the osage orange, or hedgeapple, tree. This is not a native Ohio tree. It was imported and planted by farmers, usually in rows, as a hedge or fencerow. Its thorny, rot-resistant, intertwining branches kept livestock from fleeing a field.

Barbed wire replaced osage orange as a fence, but the tree survives as a relic. Pioneers put the fruit in their cabins as an insect repellent. Today, squirrels and quails munch on the seeds.

You also will see honey locust and black locust trees, distinguished by their thorns and rows of small leaves. Don't lean on a honey locust. In spite of its sweet-sounding name, its thorns, or spikes, can pierce your flesh. The thorns have been used as pins and fish hooks.

Numerous vines creep alongside the Hedgeapple Trail. Poison ivy (whose oil makes your skin itch) and Virginia creeper often grow side by side up the trunk of a tree. Five leaves spring from the stem of the Virginia creeper, three from the poison ivy vine.

Wild grape vines, the thick, woody, "Tarzan" vines we swung on as youngsters, produce dark blue or purple grapes that are enjoyed by wildlife, especially raccoons. Sweet-scented white or yellow blossoms appear from the tendrils of Japanese honeysuckle, a non-native vine imported to control soil erosion. The plant has become overabundant in some areas and suffocates native plants.

Elsewhere in the park, oaks called black, shumard, pin, and yellow thrive, along with beech, hackberry, red cedar, cottonwood, ailanthus (tree of heaven), redbud, ash, black willow, box elder, silver and black maple, black walnut, shagbark and bitternut hickory, and others.

The park's diverse wildflower assemblage includes beauties found in woodlands and meadows. Look for these—Virgin's bower, thimbleweed, black nightshade, black snakeroot, moth mullein, spring beauty, St. John's wort, wild bergamot, sessile trillium, jack-in-the-pulpit, white and purple dwarf larkspur, jewelweed (touch-me-not), catnip, giant hyssop, and many others.

The ponds on the Hedgeapple Trail differ slightly. As noted above the vernal pond teems with life—insect larvae and tadpoles—when water fills it in the spring. By mid-summer the pond is empty, but dragonflies feast on swarming mosquitoes, and the great crested flycatcher preys on dragonflies.

The woodland pond is shaded and keeps it water year-round. It is a watering hole for animals, a place for turtles to bask, and for salamanders, frogs, and toads to hibernate.

Bullfrogs croak in raspy-basso notes at the cattail pond, more open than the neighboring woodland pond. Red-winged blackbirds nest in the cattail stands. Freshwater snails in the ponds provide meals for nocturnal visitors.

At the last count 20 species of amphibians and reptiles have been recorded in the park, such as the hognosed (becoming rare), black rat, and rough green snakes, and the slimy and ravine salamanders.

The ridgetops are proven viewing spots for hawks, vultures, waterfowl, and other migratory birds. The park attracts the usual crowd of warblers and sparrows, plus regulars like cardinals, robins, bluejays, and crows. The meadows fill with butterflies in summer, notably the tiger swallowtail and monarch.

History

It is possible that ancient people called the Palaeo Indians roamed atop these hills 14,000 years ago. Later groups (so-called Archaic, Woodland, and Fort Ancient Indians) occupied the slopes, according to the park district. Ten sites discovered in the park—small villages, campsites, two mounds, and the Eight Mile Earthworks—remind us of their presence. (See Shawnee Lookout.)

The Miami and Shawnee people moved into Ohio in the early 1700s, a few decades before the first whites began to explore the region. The nearby Ohio River, of course, was a major transportation route for Native Americans and white pioneers.

According to early pioneer diaries, the park land in 1750 was 95 percent forested, with some trees boasting girths of six feet and heights of 100 feet. By the 20th century the forest had been cleared. Elk, bison, black bear, wolf, mountain lion, and bobcat had been killed off.

The park district "penciled in" a park for this area on a 1934 master plan, but scant resources delayed the project until 1974. By 1976 some 700 acres had been acquired. The park opened on July 20, 1980, marking the park district's 50th anniversary.

The Weston Amphitheater is named after Mrs. Sara K. Weston whose donation of 40 acres in 1976 helped the district obtain a matching federal land grant. The nature center opened on May 19, 1990.

Spring beauty

HUESTON WOODS STATE NATURE PRESERVE

Sit beneath an ancient beech and let the primeval world enter your soul. This is the mammoth beech-maple forest that greeted Matthew Hueston when he arrived here in the late 18th century.

Location

Preble County, Israel Township, and Butler County, Oxford Township. The nature preserve lies within Hueston Woods State Park.

From Oxford travel north about four miles on Brown Road, which deadends in the preserve. Traveling southeast on State Routes 732 and 177 (temporarily sharing the same road bed), turn right on SR 732 (going toward Oxford), then right at the park entrance in a half mile. Turn left at the first fork, marking the start of the state park loop road. Drive beyond the Acton Lake Dam, and two picnic areas. Turn right into the next parking lot labeled for the preserve and the Blue Heron Trail. (If you reach Brown Road, you have gone too far.)

Size & Designation

This 200-acre forest became an interpretive nature preserve on October 2, 1973. The U.S. Department of the Interior added the site to the National Registry of Natural Landmarks in March 1967.

Ownership

Ohio Department of Natural Resources, Division of Parks and Recreation owns the preserve, and co-manages it with the ODNR Division of Natural Areas and Preserves.

Nearby Natural Attractions

Hueston Woods State Park surrounds the preserve. Rush Run Wildlife Area is nearby in Preble County. Pater Wildlife Area is in Butler County.

Access

The Blue Heron Trail begins on the right side of a paved circle at the end of the parking lot. Note the plaque set in stone which commemorates the forest as a National Natural Landmark. The path descends a gentle slope toward Acton Lake. An intermittent stream will be at your left.

Near shore, the Blue Heron Trail joins the West Shore Trail which originates in the state park. Go left and follow the lakeshore trail a bit. (A right turn on West Shore Trail leaves the preserve and concludes at the dam.)

Take your next left, a path shared by the Blue Heron and Sugar Bush trails. (Continuing straight takes you to a sugar house, a place where maple syrup is made.) This path ascends the slope on the other side of the stream. Another intersection greets you at the top of the ridge. Go left, on the Blue Heron Trail, to return to the parking lot. However, bigger trees await and I recommend going straight on the Sugar Bush Trail, then hiking the Big Woods Trail.

The trail gets tricky when it reaches Brown Road. Sugar Bush Trail continues across the street and heads to the right. You want to go left a few paces to what looks like a small, gravel parking area for service vehicles. A service road does go off to the right, paralleling Sugar Bush Trail. Ignore it. Take the path that wanders into the woods on the left side of this spot.

The Big Woods Trail snakes up and down several ravines and is more strenuous than the Blue Heron. But it is worth the extra work—just for the trees. Wooden bridges and stairs assist the hiker. The path empties into a parking lot.

Here, most people retrace their steps to the Sugar Bush Trail and return to the parking lot via the last leg of the Blue Heron Trail. That route stays within the preserve and completes a 2.6-mile ramble.

The Big Woods Trail does continue on the other side of the parking lot. It leaves the preserve, crosses the state park loop road, and joins the Hedge Apple Trail.

The state park offers a number of other hiking trails. Maps are available at the state park lodge.

The nature preserve is open every day from sunup to sundown. Drinking water is available at the start of the Blue Heron Trail, and a restroom is found at the parking lot for the Big Woods Trail.

You'll find other human comforts at Hueston Woods State Park, a resort park with a lodge, restaurant, cabins, marina, nature center, bridle trails, golf course, picnic areas, camping, fishing, swimming beach, swimming pools, and a pioneer farm museum. The nature center, near the marina, is certainly worth a stop.

For more information contact the Ohio Department of Natural Resources, Division of Natural Areas and Preserves, Fountain Square, Building F-1, Columbus, Ohio 43224-1331; phone (614) 265-6453.

Geology

Some 450 million years ago (Ordovician geological period) this area was covered by a sea teeming with small creatures. The accumulated remains of the animals (brachiopods, gastropods, trilobites, cephalopods, etc.) mixed with the mud and sand on the sea floor. This soup later turned into limestone and shale.

Sometime during the Silurian times (395–430 years ago), the land heaved and formed what is known as the Cincinnati Arch, a gentle roll, or wave, stretching from Toledo to Kentucky. The movement probably occurred in response to the uplifting that created the Appalachian Mountains to the east. Hueston Woods lies just a little west of the arch's crest.

The swelling lifted the Ordovician and Silurian rock layers toward the surface. For the next 300 million years or so, weathering and erosion removed overlaying sediment, flattened the crest, and exposed the rock layers.

During the Ice Age, which started about a million years ago, at least three and possibly four continental glaciers covered much of Ohio. The last glacier, the Wisconsinan, visited the area roughly 15,000 years ago and covered it with a thick layer of till, a blend of gravel, sand, clay, silt, and boulders.

Streams fed by the meltwater of the withdrawing glacier immediately began to wash away the till and excavate new valleys. One of these currents was Four Mile Creek, which runs through the state park. Over many millennia the creek, and some of its tributaries, reached the Ordovician bedrock of the Cincinnati Arch.

This ancient rock is exposed in the tiny rill alongside the Blue Heron Trail. Notice the fossilized remains of the marine life embedded in the rock. Supposedly, more than 250 species of sea life have been counted in the fossil rocks around Hueston Woods.

Look, but do not collect. Please leave the rocks in place. The state park has established two fossil collecting areas, near Acton Dam and on Hedge Row Road.

The glacial till spread across this landscape became the host for the verdant forest preserved at Hueston Woods.

Wildlife

Hueston Woods is one of only a few forests in Ohio that has been left in its original, primeval state. Here giant-sized American beeches and sugar maples are the kings of the forest. This type of woods, the beech-maple forest, is near its southwesternmost limit in Ohio. Just a few miles down the road these trees will no longer hold sway over their brethren.

Beech trees occupy 44 percent of the forest canopy (treetop level), sugar maples 28 percent, and white ashes 19 percent. The tulip tree has had some success, and so has black walnut, red oak, sycamore, shagbark hickory, and honey locust but their numbers are small. Beneath these grow spicebush, pawpaw, hackberry, elderberry, and prickly gooseberry.

There is more to this old forest than old trees, of course. Numerous brands of wildflowers brighten the forest floor. Scientists who have compiled lists over the years have reported seeing three-birds orchid and harebell, both threatened species, and jack-in-the-pulpit, a rarity.

It is no surprise that beechdrops are plentiful in this forest. This parasitic flower blooms beneath beech trees from August to October, and gets its nourishment from tree roots.

See if you can find showy orchis, climbing nightshade, low larkspur, field pussytoes, Venus' looking-glass, hoary puccoon, and yellow corydalis (yellow harlequin). One researcher counted 20 kinds of lichens and 80 varieties of bryophytes (mosses), signs of a healthy forest.

Birders can search for some 150 different species that have been sighted in the area. These include the pileated and redheaded woodpeckers, the cerulean and Kentucky warblers, the red-eyed and yellow-throated vireos, the great horned and barred owls, scarlet tanager, yellow-billed cuckoo, rufous-sided towhee, Louisiana waterthrush, great crested flycatcher, indigo bunting, and others. Acton Lake attracts several species of waterfowl.

The black racer, eastern milk, fox, garter, black rat, and northern water snakes slither in the area. The usual group of mammals—deer, raccoon, skunk, fox, opossum—roam the woods.

Hueston Woods' purity has inspired scientists and students from many disciplines to conduct research here. Their studies enhance our understanding of the natural forces at work in the forest.

History

Though most stories on the history of Hueston Woods begin with Matthew Hueston, he was not the first human inhabitant in the area. Artifacts such as arrowheads, tools, and corn grinders point to a Native American settlement at the nearby confluence of Four Mile and Talawanda creeks. An Indian mound also rises about a mile south of the dam. The Miami people lived here when white settlers arrived.

Hueston's tale begins in 1794 when he marched as a soldier in General "Mad" Anthony Wayne's frontier army. Hueston remembered the vast forest and rich soil in southwestern Ohio as the army journeyed north to the Battle of Fallen Timbers. Wayne defeated the Indians and made the frontier temporarily safe for more white settlers. After completing his service, Hueston began buying land in the area. This particular woods was part of a 310-acres tract he acquired in 1797.

Hueston has been called Ohio's first conservationist because he refused to clear the tall trees along the west bank of Four Mile Creek. It could be, however, that the creek valley was simply too steep for farming and logging, and perhaps the sugar maples were more valuable as syrup producers than as timber products. Or, it could be that Hueston considered himself prosperous enough to leave part of his holdings wild (the part too tough to clear).

Whatever the reason, the Hueston clan, generation after generation, kept this forest standing. When the last family member died in 1935, Morris Taylor, a Hamilton banker, purchased the acreage and held it in trust until the state could buy it.

In 1940, State Representative Cloyd Acton of Eaton persuaded the state legislature to begin acquiring the Hueston estate. Taylor sold the land to the state in 1941. The parcel was first designated as a state forest. More land was purchased in 1945.

The Oxford Honor Camp, which housed honor prison inmates, operated here for 12 years beginning in 1952. A 1,200-foot earthen dam was built across Four Mile Creek in 1956, a major step toward establishing the state park. The impoundment created Acton Lake, named after the legislator, the following year. The water filled in a portion of the steep and scenic Four Mile Creek valley.

The state park opened a short time later. The lodge was finished in 1967. That year, in March, the U.S. Department of the Interior listed Hueston Woods on the National Registry of Natural Landmarks. The 200-acre site became the state's 14th nature preserve on October 2. 1973.

Indian Mound

INDIAN MOUND RESERVE

You pay tribute to early Ohioans in this compact natural setting which features Adena earthworks, a pioneer's log cabin, a picturesque gorge, a waterfall, a marsh, and a wooded floodplain.

Location

Northeast Greene County, Cedarville Township.

From Cedarville, travel west (or south) toward Xenia on U.S. Route 42. Just beyond the outskirts of town the first of three parking areas for the reserve appears on the right. Stop here to view Cedar Cliff Falls (manmade) and the small gorge carved by Massie Creek. To visit the Indian sites continue on Rte. 42 to the next parking lot, about a half mile down the road on the right.

From Xenia, go northeast on Rte. 42 past Wilberforce. The reserve will be on the left just before you reach Cedarville.

Ownership

Greene County Park District.

Size & Designation

Important sites of human cultural history are protected in this 165-acre preserve. The Williamson Mound and Pollock Works (Enclosure) are national historic sites.

Nearby Natural Attractions

Greene County is packed with natural adventures. Clifton Gorge State Nature Preserve, Glen Helen Nature Preserve, and John Bryan State Park are just a few miles away near Yellow Springs. The southwest quarter of the county boasts The Narrows Reserve (described below), Sugarcreek Reserve (a Dayton metropark), and Spring Valley State Wildlife Area. The Little Miami River, Ohio's first designated national scenic river, cuts a swath through the county.

Access

If you are traveling on SR 42 from Cedarville, pull in to peek at Cedar Cliff Falls (on the right). The spot has several observation points where you can gaze upon this manmade cascade, once the site of a flour mill. The bridge arching over Massie Creek entertains visitors of all ages and presents a clear view of the falls and the dolomite gorge. You can hike to the Adena Indian ruins from here by following Cedar Cliff Trail downstream (west) after crossing the bridge.

Scaling the falls and gorge walls is prohibited. Restrooms and picnic tables are located in the parking area.

Motorists proceed west on Route 42 to the next entrance on the right. This middle section of the reserve contains the ruins left by the first Ohioans. The first large artifact you see is a restored log cabin in the parking lot.

The trail to the ancient Indian site begins at the right on the far side of a grassy area. Bear left at the first fork, following the Marsh Trail and arrows to the earthworks. After passing a small cattail marsh, stay left and enter the inside of a circular Indian earthwork known as the Pollock Works (Enclosure). A short trail loops within the earthwork.

If you follow the left leg of this loop, you will find another trail going left through a gap in the mound—the Wall View Trail. This path descends into the floodplain and leads to Massie Creek where stepping stones help you across a ford. On the north bank, turn left on the Dolomite Trail and go downstream. (The Cedarcliff Trail merges from the right.)

Notice the dolomite wall, 20–40 feet tall, on the right. Soon you will walk on a ridge (a dike really) separating two sunken areas which used to be reservoirs. After crossing a wooden bridge over a tributary of Massie Creek, turn right at the next intersection. This trail, the Mound Trail, leads to a field and the Williamson Indian Mound.

Sixty-two steps (count them) lead to the top of this memorial. Retrace your steps to the bridge, only turn right before the footbridge and follow the wide Mound Trail back to an access road and the parking lot. Go left when you reach the gravel road.

Figure on walking about two miles. The trails are well-marked and easy to follow, and the terrain is relatively flat with some low riverbanks to climb. The trail becomes thin and rocky around the earthworks. Your feet may get wet crossing Massie Creek at the ford.

Restrooms, drinking water, and picnic tables are located in the parking lot. The reserve opens at 7 a.m. and closes at dark.

For more information about Indian Mound Reserve (and The Narrows Reserve described next) contact the Greene County Park District, 651 Dayton-Xenia Road, Xenia, Ohio 45385; phone (513) 376-7445.

Geology

During its withdrawal from Ohio some 12,000 years ago, the Wisconsinan continental glacier bore rivers of melting ice. One of these currents was Massie Creek, a tributary of the Little Miami River.

Since its birth, Massie Creek has removed the bed of loose glacial till (gravel, stones, sand, and clay) that laid in its path. It also has cut a gorge into the hard dolomite rock formed 425 million during the Silurian geological period. Sometimes confused with limestone, dolomite contains high concentrations of calcium-magnesium carbonate derived from the remains of small marine creatures. Unlike limestone, however, dolomite contains few fossils because the remnants dissolved in the rock. The dissolution of the fossils accounts for the porosity of this sedimentary rock.

You can see outcroppings of dolomite (once known as dolostone) at the Falls Overlook (though the Cedar Cliff Falls is man-made) and along the Cedarcliff and Dolomite Ridge Trails.

Massie Creek flows through the gorge in a relatively straight channel contained by the dolomite. However, downstream, near the circular earthwork, the dolomite disappears, enabling Massie Creek to follow a freer snaking course.

Wildlife

The reserve protects two rare trees. One is arbor vitae, or northern white cedar, a potentially threatened species in Ohio. The other is mountain maple. Both trees are much more common in the boreal forests in Canada. They probably followed the vanguard of the Wisconsinan glacier (15,000 years ago) when the climate in Ohio was much cooler. After the glacier retreated, these survivors found a congenial, but tiny, habitat in the reserve.

Common flowers are large-flowered trillium, nodding trillium, wild columbine, Dutchman's breeches, and squirrel corn, similar to the breeches only its flower is heart-shaped. The "corn" name derives from its root tubers which resemble corn kernels.

Warblers arrive en masse in the spring and stay until early autumn. Look for the prothonotary, common yellowthroat, and black-throated green warblers. Great blue and green herons favor the creek, while great horned, barred, and screech owls prefer the forest.

The reserve supports the common furry critters. One special resident is the coyote.

History

Indian Mound Reserve is rich in human history, as well as natural history. Ancient people called the Palaeo Indians probably migrated to this area as the Wisconsinan glacier withdrew, about 10,000–12,000 years ago. They hunted mastodons, mammoths, giant beavers, muskox, and caribou.

Descendents of the Palaeo people, known as Archaic Indians, lived in this vicinity around 9,000 years ago. They, too, were hunters, though their quarry, instead, may have been deer, bear, wild turkey, and fish. Plants became part of their diet.

The Williamson Mound is a relict of the Adena Culture, 1,000 B.C.–800 A.D. Though the mound has never been excavated (and I hope it stays that way), experts believe it is the grave of tribal leaders.

The Pollock earthworks were built by ancient people called the Hopewell Indians, who established villages in Central and Southern Ohio between 100 B.C.–600 A.D. The Hopewell people raised corn to supplement their diet. They are known for their well-crafted decorative art on tools, weapons, household items, and personal possessions, and for their numerous earthen structures—circles, squares, octagons, and crescents.

The Pollock Works are small compared to other sites, where 100 acres may be enclosed. The purpose of the earthworks remains a mystery. At first they resemble military forts, but most students today think they might be gathering places for religious ceremonies or commercial activities (trading, markets).

The people of the Miami and Shawnee nations later settled in the region, but as the losers in frontier wars they had to give up their holdings to the victorious white settlers.

Mills grew up on the banks of Massie Creek after the Civil War. In 1868, Harbison Mill, a flour mill, was built on the south bank, just west of the waterfall. A 40-foot dam was erected in 1887 for turbine power and to divert water to a mill race. Notice that the dam arches upstream so that the force of water presses the stones together.

The Harbison mill stayed in business until 1917. Later, several rows of stone were removed from the top of the dam so that Massie Creek would cascade over it. The Williamson family donated the land containing the Adena mound to the public in the 1920s.

The Hager Straw Board and Paper Company occupied the site in the 1930s. Pipes, sluiceways, and ditches carried toxic effluent to settling ponds located west of the waterfall. The pools are the sunken areas beside a levee now serving as part of the Dolomite Ridge Trail. Some of the contraptions of this sewage system are evident on the trail.

The park district began acquiring the land for the park in 1968. The parcels are now returning to their normal, natural state, and the Indian earthworks are protected from industrial waste.

Journal

Grownups are commanded to leave their "hangups" at the foot of the mound. As I climbed the steps, I pretended that I was the high priest of a native community about to perform a ceremony. My walking stick was the tribal staff, and my speech (mutterings to the contemporary ear) from the summit generated nods of approval. I wore a deerskin robe decorated with turkey feathers. I got my Mojo working and started to dance . . . "Mom, what is that man doing up there?" "Must be an actor from Blue Jacket," she surmises. "Hmm. We'll come back another time, dear. Race you to the car!"

Great blue heron

THE NARROWS RESERVE

The reserve's name suggests that the Little Miami River must fit through a tight squeeze of rock walls and boulders. It doesn't. The "narrows" refers more to the slender shape of the park property rather than the shape of the land. The river flows by placidly, sometimes languidly, in a U-shaped ravine that few could deny is scenic—except the narrow-minded. The preserve's riverside trail offers some of the best views of this national and state scenic river and its comforting riparian woodland.

Location

Western Greene County, Beavercreek Township.

Take Bellbrook Road (not Lower Bellbrook Road) southwest from downtown Xenia. In a little more than four miles, turn right (northwest) on Indian Ripple Road for about 1.5 miles. Just after crossing the Little Miami River, turn left into the reserve parking lot (for canoe launch and hiking trails). The entrance to the nature interpretation center is the next left.

Ownership

Greene County Park District leases the land from the Ohio Department of Natural Resources.

Size & Designation

The Narrows Reserve has been designated as a 162-acre natural area by the park district.

Nearby Natural Attractions

See Indian Mound Reserve.

Access

There are numerous trails in the preserve. I recommend heading for the river (the canoe launching area) and turning right (downstream) on the River Trail. This trail parallels the river and has several side paths to the water, good spots for nature viewing, wading, or napping.

Ignore all trails to the right, and stay left at all intersections. The River Trail eventually empties into a meadow. Cross the meadow, keeping to the left, and reenter the woods. Again, bear left at the next fork where a trail sign indicates the Big Wood Trail. The path continues south to the reserve boundary then bends right (west) and climbs a moderately steep riverbank to the Big Wood.

Now the path rambles through the Big Wood area of the preserve. Notice the chimney of an old home, and a thicket of young sugar maples, before returning to the floodplain and the meadow. Bear right at the next merger, taking a short path that returns to the River Trail.

Follow the River Trail upstream toward the starting point. Folks who want to visit the interpretive center should turn left on the Vista Trail, mount the steep bluff, and go left on the Old Road Trail to the center. Follow the Old Road Trail back to the parking lot.

The River Trail is wide, flat and easy to read, though it does narrow after crossing the meadow. I suspect many hikers turn around at the meadow after picnicking. The walk up to the bluffs is relatively steep.

Back at the parking lot you will find picnic tables, and a restroom. Fishing, canoeing, and primitive camping (by permit) are allowed in the reserve. The interpretive center has nature exhibits.

The grounds are open daily from dawn to dusk. For more information contact the Greene County Park District, 651 Dayton-Xenia Road, Xenia, Ohio 45385; phone (513) 376-7445. Also, try The Narrows Reserve, 2575 Indian Ripple Road, Beavercreek, Ohio 45385 (513) 429-9590.

Geology

Like neighboring Clifton Gorge (which does have narrow canyons) the Little Miami River flows through The Narrows. Like Indian Mound Reserve, the bedrock exposed in places is dolomite, dating back 425 million years to the Silurian geological period.

The Wisconsinan glacier covered the bedrock with a thick layer of till, an unsorted mixture of gravel, sand, silt, and boulders. As the glacier retreated northward, around 12,000–15,000 years ago, its meltwater created the Little Miami River. Since then the Little Miami has worn a path through the till and into the ancient bedrock.

Wildlife

The Narrows boasts a collection of wildlife similar to the Indian Mound Reserve, only it lacks the northern white cedar and mountain maple trees.

The Little Miami has a large variety of fish, largemouth and smallmouth bass, bluegill, suckers and shiners, and Johnny and greensided darters are common.

History

An "open space" master plan developed by the regional planning commission in the 1960s targeted this location for a nature park. After the Little Miami River's national and state scenic river designation, the Ohio Department of Natural Resources acquired "the narrows," and in the mid-1970s leased it to the park district.

NORTHWESTERN OHIO

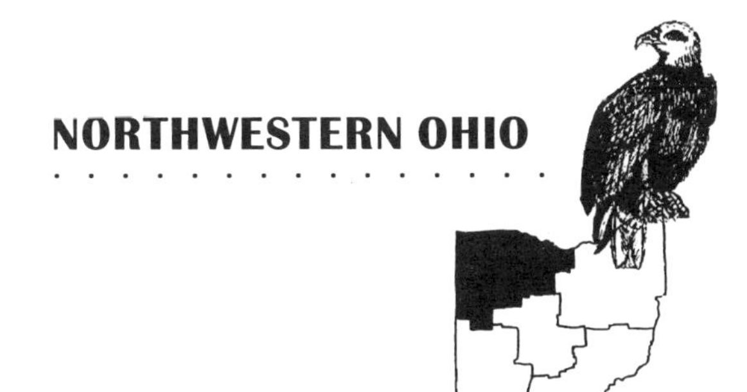

Silvery checkerspot

CEDAR BOG STATE MEMORIAL

"Welcome to the Ice Age," says Site Manager Terry Jaworski, beginning his tour at Cedar Bog State Nature Preserve. The greeting is appropriate. Cedar bog takes you back in time, to a chilly period when Ohio was covered by ice. In spite of its name, this 428-acre preserve in Champaign County is not really a bog, but a rare and fragile fen.

Location

Southern Champaign County, Urbana Township.

From Urbana, travel south on State Route 68 about 4 miles, then one mile west on Woodburn Road. Look for the entrance and parking lot on the right, just past the railroad tracks. The preserve is a little more than 9 miles north of Springfield on SR 68.

Ownership

The site is jointly owned by the Ohio Historical Society and Ohio Department of Natural Resources, Division of Natural Areas and Preserves. It is managed by the Ohio Historical Society.

Size & Designation

Fifty-three acres of this boreal-prairie fen remain protected as a scientific preserve, while 90 acres is designated interpretive. The rest of the property, 285 acres, is a scenic nature preserve open to the public at scheduled times. The historical society has dedicated the refuge as a state memorial. Cedar Bog also is a National Natural Landmark.

Nearby Natural Attractions

In Champaign County, you can explore Kiser Lake State Park, plus Davey Woods and Siegenthaler Esker state nature preserves.

Access

The fragile ecosystem of the fen requires careful protection—and careful explanation. That's why the resident site manager leads you on a tour along a boardwalk trail measuring $^{8}/_{10}$ miles.

It is always best to make an appointment to visit this preserve, but it isn't necessary. From April 1–September 30 the preserve is open from 9 a.m.–5 p.m., Wednesday–Sunday (closed Monday and Tuesday). Wait for the site manager, but if he does not appear in a short time, drive to the residence at the end of the entrance lane and fetch him. Interpretive tours also are scheduled at 1 p.m. and 3 p.m. on Saturday and Sunday during these months.

From October through March, advance registration is required to visit the bog. For more information, contact Cedar Bog State Nature Preserve, 980 Woodburn Road, Urbana, Ohio 43078, (513) 484-3744 (site manager); or 1-800-686-1541 or (614) 297-2606 at the Ohio Historical Society, 1982 Velma Avenue, Columbus, Ohio 43211-2497.

A restroom is located in the parking lot, but drinking water is not available. Carry a small canteen. The fen water sometimes rises above the boardwalk trail, so be advised that the path can be wet and slippery in places.

Geology

Cedar Bog's special geological history creates the unique habitat for the wildlife thriving here. It is a remnant of a series of fens, swamp forests, and wet prairies that once stretched across the broad Mad River Valley, which itself was formed by the runoff from the Wisconsinan ice sheet 12,000–18,000 years ago. The Wisconsinan was the last of at least three (possibly four) continental ice sheets that blanketed Ohio during the Ice Age.

The melting glacier removed hilltops, rerouted streams, and scoured bedrock. In southern Champaign County, it dumped hundreds of feet of gravel into the abandoned tributaries of the ancient Teays River, a northwesterly flowing stream which, in its preglacial heyday, rivaled the potency of the Ohio River. (The Teays River was long gone before the arrival of the Wisconsinan glacier.) Two long ridges of this gravel debris, or moraines, flank a valley where Cedar Bog is situated.

The groundwater which seeps down the Mad River Valley and the smaller Urbana Outwash percolates through the calcium-magnesium-enriched gravel and surfaces as springs northeast of the preserve. These fountains—cool because they have not been warmed by the sun—keep the water flowing through the fen year-round, and at a relatively constant temperature (54º Fahrenheit) and volume.

The "hard" water is charged with dissolved bicarbonates of calcium and magnesium. These compounds combine with mud to form a lime-rich soil called marl. Only specialized plants can survive in this rather harsh habitat of cool water and marl.

The spring water "flushes" the fen and refreshes Cedar Run as it meanders throughout the preserve. This flushing action is the trademark of a fen. In contrast, a bog sits in a basin and catches precipitation. Water leaves a bog through evaporation. (See the comparison of a bog and a fen in this chapter.)

The water supports the site's delicate ecosystem. The fen shrinks whenever the flow has been interrupted by prolonged drought, mining of the gravel, or diversion (draining or ditching) for farming, transportation, recreation, or housing developments.

Cedar Bog is $^{1}/_{16}$ its original size. Long ago it swamped 7,000 acres. Scientists have figured that 15 of Ohio's 52 original fens have vanished, and that the survivors, like Cedar Bog, are tiny shadows, mere relics, of their former glory. Ohio has lost 95 percent of its wetlands since the settlement of white people.

Left to nature's slow pace, fens and bogs eventually would fill with natural debris (soil and plant matter) and turn into forests. Somewhere else, new wetlands would emerge and continue the life cycle. However, human activities have severely disturbed this process of regeneration. We can say reliably that a new bog will not be born when one meets its natural death. Consequently, Cedar Bog and other rare fens must be "saved" from natural forces, and managed for preservation.

Wildlife

At first, the fen's saline water (calcium carbonate) and cool temperature discouraged plant life. Eventually, though, sedge (a marsh grass) took root on the marl flats. Repeated growths of sedge formed a peat-like deposit and sponsored the encroachment of northern white cedar, which gives the preserve its name. Northern white cedar, or arbor vitae, a common tree in colder, northern climes, came into Ohio in the vanguard of the glacier. This tree, designated as potentially threatened in Ohio, survives in pockets that encourage its growth. These sturdy specimens were prized for railroad ties and as Christmas trees.

Oddly, the fallen needles of the cedar produce an acidic soil enabling partridgeberry, bulblet fern, Canada mayflower, starflower, and green woodland orchid (potentially threatened species) to flourish.

Thirty-two other Ice Age imports dwell here, including shrubs like the scrubby cinquefoil and the state-threatened northern dwarf or swamp birch, which survives to the Arctic Circle but reaches its southern extreme here. Some eastern hardwoods have gained a foothold on the periphery, notably butternut, a potentially threatened tree whose nut attracts deer.

Other shrubs are represented by the common spicebush, ninebark, willows, huckleberry, and alder-leaved buckthorn. These communities, once more numerous, are being crowded by the arbor vitae.

Wild orchids from the temperate areas—small yellow lady's slippers (endangered) and grass-pink (potentially threatened)—mix with prairie blossoms, such as blazing star and prairie dock, which entered the scene during a dry, warm spell, the so-called Xerothermic Period, about 4,000 years ago. Like Ohio's wetlands, the state's prairie meadows enjoyed a greater range and collection of flora.

As you hike, look for large-flowered trillium, marsh marigolds, Johnny jump-ups, rue anemone, three kinds of Solomon's seal, round-leaved sundew (potentially threatened), Riddell's goldenrod, coreopsis, prairie valerian (endangered and at its eastern limit), dog violets, queen-of-the-prairie, bellflowers, skunk cabbage, Canadian burnet (a.k.a. white swamp candles), grass-of-parnassus, Kalm's lobelia, and the potentially threatened fringed gentian, a late-summer and autumn bloomer.

All totaled, 59 protected species (endangered or otherwise) have taken up residence at Cedar Bog. One of them is the venomous massasauga rattlesnake, known to nest in a field of Kentucky fescue, a hybrid grass. Another is the spotted turtle (look for spots on its shell), an elusive reptile that dives to safety when it senses danger. Both of these critters are designated "special interest" by the Division of Wildlife, a listing roughly equal to "potentially threatened."

Several butterflies commonly seen flitting about at

Cedar Bog are rarely found anywhere else in Ohio. These are the swamp metalmark (endangered), Milbert's tortoise shell, and silvery checkerspot.

Cedar Bog provides a habitat for more than 100 bird species. One rarity that has been observed here is the yellow rail, which breeds only in tiny, widely scattered areas in the Great Lakes and Canada.

Eighteen kinds of fish swim in Cedar Run. Two rare swimmers are the endangered tongue-tied minnow and the brook trout, the latter designated "special interest." The cool waters of spring-fed Cedar Run is one of the few places the brook trout survives in Ohio. The Mad River sponsors trout too, but most other Ohio streams are too warm for this prized game fish. Other unusual fish include the American brook lamprey, mottled sculpin, brook stickleback, and central mudminnow. Of course, fishing in the preserve is unlawful.

History

Though much of the original fen—known at various times as Cedar Swamp, Urbana Bog, Dallas Cedar Swamp, and Dallas Bog—became farmland, a few landowners protected this unique land. One of them was Russell Randall, who guarded his showy lady's slippers (wild orchids) with a shotgun in the 1920s.

In 1922, wildflower artist and Cincinnati Tree Council founder Florence Murdoch, owner of some of the wetland, tried to get the fen protected by the Ohio Department of Forestry. Others took up the cause later, notably the Urbana Women's Club. Finally, the state set aside $10,000 to buy the fen in 1938, but just as the transaction started, Governor Martin L. Davey (Davey Woods preserve in Champaign County is named after him) vetoed the deal.

Florence Murdoch, who had sold her share of the fen to a relative early in 1941, carried the torch again later that year when she discovered that one of the owners planned to drain the bog and fatten cattle in it. She enlisted the support of Edward Sinclair Thomas and Erwin C. Zepp, both curators at the Ohio Archeological and Historical Society, the precursor of the Ohio Historical Society.

Thomas talked with the new governor, John W. Bricker, who agreed not to block the purchase. Thomas and others finagled $5,000 from the state to buy an 88-acre tract of Cedar Bog for the state's first nature preserve. The purchase killed the cattle ranch scheme. The title was transferred to the historical society in 1942.

Later, the Ohio Chapter of The Nature Conservancy helped to acquire some 200 acres to form a buffer zone beside the fen. Additional land has been acquired over the years.

Greater protection came in April 1967 when the U.S. Department of the Interior declared Cedar Bog a National Natural Landmark. On February 28, 1979 the fen was designated a state nature preserve by the Ohio Department of Natural Resources.

Conservation groups led a successful campaigns in 1959 and again in 1972 against widening SR 68, the main drag between Urbana and Springfield. However, those so-called highway "improvements" resurfaced again in the early 1990s.

FEN VS. BOG

For years the words bog, marsh, fen, swamp, and quagmire were used interchangeably (except by astute students of wetlands). Now we know each has a special place in the natural process.

BOG

- Starts as a pond, formed when a chunk of ice broke from a glacier and melted in a depression.
- Water enters as precipitation and leaves through evaporation.
- Water is acidic (3.5–5.5 pH); oxygen and nitrogen deficient.
- Generally circular-shaped, and vegetation grows in rings from an "eye."
- Water temperature is usually around 54 º F.
- Northern plants like red maple, birch, hemlock, blackgum, and pines may find a habitat here.
- Most bogs in Ohio are in the northeast, but a few occur in the northwest. See Brown's Lake Bog.

FEN

- Lies in shallow areas near gravel ridges (moraines) formed by glaciers. The gravel is rich in calcium and magnesium.
- Groundwater travels through the marly gravel, surfaces as a spring, and leaves via another body of water. Though a current may be imperceptible, water flows through and flushes a fen.
- Water is slightly acidic to alkaline (5.5–8 pH); lacks oxygen and nitrogen.
- Water temperature remains fairly constant at 54 º F.
- Sedge grass and arbor vitae are common plants.
- Usually "meadowy" in shape; and plants grow in clusters, not concentrically.
- In Ohio, fens are found in the northeastern and western parts of the state. Besides Cedar Bog, visit Jackson Bog (another misnomer) and Frame Lake-Herrick Fen state nature preserves.

Trout lily

DAVEY WOODS STATE NATURE PRESERVE

Davey Woods protects one of the largest and richest stands of old growth forest in west central Ohio. An impressive 40-acre parcel of tulip trees, many reaching a height of 100 feet and a diameter of four feet, is the hallmark of this preserve.

Location

Western Champaign County, Concord and Mad River townships.

From Urbana, go seven miles west on State Route 36, then north (right turn) a mile on Neal Road to Smith Road (Township Road 65). Travel .4 mile on Smith Road, turn right on Lonesome Road (Township Road 66) for .2 mile to the parking lot on the left. Lonesome and Smith roads serve as two boundaries of this triangular-shaped preserve.

Ownership

Ohio Department of Natural Resources, Division of Natural Areas and Preserves.

Size & Designation

Davey Woods, dedicated as an interpretive preserve on May 2, 1990, comprises 103 acres.

Nearby Natural Attractions

Just a few minutes drive away is Kiser Lake State Park, Siegenthaler Esker State Nature Preserve, and Cedar Bog Nature Preserve, all in Champaign County.

Access

Two connecting trails basically trace the perimeter of the preserve. The paths were blazed by members of an archery club which used the grounds. Study the trail map posted on the information board before heading off. Walk both of them for a two-mile journey.

I started on the Conrad Trail, heading northwest (parallel to Lonesome Road) up a moderately steep ridge. The trail turns south, follows the west property line, and descends into a small picturesque valley. The path wanders along an intermittent creek, then climbs another slope.

Midway up this hill you run into the Short Loop Trail. Turn left at this intersection if you want to return to the parking lot. I recommend that you bear right, and follow the loop path around the crest of a hill, through tall timbers, and back down to the starting point.

The preserve is open during daylight hours. State naturalist-led programs are scheduled during the year. For more information contact the Ohio Department of Natural Resources, Division of Natural Areas and Preserves, Fountain Square, Building F-1, Columbus, Ohio 43224-1331; phone at (614) 265-6543.

Geology

The undulating plains of the area are characteristic of glaciated Ohio (referring to the two-thirds of Ohio whose surface was shaped by glaciers). The surface essentially is composed of glacial till, a blend of clay, silt, sand, and small rocks, deposited by the retreating Wisconsinan glacier, some 12,000–18,000 years ago. Ohio's fertile agricultural soils developed in this Ice Age sediment. Beneath the till lies Silurian-age dolomite and limestone, formed some 410–440 million years ago. Limestone and dolomite, made of compressed marine life, signal the presence of an ocean here long ago.

The preserve is drained by two intermittent streams which merge near the parking lot and flow into nearby Nettle Creek. Intermittent means water does not always flow in them year-round, perhaps only seasonally or after heavy rain. Nevertheless, the erosive power of these diminutive currents has sculpted the hollows in the woods.

Wildlife

Though by no means a virgin forest, much of Davey Woods has reached maturity (meaning the trees have reached their full size and are naturally and somewhat evenly spaced). Other portions are recovering from agricultural use, and struggle in various stages of succession. This growth, found at the start of the Conrad Trail, shows itself in thickets of young trees competing for dominance.

Besides the towering tulip trees, some 50 species of trees and shrubs thrive in Davey Woods, notably large beech, sugar maple, shagbark hickory, red oak, white ash, basswood, white oak, cherry, blackgum, and Ohio buckeye. Wildflowers carpet the grounds in the spring.

Numerous birds reside in the woods, including such favorites as the cerulean, Kentucky, and hooded warblers. Deer find refuge here. Four of them tiptoed passed me on the Conrad Trail.

History

The woods, known locally for years as Conrad Woods, survived because the Grayson Conrad family resisted the temptation to log it. The main trail honors the four-decade conservation effort of the former owners, who in the mid-1980s announced they were looking for a buyer.

Dr. Louis Laux, a biology professor at Wittenberg University in Springfield, took the cause to the Ohio Chapter of The Nature Conservancy who purchased the land in 1988, aided by a $55,000 donation from the Davey Tree Expert Company of Kent. The gift amounted to half the purchase price. ODNR agreed to pay off the remaining half of the loan and to acquire the property from The Nature Conservancy.

Monarch butterfly

ERIE SAND BARRENS

To the casual summer visitor, this seemingly God-forsaken place looks like some overgrown, weed-infested field a farmer forgot to plow. There aren't many shade trees, no boulders to climb, and no body of water in sight. So, what gives? Well, 12,000 years ago, this barren land was Lake Erie's beach. Geologically, it was called Lake Warren. Later, plants of the western tallgrass prairie rooted themselves into the harsh sandy ridges, and have somehow survived for 4,000 years.

Location

Southwestern Erie County, Oxford Township.

From State Route 4 (about 1.5 miles north of the Ohio Turnpike), in a hamlet appropriately called Sandhill, head east on Mason Road. About 7/10 mile down the road, in a village called Bloomingville, turn left on Taylor Road. A mile ahead the narrow road reaches an unmarked fork. Take the right fork, known as Scheid Road. (Taylor Road deadends ahead.) Look for the wooden preserve sign on the right and park in the small allotted space or on the berm (especially if you are driving an RV or another oversized vehicle).

Ownership

Ohio Department of Natural Resources, Division of Natural Areas and Preserves.

Size & Designation

Erie Sand Barrens is a 32-acre interpretive preserve.

Nearby Natural Attractions

Near Huron visit Old Woman Creek and Sheldon Marsh state nature preserves. Take the ferry to Kelleys Island to see Glacial Grooves State Memorial and Kelleys Island State Park. Milan, Resthaven, and Willow Point state wildlife areas also are located in Erie County.

Access

The mowed loop trail starts at the parking lot. You can't

miss it. Figure on a half-mile walk.

Summer visitors will be treated to wildflowers, butterflies, and mosquitoes, so bring insect repellent. Wear a cap and long pants. A canteen might come in handy because there is no drinking water nearby. Come here in the winter if you want to study the sand ridge.

The preserve is open every day from sunrise to sunset. For more information contact the Ohio Department of Natural Resources, Division of Natural Areas and Preserves, Fountain Square, Building F-1, Columbus, Ohio 43224-1331; phone (614) 265-6453.

Geology

To appreciate this preserve you have to go back about 12,000 years. At that time the Wisconsinan ice mass sat in a basin today occupied by Lake Erie.

Try to imagine a series of interrelated geological events. First, north-flowing water blocked by the glacier forms a new body of water called Lake Warren. Water melting from the glacier also fills the lake.

Meanwhile, a small drain opens at the eastern end of the lake, either through a gap in the ice or over a low lake bank. The shoreline of the lake, however, stays relatively constant for years because the amount of water entering the lake equals the amount escaping.

Picture the melting glacier and northbound streams carrying sand and gravel into the lake. Waves and currents produced by a cold, north wind then distribute the sand onto beaches, sand bars, and sand spits.

As the glacier melts, more water escapes through new outlets, like the St. Lawrence valley. The lake shrinks and leaves its former shoreline high and dry.

About 4,000 years ago the climate in Ohio became warmer and drier than the present climate. Scientists call that heat wave the Xerothermic Period. The existing deciduous forest shriveled and the tallgrass prairie of the Great Plains moved into Ohio. When the climate cooled again, the prairie retreated westward. The forest returned, except in scattered pockets where local conditions made it possible for the prairie to survive.

This sandy beach ridge was one of these pockets. Here plants of the prairie and the beach survive on the ancient shore of Lake Warren.

Wildlife

Plants that tolerate dry, well-drained, windswept, sandy soil thrive in the preserve. These include, in wet depressions, Ohio's only colony of least St. John's-wort, an endangered species. Here lives variegated scouring rush, flat-leaved rush, olivaceous spikerush, dwarf bulrush, twisted yellow-eyed grass, and field sedge, all threatened plants; and potentially threatened specimens named grooved flax, tall St. John's-wort, lance-leaved violet, and Virginia meadow-beauty. The latter plant has few kin in Ohio—one community in Gallia County, another in Jackson County. Sand panic grass, common in the Great Plains, grows here at its easternmost limit.

Specimens like the striking partridge pea, prairie milkweed, and sand panicgrass occupy the driest and highest ground. Other rarities growing here are western ironweed, variegated horsetail, slender knotweed, arrow-leaved violet, and hairy milkweed. See if you find sweet everlasting, heath aster, and boneset.

In August, the time of my visit, butterflies swirled about like wind-tossed confetti. The orange, black-veined monarch butterfly was numerous. This beauty winters in one concentrated area of Mexico and migrates north in the spring. It would not survive without the milkweed, the host plant for the monarch's summer life cycle—from egg laying to caterpillar to full-fledged butterfly.

In spite of its bright coloring and slow, clumsy flight, which appears to make it an easy target for predators, the monarch population is wholesome. That's because it is toxic to predators. The monarchs have learned to tolerate and store cardiac glycosides, a mild poison absorbed from its host plant.

Birds which mistakenly eat a monarch caterpillar or butterfly get sick. The striking orange wings of the monarch alert predators to leave the insect alone.

The nonpoisonous viceroy butterfly mimics the monarch to survive. It hopes that predators think it is a distasteful monarch. Viceroys are not as abundant as monarchs. If they were equal or greater in number than monarchs, birds would not become trained to avoid the orange and black flyers.

Cows shun milkweed because of its ill effects. Digitalis, another cardiac glycoside, can be extracted from purple foxglove, another plant found in the preserve.

History

Early white settlers thought this "barren" land was worthless, and unfit for the plow. But as the population grew, even this "barren" land got farmed and grazed.

The Erie sand barrens owe their preservation to a local botanist and the U.S.

Army. Turn-of-the-century botanist E. L. Moseley discovered the geological and botanical importance of the land he called Oxford Prairie. During World War II, the U.S. Army bought most of the prairie, then largely under the plow, for an ammo dump. The army, now holding the land, stopped farming and let unused portions of the land grow back into a prairie.

The National Aeronautics and Space Administration acquired the 6,000-acre tract in 1958 and established the Plum Brook Station, a research facility still occupying neighboring land. (Taylor Road stops at the fence that surrounds this NASA site.)

In the early 1980s, 1,600 acres of the station became government surplus. The U.S. Department of Defense, with the help of the Ohio Chapter of The Nature Conservancy, transferred 32 acres to the Division of Natural and Preserves in May 1983.

Journal

August 1993. Temperature, 90º. I shake the canteen for its last drop, slap bloated mosquitos on my leg, and wipe the sweat off of my neck. Today would be the day to turn back the clock 12,000 years, when cool waves of Lake Warren would be just a few feet away. I rummage through the car for refreshment and find a strawless Hi-C juice box under the front seat. The liquid is body temperature—car body temperature. It will do until I reach the pop machine at the crossroads on Route 4. I would've missed my Coke 12,000 years ago.

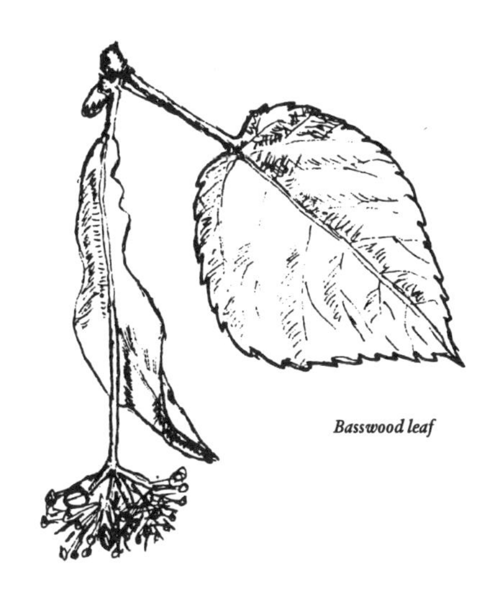

Basswood leaf

GOLL WOODS STATE NATURE PRESERVE

We are indebted to five generations of the Goll family who resisted the temptation to flatten the luxuriant forest they called the "big woods." Some of Ohio's oldest oaks preside over Goll Woods, a virgin thatch of hardwoods and a remnant of the vast Great Black Swamp. The woods is now an isolated island, and Fulton County's only link to its original natural past. ★ ZZZ

Location

Western Fulton County, German Township.

From Archbold, go 2.5 miles north on State Route 66, then west (left) on County Road F for three miles. At the intersection with County Road 26, head south (left turn) for 1/4 mile and pull into the parking lot on the east side. CR 26 runs through the middle of the woods. Another smaller parking facility is located on CR F, west of the intersection with CR 26.

Ownership

Ohio Department of Natural Resources, Division of Natural Areas and Preserves.

Size & Designation

In December 1974, Goll Woods joined the National Registry of Natural Landmarks, administered by the U.S. Department of the Interior. A month later, in January 1975, it was dedicated as a state scenic nature preserve by the Ohio Department of Natural Resources. The preserve protects 320.6 acres. The Society of American Foresters also has declared Goll Woods a natural area.

Nearby Natural Attractions

Harrison Lake State Park, just a few miles north of Goll Woods, offers hiking, camping, swimming, and other outdoor recreation opportunities.

Access

Tree lovers get ready. For the next 3.5-miles you will journey through a cathedral of tall timbers the likes of which you will not find in many places in Ohio. You are going to see trees the size of smokestacks. One giant oak is believed to be 500 years old.

After visiting the East and West Woods, you will pass the Goll family burial grounds, enter the floodplain of the Tiffin River (the home of buxom sycamores and cottonwoods), and wind through a mature pine plantation. The adventure begins at the parking lot on CR 26.

Study the bulletin board beside the parking lot before departing. We are going to walk the perimeter of the preserve. A plaque commemorating Goll Woods as a National Natural Landmark hangs on the flip side of the board.

Ignore the arrows on the trailhead signpost which point to the Cottonwood, Burr Oak, and TulipTree trails. Instead, follow the path at the left, heading east. This is the north leg of the Cottonwood Trail.

Skip the Burr Oak Trail that goes right and cuts across the East Woods to the south leg of the Cottonwood Trail. Our path continues east, then heads south (near a forest pond) into the ancient forest, and finally west. Again, the Burr Oak Trail joins from the right. Again, skip it, and keep going straight.

As you near CR 26, the path forks. A right turn, the Cottonwood Trail, returns to the parking lot completing a 1.75-mile loop. But we will bear left and follow the Tulip Tree Trail into the West Woods. The path crosses CR 26, continues west until it nears CR F, then swings north and links with Toadshade Trail, entering from the right. The Tulip Tree Trail ends here.

Continuing north on a parallel route with the road, Toadshade Trail crosses CR F just south of the Goll Cemetery and enters the floodplain of the Tiffin River. Ahead, relax awhile at the deck perched above the river (more a creek than a river). It's also a good place to observe wildlife.

Back on your feet, you'll see the trail curve to the right, recross CR F, and wind through rows of planted pines to CR 26. Your car is parked across the road.

Goll Woods is a swamp forest growing on horizontal land. Consequently, the trails are often muddy and slippery, so wear appropriate footwear. All of the paths are wide and easy to follow. Insect repellent is recommended during the summer. I regretted wearing shorts during my early September visit because of nettles at the edge of the paths.

The preserve is open from sunup to sundown. Restrooms are located in the CR 26 parking lot, which easily accommodates school buses. You can spread a picnic blanket on the lawn, but remember to dump your trash in the garbage barrel near the toilets. A drinking water pump is located at the bulletin board.

Interpretive nature programs are held at the preserve throughout the year. For more information contact the Ohio Department of Natural Resources, Division of Natural Areas and Preserves, Building F-1, Columbus, Ohio 43224-1331; phone (614) 265-6453.

Geology

The story of Goll Woods begins 12,000 years ago, when the latest continental ice sheet, the Wisconsinan glacier, was parked in the neighborhood of Canada. The frozen mass had recently covered two-thirds of Ohio. With climate now warming, it was retreating northward at a snail's pace.

A huge lake refreshed by glacial meltwater and northbound runoff filled the basin south of the glacier. The lake level swelled to 200 feet above the current level of Lake Erie and once boasted a shoreline that reached into Allen and northeastern Mercer counties.

The shoreline of this lake fluctuated. Whenever the glacier temporarily advanced the lake inundated and submerged the existing beach ridge. A new beach then would form, but its contour depended on the position of the glacier. Names have been given to each stage of the lake: Maumee, Whittlesey, Warren, and Erie.

The three major natural phenomena of Northwestern Ohio—the Great Black Swamp, the oak openings, and the marshes of Lake Erie and Sandusky Bay—trace their origins to these glacial lakes and the ensuing events. Goll Woods is a remnant of the Great Black Swamp, our interest in this chapter.

The water reached its current level (Lake Erie) after the Niagara-St. Lawrence outlet opened through the wall of ice. That left the old sandy shorelines high and dry. Much of the former lake bottom became a great, exposed plain. It measured about a 120 miles in length and 30–40 miles in width, roughly parallel to the Maumee River.

The powdery clay deposit that sifted to the old lake floor, now serving as an impervious subsoil beneath a more porous topsoil, refused to let water soak deep into the earth. The poor drainage on this flat terrain did not help matters. Muddy, flooded, gooey conditions prevailed and gave rise to the "Great Black Swamp," as it was called beginning in 1812. The "black" referred to either to color of the soil, the shadow beneath the forest canopy, or the fortunes of those who ventured into it.

Wildlife

Though still affected by the glacier, vegetation quickly occupied the chilly swamp. Lichens, mosses, and sedges appeared first, but they gave way, as the climate warmed, to conifers (spruce, pine, tamarack, hemlock) and eventually to the familiar deciduous trees (oak, beech, birch, maple, etc) that dominate today.

Humans began draining water from the swamp as a goal of public policy in the mid-19th century. The former forest wetland, converted to cropland, shrank to a few isolated islands of tall timbers. Goll Woods is one of the last vestiges of that primeval realm. An 80-acre section of the East Woods is considered an undisturbed, virgin woodland. It is this woodlot that draws the most attention.

A booklet on the preserve claims the forest probably evolved from a reed swamp to a sedge meadow, then to a dogwood-cottonwood community, and eventually to a swamp forest. Goll Woods continues to evolve. A discerning eye will notice four types of forest in the preserve: the swamp forest; a community supporting a mixed bag of species (called a mixed mesophytic forest); a beech-maple forest; and a plantation of maturing pines, sowed in rows back in the mid-1960s. The pine forest did not occur naturally.

Pockets of the swamp forest exist throughout the woodlot. Water lies on the surface most of the year, thanks to the subsoil of impenetrable clay. Trees that can tolerate wet ground live here, such as black ash, red and silver maples, and swamp oak. Scientists refer to this grouping of trees as the elm-ash-soft maple swamp forest. Dutch elm disease killed the elms that once stood shoulder to shoulder in the canopy. Shade-tolerant, moisture-loving pawpaw and spicebush grow in the understory.

The mixed mesophytic forest is most apparent on the west side of the East Woods. Long ago it was a swamp forest, but as the land drained new species entered the scene. Today, it is a collection of oaks (bur, white, chinkapin), walnut, shagbark hickory, basswood, tulip tree, and some white ash and sugar maple.

One behemoth bur oak from this assemblage, estimated to be 500 years old, measures five feet, two inches in diameter. Foresters have calculated that a pair of huge white oaks from this grove would provide enough lumber to build a small house.

Towering, erect specimens of tulip tree (a.k.a. whitewood and yellow poplar) rise in these woods. Pioneers often built log cabins from tulip trees because the young tree prunes itself resulting in a straight trunk.

A beech-maple community thrives in a cluster in the eastern part of the East Woods. These trees reside on what remains of a beach ridge formed by old Lake Whittlesey around 11,000 years ago. (See geology section above.) Though barely discernible, this slight elevation provides enough drainage for these species to gain a foothold. Naturalists call this stable condition a climax forest.The beeches and maples may enlarge their domain if the woods continues to drain.

You will have to look above the top of the understory trees and the saplings to find the limbs of most of these giants. The branching starts about 50–60 feet above the ground.

Goll Woods also safeguards blue and green ash, bigtooth aspen, black gum (black tupelo, sourgum), black maple, two types of dogwood, ironwood, Ohio buckeye, bitternut and pignut hickories, redbud, hackberry, hophornbeam, box elder, and others. Sycamores and cottonwoods arch over the Tiffin River.

Wildflowers steal your eyes from the trees in the warm months. These include appendaged waterleaf, false spikenard, nodding trillium, perfoliate bellwort, avens, bastard toadflax, jimsonweed, and turtlehead. Three protected plants hide in preserve—three-birds orchid (threatened), spotted coral root, and jack-in-the-pulpit (both potentially threatened).

Prominent ferns found here include Christmas, Goldie's, rattlesnake, fragile, lady, sensitive, glade, maidenhair, and spinulose woodfern. During the Carboniferous Period (280–345 million years ago) ferns grew as tall as trees.

Birds, plenty of them, nest in these peaceful woods. For a challenge, look for the Baltimore orioles, eastern wood pewee (listen for its pee-a-wee song), red-bellied woodpecker, redstart, rose-breasted grosbeak, scarlet tanager, towhee, and barred owl. The endangered hermit thrush might be seen here too.

Dr. Roy W. Rings of the Ohio Agricultural Research and Development Center in Wooster collected 213 insect species from Goll Woods in 1988 (the year ODNR stopped limited insect hunting in the preserve). One common insect was the tiger swallowtail butterfly. Another carried the name "olive-shaded bird dropping moth."

Elk roamed in the area until the 1830s. Mountain lions disappeared in the 1840s, while bears and wolves stayed into the 1870s, and raven into the 1880s. Deer, raccoons, and red fox are the biggest furry critters found here now. The latter's tracks resemble a small dog's. Note the direction of the tracks. If they go straight they probably belong to a fox. Dog trails tend to zigzag, and the tracks appear to be staggered or out of line (hence, dogtracking).

The forest ponds harbor fairy shrimp, crayfish, scud, frogs, and salamanders, a food source of raccoons, skunk, and opossums.

History

The Ottawa, Chippewa, Delaware, Pottawatomie, and perhaps Wyandot Indians hunted in the Great Black Swamp. These were Indians living in the region explored in 1679 by Chevalier Robert de la Salle, a French fur trader.

In 1834, more than a half century after the American Revolution, German pioneers settled in the area, hence German Township. Arriving in 1836, among a second wave of immigrants, was Peter Goll and his family from Dobs, France. Goll purchased 80 acres for $1.25 an acre the following year. Over time his acquisitions grew to 600 acres.

In the 1960s, the preservation of Goll Woods became a goal of the Northwestern Ohio Natural Resources Council, Toledo Naturalists Association, and the Ohio Chapter of The Nature Conservancy. The Ohio Department of Natural Resources bought the property from the Goll family in 1966, and dedicated it as an interpretive preserve in January 1975. A month earlier, in December 1974, the U.S. Department of theInterior listed Goll Woods on the National Registry of National Natural Landmarks.

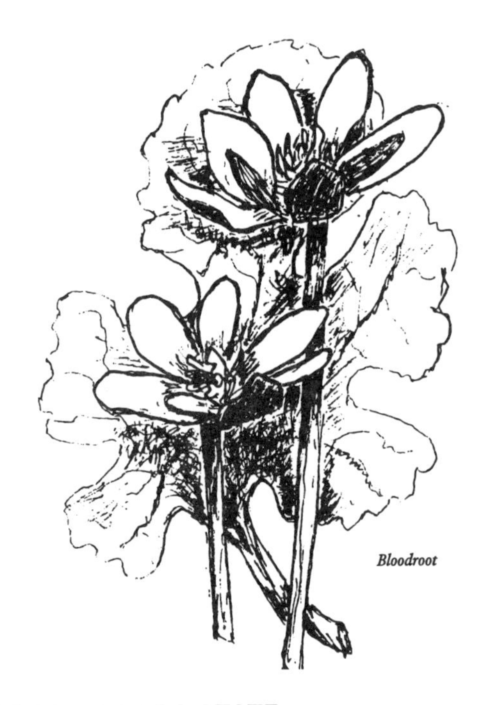

Bloodroot

GROSS WOODS STATE NATURE PRESERVE

For generations, this thick mat of trees was called "Grandpa's Woods." Grandpa was Samuel Gross, who vowed to keep this 40-acre swamp forest looking exactly as it did when he inherited it from his father, Nicholas. Grandpa's descendents continued that conservation ethic. Now the Ohio Department of Natural Resources is entrusted to keep the place looking as Nicholas Gross first saw it. ZZZ

Location

Northeast Shelby County, Jackson Township.

Leave Interstate 75 at the Botkins Road exit and travel on Botkins Road about six miles to the preserve parking lot on the left side of the road. It is the largest patch of woods around.

Ownership

Ohio Department of Natural Resources, Division of Natural Areas and Preserves.

Size & Designation

This 40-acre woodland became a state interpretive preserve on May 4, 1982.

Nearby Natural Attractions

Visit Lake Loramie State Park in western Shelby County, or Indian Lake State Park, a stone's throw away in Logan County. Greenville Falls State Nature Preserve is located just few miles across the county line in northwestern Miami County. Siegenthaler Esker State Nature Preserve lies in northwestern Champaign County.

Access

A 3,000-foot boardwalk trail built in 1985 loops through the wet preserve. The path begins and ends at the parking lot which can accommodate several vehicles, including recreational vehicles.

Since this site is a swamp forest, visitors should protect themselves from insect pests in the summer. Please don't ride bicycles on the boardwalk. Splinters await the feet of barefooted strollers.

For information about Gross Woods and nature programs held there, contact the Ohio Department of Natural Resources, Division of Natural Areas and Preserves, Fountain Square, Building F-1, Columbus, Ohio 43224-1331; phone (614) 265-6453.

Geology

This part of Ohio is as flat as plywood, though a few rolling hills break the monotony. Gross Woods lies atop poorly drained till, a rich mixture of clay, gravel, sand, and rocks deposited by Wisconsinan ice sheet some 12,000 years ago. In the spring, shallow, black pools form in the depressions.

To the northwest, outside the preserve, stretches the Mississewa end moraine, a slightly elevated till ridge showing us where the glacier stalled and unloaded sediment in its vanguard.

If you dig down deep enough you will uncover dolomite, a sedimentary rock made of marine life that settled to the bottom of an ocean during the Silurian geological period, some 420 million years ago.

Wildlife

Gross Woods is one of the last mixed-species swamp forests in Western Ohio. By "mixed" scientists mean the diversity of trees in the woods is unusual and extraordinary. And, you won't find many (if any) 40-acre mature woodlots standing in these parts.

Gross Woods is a bur oak-basswood swamp forest, though 25 varieties of trees grow here. Buxom specimens of these deciduous hardwoods dominate the wettest spots. Mammoth beeches and red oak grip the higher ground—here, measured in inches.

Some of the trees are more than 200 years old. Notice how the trunks of these giants rise straight above the canopy of understory species, such as sugar maple. The branches on some of the tall ones don't appear until the 50-foot mark, evidence of the maturity of this woods. Trees which grow in open areas sprout branches much closer to the ground.

Healthy groups of shagbark hickory, black walnut, white oak, and ash are easily found here too.

Some 150 kinds of wildflowers have been identified, notably the delicate miterwort (bishop's cap), swamp buttercup, wild geranium, toadside trillium, cleavers (used by pioneers for bed ticking), and bloodroot. Come here in the spring for this floral show.

A group of great blue herons once had a rookery (nesting area) along the western edge of the preserve. They abandoned the woods a few years ago, perhaps moving to a site closer to their feeding spot at Indian Lake.

The usual cast of four-legged forest critters frolics in the forest. And a normal bevy of songbirds sprinkles the air with merriment in the spring and summer.

History

The preserve honors Samuel Gross (1852-1937) and his seven children who kept this woodlot as near to pristine as could several farming generations. Their "disturbance" amounted to removing several oaks for barn timbers, and collecting some downed wood for warmth. Grandpa Gross also harvested game in his woods and gathered edible mushrooms.

In 1972 the Gross family donated the parcel to the Ohio Chapter of The Nature Conservancy which turned it over to ODNR in 1976.

Journal

In "A Pilgrim at Tinker Creek," Annie Dillard wrote, "Big trees stir memories." Indeed, they do. Here, every tree stands as a memorial to Samuel Gross and his descendents. There are not many tree stands left in northwestern Ohio. Imagine a hairbrush with just three bristle clusters or a comb with four teeth.

Gross woods stirs memories of the thick thatch of trees that once covered Ohio. I imagine standing in the middle of it when it's at its fullest—midsummer. My eyes might be able to penetrate it a mere 100 yards. I play "choices." Imagine coming here as a pioneer and never being able to see farther than a hundred yards wherever I stand in an endless forest. I think about never being able to see the sky even on its brightest, bluest day. That was Ohio 300 years ago. Now, I picture myself, midsummer, in the mall parking lot looking for my car. Where would I rather be? (I guess it isn't fair thinking about what I just got on sale.)

Spotted turtle

IRWIN PRAIRIE STATE NATURE PRESERVE

Five distinct plant communities thrive in this preserve, variously described as a wet prairie, and an oak savanna. The rare wildflowers and grasslike plants make this a special place—one of the last sedge meadows in the state.

Location

Northwest Lucas County, Spencer Township.

From Interstate 475, head west on U.S. Route 20 about four miles, then go south on Crissey Road to Bancroft Street. Turn right on Bancroft Street and travel west about 1.5 miles (passed Wolfinger and Irwin roads) to the parking lot on the left.

Ownership

The Ohio Department of Natural Resources, Division of Natural Areas and Preserves.

Size & Designation

This 187-acre prairie was dedicated as an interpretive nature preserve on December 27, 1974.

Nearby Natural Attractions

Irwin Prairie borders Secor Metropark which has entrances on US 20 and Wolfinger Road. Visit these Toledo Metroparks: Swan Creek Preserve, Oak Openings Preserve, Pearson, and Wildwood Preserve.

Lucas County also boasts Maumee Bay and Crane Creek state parks, Ottawa National Wildlife Refuge, Maumee State Forest, and Magee Marsh and Metzger Marsh state wildlife areas.

Access

A boardwalk trail starts from the parking lot and heads south through a stand of mixed oaks (around the parking lot, actually), a shrub swamp, and a edge meadow. The walk bends left (east), crosses Irwin Road, and snakes through another sedge meadow, a small pin oak forest, and finally to a viewing platform that gazes upon a grassland. There is a fork in the trail just before you reach the observation tower. Choose either leg of this loop—each leads to the platform.

Exit by retracing your steps. This easy, flat ramble covers a little more than two miles. Summer hikes require precautions against insects. You may be tempted to walk barefooted in the summer. *Don't! The hot boards can scorch your feet.*

Signs tell visitors not to ride bicycles on the boardwalk. But I discovered, during my tour of the preserve, that adult and teenaged bicyclists ignore the sign. Walkers should be careful but assertive. After all, the boardwalk was designed for foot travel. Please keep two-wheelers off the boards.

Irwin Prairie can be visited during daylight hours every day. Drinking water and restrooms are located in the parking lot.

ODNR has published a booklet on the natural history of Irwin Prairie. To obtain a copy, and for other information (such as nature programs) contact the Ohio Department of Natural Resources, Division of Natural Areas and Preserves, Fountain Square, Building F-1, Columbus, Ohio 43224-1331; phone (614) 265-6453.

Geology

Irwin Prairie lies in a yellow-brown sand belt known as the Oak Openings which once stretched from Detroit, Michigan, into Lucas County, and parts of Fulton and Henry counties. In Ohio, the Oak Openings region measures 25 miles in length, and anywhere from 3.5–7 miles in width.

Geologists think the sand came from Michigan on the heels of the retreating Wisconsinan glacier, around 10,000–12,000 years ago. A river fed by the meltwater of this glacier transported the sand (a glacial deposit) into Lake Warren, the Ice Age ancestor of Lake Erie.

The shore of Lake Warren reached much farther inland than today's Lake Erie because the glacier blocked the water outlet (the Niagara-St. Lawrence valleys) to the sea. The longshore currents of Lake Warren, moving westward and parallel to the shore, carried the sand to the southwestern shore, building beaches and sand bars.

When the outlet finally unplugged, Lake Warren shrank roughly to the size of the current Lake Erie. The abandoned beaches and sand bars became windswept sand dunes. (See Oak Openings, Sheldon Marsh.)

The sand deposits varied in depth. Above thick deposits, a few scrubby plants, like black oak (thus the name "oak openings"), survive on the dry earth. At Irwin Prairie, however, the sand layer is thin, and the surface water is trapped above an impervious strata of clay. Consequently, wet conditions prevail year-round, allowing the vegetation of a wet prairie to grow in this unique habitat. The swampy, flooded environment also discourages encroachment by most trees which tend to settle on the higher ground.

Wildlife

Irwin Prairie is one of the last and largest of the wet prairies in what is left of the Oak Openings in Ohio. A century and a half ago this timberless wetland may have been a mile wide and seven miles long. But extensive drainage since the last half of the 19th century has bled the land so that farms and villages could be established.

The siphoning ditches lowered the water level, and let cottonwoods and aspens march into the meadows. Only about 50 acres of the original Irwin Prairie remains.

The stroll along the boardwalk takes you to five of the six distinct plant communities. (Botanists debate the boundaries and classifications of these groups.) The parking lot is surrounded by oaks, mostly pin oaks. The branches of this sturdy tree "pinned" or bound barn timbers—hence the name. A shrubby swamp of willows and dogwoods is followed by a clearing that boasts characters typical of the western tallgrass prairie.

A large sedge meadow lies on the east side of Irwin Road. Visually, the spot briefly recalls the savannas of Africa and South America. The main plant, twig-rush (potentially threatened in Ohio), is really a sedge. A sedge has a triangular, solid stem (especially at the top), while a rush stem is hollow and never three-sided.

Ahead, you venture through a tiny stand of pin oaks, another thicket of shrubs, and then a field of blue-joint grass and northern reed grass. In the spring, this field becomes a shallow pond which attracts waterfowl, thousands of frogs, and the dainty fairy shrimp.

You may also see elm (American and red), red maple, swamp white oak, sassafras, and black cherry trees on the way. Check out the shrubs named ninebark, meadowsweet, prickly ash, and bristly greenbrier.

Forty-four wildflowers are listed in ODNR's booklet on the preserve. The prairie collection boasts spiked blazing star, tall coreopsis, wild bergamot, and big bluestem (a grass). Five kinds of goldenrod wash the meadow with "gold." Look for butterfly-weed, white beardtongue, ladies' tresses, mermaid weed, small-fringed gentian (potentially threatened), swamp candles, and wild carrot (a.k.a. Queen Anne's lace).

Lucky observers might spot a least bittern (an endangered bird), a Virginia rail or sora (each a "special interest" bird, or potentially threatened), a pied-eyed grebe, and a common snipe. Find a marsh wren (becoming a rarity in Ohio) in your binoculars, or an endangered sedge wren.

Muskrat, mink, raccoons, opossums, red fox, skunk, and deer live or browse here. The rare spotted turtle (perhaps resting beside a drainage ditch) and ribbon snake (seen by the author slithering between the planks of the boardwalk at the trailhead) represent some of the reclusive reptiles.

History

Native Americans found a rich bounty of wildlife in this verdant savanna. Canoes could slide into its nook and crannies during periods of high water, but at other times the swampy conditions made hunting, fishing, and gathering strenuous.

Early French explorers may have trapped fur-bearing critters in the area. Later settlers found the land too waterlogged and treeless for settlement. That changed in 1859 when the Lucas County Commissioners began draining the wetlands for farming. The slow work of bleeding the area continued well into the 20th century.

In 1960, John Stophlet, a local naturalist, persuaded Dr. J. Arthur Herrick, boss of the Natural Areas Inventory Project for the Ohio Biological Survey, to visit this place. Herrick declared it "one of the rarest of gems in Ohio."

In June 1964, members of the Toledo Naturalists Association began a study of the site they named Irwin Prairie (after a pioneer named William Irwin who settled here in 1865). Their findings confirmed Herrick's conclusion, and led to the creation of a grassroots organization.

In 1971, the Ohio Chapter of The Nature Conservancy started raising money to buy the prairie. By 1974 the conservancy and the Ohio Department of Natural Resources had acquired the funds to buy Irwin Prairie. On December 27, 1974 Irwin Prairie became a state nature preserve.

Pawpaw tree

KENDRICK WOODS METROPARK

The former owners of Allen County's largest woodlot almost turned it into a trailer court. But, at the last minute, they were persuaded to sell. The action saved a grove of venerable, regal oaks who have lived here for three centuries. These trees saw the militia of General "Mad" Anthony Wayne march on the Defiance Trail to the Battle of Fallen Timbers. The army that defeated the Indians also brought on white settlers who, in turn, defeated the forest.

Location

Southwestern Allen County, Amanda Township.

From downtown Lima go west on State Route 81 about 12 miles. Immediately after crossing the Auglaize River turn right (north) on Defiance Trail. The park entrance is a half mile ahead on the left. Park to the right of the restrooms, near the trailhead.

Ownership

Johnny Appleseed Metropolitan Park District.

Size & Designation

Kendrick Woods, encompassing 159 acres, is one of newest state nature preserves, dedicated on May 26, 1992. The park includes 218 acres.

Nearby Natural Attractions

Kendrick Woods is one of seven facilities managed by the park district. The others are McLean Teddy Bear Park, Allen County Farm Park, Agerter Road River Access, McElroy Environmental Education Center, and Ottawa Metropark.

Access

The park, open daily during daylight hours, offers five miles of trails, picnic area, playground, fishing and ice skating pond, restrooms, and drinking water. Folks in wheelchairs or pushing strollers can take the boardwalk, or All People's Trail.

The journey described below visits most of the natural attractions open to the public. Pick up an interpretive guide for the South Trail at the trailhead.

Bear left as you enter the woods, and left at the next fork. Follow this path westerly along a creek. Skip the next left which crosses the creek near Stop 1 in the trail guide. Instead, continue ahead, then go left (west) at the next intersection. Cross the bridge over an unnamed tributary of Six Mile Creek. (You will be skipping Stop 2 in the trail guide.)

This path, known as the Hickory Trail, loops through the northwest section of the park, an oak-hickory forest. During my visit in early September a whipping wind shook the canopy and showered me with acorns and hickory nuts. Soon the woodland route bends left (south), then east with a corn field on the right. Take your next left (northerly) through the woods, leaving the Hickory Trail. This short path joins the South Trail near Stop 3 where you can admire a beech tree. Turn right (east) here and enjoy Stop 4 (humus).

Skip the next path going left unless you must return to the parking lot. Ahead, the Hickory Trail, entering from the right, merges with the South Trail. Heading south now (with Six Mile Creek on the left), the trail reaches a fork. The trail guide (Stop 5) notes the pawpaw tree at the left. Its odd, sweet potato-shaped fruit hung heavily from the branches when I reached the spot. Supposedly the fruits tastes like papaya, but you will have to harvest them before the raccoons, opossum, squirrels, and mice.

Bear left at the fork, following the bank of the creek. Soon you will reach a sulfur spring (Stop 6) on the right (though you are apt to smell it first), then the white oak stand (Stops 7 and 8). Ahead, the South Trail hooks right, completes the loop, and continues north passed stop 9 and 10 in the guide.

Stay to the right where the South and Hickory (at the left) trails meet. Go right at the next intersection, cross the wooden bridge, and return to the parking lot. Restrooms will be on your left when you leave the woods.

The park district schedules nature walks and programs at Kendrick Woods during the year. For more information contact the Johnny Appleseed Metropolitan Park District, 2355 Ada Road, Lima, Ohio 45801; phone (419) 221-1232.

Geology

An issue of the park district's newsletter, *Cider Press,* acknowledges that the region lacks "the scenic hills and gorges of southern Ohio. Our rivers do not measure up to the mighty Ohio. We don't even have rocky hillsides or scenic overlooks."

Still, visitors can find beauty in this flat land from a different perspective. Here you have the feeling of being at the bottom of the sky, rather than at the top of the Earth.

Frozen tidal waves called continental glaciers shaped the surface into elongated undulations and spread a thick blanket of till (gravel, sand, clay, and other sediments) which became the fertile ground for the forests and farms of the region.

Certainly, there are slight changes in elevation, and nature has taken advantage of these thin distinctions. Your job is to detect the subtleties in this wild realm.

The water currents crawling through this level preserve, Six Mile Creek and the Auglaize River (forming the eastern border), appear vapid and cloudy most of the year. Auglaize means muddy, in French, the language of the Europeans who put new names on the streams. The sleepy streams, of course, become devilish torrents after thaws and heavy rains.

As you traipse along the South Trail you cannot miss the whiff of sulfur. The odor comes from an artesian spring gurgling at the surface. According to the trail guide "the spring was formed when the water-bearing rock layer underground, called the aquifer, was either drilled into or naturally met the surface of the ground. A bubbling, flowing spring like this one indicates that the aquifer is under pressure from the layers of soil and rock above, thus causing the water to constantly flow out."

The swamp around the spring results from water seeping to the surface and spreading over the ground year-round. Grazing cattle drank from this water hole.

Another sulfur spring emerges near the Auglaize River. Local folks filling jugs at the spot called it the "Fountain of Youth" and claimed the water was good for health.

Wildlife

Somehow a small community of aged white oaks, about 12–15 trees, avoided the axe. Others were not as lucky and their rotting stumps stand as tombstones. They are all that remains of the thick, mature forest that once covered Allen County.

They are joined by 55 other kinds of trees and shrubs in this predominant oak-hickory woodland. Six other oaks (red, swamp white, pin, bur, black, and chinkapin) and three types of hickory (shagbark, pignut, and bitternut) grow in the deep woods. Sycamores, their branches reminiscent of crossed swords, arch over Six Mile Creek. Their partners in the floodplain include cottonwood, box elder, Ohio buckeye, black walnut, and silver maple, among others.

You will find basswood, honeylocust, beech, bigtooth aspen, white and green ash, American and slippery elm, and pawpaw. Some of the shrubs represented are nannyberry, trumpet honeysuckle, and running strawberry bush.

Naturalists have counted more than 65 types of wildflowers on the forest floor. For a challenge, look for false mermaid, Greek valerian, lopseed, enchanter's nightshade, heart-leaved skullcap, and horsebalm. Wild columbine is supposedly abundant here. A three-acre prairie, planted in 1987, returns these blossoms to Allen County.

Birds are plentiful—85 species have been spotted, even a bald eagle, hermit thrush, yellow-crowned night heron, and yellow-bellied sapsucker. These creatures are endangered in Ohio.

Birders can fix their field glasses on these warblers: black-throated green, yellow-throated, myrtle, blackburnian, black and white, baybreasted, chestnut-sided, and American redstart. Try to find the redheaded woodpecker, ruby-crowned kinglet, rose-breasted grosbeak, eastern meadowlark, and many others. Hawks include the American kestrel, Cooper's, and red-tailed.

The streams harbor reptiles such as the five-lined skink and northern water snake. The smallmouth salamander, an amphibian, inhabits these woods. The common woodland mammals thrive here—deer, squirrels, fox, mink, muskrat, raccoon, opossum, and the rest.

History

The preserve is located along the historic Defiance Trail, the path taken by General "Mad" Anthony Wayne to the Battle of Fallen Timbers on the Maumee River in August 1794. Avenging an American loss three years earlier, Wayne defeated a combined Indian force commanded by Tecumseh and Blue Jacket. Wayne's victory opened the area for white settlers already pouring into the Northwest Territory. The new human inhabitants cut down the forest for farms, cities, roads, railroads, and industries.

By the 1960s, this woodlot, known as Strayer's Woods, became an anomaly, an isolated copse of tall timbers surrounded by a flat, open, checkerboard region of farms and small towns. When word got around that the landowners wanted to build a mobile home village here, conservationists persuaded the owners to sell the woods to the park district.

Using money from the estate of Florence Kendrick (in memory of her husband Ray) the park district purchased the property in 1976. The metropark opened in 1987. The Ohio Department of Natural Resources designated the woods, now called Kendrick Woods, a state nature preserve in May 1992.

Journal

Early September 1993. I've been stoned by the hardwoods. They hurled acorns and hickory nuts whenever a gusty wind shook the branches. Good thing I have a hard head.

Lakeside daisy

LAKESIDE DAISY STATE NATURE PRESERVE

The Lakeside daisy is the rarest of the 206 endangered species in Ohio. It survives naturally, and barely, in only three places on earth—in a limestone quarry on the Marblehead Peninsula, and in two spots on Ontario's Lake Erie shore. In Ohio, humans can view this rare jewel in its preserve only once a year—in May—when its yellow blossoms religiously obey the sun's golden rays.

Location

Ottawa County, Danbury Township, near Lakeside on the Marblehead Peninsula.

Driving west on State Route 2, exit northbound on State Route 269, and take this road over Sandusky Bay, through Danbury to its junction with State Route 163. Turn right (east) on SR 163 and travel to Lakeside. In the village, turn right on Alexander Pike (town hall and firehouse on the corner) to the preserve.

Ownership

Ohio Department of Natural Resources, Division of Natural Areas and Preserves.

Size & Designation

The endangered flower lives in a 19-acre scientific preserve which is off-limits to humans, except in May.

Nearby Natural Attractions

Ottawa County boasts four state parks, three state wildlife areas, and part of a national wildlife refuge. The state parks are East Harbor, Catawba Island, Crane Creek, and South Bass Island. You also can visit these state wildlife areas: Magee Marsh (reviewed in this book), Tousaint, and Little Portage. The Marblehead Peninsula is famous for its lighthouse, marinas, wineries, fishing, beaches, and ferry to the islands.

Access

The preserve is open to visitors *only* in May. A permit must be obtained from the Division of Natural Areas and Preserves to visit the preserve any other time. Visitors must park on the berm and stay in designated areas. There is no trail for May visitors, so you are free to roam about—only be careful not to step on the plants.

For more information contact the Ohio Department of Natural Resources, Division of Natural Areas and Preserves, Fountain Square, Building F-1, Columbus, OH 43224; phone (614) 265-6453.

Geology

The tough Lakeside daisy has chosen to live on bare, limestone rock which 375 million years ago (Devonian geological period) was an ocean floor. When the ocean receded this bottom stew of sea creatures and mud hardened into a rock that geologists call Columbus limestone. It contains the fossils of ancient shellfish and fish, some of which grew to lengths of 25 feet.

In Ohio, this slab of limestone stretches from Columbus to the Lake Erie Islands. In places it's 100 feet thick. The top half of the strata, almost pure calcite, is quite valuable, and has been extensively mined throughout its range.

Wildlife

The Lakeside daisy's existence in Ohio is a conundrum. The plant belongs to the genus Hymenoxys which claims 14 native species in North America. Thirteen members of this clan reside in the southern Rocky Mountains and western Great Plains, south as far as South America. Why, then, does one isolated species live east of the Mississippi River? How did it get here? When did it arrive?

Scientists do not really have answers. While some attribute its appearance to traveling Indians or to early 19th century cattle drives (seeds transported in cow manure), others believe it arrived several thousand years ago with the tide of the tallgrass prairie and got left behind.

The Lakeside daisy lives in a harsh and fragile environment—on bare, windswept, sun-baked, storm-pounded limestone or dolomite rock. In early May, the bright yellow petals of the perennial flower open atop a solitary, leafless stem measuring 6–ll inches. The leaves of the plant form a tight, fleshy rosette on the rock surface. Each community of daisies blossoms about the same time.

The daisies are heliotropic, meaning all the flowerheads obediently follow the path of the sun in unison. At sunset, the double-notched petals point west, and at dawn they salute the eastern rays. The blossoms pay homage to the sun for about a week, then begin to drop their petals.

Though the plant disperses seeds in mid-June, it also reproduces by spreading its underground stem (called a rhizome) from the rosette.

The Lakeside daisy has been called the four-nerved starflower, the stemless rubberweed, and the mountain sunflower. The latest name was adopted by Clarence M. Weed, a researcher at the Ohio Experimental Station who conducted the first studies of the plant in May 1890. He named it after the nearby village, Lakeside, and the name stuck.

The common name aside, scientists continue to wrestle with the plant's precise scientific name. This taxonomic tug-of-war has produced a half dozen Latin names since Clarence Weed's day. ODNR has settled on one chosen by a veteran naturalist, Allison Cusick, who believes our rare daisy is a species all its own, called Hymenoxys herbacea.

Although Hymenoxys herbacea is the floral star attraction, the small preserve also protects 11 other rare plants, such as rock sandwort, balsam squawweed, and Great Plains ladies'-tresses. Other prairie favorites—notably spiked blazing-star and stiff goldenrod—grow here too. Most of these wildflowers blossom two months after the Lakeside daisy (mid-July) when the preserve is closed to the public.

History

While Clarence Weed is credited for naming the daisy and bringing it to the attention of the scientific community, it was Ruth E. Fiscus of Cleveland Heights who carefully observed the plant and crusaded for its protection for more than 40 years. Later, Marblehead resident Colleen "Casey" Taylor led a statewide effort to preserve the quarry.

In 1988, ODNR bought 19 acres of abandoned quarry from Standard Slag Company, now a subsidiary of Lafarge Corporation of Paris, France. The following year, the state agency began monitoring the plant's growth, and transplanted a few flowers to a quarry in nearby Kelleys Island State Park.

Other research avenues are being traveled in Illinois which lost its last natural daisy habitat in 1981. Fortunately, biologist Marcella DeMauro rescued a few plants and reestablished them in protected sites. Later, she crossbred the Illinois and Ohio survivors and planted the offspring in selected locations.

Pintail duck

MAGEE MARSH STATE WILDLIFE AREA

Magee Marsh protects birds who may be at the end of their ecological line. Twenty of 25 endangered Ohio bird species, and 16 of 18 potentially threatened ("special interest") birds have been seen is this fertile wetland. Here is your chance to see them.

Location

This state wildlife area straddles the border of Lucas and Ottawa counties.

From State Route 2, take the entrance road to Crane Creek State Park. Magee Marsh sprawls out on both sides of the road. Stop at the contemporary rustic lodge serving as the Sportsmen Migratory Bird Center and Crane Creek Wildlife Experiment Station. The road continues to the state park.

Ownership

Ohio Department of Natural Resources, Division of Wildlife.

Size & Designation

This 1,821-acre refuge is a state wildlife area.

Nearby Natural Attractions

Magee Marsh borders Ottawa National Wildlife Refuge and Crane Creek State Park, where you can swim in Lake Erie and picnic under cottonwood trees.

In Ottawa County visit Lakeside Daisy State Nature Preserve (May only), East Harbor, Catawba, and South Bass Island state parks, and Little Portage and Toussaint state wildlife areas.

Lucas County features Irwin Prairie State Nature Preserve, Maumee Bay State Park, Metzger Marsh State Wildlife Area, Maumee State Forest, and these Toledo Metroparks: Oak Openings, Pearson, Wildwood, Secor, and Swan Creek.

Access

The road to the state park beach offers rewarding views of the marsh and its inhabitants. Hint: Stay in your car when observing the birds. Parking and unloading, noisy and intrusive actions, almost always causes the critters to flee. (The birds near the road are used to cruising cars, but the approach of humans harasses them.) For best results, roll down the windows, drive slowly, avoid loud talking, and keep the motor idling if you must stop.

Keep other autos in your sights too. Cars behind you may not be interested in watching a great blue heron wade in the water. Wave those cars ahead. Also, geese and ducks frequently cross the road. Give them plenty of room. Driving closer often confuses them, delaying their crossing and your progress.

The Sportsmen Migratory Bird Center is a must stop. It has some excellent exhibits of the wildlife that thrives in the Lake Erie marshes. Hunters will enjoy the duck hunting displays and the center's collection of decoys. A "touch table" challenges children to handle bones, skulls, feathers, and fur of marsh animals.

A state wildlife officer is usually on duty to answer questions, and you will find written information about the marsh at the information desk. The center has restrooms, and on hot summer days its air-conditioned atmosphere and cold drinking fountain are refreshing. The center is open Monday through Saturday from 8 a.m.–5 p.m., Sunday, noon–6 p.m. In winter, the center is closed on weekends.

You can view the marsh from the porches (two levels) of the center. A 100-yard boardwalk trail (wheelchair and stroller accessible) along the edge of a marsh pond leads to a three-story observation tower. The tower, however, was closed for repair in 1993.

The Magee Marsh Bird Trail, a boardwalk measuring 6/10 of a mile, begins at the beach entrance of Crane Creek State Park. Look for the wooden sign on the left, and park in the lot. Folks in wheelchairs and those pushing strollers can negotiate this flat trail. Keep bicycles and tricycles off the path, please. Roundtrip: 1.2 miles.

Insects attack with vigor in summer, so pack repellent and wear a cap, long pants, and socks. Sunscreen lotion is advised. A summertime visit should include a dip into Lake Erie at the state park beach and a stroll along the shore to admire shells.

The Crane Creek Wildlife Experiment Station is housed in the nature center, the state headquarters for wetlands wildlife research. Some of the station's numerous duties are developing and managing the wetlands habitats, increasing wildlife populations (Canada geese, bald eagles and beavers, for example), and to study wetlands ecology.

Boating in Magee Marsh is not allowed, unless special permission is granted. Waterfowl hunting is limited to a small number of hunters selected in a drawing. Likewise, trapping for muskrats is restricted.

For more information about Magee Marsh contact the Ohio Department of Natural Resources, Division of Wildlife, District Two, 952 Lima Avenue, Box A, Findlay, Ohio 45840; phone (419) 424-5000 or (419) 898-0960 (area manager).

Geology

Magee Marsh is part of a once enormous marshland called the "Great Black Swamp." The swamp stretched from Detroit, inland to Fort Wayne, Indiana, and eastward to Sandusky, roughly the shoreline of old Lake Maumee, the precursor of Lake Erie.

Lake Maumee was formed by the meltwater of the Wisconsinan glacier, about 12,000–10,000 years ago. As the glacier retreated northward, water rushed through the Niagara-St. Lawrence valleys and shrunk Lake Maumee approximately to the size of Lake Erie today. The poorly drained plains south and west of this new shoreline became the Great Black Swamp, a paradise for wildlife but a place largely unsettled by Native Americans.

The size of the marsh depends on the water level of Lake Erie which derives 90 percent of its water from the upper Great Lakes (Huron, Michigan, and Superior). The water level, of course, fluctuates seasonally (lowest in February, highest in June), and decade to decade. A record peak level was reached in 1973, followed by a period of recession, then increases in the late 1980s.

During periods of high water the marsh swells inland, but it shrivels up again when the level drops.

Barrier beaches (sand spits and sandbars) protect marshes by impounding water and absorbing Lake Erie's crashing waves. The beach at Crane Creek State Park serves as a barrier beach. However, these natural dams sometimes lose their effectiveness when the lake level rises, or during violent storms.

All but a small fraction of the swamp and marshland has been drained for agricultural and human developments. Still, nature may have the last laugh. Geologists have discovered that the land in the southwestern end of Lake Erie is gently sinking about two feet per century. If left undisturbed, Lake Erie's shoreline and the marsh will be located farther inland in the 23rd century.

Wildlife

For many years humans viewed marshlands as barren, featureless, and lifeless wastelands. Just the opposite is true. Acre for acre, marshes and other wetlands produce more wildlife than any other kind of habitat.

The most visible representative of this bounty are the migratory birds who come here in the thousands in the spring and fall. Magee Marsh is one of the important stops for waterfowl and warblers winging on the Mississippi Flyway, the invisible highway-in-the-sky that birds have flown for millennia. It also is a vital habitat for the protected birds who have been seen in Magee Marsh.

ODNR's check-list includes 303 birds. In season, you will likely see the pied-billed grebe, tundra swan, dunlin, Bonaparte's gull, common nighthawk, bay-breasted warbler, and snow bunting. Sharp eyes may spot the snow and blue goose, willet, glaucous gull, whippoorwill, ruby-throated hummingbird, Brewer's blackbird, and lapland longspur. But don't forget to look for the bald eagle, American bittern, magnolia warbler, short-eared owl, upland sandpiper, and dozens more.

Muskrats are abundant. Deer, skunk, mink, raccoon, fox, rabbit, woodchuck, and opossum flourish here. Look for these snakes—fox, northern brown, common water, garter, Kirtland's, and queen. Turtles are represented by the snapping (some up to 50 pounds), painted, and Blanding's. Listen for these frogs—bullfrog, green, leopard, striped chorus, cricket, and spring peeper. Salamanders include the mudpuppy, Jefferson, spotted, and red-backed.

Wildflowers bloom in summer, notably pink rose mallow, Joe-pye weed, arrowhead, water lily, blue skullcap, pickerel weed, American lotus, and bur marigold.

History

The successive tribes of Indians who have lived in this area relied on the rich marshland for food and furs. The Ottawas, who moved to the shore in the 1740s, swapped furs for European goods with French and other traders.

A French explorer named Etienne Brule was probably the first white man in these parts. He landed at the mouth of a nearby stream on All Saints Day in 1615, and named the stream Toussaint Creek (All Saints Creek). The French who settled here built primitive bark huts lived off the land, doing little to civilize the marsh.

Later, settlers drained the wetlands for farms. A different kind of harvesting began in the 1850s when hunting clubs started shooting ducks and geese for market. Members of the Crane Creek Shooting Club traveled from Cleveland, Pittsburgh, and Detroit to enjoy the hunt. The ducks were salted and shipped to market in wooden barrels.

When attempts to convert the marsh to farmland in the early 1900s failed, the land was allowed to return to marshland for waterfowling and muskrat trapping. From the late 1920s through 1950, hunters in the private club here bagged 2,500 ducks a year. Trapping yielded 97,000 muskrats from 1939–1951.

Maintaining the marsh habitat became costly for the hunting club. ODNR bought it in 1951, including the beach, and started controlled waterfowl hunting. The Crane Creek Wildlife Experiment Station was established in 1956. The Sportsmen Migratory Bird Center was constructed in 1970.

Ducks Unlimited and the Ohio Decoy Collectors and Carvers Association have been helpful in providing money for marsh development.

Journal

August 18, 1993. Shoot. The observation tower is boarded up. The kids would rather look at the marsh from the tower than from the road. Truthfully, they'd rather be swimming at the beach a mile away.

Smallmouth bass

OLD WOMAN CREEK STATE NATURE PRESERVE

Here, the waters of Old Woman Creek and Lake Erie churn together to make a chemically different body of water–an estuary–and a habitat filled with creatures who live in the deep, the creek, the swamp, and the woods. For 9,000 years, the first Ohioans occupied a village on a nearby bluff and harvested the bounty from the estuary. Today, scientists housed on a different bluff, try to uncover the secrets of the estuary, the most studied natural area in Ohio.

Location

Erie County, just east of Huron.

The preserve is about two miles east of the city limits on U.S. Route 6. Look for the main entrance on the right, just after you cross a stream, which happens to be Old Woman Creek.

Ownership

Ohio Department of Natural Resources, Division of Natural Areas and Preserves.

Size & Designation

The site is an interpretive preserve of 571 acres. The estuary also is protected as a national estuarine reserve. Scientists studying the estuary's ecology hope to better understand the function and importance of this kind of coastal marsh.

Nearby Natural Attractions

Combine a visit to Old Woman Creek with a stop at Sheldon Marsh State Nature Preserve, just a mile west of Huron. Erie Sand Dunes State Nature Preserve is located in southwestern Erie County. Take the ferry to Kelleys Island to see Glacial Grooves State Memorial (a National Natural Landmark) and Kelleys Island State Park. Sportsmen should check out Willow Point, Milan, and Resthaven state wildlife areas.

Access

Unlike other state nature preserves which are open from sunrise to sundown, visiting hours for Old Woman Creek are 8 a.m.–5 p.m. daily. The visitor center is open Wednesday–Sunday, from 1–5 p.m. The center is closed on Monday and Tuesday.

If it's open, the visitor center should be your first stop. The nature exhibits, including an aquarium and other displays, will give you a great picture of the geology, history, and wildlife of the estuary. Children love the "living stream" aquarium featuring the fish that live in the estuary. Fresh water actually flows through this aquarium, and recreates the habitat of the fish.

You also will find various brochures on the preserve, and a bird checklist. Restrooms and drinking water also are available.

After the visitor center, follow the paved path, the Edward Walper Trail, that leaves the northwest corner of the parking lot. This wheelchair and stroller accessible trail descends a quarter mile through woods to an observation deck that gazes up on the estuary. Please stay on the trail, and discourage kids from climbing on trees that have fallen into the estuary. Besides the obvious dangers, their sudden appearance "out on the limb" may force wildlife to flee from their feeding or nesting place.

The pavement ends at the observation deck. The continuing gravel trail, unfortunately, is too difficult for wheelchairs. This path traces the edge of the estuary for a while (go slow and look for herons and other beasties on the far shore) then enters a marshy woods. Here the trail splits. A left turn climbs a brief slope and returns to the parking lot and visitor center. I recommend that you bear right and stay on the Walper Trail, which winds through a wooded area, old farmland in various stages of succession (look for the rusting farm equipment along the way), a wet meadow, and back to the parking lot. The whole journey measures about a mile.

There is more—the barrier beach at the mouth of Old Woman Creek. Turn left (west) onto Route 6 at the end of the drive, heading toward Huron. Immediately after crossing the bridge over Old Woman Creek, turn right into the first driveway. Park in the small designated lot at the left. A white building will be at the right.

Backtrack a bit and walk around the barn to the creek then stroll to the barrier beach. The homes that you see on the grounds are dormitories for visiting researchers.

Go ahead and take off your shoes and wade along the shore. That's it, though. Swimming is forbidden. Also, please refrain from collecting natural artifacts and picnicking. Keep this beach as natural and as undisturbed as possible. One more rule: don't wander onto private beaches. To the west, the preserve beach ends where the sand ends. Signs posted on the trees behind the beach mark the boundary of the preserve. To the east, a wooden sign designates the location of a private beach.

Special education programs and workshops are available for individuals and groups. For more information contact Old Woman Creek State Nature Preserve, 2514 Cleveland Road East, Huron, Ohio 44839; phone (419) 433-4601. You can also contact the Ohio Department of Natural Resources, Division of Natural Areas and Preserves, Fountain Square, Building F-1, Columbus, Ohio 43224-1331; phone (614) 265-6453.

Geology

Old Woman Creek is a special kind of estuary. Traditionally, an estuary holds brackish water, a mixture of saltwater from the sea and freshwater from a stream. In this type of estuary the salinity of the water depends on the amount of freshwater flowing into the estuary, and the water's distance from the sea. The water level of a saltwater estuary fluctuates daily according to the strength of lunar tides.

Old Woman Creek estuary, however, is a freshwater estuary. Though Lake Erie (actually an inland sea) and Old Woman Creek are both freshwater, their chemical compositions are not the same. A different chemical mixture is produced where these waters meet. Estuarine water near the mouth of the creek is more like that of Lake Erie, but inland its characteristics are closer to those of the creek. Precipitation and other weather conditions, far more than tides, influence the water level at Old Woman Creek. The changes in the water level are subtler than those experienced in saltwater estuaries.

The estuary filters out sediment and pollution headed for Lake Erie (though there are limits to how much purification the estuary can accomplish). It also can hold floodwater after heavy rains.

As its name suggests, the barrier beach at the mouth of the creek acts as a barrier that separates the lake from the creek. In a sense, it regulates the flow of water. Take away the beach, and the estuary disappears.

Spring rains swell Old Woman Creek, flush the estuary, and force creek water over the barrier beach. Storm waves breach the beach and spill lake water into the estuary. The waves also push sand back on the beach.

By midsummer, the beach has closed the creek's mouth. Still, lake water percolates and seeps through the sand and into the estuary.

The beach fattens and shrinks, and this affects the water content in the estuary. In the last dozen years, the beach has been thicker, and thinner, than its current size.

Wildlife

Like nearby Sheldon Marsh State Nature Preserve, Old Woman Creek teems with life. Many species, dwindling in numbers in Ohio, find refuge in the preserve.

Let's start with the critters best viewed under a microscope—plankton. These tiny plants and animals—billions of them—serve as the foundation of the life cycle in the estuary. They are consumed by small fish which like to spawn in the warm shallows around lotus beds. Bigger fish (bass, walleye, etc.), as well as herons and egrets, eat the small fry. Eagles, terns, and gulls then feast on the game fish.

The estuary, beach, meadows, and woodlands attract almost 300 species of birds, including ducks, herons, raptors, shorebirds, and warblers. A bird checklist for Old Woman Creek and Sheldon Marsh is available at the visitor center. (Also see the chapter on Sheldon Marsh.)

As you can imagine, amphibians and reptiles are abundant. Amphibians are represented by the American toad (able to eat 10,000 bugs in a three-month span), spring peeper (known for its spring melody and the "X" mark on its back), leopard frog (like the cat this frog is spotted), and red-backed salamander (which breathes through its skin, not lungs).

Reptiles commonly seen are the eastern fox snake (mistaken for the venomous copperhead), eastern garter snake (the most widely distributed snake in the U.S.), northern brown snake (likes snails, slugs, worms), northern water snake, snapping turtle (don't try to pet it), eastern box turtle (distinctive yellow and brown patterns), midland painted turtle (plain looking except for the painted red design on the edge of its shell), and Blanding's turtle (potentially threatened; look for a yellow chin).

Forty kinds of fish live in the estuary, an ideal spawning location for many. They include the largemouth bass, carp, sunfish, perch, shiners, and shad.

Enriching the largesse of the estuary are 14 protected plants, such as the endangered clasping leaf dogbane, bushy aster and narrow-leaved bluegrass. The following residents are threatened species—beach wormwood, leafy tussock sedge, Bebb's sedge, slender sedge, plains frostweed, and Lake Erie pinkweed. Five are potentially threatened—inland sea rocket, seaside spurge, early buttercup, Great Plains ladies' tresses, and purple sand grass.

Nature occupies every niche. On open water you'll find American lotus (mistaken for water lily) in abundance, along with pond and water lilies, arrow arum, pondweed, and swamp rose mallow.

History

Around 11,000 years ago ancestors of the First Ohioans reached the shore of Lake Erie. The continental ice sheet known as the Wisconsinan glacier had withdrawn into Canada. These settlers, the Paleo Indians, hunted mastodon (an elephant), caribou, and probably elk. They also fished the waters of Lake Erie, its marshes, estuaries, and streams.

Just north of where State Route 2 crosses Old Woman Creek (south of the visitor center) Kent State University researchers uncovered artifacts of the First Ohioans at excavations called the Anderson site. Archeologists figured the Paleo-Indians lived there 9,000–10,000 years ago. The camp was occupied at various times during the past 10,000 years, the last native people perhaps being the Ottawas.

The Anderson site was carefully selected. It is located on a bluff where the creek empties into the estuary. The rich resources of the estuary, the lake, and the forest were within arm's reach.

As the climate warmed, the evergreen forest of the cold, glacial era was replaced by the deciduous (leaf-losing trees) hardwood forest that moved in from the south. This ecological transformation inspired technological changes among the Archaic Indians, the people who lived here between 9,000 and 3,000 years ago.

The last 3,000 years, the Woodland Period, produced profound changes. The Indians began to cultivate plants to supplement the food they secured from hunting, gathering, and fishing. As they became more dependent on agriculture (around 900 A.D.) native crops were abandoned for corn, beans, and squash which all originated in Mexico.

A major settlement was established at the Anderson site during the 15th century. Though these Ohioans (late Woodland Indians) planted maize (corn), hunting, fishing, and gathering still seemed to be more important.

The white-tailed deer was the most important game animal, providing meat, clothing, tools, utensils, and other items. Elk, turkey, bear, raccoon, and rabbit also were hunted. The wetlands gave them waterfowl, beaver, and muskrats.

The Treaty of Green Ville in 1794 marked the end of the Indian culture in northwestern Ohio. The people who valued the land were replaced by immigrants (Europeans and Americans) who valued what they *did* to the land, like cut down the dense forest.

In 1805, Almon Ruggles surveyed this neighborhood for the government. This region became known as the Firelands, land reserved for Connecticut Yankees displaced during the American Revolution. J.K. Thompson constructed the first gristmill on Old Woman Creek near Berlin Heights. Soon there were six sawmills, two more gristmills, and five sandstone quarries.

The giant oaks along the creek fell. They were transported to Huron which, in the 19th century, became a large shipbuilding city, Strawberries, raspberries, grapes, and other fruits became important agricultural crops.

Fortunately, several landowners in the 20th century—the Anderson and Hartley families—resisted offers to build homes and recreational developments on the shores of Old Woman Creek. Oberlin College has protected part of the beach and east shore since 1913.

Old Woman Creek estuary became a state nature preserve on September 5, 1980. Much of the property is designated for scientific research. It also is protected as a national estuarine sanctuary.

Research is partially funded by the National Estuarine Reserve Research Program, created by Congress to help the state save the last few natural estuaries. The program is administered by the National Ocean Service, Office of Ocean and Coastal Resource Management, an agency of the National Oceanic and Atmospheric Administration of the Department of Commerce.

The buildings above the barrier beach are living quarters for researchers studying the waters, wildlife, and wonders of Old Woman Creek estuary.

Bald eagle

OTTAWA NATIONAL WILDLIFE REFUGE

Endangered bald eagles rule as the titular monarchs over this flat realm which harbors more protected birds than any other preserve in Ohio. More visible than the reclusive eagles are the waterfowl, shorebirds, and warblers who populate the marsh at the edge of the "Great Black Swamp." Thousands of migratory birds use the refuge as a roadside rest during their annual journeys on the Mississippi Flyway. 

Location

Ottawa National Wildlife Refuge Complex encompasses five sites in Lucas and Ottawa counties, but only one is open for people.

Visitors can hike at the Ottawa headquarters located off State Route 2 in Ottawa County near the border with Lucas County. Permission is required to visit the other four sites: West Sister Island, Cedar Point, Navarre Marsh, and Darby.

Ownership

The U.S. Department of the Interior, Fish & Wildlife Service (FWS) owns the Ottawa, Cedar Point, West Sister Island, and Darby sites. Navarre Marsh, next to the Davis-Besse nuclear power plant, belongs to the Centerior Energy Corporation, but the FWS administers it.

Size & Designation

This 8,316-acre wetland is the only national wildlife refuge in Ohio. The complex also comprises the largest parcel in Ohio set aside for nature. West Sister Island is Ohio's only national wilderness area.

Nearby Natural Attractions

Magee Marsh Wildlife Area and Crane Creek State Park border the national refuge. The Lake Erie beach at the state park certainly will be refreshing after a midsummer's hike through the refuge. Lakeside Daisy State Nature Preserve and Metzger Marsh, Toussaint, and Little Portage state wildlife areas also are located in Ottawa County.

In Lucas County, visit Irwin Prairie State Nature Preserve, Maumee State Park, Maumee State Forest, and these Toledo Metroparks—Oak Openings, Swan Creek, Pearson, Secor, and Wildwood.

Access

Don't come here if you are seeking shade, waterfalls, big trees, a gorge, rugged terrain, or a babbling brook for skinny-dipping. They don't exist.

But if birds are your passion (or you are looking for a change of pace), this is your destination. Though the refuge is primarily a haven for waterfowl, shorebirds, raptors, and other wildlife, it also is a paradise for birders toting binoculars, field guides, and checklists. A small, illustrated checklist of birds appears on the back of the trail guide. A complete checklist is available at the refuge office (or write for one before you visit).

The Ottawa site offers four interconnecting hiking trails, totaling seven miles. The refuge is open every day from sunrise to sundown. The terrain is flat and open, and the trails are easy to follow. You will find maps at an information board in the parking lot, or at the headquarters beside the parking lot. Restrooms (vault toilets) are located a few paces west of the parking lot.

The Swan, Yellowlegs, and Mallard trails are rectangular-shaped and follow the ridges of levees that crisscross the marshes. The Blue Heron Trail traces levees too, but it also traipses through fields, woodlots, and a marsh. An observation deck equipped with a permanent telescope is located on the north loop of the Blue Heron Trail (south leg of the Swan Loop).

The Swan Loop (1.75 miles) gives folks with limited time a good view of this unique wetland. Walk the Yellowlegs and Mallard loops to improve your chances of glimpsing a bald eagle.

The levees act as observation mounds, allowing you to see for thousands of yards across this expanse. (This is the place to go if you like that "big sky" feeling.) Binoculars are essential because the wildlife, given tons of space, simply will not cooperate by staying close to the trails.

Though the terrain is easy, the sun and wind can be your biggest challenge in the summer. Pack insect repellent, sun screen lotion, visor caps, sunglasses. Water canteens are strongly advised for summer hikes. I don't recommend a long walk for kids who are mosquito magnets. Hike to the observation deck and back—less than mile roundtrip. Though the trails stay on top of levees and remain relatively dry, sections of the path can get soggy and slippery.

If you can choose your season, by all means come in the spring (March, April) and autumn (October, November) when the populations of winged migratory creatures peak. The weather is apt to be more pleasant too.

Nature education programs are held at the refuge headquarters throughout the year. For information about education programs, visiting other sites, or trails contact: Refuge Manager, Ottawa National Wildlife Refuge Complex, 14000 W. State Route 2, Oak Harbor, OH 43449; phone (419) 898-0014.

Geology

Lake Maumee, the forerunner of Lake Erie and one of a series of glacier-fed lakes that occupied the basin, swamped much of northwestern Ohio some 13,000 years ago. (The lake actually stretched from western New York to Fort Wayne, Indiana.) The Wisconsinan glacier, whose meltwater refreshed the lake, blocked its drainage outlets. Eventually, the ice mass retreated northward and unplugged its outlets. Lake water drained northeast through the Niagara-St. Lawrence valley.

Lake Maumee shrunk roughly to the current size of Lake Erie. The former lake bed, smoothed out by wave action and gentle currents, became the "Great Black Swamp," a flat plain measuring 120 miles in length and 30–40 miles in width. Picture a broad, muddy swamp from Fort Wayne to Detroit to Sandusky. Two factors kept the area wet—flat terrain slowed drainage to a snail's pace, and a clay subsoil stopped water from absorbing into the earth.

Marshes emerged between the swamp and Lake Erie. The water level of the lake determined the size of the marsh. The marsh moves inland during periods of high water, and retreats when the water level falls. Ottawa refuge protects remnants of The

Great Black Swamp and the Lake Erie marshes.

Today, man-made dikes (doubling as hiking trails) control water levels according to a long-term wildlife management plan. The pools are drained in the summer, and flooded in autumn.

Wildlife

The following facts tout the importance and vitality of Ottawa National Wildlife Refuge. It is the kingdom of birds.

- Eighteen of the 25 birds listed as endangered in Ohio, one threatened bird, and 14 of the 18 birds designated as being of "special interest" (potentially threatened), *have been observed here.*
- Seven endangered, eight special interest, and one threatened species *nest here.*
- Seven endangered species are listed as *"commonly seen" or "fairly commonly seen"* on the refuge's checklist. Six special interest birds are similarly listed.
- Forty-nine varieties have been *seen only a few times* and are classified as "accidentals."

All totaled, 274 species of birds are regular visitors at the refuge, which lies beneath a branch of the Mississippi Flyway, one of those invisible highways-in-the-sky that birds have instinctively followed for millennia.

One of most dramatic arrivals in late winter and early spring is the all-white tundra swan (or whistling swan), returning to its Arctic nesting ground after wintering in the Chesapeake Bay. In a good spring, as many as 5,000 of these graceful birds may be seen in the marshes of southwest Lake Erie. They return in the fall, but their numbers are fewer and less concentrated. The call of the tundra swan, also known as the whistling swan, is a shrill bark resembling "wow, wow-wow."

The area north and east of the refuge office is called the Goosehaven because Canada geese assemble here in March en route to their northern nesting areas. Some female geese, however, do bed down and raise their young here. Before flying across the lake the geese beef up on grass shoots, pondweeds, and crops such as corn, sorghum, and buckwheat which have been sowed here just for them.

Warblers also arrive in the spring. Look for these little beauties in the woods—the Tennessee, Kentucky, Connecticut, yellow-rumped, blackpoll, Wilson's, and palm.

Though eagles are seen year-round they are best viewed from February, when nesting begins, until the fledging of eaglets in July. The nest resembles a platform of branches and sticks set atop a tall tree. While one adult hunts, the other stays in the nest with the young until they have fledged.

Look for these noble birds flying above treelines (nest sites). They have white, or "bald," heads, and striking white tail feathers. Listen for their distinctive, piercing screech. They dine on fish, but may attack small animals if hungry.

Bald eagles used to be much more numerous on the Lake Erie shoreline. Lakeshore development, logging, and pesticides reduced the flock to just four nesting breeding pairs statewide in 1979. In 1992, the number of nests statewide reached 20 and 31 eaglets fledged, thanks largely to a restoration program by the Ohio Department of Natural Resources. As many 25–30 eagles were seen at a time that year at Ottawa National Wildlife Refuge.

Though the news has been heartening, the bald eagle still faces extinction in Ohio. Further lakeshore development is reducing habitat, and the level of toxic chemicals affecting reproduction in eagles (DDT and PCB) remains high even though they have been outlawed for more than two decades.

Besides eagles, ducks, geese, and swans, the refuge attracts the great blue heron and great egret, both commonly seen, plus pheasant, deer, rabbits, owls, hawks, and muskrats (abundant).

Controlled hunting and trapping manages the populations of geese and muskrats. Hunters and trappers are selected through annual drawings.

History

Though the Native American who lived along Lake Erie found the swamp and marsh foreboding, they managed to feed and clothe themselves on the game found here, and no doubt acquired valuable eagle feathers. Those who exchanged furs for the white man's tobacco and corn called themselves "ottawas," their word for trader.

Driven from their homes in Canada and northern Michigan, the Ottawas settled in the southwestern Lake Erie area in the 1740s, living at the edge of the Great Black Swamp. French trappers also journeyed into this area. In 1763 the great Ottawa chief, Pontiac, organized regional tribes but failed to drive out the British.

For a time, the Great Black Swamp proved impenetrable to white settlers. Eventually, the vast swamp and marshes were drained and subdued for agricultural, industrial, commercial, and residential developments.

Only pockets of the Great Black Swamp survive (see Oak Openings Metropark, Goll Woods) and the marshland, once, over 300,000 acres, has shrunk to 15,000 acres, much of it protected by federal and state governments.

In 1938, President Franklin Roosevelt declared the 82-acre West Sister Island a national wildlife refuge. This patch of land in Lake Erie is a priceless rookery for black-crowned herons, great blue herons, and great egrets. The island became Ohio's only national wilderness area in 1975. It's closed to the public.

The federal government began acquiring marshland for a refuge in the 1960s. More than 8,000 acres have been protected so far.

Journal

August 18, 1993. I scan the treeline along Crane Creek hoping to see a bald eagle—even for just a second. No luck. The sky is empty. This is my sixth visit to the refuge and I have yet to see an eagle. I feel like a crest-fallen tourist who has failed to see a movie star while in Hollywood. As I drive out of the sanctuary, I recall a coincidence involving an eagle's nest that happened 30 years earlier near Vermilion.

Following his routine, biologist John M. Anderson, manager of the Winous Point Club, drove his car on the long, dusty driveway to the mailbox. As usual, he glanced at the vacant eagle's nest atop a dead elm tree. He hoped the bird would someday return to the aerie. When he reached the mail box, news of the assassination of President Kennedy came over the car radio.

Anderson lingered awhile listening to more news. Driving back, his eyes drifted to the old elm. The nest was gone. The eagle's nest had fallen the same hour that President Kennedy was shot.

Skunk cabbage

SHELDON MARSH STATE NATURE PRESERVE

The locals once called this place Sheldon's Folly. They just couldn't figure out why a Sandusky doctor would spend his money on a slim spit of sand that attracted bugs and, half the time, was washed over by Lake Erie. And those pretentious iron gates at the entrance were eerie, as if a dowager's vine-covered estate lay in ruins behind a row of creaking oaks. But Dr. Dean Sheldon was more interested in wildlife than local gossip. He knew that his marsh was an important stopover for migratory birds flying across Lake Erie, and that the spit was one of the last undisturbed barrier beaches along Ohio's north coast. ★

Location

Sheldon Marsh is located a few miles west of Huron in Erie County.

From Huron, head west on State Route 2, exit north on Rye Beach Road to the intersection of U.S. Route 6, then go west on US 6 about 1/2 mile to the preserve (north side). Look for the iron fence on the right.

Ownership

Ohio Department of Natural Resources, Division of Natural Areas and Preserves.

Size & Designation

The state dedicated this 387.3-acre marsh and barrier beach an interpretive nature preserve on February 5, 1980.

Nearby Natural Attractions

Old Woman Creek and Erie Sand Barrens state nature preserves are a few miles away in Erie County. You can also visit Milan, Willow Point, and Resthaven state wildlife areas, also in Erie County. Kelleys Island State Park, on Kelleys Island, protects the rare formations at Glacial Grooves State Memorial, a national natural landmark. Ferry service to the island is available from Sandusky.

Access

From the parking lot off State Route 6, follow the paved path at the left which once was the driveway to Cedar Point amusement park. At the former Sheldon home, the pavement ends but the trail remains wide and smooth. It appears to be manageable for folks in wheelchairs or pushing strollers.

The marsh will soon appear on the left. Ahead, the trail joins a paved lane (from the right) and continues north toward the beach. The road leads to an observation deck on the left and to the National Aeronautical & Space Administration pump station at the beach. The observation deck, with benches, offers an excellent panorama of the marsh all year.

At the pump station, look for the narrow trail heading into the woods. This wild, narrow path through a dense thicket of reeds ends at the barrier beach. I strongly recommend that you walk this brief trail in the summer to experience the jungle-like vegetation growing on the sand spit. The barrier beach stretching to the west is a good place to rest a spell and soak in the sun, listen to the waves, and search the sky for bald eagles.

Backtrack to the exit. You might want to take the blacktopped left fork back to the start. If so, follow the trail to the end, then take the path at the right. It leads across a lawn to the parking lot.

If you took the right fork, along the marsh and through the forest, consider a short loop trail to the right just past the ranger's house. It returns to the driveway.

The site is open daily from sunrise to sunset, April–October. Permission is required for visits from November–March. For information and winter access, contact the preserve manager, c/o Old Woman Creek State Nature Preserve, 2514 Cleveland Road East, Huron, OH 44839; phone (419) 433-4601 or 443-7599. Or, get in touch with the Ohio Department of Natural Resources, Division of Natural Areas and Preserves, Fountain Square, Building F-1, Columbus, OH 43224-1331; phone (614) 265-6453.

Geology

The narrow finger of land stretching west into Lake Erie is a sand spit. It acts as a barrier beach and protects the wetland marsh from the heavy waves of the lake.

Geologists suspect this sand spit began to develop about 4,500 years ago when the water level of the lake increased and flooded the shore. The sand and mud of the old shoreline that washed into the lake during this inundation was later hurled back toward the land by waves and deposited as an offshore sandbar—the foundation for the spit.

In western Lake Erie the close-to-shore current that transports sand and other sediment (called a littoral drift) flows from east to west. When littoral drift is slowed by an obstruction—the shore, a bay, the mouth of a river, a sand bar, a shallow basin, or a beach—the sand it carries begins to settle.

At this spot on the coast the drift moves toward the shore at an oblique angle. The spit was born where the current struck land. It grew into the lake in the direction of the littoral drift, toward the west. A marsh evolved in the calm water between the spit and land.

Like a desert sand dune, a sand spit shifts position. It widens toward the lake when the water level drops, but during high water it thins out and heads for land. Lake Erie's water level is considered high at this time, and consequently the spit at Sheldon's Marsh is very narrow.

Twenty years ago the western tip of the spit was connected to the eight-mile-long Cedar Point spit. During a furious storm in November 1972, waves crashed through the barrier and created a channel. Since then, Lake Erie's waves have shoved the Sheldon Marsh spit landward some 1,000 feet. A January 1993 storm breached the barrier again, about 1,000 feet east of the tip.

The breakthroughs occur because a series of longwall piers constructed east of the preserve in Huron from 1827–1932 traps sand heading for the spit. Barrier beaches and spits weaken if they are not replenished with sand. They dissolve when big storm waves pound the beach and open passages.

Plants trying to gain a toehold on the spit face a tough environment of high waves, strong winds, and burning sun. The eastern end of the spit, anchored to the mainland, is more stable because driftwood and vegetation stop the waves, collect sediment, build up the sandy soil with their roots and rotting material, block the wind, and provide shade for plants that need it.

Still, the spit rises only six feet above the lake level at its highest point.

Small lobes growing southward from the tip actually are tiny deltas created by the runoff of waves that wash over the beach. This erosion by waves explains how the spit has curled inward and drifted toward land.

Under present circumstances the spit is doomed.

So is the marsh, which shrinks as the beach drifts toward land. Eventually, waves will push the beach into the mainland, and kill the marsh. Human intervention might save the spit. Jetties and offshore barriers would slow down waves and capture much needed sediment for the sand-starved beach. However, such "beach nourishment" projects could harm a new residential development and marina on the nearby Chaussee Road/Cedar Point causeway. Developers have deepened the channel opened by the 1972 storm for pleasure boats.

Wildlife

Few places on the Lake Erie coast can match Sheldon Marsh's accommodations for wildlife, especially its various wetlands which include a large lake (Lake Erie), a bay, a cattail and sedge grass marsh, woodland swamp, and a pond. These moist habitats, and the barrier beach, serve as sanctuaries for a vast assemblage of birds, fish, amphibians, reptiles, and plants, many of them endangered or threatened.

For the birds who must journey across Lake Erie every equinox Sheldon Marsh is a welcomed stopover for rest, food, and shelter. More than 300 species of birds, most of them migratory, have been spotted here, ranging from the majestic and endangered bald eagle to the diminutive ruby-throated hummingbird.

An ODNR checklist of birds indicates that you might see 23 of the 25 birds listed as endangered in Ohio, including: the peregrine falcon, bald eagle, magnolia,common and black terns, Kirtland's and Canada warblers, northern waterthrush, and dark-eyed junco.

Fifteen of the 18 species listed as "special interest" (roughly meaning potentially threatened) by the Division of Wildlife have been spotted here. These include double-crested cormorant and northern saw-whet owl.

Twenty-six varieties of waterfowl (notably the white tundra swan) and 35 kinds of warblers have been counted. Carefully located bird boxes attract wood ducks, bluebirds, kestrels (hawks), and tree swallows.

Some 44 members of the fish world live around the preserve, such as walleye, perch, catfish, bullhead, minnow, shiner, and bluegill. Fishing, of course, is prohibited.

Reptiles and amphibians, represented by 32 species, are abundant here. This population includes turtles (Blanding's—special interest), salamanders (red-backed, Jefferson), frogs and toads (American toad, bullfrog, spring peeper, leopard), and snakes (blue racer, northern water, northern brown, eastern garter).

Keen observers might see some of the 22 mammals that have resided here, like deer, raccoon, least weasel, muskrat, mice, and moles.

In the forest, look for oaks and shagbark hickory on higher ground; elm and ash closer to the marsh. These are joined by cottonwood, willows, mulberry, silky dogwood, maples, basswood, bald cypress, dawn redwood, aspen, and ginko, the last introduced by Dr. Sheldon.

Many endangered, threatened, or potentially threatened plants live in the preserve. The list, partly based on a 1990 survey, includes beach wormwood, inland sea rocket, low umbrella sedge, Engelman's umbrella sedge, Schweinitz's umbrella sedge, matted spikerush, seaside spurge, bushy cinquefoil, jack-in-the-pulpit, and sand dropseed.

From mid-April through June, wildflowers such as trillium, marsh marigolds, cut-leaved toothwort, wild geranium, trout lily, and cardinal flower color the forest floor. Marsh mallow, American lotus, and water lily are abundant in late summer.

History

The gates at the entrance to the preserve are all that remain of the original car entrance to Cedar Point Amusement Park. The drive was abandoned in the 1930s because the lake too often washed away the road on the narrow spit. The park entrance was moved farther west, but the gates stayed.

The marsh, bay, and beach became a favorite waterfowl hunting and fishing spot for local sportsmen. The site was one of only a few undisturbed coastal properties.

In 1954 Dr. Dean Sheldon, a Sandusky physician and conservationist, purchased 56 acres of this tract and managed some of it as a nature sanctuary. He and his family built the farm pond near the entrance, planted trees (some of them exotic species), and placed birdhouses throughout the property.

The Ohio Department of Natural Resources acquired the Sheldon land in 1979 and combined it with adjoining tracts to create the nature preserve in 1980.

An adjoining marsh recently purchased by the Ohio Chapter of The Nature Conservancy (TNC) more than doubles the wetland area now protected for nature. This TNC preserve (not open to the public) will be known as the John B. and Mildred A. Putnam Memorial Preserve, honoring the family that bequeathed $37 million to the conservation group.

Esker

SIEGENTHALER ESKER STATE NATURE PRESERVE

This sausage-shaped ridge was once a creek flowing beneath a mountain of ice, a veritable glacial storm sewer, that left behind a sinuous mound of clay, sand, and gravel.

Location

Champaign County, Harrison Township.

Starting from Urbana, travel north on State Route 29 about 10 miles. Turn right on Calland Road for 2.5 miles, then right on Couchman Road for a half mile. Park on the south side of the road.

Ownership

Ohio Department of Natural Resources, Division of Natural Areas and Preserves.

Size & Designation

This interpretive preserve of 36.8 acres was dedicated on June 21, 1978.

Nearby Natural Attractions

In Champaign County, see Cedar Bog State Nature Preserve, Davey Woods State Nature Preserve, and Kiser Lake State Park.

Access

The trail from the parking lot heads straight south along a fencerow for several hundred yards, then turns right down a slope and up to the spine of the esker. The short loop trail begins and ends here. Go in either direction, for the path follows the ridge then circles along the base of the formation and back up the ridge. You'll walk about a mile.

Stay within the fenced area. The preserve is open from sunup to sundown every day. For more information contact the Ohio Department of Natural Resources, Division of Natural Areas and Preserves, Fountain Square, Building F-1, Columbus, Ohio 43224-1331; phone (614) 265-6453.

Geology

Few vantage points in Ohio offer such a variety of glacially shaped features. The footpath leads to a 15-foot-tall esker, a glacial deposit composed of sand, clay, and gravel. A stream flowing through a tunnel at the base of the Wisconsinan glacier (15,000 years ago) gave this esker its shape. When the ice mass dissolved, glacial till (clay, rocks, sand, and silt) carried in the current filled the stream bed. The esker traces the course of the meltwater creek.

Look south to see another esker made by the same south-flowing glacial stream. (This ODNR-owned esker is off limits to the public.) The combined length of these twin formations is 2,000 feet. To the west rises another esker, this one created by a different stream.

Impressive as these eskers seem, they are comparatively small. An esker west of New Richmond in Logan County is more typical. It measures two miles in length and soars to 25 feet.

Those dome-shaped knolls north of the esker are kames, created when gravel carried by meltwater running on top of the glacier fell into openings in the ice. Picture sand streaming through an hourglass to get an idea how a kame came about.

Scientists think that eskers and kames show that the glacier's retreat had stalled or slowed, and that it was melting down (shrinking) as well from its face.

The marshy area to the east is an old kettle lake formed when a block of glacial ice melted in a depression. Though you cannot see it from the esker, a larger and deeper kettle lake lies to the east, on the other side of the ridge.

The flat terrain west and south of the eskers is another meltwater creation called an outwash valley, a feature resembling interconnected, fanlike alluvia. Here the meltwater flowed slowly in a broad, shallow delta.

On the walk back to the car, notice the huge boulders beside the trail in the grazed woodlot. These are erratics, foreign rocks, brought here from the north by the glacier.

Wildlife

Livestock grazed on these glacial formations for decades. The few hickories and oaks that stand on the summit remind us of the forest that once covered the esker. Nowadays, hawthorns, various berry patches, and honeysuckle are trying to take over the ridges. These plants provide ideal habitat for the many small birds darting across the ridge.

When I visited in mid-April, a small herd of deer grazing on the west esker bounded away to the woods which covered the southern esker. Canada geese nested in the soggy kettle lake.

With binoculars I watched the courtship antics of a pair of eastern meadowlarks in the grass at the base of the kames. While the female waddled and fanned her tail feathers, the male extended his wings halfway and broad-jumped 10 feet. After five or six leaps the lovers disappeared into a thicket.

Tiger salamanders, a potentially threatened amphibian, were found at the base of the esker in 1988. They did not appear when I visited their domain.

History

The preserve honors Vaughn and Freida Siegenthaler who donated these 37 acres of geological history to the OhioDepartment of Natural Resources.

American bittern

SPRINGVILLE MARSH STATE NATURE PRESERVE

Springville Marsh is the largest remnant of the Big Spring Prairie, a sprawling wetland that once stretched 15 miles from Carey to Fostoria. Forty years ago the marsh was stripmined for its muck, but nature has largely concealed that human intrusion.

Location

Southwest Seneca County, Big Spring Township.

From Carey, travel north on U.S. Route 23/State Route 199 for 3.5 miles, then head west (left) on Township Road 24. Look for the parking lot on the south side after crossing railroad tracks.

Ownership

Originally purchased by the Springville Marsh Committee and the Ohio Chapter of The Nature Conservancy, the property was turned over to the Ohio Department of Natural Resources, Division of Natural Areas and Preserve.

Size & Designation

The Ohio Department of Natural Resources dedicated the 161-acre wetland as an interpretive nature preserve on August 1, 1981.

Access

Half of the distance of the one-mile loop trail is a boardwalk that begins at the parking lot and leads to a viewing platform and an observation tower. The remaining half of the trail visits a woodland along the west edge of the preserve. Look for a preserve brochure and trail guide at the information board at the trailhead.

The observation tower presents the best view of the marsh. This is especially true in the summer when tall sedges and grasses block your vision at the ground-level platform. Visitors riding in wheelchairs and pushing strollers can probably manage the boardwalk trail.

Though wildlife can be seen any season, bird life is especially abundant during the spring and fall migrations. Visibility is best at these times because vegetation is low.

Summer hikers should guard against mosquitoes by wearing insect repellent, a ball cap, sunglasses, and long pants. Marsh plants will soar above your reach in the summer. The vegetation is so thick in July and August, I cannot imagine a human crossing the marsh without assistance.

You can view the marsh every day from dawn to dusk. Naturalist-led programs are held here, usually during the spring and fall tides of birds.

For more information contact the Ohio Department of Natural Resources, Division of Natural Areas and Preserves, Fountain Square, Building F-1, Columbus, Ohio 43224-1331; phone (614) 265-6453.

Geology

The terrain in this part of the world is flat to gently rolling, thanks to the scouring action by the Wisconsinan glacier some 12,000 years ago. The ice sheets, in other words, prepared the land for the wet prairie and unique ecology that came later.

Dolomite (the same bedrock found at Niagara Falls) lies near the surface of the slight ridges surrounding the preserve. The ridges also contain the water for the marsh and ponds. This cool, spring water (hence the names of the marsh and prairie) carries calcium derived from the bedrock. The calcium-rich, marl soil, composed of sedge peat mostly, was mined by fertilizer companies.

Technically, Springville Marsh is a fen because it is refreshed by alkaline spring water from underground sources. Cedar Bog State Memorial, described in this book, is another spring-fed fen.

Wildlife

In this dense cattail-bulrush-sedge marsh live some of Ohio's most precious plants and critters. The American and least bitterns, each endangered, find refuge here. The spotted turtle, listed as a special interest (potentially threatened) reptile, might be seen in spring basking on a log protruding from the marsh or pond. "Special interest" birds like sora and Virginia rails, and the marsh wren, are counted among the population of birds.

Grass-like pondweed, an endangered plant, attracts waterfowl, and grows near few-flowered spikerush, a threatened specimen. Little yellow sedge, twig-rush (typically found on the Atlantic coast), long-beaked willow, Ohio goldenrod, white beakrush, and shining ladies'-tresses, all potentially threatened species, thrive in this verdant wetland. Also look for the blossoms of bittersweet nightshade, Kalm's lobelia, yellow avens, and nodding ladies' tresses among the numerous fen orchids.

See if you can spot the Ice Age relicts, the small clusters of plants more common in the north—shrubby cinquefoil and grass-of-parnassus (white, green-striped flowers). Ferns are represented by the royal, northern marsh, adder's-tongue, and sensitive.

Several rarities have been planted in Springville Marsh to extend their range—swamp birch (threatened), fringed gentian (potentially threatened), small white lady's slipper, and spiked blazing star.

Cottonwoods dominate the swamp forest, which is low enough to be seasonally flooded. Big-toothed aspen, hackberry, wild cherry, and dogwood also grow here.

The marsh, forbidding to humans, is luxuriant for the 136 species of birds who live here or pass through. The nesting birds include the above-mentioned rails, common gallinule, American coot (not the human kind), blue-winged teal, wood duck, and willow flycatcher. You also might see the great blue heron, other varieties of ducks, the pileated woodpecker, and the merlin, a jay-sized falcon often mistaken for the larger peregrine falcon. The wooded areas attract warblers, goldfinches, sparrows, and other common residents.

The dome-shaped piles of cattails that you see from the observation tower are muskrat dens. Mink, fox, weasel, rabbit, and deer also reside here.

Springville Marsh preserves an extraordinary collection of wildlife living in five distinct habitats: pond, stream, cattail marsh, swamp forest, and sedge meadow.

History

Native American and early white pioneers successfully hunted and trapped in the marshland.

According to ODNR's brochure, the U.S. government gave much of the Big Spring Prairie (16,000 acres) to the Wyandot Indians in 1818 because it suited their traditional hunting and gathering ways. A more likely explanation is that pioneer farmers found the marshland unsuitable for agriculture—so they gave it to the Indians.

The Hocking Valley Railroad put a rail line through the marsh in 1877. Ditches drained the swamp so that more crops could be sowed. By 1900 the place known today as Springville Marsh was an onion farm.

The Smith Agriculture Chemical Company bought the swamp in 1937 and began dredging the calcium-rich muck from the bottom. The muck was loaded into the cars of a small-gauge railroad and transported to the nearby main rail for shipment to fertilizer companies. The mining ended in 1956, and the land quickly reverted to a marsh.

Naturalists have flocked to the marsh. At the turn of the century, Dayton-born naturalist Thomas A. Bonser documented the flora and fauna of the Big Spring Prairie in his master's thesis.

H. Thomas Bartlett, a local science teacher, has been studying the bird sat Springville Marsh since 1978. In his 1990 report, he observed 205 species, representing 77 percent of all types seen in the region.

In the late 1970s, local concerned citizens organized the Springville Marsh Committee and with the help of the Ohio Chapter of The Nature Conservancy bought the marsh. Some of the land was acquired through a gift in memory of Charles and Bertha Krejci Vanek, former landowners. The title was transferred to the Ohio Department of Natural Resources, Division of Natural Areas and Preserves in 1981.

Journal

August 17, 1993. I am struck, literally, by the height and density of the cattails and phragmites (cane-like grasses). They grow beyond my reach, eight feet tall or so. Humans don't walk through this green thicket easily. Two centuries ago, it was likely a good wildcat hideout. Now, nothing larger than a fox slinks down the skinny path from the boardwalk into the marsh.

The tall grasses are perfect cover for my son, David, who amused himself by hiding in the bush around every turn and then springing out at me. He sprinted to the observation deck and climbed to the upper level. In autumn, his energy might have scattered dozens of birds. Today, he only strew my thoughts.

TOLEDO METROPARKS

The Metropolitan Park District of the Toledo Area was created in 1928. It manages nine parks covering some 6,700 acres and includes Oak Openings Preserve, one of the largest metroparks in the state and a rare wildlife paradise. Folks longing for a walk along the Maumee River, a state scenic river, can go to Bend View, Farnsworth, Providence, and Side Cut metroparks. The metroparks are open every day from 7 a.m.-dark. There is no fee. For more information, contact the Metropolitan Park District of the Toledo area, Administrative Offices, 5100 W. Central Avenue, Toledo, Ohio 43615; phone (419)535-3050.

Oak openings

- **Oak Openings Preserve**
- **Pearson Metropark**
- **Secor Metropark**
- **Swan Creek Preserve**
- **Wildwood Preserve**

OAK OPENINGS PRESERVE

This preserve protects one of the rarest and most unique habitats in the state, if not the world—an oak opening. More than 1,000 different plants flourish in this bounteous place. The cornucopia of life includes the largest assemblage of rare and threatened plants and animals in Ohio.

With so much life at risk, it is no surprise that conservationists have declared the oak openings and nearby savannas a globally threatened habitat. ★

Location

Western Lucas County, Swanton Township.

From Interstate 475 on the west side of Toledo, travel west on State Route 2 for 8 miles. State Route 295 joins SR 2 at the Toledo airport and both roads continue west.

In a mile, the roads split. Take SR 295 south (left) for a half mile then bear right on Wilkins Road. Follow Wilkins Road for 2.5 miles to its end, then go right (west) on Oak Openings Parkway. Turn at the next right and park at the lot for Mallard Lake and the Buehner Walking Center.

Ownership

Metropark District of the Toledo Area.

Size & Designation

The sprawling Oak Openings Preserve encompasses 3,668 acres and is larger than the eight other Toledo metroparks combined. Oak Openings is one of three metropark sites designated by the park district as a preserve, or a prime natural area open to the public.

Nearby Natural Attractions

Lucas County offers many facilities for nature lovers such as Maumee Bay and Crane Creek state parks, Irwin Prairie State Nature Preserve, Maumee State Forest (bordering the preserve), and Metzger Marsh and Magee Marsh state wildlife areas.

Also visit the other Toledo Metroparks reviewed in this book—Wildwood Preserve, Swan Creek Preserve, Pearson Metropark, and Secor Metropark.

Access

Oak Openings Preserve teases the hiker with seven marked trails totaling 28.1 miles, including its famous 17-mile loop around the perimeter of the park land. Beyond this, hikers can ramble down 50 miles of unmarked fire lanes, and a 5.5-mile stone-surfaced all-purpose trail. That's nearly 85 miles of foot trails!

In addition, 23 miles of trails beckon horseback riders. The riding center is located on Jeffers Road.

The four trails that I toured visit many of the highlights and various habitats. If you can only choose one path, take the Sand Dunes Trail. Before leaving, grab a park brochure (which includes a trail map) and study the big trail map at the Buehner Walking Center.

The Sand Dunes Trail (red blazes) begins at the trailhead on the west side of the parking lot. A few steps into the woods bear right and head north through a quiet pine grove. After passing a fire lane, the trail splits, marking the beginning of its loop.

Each leg of the loop reaches the striking sand dunes located at the north end of the loop. (At that point you can follow the All-Purpose Trail east a bit to the Ferns & Lake Trail.) Generally, the west leg of the loop rambles through more open and sandy areas, while the east leg stays in a hardwood forest adorned with graceful, wholesome ferns. Return to the trailhead to finish a 1.7-mile walk.

For lovers of ferns, Oak Openings has some of the most magnificent fronds I have seen in Ohio. Take the 2.9-mile Ferns & Lake Trail, heading north from Mallard Lake and the Buehner Walking Center. Extraordinary specimens of cinnamon, interrupted, and royal fern await the walker.

This path (blue blazes) traces Gale Run, swings east and crosses a railroad grade, leads to a pond, and touches the 17-mile trail before curving south to the trailhead at Mallard Lake.

An alternate route, combining the best of the Sand Dune and Fern & Lake trails, follows the west leg of the Sand Dune Trail, the All-Purpose Trail to the west leg of the Fern & Lake Trail, then south along Gale Run to Mallard Lake.

Horseshoe Lake Trail loops around an abandoned channel of Swan Creek. To get there bear left (south) at the trailhead by the parking lot, cross Oak Openings Parkway, and enter the woods. (Ignore the All-Purpose Trail branching to the left.)

At the intersection ahead, bear right and follow the yellow blazes of the lasso-shaped Horseshoe Lake Trail, a 1.5-mile walk. From that same intersection, go straight, following silver markers if you want to hike the Ridge Trail. Ahead, you cross Swan Creek and come to the fork for the loop. Go right and climb a gentle ridge overlooking the creek. The path swings east, past some ravines with hemlocks, then descends to the creek and curves west (upstream) to the start of the loop. Retrace your steps to the parking lot. The Ridge Trail measures 2.5 miles.

Folks in wheelchairs or pushing strollers can enjoy the $^{6}/_{10}$-mile Lake Circuit Trail (aqua blazes) which circles Mallard Lake. Small kids might prefer this short hike, which features an observation deck on the west shore. Skating is permitted on Mallard Lake when the ice is thick enough. (Call first.)

The yellow-blazed 17-Mile Trail encircles the metropark. It can be hiked in a single day, but most hikers walk portions over several days. Trailheads for this path are located at Mallard Lake, and the Springbrook, Evergreen Lake, and White Oak picnic areas.

Fishing is permitted at Evergreen, Springbrook, and Mallard Lake (the latter only for children 14 years and under).

A special four-mile trail for cross-country skiers begins at Evergreen Lake. You will find restrooms and a warm fire at a shelter halfway on the trail. Call (419) 382-7669 for skiing conditions.

Generally trails are well-marked and easy to follow. The trail map on the park brochure is detailed. Merging fire lanes may cause a moment of indecision, however. Frequent visitors seeking new trails might try those unblazed paths.

The Buehner Walking Center has restrooms and drinking water. Please deposit your trash in the receptacles if you picnic at Mallard Lake. Group camping sites are available to youth and educational organizations, but reservations are required.

Oak Openings Lodge can be reserved for meetings and social events. The dormitory and food service can handle 52 guests.

Geology

To understand how this land received the gift of so much plant life, we have to journey back 10,000 years or so when water, not vegetation, covered this land.

Back then, a large freshwater lake, one of Lake Erie's predecessors, flooded much of northwestern Ohio. The lake level reached far inland because the Wisconsinan glacier blocked the Niagara/St. Lawrence outlet to the east.

Rivers and glacial meltwater carried fresh water and sediments (sand, silt, etc.) into the series of lakes on the same site, known as Lake Warren, Lake Wayne, or Lake Lundy, depending on the location of its shoreline. The water level of Lake Warren, for example, was 93 feet higher than Lake Erie's.

Sand deposited off the western and northwestern shores of the ancient lake (off the shore of eastern Michigan) traveled to the flat beaches on the southwestern and southern shores (Ohio) by way of southbound longshore currents. When the ice jam finally broke, the lake drained and left the beaches high and dry.

At first, the landscape probably resembled a flat, sandy, barren plain. Quickly, though, wind dried the plain and began blowing sand into shifting dunes. The terrain now looked corrugated, and wind swept.

In Ohio the sand belt stretched for 25 miles and varied in width from 3–7 miles. (The dunes continue into Michigan.) The sand ridges rise from 15–50 feet above their clay base. Water drains slowly (if at all) in this sandy area, and may settle within three feet of the surface. Where the sand is thin between sand ridges, swamp forests or bogs commonly form.

The soil on the crest of sandy ridges tends to be acidic, due to decomposing vegetation. However, in depressions it is usually slightly alkaline because it lays just above glacial till (gravel, silt, rocks, etc.) that is alkaline. These slight variations in soil pH levels add to the diversity and mystery of the oak openings.

Swan Creek, one of two currents naturally draining the sand belt, avoids disturbing the highest dunes as it snakes through the preserve. In places, you can see where the current has cut below the sand layer and into the clay. Dammed tributaries have created Mallard Lake, Springbrook Lake, and Evergreen Lake (the biggest pond in park).

Wildlife

The geological forces that sculpted this terrain created six distinct habitats in the oak openings.

Two of the habitats are found on the dunes themselves. One setting has widely spaced black and white oak, and some red oak, growing on the top of the ridges. Black oak seedlings grow best in dry and open areas, which explains why they have found a home on the sandy ridges. This habitat also sponsors bracken and sweet ferns, huckleberry, dewberry, shrubby St. John's wort, New Jersey tea, everlasting, wintergreen, wild indigo, chokeberry, lupine, sweet pea, butterfly weed, and others.

Prairie-type plants, like little bluestem grass, Indian grass, coreopsis, and sunflowers thrive on the dunes and abandoned farm fields. Some of these plants are remnants of the prairie vegetation that moved into Ohio during a warm spell 4,000 years ago. These plants could grow beneath the scattered oaks. Butterflies (fritillaries and monarchs), honeybees, and sand (digger) wasps are abundant in this area.

At the dunes, study the small, delicate details—the footprints of beetles (gray tiger and brown beetles) and birds, the twisting path of a hognose snake, or the thin, crescent-shaped traces of windblown grass or a tree branch on the sand. Look for ripples on the dunes, and the different colors in the sand.

Small swamp forests rise in the hollows between dunes. In this living place, you are apt to find pin oak, red oak, black cherry, blackgum, pawpaw, spicebush, and bigtooth aspen trees. The ferns (cinnamon, interrupted, and royal) grow to great heights, as do clumps of buttonbush, blackberry, spikenard, bedstraw, spicebush, white baneberry, stinging nettle, meadowsweet (spirea), and wild lily-of-the-valley.

In the scattered bogs, also found at the base of sand dunes, look for speckled alder, willows, meadowsweet, buttonbush, elderberry, berry patches, skunk cabbage, marsh marigold, jack-in-the-pulpit, spotted jewelweed (touch-me-not), yarrow, and marsh ferns.

The Swan Creek floodplain supports typical bottomland plants such as green ash, sycamore, walnut, silver maple, basswood, box elder, plus wood nettle, smartweed, giant ragweed, and lizard's tail. This type of habitat is not unique to the oak opening and can be found along other floodplains in northwestern Ohio.

The sixth habitat of the oak openings region—the wet prairie, or savanna—is best viewed at nearby Irwin Prairie State Nature Preserve or Kitty Todd Preserve (owned by The Nature Conservancy)—though some elements exist here. These moist areas look like typical wide-open grasslands with clusters of shrubs and small trees. Many plants associated with wet prairies are found in the Oak Openings Preserve.

The evergreen stands of red, white, and scotch pines, spruce, and fir were planted by relief workers nearly 60 years ago. Many have become diseased, or are dying of old age (scotch pines). Since these are not native Ohio trees, the land will be allowed to return to its natural condition.

Edwin L. Moseley studied the vegetation of the sand belt back in the late 1920s. He recorded 715 plant species in his 1929 book. Sixty-one of these plants were found in only two other Ohio counties, and 168 species were more common here than the rest of Ohio. He counted 17 kinds of asters, and 20 varieties of goldenrods. Since his report, almost 300 more plants have been discovered and recorded on the inventory.

A recent park district survey of the flora and fauna revealed the existence of 157 protected species in the preserve. That is the largest gathering of endangered and threatened life in any preserve in Ohio.

In dry areas, look for these endangered plants—Junegrass, southern club moss, plains muhlenburgia, southern hairy panic grass, Canada hawkweed, limestone rockcress, Carolina whitlow-grass, narrow leaf pinweed, prairie tick-foil, sessile tick trefoil, dotted horsemint, hoary mountain mint, one-flowered wintergreen, green-flowered wintergreen, fern-leaf false foxglove, and old field toadflax. Eighteen threatened and 17 potentially threatened plants enlarge this grouping of rarities.

Wet areas provide a sanctuary for rare sedges (Bicknell's, hay, pale umbrella), grass-like beak rush, Atlantic blue-eyed grass, Greene's and inland rush, long-bracted orchid, yellow lady's slipper, purple fringed orchid, bushy aster, Missouri ironweed, spathulate-leaved sundew, prairie gentian, soapwort gentian, Bicknell's geranium, fire weed, cross-leaved milkwort, gay wings, Canada plum, and Skinner's foxglove. Add to this list northern blue-eyed grass, thought to be extinct in Ohio, and 20 threatened and 27 potentially threatened species.

Tachysphex pechumani, a small sand wasp, is the latest discovery at Oak Openings. The insect is so rare it lacks a common name. It is known to exist only in isolated spots in New Jersey's pine barrens and Michigan's Pinckney Recreation Area.

The mostly black bug burrows into sand to lay eggs. It stuffs the tiny tunnel with insects so that young, hatching wasps have food. Close up, the male measures only $^1/_2$–$^3/_4$ inches, while the larger female grows from $^3/_4$–1 inch. Females have orange antennae, which distinguishes them from other wasps. Males have amber-colored wing bases.

Other endangered insects found here are the Persius dusky wing, frosted elfin, regal fritillary, and Karner blue butterflies, and the unexpected cycnia and brown satyr moths. The Karner blue butterfly has not been seen since 1989, however. If you see one, report it and mark its location.

The Karner blue, Persius dusky wing, and frosted elfin deposit their eggs solely on wild lupine. The plant is the larval host for these struggling butterflies. If the lupine declines, so do these beautiful aviators. To improve the chances for these butterflies, park managers must bolster the lupine population by controlling the spread of shrubs and trees by trimming and mowing.

Birders should keep their eyes peeled for a glimpse of these endangered birds—American bittern, northern harrier, bald eagle, peregrine falcon, king rail, sandhill crane, winter wren, magnolia and Canada warbler (these all being migratory, stopover birds), sedge wren, hermit thrush, golden-winged warbler, and lark sparrow, the latter being nesters in the preserve.

Some unusual birds, unusual because they are not commonly seen in northwestern Ohio, pay a visit—prairie, pine, and yellow-throated warblers, summer tanager, and blue grosbeak. The preserve, of course, claims a long list of common and unprotected birds—rufous-sided towhee, bluebird, wood thrush, and common flicker being in this company.

Though it has not been observed recently, the endangered Indiana bat dwells in the preserve, along with the evening bat, considered a rarity. The oak opening region is one of the last Ohio habitats for the badger, a special interest (potentially threatened) mammal.

The blue-spotted salamander, an endangered amphibian, finds refuge here, along with four "special interest" reptiles, notably Blanding's turtle and the poisonous eastern massasauga rattlesnake, though the latter has not been sighted for a while.

The preserve has a large herd of white-tailed deer, and its streams attract muskrat, mink, and long-tailed weasel. The red fox, gone from the region in 1900, is common again, but the gray fox is infrequently seen.

Earlier studies identified 70 kinds of fungi living in the openings. Twenty to 30 years ago, naturalists talked about the lichen prairies in the preserve—good open spots to view the stars, they said. The Evergreen Trail boasts the preserve's most colorful colonies of lichens and mosses.

History

Humans arrived at the oak openings about 12,000 years ago, judging from their discarded artifacts. But they apparently never established a permanent settlement in the sands. The sand ridges became trails for early European explorers and trappers traveling from Detroit to the Maumee River. (The paths probably were first blazed by deer.) Hiking and camping in the "opening" was easier than trudging through the surrounding swamp forest, known as the Great Black Swamp.

Settlers began "developing" the openings in the 1830s. They cleared the land of timber oaks, plowed the prairie, and drained the wetlands with a series of ditches. Because of the high degree of leaching in the sandy soil, farmers countered with great amounts of fertilizer which found its way into the soil and water.

Crushed limestone used in road building changed acidic soils to alkaline soil along roadsides. This allowed new vegetation to enter the area. Lime also blew into the preserve from adjacent farmland.

Local farmers robbed orchids from the forest and sold them for a nickel or dime in Toledo along with their vegetables and fruits. The buyers tried to plant the orchids in their own gardens, but most discovered too late that few orchids survive transplantations. The forest and dunes also were ravaged by mushroom hunters, wildflower pickers, motorcyclists, and folks who simply liked to frolic in the sand (not realizing the damage they were doing).

The coming of the automobile brought more people into the region and put greater stress on the openings. By the mid-1920s much of the original oak savanna had vanished.

The Toledo Metropolitan Park District was founded in 1928. One of its first projects was saving the oak openings. In 1932, 67-acre Springbrook Park, the preserve's predecessor, opened. More land was purchased as funds became available, and today the preserve protects 3,668 acres.

Journal

December 27, 1993. I am reading old accounts of the vanished wildlife that once lived here and enriched this land. For instance, 15 pairs of sandhill cranes nested in the area until 1875. Today, a few cranes may stop briefly to rest and refuel before continuing their migration.

A metroparks naturalist named Paul Goff wrote about the preserve "having an abundance of hognosed snakes." That was back in 1968. Today, one kind of hognosed snake, the eastern hognose, is considered a rare find in the preserve.

We mourn the loss of the creatures who have disappeared.

Red maple tree

PEARSON METROPARK

This verdant relict of the Great Black Swamp forest survives today thanks to a newspaper reporter's 20-year campaign to liberate these trees from the grip of local bankers. Long ago local folks called the place the Bank Lands because banks held it as a security on loans. Now it's public land and everybody's collateral for the future.

Location

Eastern Lucas County, City of Oregon.

Traveling on Interstate 280 southbound motorists should exit at Starr Avenue (or State Route 2, Navarre Road, see below) and head east, then right (south) on Lallendorf Road, and left into the park entrance (one-way road).

Northbound travelers on I-280 should exit at Wheeling Road and go right (north) a short distance, then right (east) on Navarre Road/SR 2, left on Lallendorf Road, and an immediate right at the park entrance. Park in the lot on the right just past the Packer-Hammersmith Center. The one-way road through the park exits on Starr Avenue.

Ownership

Metropark District of the Toledo Area.

Size & Designation

Pearson Metropark totals 320 acres.

Nearby Natural Attractions

The other Toledo metroparks in this book are Oak Openings Preserve, Swan Creek Preserve, Wildwood Preserve, and Secor Metropark. Elsewhere in Lucas County, visit Maumee Bay and Crane Creek state parks, Irwin Prairie State Nature Preserve, Maumee State Forest, Ottawa National Wildlife Refuge, and Magee Marsh and Metzger Marsh state wildlife areas.

Access

From the parking lot proceed to the modern Packer-Hammersmith Center, dedicated in 1988. Visit the "Window on Wildlife," open daily from 7 a.m.-dark (the same as the park hours) and grab a trail map before departing. Both footpaths begin at the nature center.

Heading east from the center the 1.3-mile Black Swamp Trail (orange trail markers) rambles through a remnant of the Great Black Swamp forest. Bear right at the first fork (start of the loop). Ahead, the trail splits near a gazebo, a good spot for watching wildlife.

The path to the left is a short cut that shortens the walk to 8/10-mile. I kept going straight on the Black Swamp Trail, journeyed to another gazebo deeper in the woods, then just moseyed back to the trailhead.

The Wood Thrush Trail, also 1.3 miles, heads west from the center, crosses the driveway, and visits the Pearson Memorial. Follow the blue-blazed path into an open area, and bear right at the first junction. (The path to the left goes to a lake.) The loop begins ahead at the edge of the woods. You choose the way. Each leg wanders through field and forest.

The park also features a 3.3-mile bicycle trail and a 2.9-mile jogging trail around the perimeter. These trails are designed for faster-paced folks.

Children enjoy the pedalboats that can be rented at the Lake Activities Center. In the winter, the pond is lighted for ice skating, and cross-country skiing is permitted on all trails.

Pearson Metropark attracts many people to its numerous softball fields, its tennis courts, soccer field, picnic areas, and playgrounds. Restrooms are located at the nature center, soccer field, lake activities area, and tennis courts.

Geology

Pearson Metropark is a fragment of the Great Black Swamp, a vast swamp forest that once covered much of northwestern Ohio. The forest arose on the lake floor of Lake Maumee (Lake Erie's predecessor) which stretched from western New York to Fort Wayne, Indiana some 13,000 years ago. Water running off the Wisconsinan glacier and surrounding countryside filled Lake Maumee.

When the glacier withdrew farther north into Canada outlets opened and Lake Maumee drained through the St. Lawrence-Niagara gateway. It left behind a flat plain more than 100 miles long and 30–40 miles wide. The Great Black Swamp sprawled out on this plain.

The impermeable clay soil of this plain stopped water from percolating into the earth, and the level land retarded drainage. Consequently, this flatland remained soggy most of the year. Plants took root as the temperatures warmed.

At first, the Great Black Swamp was an imposing, wild obstacle, but white settlers slowly conquered it by draining it and turning the forest into cropland.

Wildlife

The woodland canopy in this natural area boasts a variety of mature hardwoods, such as sugar and red maple, American beech, basswood (linden), swamp oak, shagbark hickory, sycamore, and cottonwood. Dutch elm disease wiped out the impressive stands of elm. Their stumps and rotting trunks remind us of their former glory.

Pawpaw, ironwood (blue beech), spicebush, redbud, and dogwood dominate the understory, the growth area between the forest floor and canopy represented by smaller trees and shrubs.

On the ground, a bouquet of wildflowers blooms according to Nature's staggered schedule. These miracles include snakeroot purple cress, stinging nettle, spring beauty, trillium, jack-in-the-pulpit, wild ginger, wild geranium, and garlic mustard.

In spring, the woods brightens with warblers. Sharp eyes may spot an endangered hermit thrush, or a northern oriole, red-eyed vireo, ovenbird, scarlet tanager, American redstart, wood thrush, downy and hairy woodpeckers, and Acadian flycatcher. The sharp-shinned hawk, designated a special interest (potentially threatened) bird in Ohio, and the great horned and screech owls are less frequent guests.

History

The metropark honors George W. Pearson, an East Toledo resident and a reporter for *The Blade*, Toledo's daily newspaper. Pearson's many articles about the swamp forest inspired hundreds of citizens to join his effort to save it as a park.

For many years the property was known as the Bank Lands because banks held it as a security on loans.

The park district bought the first parcel, a 280-acre tract, right off the auction block, using money from an anonymous donor. A fundraising scheme called "Living Memorials," where donors get their names "plaqued" and tacked to trees secured cash to buy the remaining 40 acres. The park was dedicated on August 30, 1934.

Laborers working for the Works Progress Administration and Civilian Conservation Corps built many of the park's facilities, notably the distinctive stonework. Workers dug the man-made ponds (renovated in 1986–87) with picks and shovels.

The Packer-Hammersmith Center pays tribute to a trio of school teachers whose hefty bequests built the nature education facility. The teachers were Dorothy Packer-Hammersmith, Edward Packer, and George Hammersmith. The center was dedicated in 1988.

Journal

This must be a scene from a Harold Pinter play. I pause at the gazebo. Another man joins me, but as I'm about to greet him, he averts his eyes. A third man enters and also keeps to himself. For five minutes nobody says a word, but I sense the two other men recognize each other. The first arrival suddenly departs, then the second, then me. They continue to glance back, then vanish. The wildlife is always surprising at Pearson Metropark.

Large-leaved trillium

SECOR METROPARK

It is hard to believe that the long, rolling mound yonder, the one topped by oaks and wildflowers, once was a naked sand dune on the beach of an ancient lake. Towering tulip trees also spread their roots wide in the sandy and soggy forest.

Location

Northwestern Lucas County.

From Interstate 475 travel west on U.S. Route 20 (Central Avenue) about 4.5 miles to the entrance on the left side of the highway. Follow Tupelo Way, the entrance drive, a mile to the Nature Discovery Center.

Ownership

Metropolitan Park District of the Toledo Area.

Size & Designation

Secor Metropark is the second largest Toledo metropark, comprising about 600 acres.

Nearby Natural Attractions

Secor Metropark is one of nine Toledo metroparks. The other metroparks described in this book are Oak Openings, Wildwood, and Swan Creek preserves, and Pearson Metropark.

Also in Lucas County, see Irwin Prairie State Nature Preserve (bordering Secor), Maumee Bay and Crane Creek state parks, Maumee State Forest, Ottawa National Wildlife Refuge, and Magee Marsh and Metzger state wildlife areas.

Access

Obtain a park brochure at the Nature Discovery Center (more on this facility later) and go to the trailhead for the Woodland, Forested Dune, and Trillium trails, located behind and to the right of the center. Follow the blue markers of the Woodland Pond Trail.

First stop is the wooden deck offering a view of Woodland Pond. The dark brown color of the water derives from the tannic acid in oak leaves that fall into the water. Continue on the path that follows the shore of the pond.

Turn right at the next junction, taking the shared path of the Forested Dune (silver markers) and Trillium trails. (A left turn returns to the starting point.) At the intersection ahead, follow the Forested Dune Trail (silver) which splits off to the left. In a few paces this trail forks, signaling the start of a loop. Bear left at the fork, and notice the old beach dunes on your left.

After completing the loop, backtrack a few steps to the next intersection. Turn left here on the Trillium Trail marked by yellow blazes. This path crosses Tupelo Way and comes to a "T" after reentering the woods. Go right (north) sticking with the yellow markers. As it winds north, parallel to Tupelo Way on the right, the Trillium Trail crosses the driveway into the Lone Oak Picnic Area.

To peek at Prairie Creek, bear left at the next fork. The path passes through a clearing behind the Shepherst Memorial and meets the All-Purpose Trail where you will turn right and return to the Nature Discovery Center.

This ramble, covering about two miles, crosses flat terrain which can be mushy in spring and after heavy rain. The paths are wide and easy to follow.

If you have time, hike the Swamp Forest Trail (1.2 miles), leaving from the Meadowview Picnic Area; or the mile-long Meadow Trail, branching from the All-Purpose Trail by the Wolfinger Cemetery; or the half-mile Prairie Trail, stemming from the All-Purpose Trail across the road from the nature center.

The All-Purpose Trail (3.4 or 2.7 miles) is designed for joggers, bicyclists, and for visitors traveling in wheelchairs and strollers.

The nature center, rededicated in 1990 after a facelift, brings people, especially children, closer to nature. Toddlers can crawl through a chipmunk tunnel; a treehouse teaches children about life in the forest canopy. Birds and other critters can be observed at the "Window on Wildlife," a picture-window looking out on birdfeeders and other critter attractions.

The building is open Wednesday through Sunday from noon–5 p.m. The Window on Wildlife is open every day from 7 a.m.–sundown. Hands-on exhibits, drinking water and restrooms also are located in the center.

The park has three picnic areas, featuring open spaces for outdoor games, a playground (Walnut Grove only), toilets, and drinking water.

Geology

This park lies at the edge of the oak openings region of northwestern Ohio, a land characterized by forested sand dunes and shallow, swampy areas. You will walk beside some of these dunes on the Forested Dune Trail.

For about 10,000 years, the lakeshore of Lake Erie's predecessor, Lake Warren, extended farther inland because the Wisconsinan glacier blocked the natural outlet (the Niagara-St. Lawrence valley) for accumulating water.

Glacial meltwater and rivers to the north (Michigan) dumped sand and heavier sediment into the lake. Southbound longshore currents carried the lightweight sand to the southwestern coast of the lake, then waves distributed it on flat beaches and offshore shallows.

When the ice jam broke the lake drained, leaving its former beach and shore high and dry. Wind then dried the sand and tossed it into shifting dunes. Eventually, vegetation sank roots and stabilized most of the dunes. (See Oak Openings Preserve.)

Prairie Creek courses through the northwestern third of the park before entering Tenmile Creek. One of its diminutive tributaries, Wiregrass Creek, has traced a shallow trough in the southwestern corner of the park. Both of these currents expose the layer of sandy topsoil on their banks. Beneath the sand is a bed of impermeable clay which explains why water collects in the hollows between sand ridges and gives rise to the trees of the wet woods.

Wildlife

The wet forest in Secor Metropark sponsors the growth of buxom tulip trees, black cherry, beech, basswood (linden), black walnut, sprinkled with some oaks on the ridgetops. Note that many of these trees have buttressing trunks, meaning their roots have spread farther than normal for extra support in the unstable sandy topsoil.

Various oaks rim Woodland Pond. Their decomposing leaves emit tannic acid and give the pond its dark color. A pair of white oaks, the oldest trees in the park, stand sentry in front of Wolfinger Cemetery.

The understory, the trees growing below the forest canopy, consists of black gum, spicebush, pawpaw, sassafras, and flowering dogwood. Secor, in fact, boasts the largest concentration of native dogwoods in northwestern Ohio.

At ground level, ferns (cinnamon, interrupted, royal) and wildflowers called bloodroot, cut-leaf toothwort, garlic mustard, jack-in-the-pulpit, jewelweed (touch-me-not), white baneberry (doll's eyes), mayapple, wild geranium, and stinging nettle display their colors and shapes.

Common woodland animals dwell here—raccoon, downy woodpecker, flicker, tufted titmouse, and fox squirrel, among others. Tracks in the sandy soil gave away the presence of deer.

In the meadow are dogwoods, milkweed, Queen Anne's lace, yarrow, sensitive fern, berry patches, asters, thistles, common vetch, and others. Black oak (which likes open areas), blazing star, tall coreopsis, bergamot, prairie dock, lupine, puccoon, and big and little bluestem grasses flourish in the planted prairie.

The prairie blossoms arrived en masse during a warm spell 4,000 years ago. Though temperatures later cooled, sparking the comeback of the deciduous forest, the prairie persisted in isolated pockets. Settlers wiped out most of the native prairie remnants in Lucas County.

In these open areas, you might see birds like the woodcock (spring), red-winged blackbird, goldfinch, bobwhite quail, ring-necked pheasant, brown thrasher, bluebirds, and sparrows. Hawks may fly overhead hunting for field mice.

Other aviators include swallowtail, monarch, crescent, cabbage white, and sulfur butterflies. Grasshoppers, honeybees, ladybugs and garter snakes reside in the fields too. Furry critters such as the red fox, ground hog, and cottontail rabbit prefer this habitat.

History

Oddly, the metropark owns a parking lot at the corner of Jefferson and Erie in downtown Toledo. That busy corner was given to the park district in 1941 by Arthur J. Secor in memory of his parents Joseph K. and Elizabeth T. Secor.

The profit from the parking lot paid for the park land in 1949. The park opened in September 1953, followed in 1959 by the Nature Discovery Center. The proceeds from the 1985 sale of the parking lot funded most improvements at the Nature Discovery Center, rededicated in 1990.

The Wolfinger family used to live on this land. Their family cemetery is preserved on the park grounds.

The Shepherst Memorial pays tribute to J. Max Shepherst, the park district's first director-secretary. Shepherst was one of the leading advocates for the preservation of the oak openings region.

Journal

July1993. If you've been in the field all day, you notice the particular calm that takes place between sunset and dark. It's like all of the wildlife has gone home to eat dinner and watch the evening news. The woods dims and becomes still. By the time I reach the car, night has taken over, a barred owl booms, glow worms glow, and all seems right in this particular place . . .I hope I have enough gas to get home.

Beech tree leaves

SWAN CREEK PRESERVE

Don't be fooled by the placid pace of meandering Swan Creek. Like a restless snake, this current has shed its skin, scattering fragments of flesh in the form of oxbow-shaped wetlands in its floodplain. Examining these oxbows—sometimes ponds, sometimes morasses, sometimes dry—is one of the treats in this suburban metropark.

Location

South Toledo, Lucas County.

Leave Interstate 475 at the exit for State Route 2 (Airport Highway) and travel east a little more than a couple of miles to the entrance on the right. Park at the lot for the Yager Center. Another entrance is located on Glendale Avenue.

Ownership

Metropark District of the Toledo Area.

Size & Designation

Swan Creek Preserve encompasses 417 acres. It is one of nine Toledo Metroparks.

Nearby Natural Attractions

Besides Swan Creek Preserve, visit Oak Openings Preserve, Secor Metropark, Wildwood Preserve, and Pearson Metropark, the Toledo metroparks reviewed in this book.

Lucas County also boasts Irwin Prairie State Nature Preserve, Maumee State Park, Maumee State Forest, Ottawa National Wildlife Refuge, Crane Creek State Park, and Magee Marsh and Metzger Marsh state wildlife areas.

Access

After parking, pick up a park brochure and trail map at the Yager Center, which features outdoor nature exhibits, the indoor "Window on Wildlife," drinking water, and restrooms with outdoor entrances. The park has five nature paths, none measuring more than 1.5 miles, and a 3.3-mile All-Purpose Trail for bicyclists, joggers, and recreational walkers.

The longest footpath, the North Trail, begins to the left of the Yager Center, and swings northeast (follow blue blazes) to pavement and a wooden observation deck that overlooks Swan Creek. Folks in wheelchairs and pushing strollers can reach this spot too. Birdwatching is a favorite pastime at this view.

The trail bends left at the deck. In a few paces you will reach an intersection. Turn right to visit an oxbow; left if the parking lot or another trail is your destination.

Now the North Trail hooks eastward behind some apartment buildings and along a meadow. After a gentle descent into the floodplain bear right at the fork, the beginning of a loop that visits an oxbow. The abandoned stream begins as a shallow pond in the spring and early summer, but by summer's end the murky soup has dried up. Finish the loop and retrace your steps to the trailhead to complete a 1.5-mile journey.

The Brown Connecting Trail (.7 miles) heads south behind the Yager Center, crosses Swan Creek via a bridge, and ends at the parking lot of the Glendale Avenue entrance. Branching from this spur are the

Meadow, Big Woods, and Floodplain trails.

Departing from the Yager Center, the All-Purpose Trail wanders into the northwest section of the park. Another connecting spur travels to the Glendale Avenue entrance. Cross-country skiers can use all the trails.

Geology

Swan Creek makes curling brushstrokes as it wanders through this preserve. The scenic S-shaped curves are called meanders, which occur only when a stream passes over flat terrain.

Though Swan Creek looks peaceful it continues an earth-moving process that it has carried out for centuries. Look carefully at the creek bank. The current quickly washes away loose bits or chunks of dirt, largely clay. This soil is composed of fine clay particles and silt that washed into a large lake (Lake Erie's predecessor) that grew in front of the stalled Wisconsinan glacier around 10,000 years ago. Tree roots, relieved of soil by the creek, dangle over the water.

The sediment lifted by the current upstream may be dumped downstream at places where the water slows, such as the inside of bends or behind logs and other obstacles that fall into stream. Sand bars, tiny islands, new banks, or small beaches may form in these slack areas.

During the spring flood period and after heavy rains Swan Creek becomes a wild current. It will overflow its banks and inundate the floodplain. It might even form a new channel, as it has done many times already, by cutting through the neck of a curve. The abandoned, horseshoe-shaped channel, like a snake's discarded skin, becomes a stagnant oxbow pond.

Floods may occasionally freshen some of these ponds; some become intermittent pools. Those farthest from the everchanging current may dry up entirely and host lush vegetation.

Water takes a long time to drain from and percolate through the clay-based floodplain soil. This creates swampy conditions.

Wildlife

The soggy swamp forest at Swan Creek sustains plants that can stand being flooded from time to time. These include trees like sycamore, willow, black walnut, cottonwood on the creek banks, and elm, ash, and red maple. Aspen, beech, dogwood, black cherry, mulberry, Ohio buckeye, bladdernut, tulip tree, and butternut (a potentially threatened species) reside in the preserve. Combined, 44 types of trees have been counted.

Arrowhead, purple cress, and stinging nettle might be some of the first wildflowers to settle in the swamp area. More than 180 species of blossoms have been recorded, notably jack-in-the-pulpit and beauties called poor man's pepper (peppergrass), deadly (climbing) nightshade, Virginia creeper, lizard's tail (look for an arching flower-head), gall-of-the-earth, beggartick, twisted stalk (a tiny lily with a twisting stalk), black snakeroot (supposedly a healer), and white snakeroot (supposedly a killer if cow's milk containing its toxin is consumed by humans).

Nine ferns thrive here. Look for the interrupted, ostrich, and rattlesnake ferns.

Sometimes a badger (a protected mammal in Ohio) lives in the preserve. Otherwise, expect the regulars—red and gray fox, deer, woodchuck, rabbit, mink, striped skunk, and others.

Along the creek you are apt to see a belted kingfisher swooping for food, or a great blue heron stabbing the current with its beak. Seventy-four other birds join the preserve's checklist. Try to find the Swainson's thrush, the nighthawk, scarlet tanager, evening grosbeak, indigo bunting, wood duck, northern oriole, golden-crowned kinglet, and bobwhite quail.

Thirteen reptiles (turtles and snakes) and 11 brands of amphibians might be identified by the keen observer.

History

Back in 1928, wishful park planners zeroed in on this acreage, but money for its purchase did not become available until the 1960s. This once-rural setting now had become suburban.

Some of the funds for the park land came from the federal government—compensation for the loss of Toledo park land during the construction of interstates 75 and 475. After additional purchases, the park opened on October 27, 1973.

The Yager Center is named for the late Joseph A. Yager, a park district board member, and his son, John W. Yager, a park board member and a board president.

The Mary Jane Gill Picnic Shelter honors a board member who retired in 1987.

Journal

What's in a name? Swan Creek is a misnomer. This twisting creek becomes a raging torrent after a heavy spring rain. It overflows its banks and floodplain, sometimes forming new channels. It should have been named Snake Run or Serpentine Creek. But then again, places with those names don't sound like they're worth saving.

Great horned owl

WILDWOOD PRESERVE

Wildwood Preserve once was the estate of a millionaire who made his fortune selling spark plugs. But the "spark" to protect this natural land was ignited in the early 1970s when a developer revealed a plan to carve up the place into luxury housing lots. Citizens and conservation groups persuaded voters to buy it. The effort restored a stately manor house, saved the upland and floodplain forests, kept the meadows alive for birds, and gave people a striking view of the Ottawa River—something to cherish for a long time.

Location

North Central Lucas County.

Leave Interstate 475 from either the U.S. Route 20/Central Avenue or Talmadge Road exits. If you exit I-475 at Central Avenue, travel east about a mile to the entrance on the left. From the latter exit, head south on Talmadge Road, then west (right) on Central Avenue to the park drive on the right. Park in the main lot serving the visitor center and estate.

Ownership

Metropark District of the Toledo Area.

Size & Designation

The preserve comprises 460 acres. The Stranahan Manor House and the administrative offices of the park district are located in this park.

Nearby Natural Attractions

Wildwood Preserve is one of nine Toledo metroparks. The other metroparks reviewed in this book are Oak Openings Preserve, Swan Creek Preserve, Secor, and Pearson.

In Lucas County you also can visit Irwin Prairie State Nature Preserve, Maumee Bay and Crane Creek state parks, Maumee State Forest, Ottawa National Wildlife Refuge, and Magee Marsh and Metzger Marsh state wildlife areas.

Access

Wildwood's five nature trails visit different habitats. All of them can be reached from the trailhead behind the Visitor Center. The All-Purpose Trail (1.6 miles) for bicyclists, joggers, and visitors in wheelchairs and strollers starts in the parking lot. Cross-country skiers can use all the trails in the winter.

Let's begin on the 2.3-mile Upland Woods Trail, the longest at Wildwood. Enter the woods and track the red markers for the Upland Woods Trail. Skip the Floodplain Trail, branching to the right, and the Prairie Trail, heading left.

The wide, smooth, sandy trail journeys northwest through a hardwood forest. The trail suddenly becomes paved where it spans a ravine, but it soon resumes its dirt base. At the half mile pole you reach the beginning of a meadow. A few paces ahead you will come to a fork, signaling the beginning of the loop. An arrow on the trail post points to the left.

At the end of the meadow the trail turns right into the woods. The trail wanders to the north border of the park where the roar of traffic from I-475 can be distracting. A boardwalk lifts walkers over soggy areas in the forest.

The path hooks right (southeast) when it reaches a bluff above the Ottawa River. Ahead stand two viewing platforms, ideal places for wildlife observation and resting. Waist-high ferns and tall oaks surround the second deck. At the end of the loop, turn left and head back toward the Visitor Center.

Take the next left (north), following the blue blazes of the Floodplain Trail. This path descends to the Ottawa River (also known as Ten Mile Creek) and follows the current downstream. (The green-blazed Ridge Trail loops from the Floodplain Trail.)

The trail becomes a boardwalk near the Manor House. Here you climb the stairs to the Manor House and follow the yellow blazes (Meadow Trail) back to the trailhead; or continue downstream and back to higher ground where you can tour the mansion or return to the parking lot.

The Prairie Trail (a mile lasso-shaped trail) visits a remnant of the once vast tallgrass prairie, located in the southwestern part of the park. Stroll down this lane from mid-July to Labor Day when the prairie flowers fully bloom.

The mile-long Meadow Trail visits a clearing south of the Manor House, a good spot for viewing seed-eating birds, wildflowers, and butterflies.

After traipsing through the wild, dust off your hat, wipe your feet, and tour the Manor House, the former estate of Robert A. Stranahan. The mansion is open Wednesday through Sunday from noon–5 p.m.

The Visitor Center, the former stables of the estate, has a wildlife viewing window, outdoor nature education panels, restrooms, and drinking water. The Window on Wildlife is open daily from 8 a.m. to dusk. Park offices are located here. Picnic tables and a play area are nearby.

Metroparks Hall boasts nature art exhibits, a gift shop, and offices for the Citizens for Metroparks. The building, open Wednesday-Sunday from noon to 5 p.m., used to house Stranahan's limousines.

Geology

The sand beneath your feet in the forest was once either part of an ancient beach, sand dune, or sand bar.

About 10,000 years ago, the last continental glacier that scraped across Ohio, the Wisconsinan glacier, rested in a huge basin to the north. The ice sheet plugged the St. Lawrence-Niagara outlet, so glacial meltwater and runoff from streams formed huge lakes, known to geologists as Lake Maumee, Lake Warren, Lake Wayne, and Lake Lundy. These lakes preceded Lake Erie.

The waters of these lakes flooded much of northwestern Ohio. Waves, shoreline currents, and wind deposited sand in depths of 15-50 feet. When water began escaping to the ocean through the Niagara and St. Lawrence valleys, the lake shrank roughly to the size of today's Lake Erie.

That left the former beaches and sand bars high and dry. The land was barren, and for a while wind whipped the sand into shifting dunes, creating a corrugated terrain. Eventually, vegetation gripped the land and slowed the movement of sand.

The Ottawa River, a postglacial stream, curls through the park. In places it has eroded through the sand and exposed the layer of clay beneath it. Spring floods reshape the banks, lick new channels, and deposit new sediments—actions which redistribute and replenish the plant life in the floodplain.

Wildlife

Some 32 types of trees grow in Wildwood Preserve. Red and white oak rule in the upland woods. Here you also find sugar maple in abundance, and healthy specimens of wild black cherry, bitternut hickory, sassafras, viburnum, and pin oak.

Sycamore and cottonwood preside over the floodplain. Ohio buckeye, black walnut, box elder, silver maple, willow, and river birch also occupy this moist habitat.

Fifty-nine varieties of wildflowers have been counted. After spring floods look for wild phlox, bittercress, and buttercups along the river. In summer, these are replaced by nettles, coneflowers, cup plant (a member of the sunflower family), and others.

The upland forest yields many blossoms, including sweet cicely, trout lily, spring beauty, and white baneberry (also known as doll's eyes), whose white berries are poisonous.

The prairie hosts grasses, like big bluestem and Indian grass, which can grow to 10 feet, and blossoms named bergamot, black-eyed Susan, and blazing star.

In the meadows, look for the swaying doily of Queen Anne's lace and vetches on the higher terrain. Joe-pye weed and ironweed will occupy the lower ground.

The resplendent, feathery wings of ferns appear everywhere. Representatives include the sensitive, interrupted, bracken, and maidenhair ferns.

Fox, owls, and hawks will hunt for mice, voles, and small birds in these clearings. Deer browse throughout the park. You are likely to see the tracks of raccoons on the banks of the Ottawa River. This furry critter, and the great horned owl, find homes in the hollows of tall trees.

An old "walker's companion" published by the park district listed the 68 different birds that had been seen in Wildwood Preserve. The checklist included two endangered species—the dark-eyed junco and magnolia warbler.

The platforms along the Upland Woods Trail are excellent places to observe birds of the forest, such as the pileated woodpecker, chickadee, and nuthatch. The floodplain attracts the belted kingfisher, eastern phoebe, and great blue heron. The fields hide the eastern meadowlark, woodcock, and eastern bluebird.

History

Only a few sand dunes, if any, remained uncovered by the time French explorers reached northwestern Ohio. Since then, human development has altered the land substantially.

Wildwood Preserve encompasses the former estate of Robert A. Stranahan, Sr., co-founder of the Champion Spark Plug Company. The Stranahan Mansion (now called Manor House), styled after the Georgian Colonial homes of the 18th century, was completed in 1938. An Italianate formal garden with brick walkways and gazebos lies east of the home.

The Ohio Chapter of The Nature Conservancy bought the property in 1973 and served as an interim owner. Voters approved a levy in 1974 to buy back the land from the conservancy. The estate reopened on Memorial Day 1975 as Wildwood.

OHIO'S SCENIC RIVERS

Ohio established a national trend in 1968 by adopting the nation's first state scenic rivers act. The legislation and the programs Ohio created to preserve and restore its rivers and streams have become models for other states. So far, 10 waterways, totaling 635 miles, have been designated state scenic rivers by the Ohio Department of Natural Resources, Division of Natural Areas and Preserves (ODNR). Two rivers have earned national scenic river status from the U.S. Department of the Interior. Designation is based on the level of human development influencing the flow, water quality, natural diversity, use, and riparian habitat of the stream. Usually, only portions of a river's length meet the qualifications. Rivers designated "wild" boast heavily forested river corridors, little human intrusion, high water quality, and thriving aquatic communities. "Scenic" designations go to streams whose corridors are less pristine in most categories than wild rivers. "Recreational" rivers have significant cultural, historical, and natural attributes worth preserving. Scenic river designation does not alter land ownership nor restrict use of the stream for boating, fishing, photography, nature study, etc. However, these activities are subject to local restrictions. In other words, canoes should enter and leave streams only in designated areas; fishing can occur only in designated areas; and permission of the landowner must be obtained. For details on river designation, preservation programs, and use of designated streams contact the ODNR, Division of Natural Areas and Preserves, Fountain Square, Building F-1, Columbus, Ohio 43224-1331; phone (614) 265-6453.

Chagrin River

Though surveyor and explorer Moses Cleaveland was chagrined to discover this river was not the Cuyahoga River, the river's name does not reflect his disappointment. Actually, the name comes from the Indian word "shagarin" meaning "clear water."

Designation

Scenic. The Chagrin River became Ohio's ninth scenic river on July 2, 1979. Total miles designated—49 miles.

Watershed

The main stem of the river originates in northern Geauga County. It flows southwest into Cuyahoga County, then north through Cuyahoga and Lake counties. The Aurora Branch arises in northwest Portage County and joins the main stem in southeastern Cuyahoga County. The East Branch snakes across northern Geauga County and meets the main stem in Lake County (Willoughby). The river empties into Lake Erie.

Designated Portions

Main stem, 23 miles, from its confluence with the Aurora Branch downstream to the U.S. Route 6 bridge; Aurora Branch, 11 miles from the State Route 82 bridge to its merger with the main stem; East Branch, 15 miles, from the confluence with the main stem upstream to the Heath Road bridge at the Lake-Geauga county line.

Nearby Natural Attractions

The Chagrin River flows through South Chagrin and North Chagrin reservations (Cleveland metroparks) and Hach-Otis State Nature Preserve (East Branch). Also, visit The Holden Arboretum, and Penitentiary Glen and Chapin Forest reservations (Lake Metroparks).

Grand River

The Grand River wears two faces. It lolls and plods through Ashtabula County, then rides a wild roller-coaster around steep banks in Lake County.

Designation

The Grand River was designated scenic and wild on January 17, 1974. Total designated miles—56 miles; 23 wild, 33 scenic.

Watershed

The Grand River starts in southeastern Geauga County, swings into northwestern Trumbull County and north into Ashtabula, then west through Lake County and into Lake Erie.

Designated Portions

From U.S. Route 322 in Ashtabula County to the covered bridge in Harpersfield (Ashtabula County) the river is designated scenic, but from the covered bridge to the Norfolk & Western railroad trestle south of Painesville (Lake County) it is wild.

Nearby Natural Attractions

These Lake Metroparks—Helen Hazen Wyman Reservation, Masons Landing, Indian Point Reservation, Hidden Valley Reservation, Riverview Reservation, Hogback Ridge Reservation; and Harpersfield Covered Bridge, Ashtabula metropark; and Mentor Marsh and Headlands Dunes state nature preserve.

Little Beaver Creek

Ohio's first wild-designated river also may be its most pristine and primeval. The first Ohioans arrived in this green valley 10,000 years ago. Those who have ever canoed this creek find its currents tricky.

Designation

Little Beaver Creek became Ohio's first wild river on January 15, 1974. It became the state's second national scenic river (34 miles) in October 1975. Total designated miles —36 miles; 20 wild, 16 scenic.

Watershed

Little Beaver Creek comprises three forks. The North Fork travels in an arch from southeastern Mahoning County into Beaver County, Pennsylvania, and Columbiana County, and joins the main stem at Fredericktown. The Middle Fork flows southerly from southern Mahoning County and joins the West Fork, coming from Guilford, in Williamsport. The creek spills into the Ohio River, just east of the Ohio-Pennsylvania state line.

Designated Portions

A portion of each fork is designated wild and scenic. The wild portion includes: West Fork from Y-Camp Road downstream to the confluence with the Middle Fork; North Fork from Jackman Road to the main stem (east of the confluence of the west and middle forks); main stem from the confluence of the west and middle forks to 3/4 miles north of Grimm's Bridge.

The scenic section comprises: North Fork, from the Ohio-Pennsylvania border to Jackman Road; Middle Fork from Elkton Road to the merger with the West Fork; and main stem from 3/4 mile north of Grimm's Bridge to the state line.

Nearby Natural Attractions

Little Beaver Creek flows through Beaver Creek State Park.

Upper Cuyahoga River

Some 2,500 years ago ancient people called Mound Builders inhabited the upper Cuyahoga River, but they suddenly and inexplicably vanished after living there a century or so. Another mound building culture—beavers—arrived later, only to be exterminated by white settlement. The beavers, however, have returned and resumed their mound building in the wetlands and swamps that recharge this river.

Designation

The Upper (upper meaning close to the river's source) Cuyahoga River was designated a state scenic river on June 26, 1974. Total designated miles—25 scenic miles.

Watershed

The west and east branches of the Cuyahoga River begin in northern Geauga County. Both branches flow south through the county and join south of Burton. The river continues south, cuts a swath across northwestern Portage County, then swings west and north through Summit County, Akron, and Cuyahoga County. It concludes its journey at Lake Erie in Cleveland.

Designated Portions

The river is designated scenic from the Troy-Burton township line in Geauga County to U.S. Route 14 in Portage County, a 25-mile stretch.

Nearby Natural Attractions

Marsh Wetland State Nature Preserve, Nelson-Kennedy Ledges State Park, Tinkers Creek State Nature Preserve and State Park, Eagle Creek State Nature Preserve.

SOUTHWESTERN OHIO 

Little Miami River

The entire length of this river is designated scenic. Rich in human and natural history, its currents have bathed the likes of the Fort Ancient Indians, Daniel Boone, Tecumseh, and Simon Kenton. The waters also have carved the spectacular ancient dolomite walls in Clifton Gorge. It is Ohio's first state-designated scenic river and its first national scenic river.

Designation

This current was dedicated in stages from April 23, 1969 to October 21, 1971. National designation got underway in August 1973 and was completed in January 1980. Total miles dedicated—105 state scenic; 92 national scenic.

Watershed

The source of the Little Miami River is in rural southeastern Clark County. From there it flows through Greene, Warren, Clermont, and Hamilton counties into the Ohio River, east of Cincinnati.

Designated Portions

The entire length of the river, and part of its north fork, is designated scenic. It is a national scenic river from Clifton to its confluence with the Ohio River.

Nearby Natural Attractions

Clifton Gorge and Caesar Creek state nature preserves, Glen Helen Nature Preserve, John Bryan and Little Miami state parks, The Narrows Reserve, Fort Ancient State Memorial, Spring Valley State Wildlife Area, and Cincinnati Nature Preserve.

Stillwater River–Greenville Creek

For most of its journey the Stillwater River, as its name implies, meanders so gently that its water appears motionless. In places, the stillness is solid enough to reflect the sycamore branches that lazily arch over the current.

During his military campaign to wipe out Indians, General "Mad" Anthony Wayne built a fort on a tributary of Stillwater River. He called it Fort Greene Ville. The treaty signed at the fort in 1794 opened the southern half of Ohio to white settlers.

Designation

The rivers were dedicated in stages from July 1975 to Apri, 1982. Total designated miles —93 miles; 83 scenic, 10 recreational.

Watershed

Stillwater River originates in western Darke County near the Indiana border and flows eastward. Greenville Creek begins in Indiana and proceeds east to its meeting with the Stillwater at Covington in Miami County. The Stillwater River continues southeast and merges with the Great Miami River in Dayton.

Designated Portions

Greenville Creek is a scenic river from the Ohio-Indiana border to its merger with the Stillwater River. From the Riffle Road bridge in Darke County to the Englewood Dam (Montgomery County), the Stillwater River is scenic. It is designated recreational from the dam to its demise in Dayton.

Nearby Natural Attractions

Greenville Falls State Nature Preserve, Stillwater Prairie Reserve, Englewood Reserve, Aullwood Audubon Nature Center, Charleston Falls Reserve, and Brukner Nature Center.

CENTRAL OHIO 

Big and Little Darby Creeks

Many endangered fish and mollusks live in these waters cleansed by the prairies of the Darby Plains. The habitat is so valuable that The Nature Conservancy, a leading land preservation organization, has declared this watershed one of its "Last Great Places."

Designation

These streams became state scenic rivers on June 22, 1984. Total miles dedicated—82 miles. The U.S. Department of the Interior was considering a national designation in early 1994.

Watershed

Big Darby Creek starts in southeastern Logan County and journeys through Champaign, Union, Madison, Franklin, and Pickaway counties. From southeastern Champaign County, Little

Darby Creek goes through Union and Madison counties before connecting with Big Darby Creek in western Franklin County.

Designated Portions

Big Darby's scenic designation runs from the Champaign-Union county line to its confluence with the Scioto River in Circleville. Designation for Little Darby begins at Lafayette-Plain City Road (County Road 5) in Madison County to its merger with Big Darby in Franklin County.

Nearby Natural Attractions

Battelle-Darby Creek Metropark, Bigelow Cemetery, Smith Cemetery, Stage's Pond, and Milford Center Prairie state nature preserves, Deer Creek and A.W. Marion state parks.

Olentangy River

This river briefly slices a path along the border of 350 million-year-old shale and limestone, and below a steep bluff it washes mysterious, round "ironstones" (concretions), some the size of wrecking balls, that have rolled into its current.

Designation

The Olentangy became Ohio's third scenic river on August 24, 1973. Total miles designated—22 miles.

Watershed

This stream runs from the Crawford-Richland county line, through Crawford, Marion, Delaware, and Franklin counties. It empties into the Scioto River in Columbus.

Designated Portions

Twenty-two miles of the river is designated scenic from the Delaware State Park Dam in Delaware County to Wilson Bridge Road in Worthington, Franklin County.

Nearby Natural Attractions

The Olentangy River flows through Highbanks Metropark (scenic portion) and Delaware State Park.

NORTHWESTERN OHIO

Maumee River

The blood of American, Indian, British, and French soldiers stained this river during the frontier wars of the 18th and 19th centuries. The Maumee flowed beside a vast wetland known as the Great Black Swamp, but like the warriors themselves, the swamp has been reduced to a mere memory.

Designation

The Maumee River earned scenic and recreational river status on July 18, 1974. Total designated miles—97 miles; 53 recreational, 43 scenic.

Watershed

The St. Joseph and St. Marys rivers converge in Ft. Wayne, Indiana to form the Maumee River which then shoots northeast through Paulding, Defiance, Henry, Wood, and Lucas counties, and into Lake Erie.

Designated Portions

The scenic portion of the river runs from the Ohio-Indiana border to the U.S. Route 24 bridge, west of Defiance. From that spot to the State Route 20 & 25 bridge in Perrysburg the river is designated recreational.

Nearby Natural Attractions

Independence Dam and Mary Jane Thurston state parks, Fallen Timbers State Memorial, and Providence, Bend View, and Farnsworth metroparks.

Sandusky River

Though better outfitted than their Seneca and Wyandot predecessors, modern fishermen gather along this river's banks during the migration of walleye and white bass from Sandusky Bay. The river winds through some of Ohio's most fertile farmland, a product of the glacier that deposited rich soil 12,000 years ago and the litter of the forest that once grew on the surface.

Designation

The Sandusky River was declared a state scenic river in January 1970. Total miles designated—70 miles.

Watershed

From its headwaters in southeastern Crawford County, the Sandusky River heads west across Crawford County, then north into Wyandot, Seneca, and Sandusky counties. It drains into Sandusky Bay.

Designated Portions

Scenic river designation runs from U.S. Route 30 in Upper Sandusky (Wyandot County) to Roger Young Memorial Park in Fremont, Sandusky County.

Nearby Natural Attractions

Howard Collier State Nature Preserve (south-central Seneca County), Spiegel Grove, home and library of President Rutherford B. Hayes, Fremont.

OHIO DEPARTMENT OF NATURAL RESOURCES

Division of Wildlife

Besides nature, the beauty of a state wildlife area is that you don't have to stay on the trails (if trails even exist). The Ohio Department of Natural Resources, Division of Wildlife, administers 84 wildlife areas with 151,294 acres of land and nearly 24,000 acres of water (total includes several state parks) at your disposal. Hunting, trapping and fishing are permitted on these parcels. Maps (up to 6, free) for some of these sites are available from the Ohio Department of Natural Resources, Division of Wildlife, 1840 Belcher Drive, Columbus, Ohio 43224-1329; phone (614) 265-6300.

State Wildlife Areas

Aldrich Pond *(Seneca)*
Aquilla Lake *(Geauga)*
Auburn Marsh *(Geauga)*
Beach City *(Tuscarawas)*
Beaver Creek *(Williams)*
Berlin Lake *(Stark)*
Big Island *(Marion)*
Bott *(Brown)*
Brush Creek *(Jefferson)*
Caesar Creek *(Warren)*
Clark Lake *(Clark)*
Cooper Hollow *(Jackson)*
Darke *(Darke)*
Deer Creek *(Fayette)*
Delaware *(Delaware)*
Dillon *(Muskingum)*
East Fork *(Clermont)*
Fallsville *(Highland)*
Fox Lake *(Athens)*
Fulton Pond *(Fulton)*
Grand River *(Trumbull)*
Grant Lake *(Brown)*
Green Island *(Lucas)*
Greenfield Lake *(Fairfield)*
Highlandtown *(Columbiana)*
Indian Creek *(Brown)*
Kaul *(Jefferson)*
Killbuck Marsh *(Wayne)*
Killdeer Plains *(Wyandot)*
Knox Lake *(Knox)*
Kokosing Lake *(Knox)*
Lake La Su An *(Williams)*
Lake Park *(Stark)*
Leesville Lake *(Carroll)*
Liberty *(Jackson)*
Little Portage *(Ottawa)*
Magee Marsh *(Ottawa)*
Mercer *(Mercer)*
Metzger Marsh *(Ottawa)*
Meyerholtz *(Henry)*
Milan *(Erie)*
Miller Blue Hole *(Sandusky)*
Missionary Island *(Lucas)*
Mohican *(Knox)*
Mosquito Lake *(Trumbull)*
New Lyme *(Ashtabula)*
Oakthorpe Lake *(Fairfield)*
Oldaker *(Highland)*
Orwell *(Ashtabula)*
Ottoville Quarry *(Putnam)*
Oxbow Lake *(Defiance)*
Paint Creek *(Highland)*
Pater *(Butler)*
Powelson *(Muskingum)*
Resthaven *(Erie)*
Rock Mill *(Fairfield)*
Ross Lake *(Ross)*
Rush Run *(Preble)*
Salt Fork *(Guernsey)*
Shenango *(Trumbull)*
Shreve Lake *(Wayne)*
Spencer Lake *(Medina)*
Spring Valley *(Greene)*
Sunday Creek *(Athens and Hocking)*
Toussaint *(Ottawa)*
Tranquility *(Adams)*
Trimble *(Athens)*
Tycoon Lake *(Gallia)*
Veto Lake *(Washington)*
Waterloo *(Athens)*
Wellington *(Lorain)*
Willard Marsh *(Huron)*
Willow Point *(Erie)*
Wolf Creek *(Morgan)*
Woodbury *(Coshocton)*
Wyandot *(Wyandot)*
Zepernick Lake*(Columbiana)*
Zoar Lake *(Tuscarawas)*

OHIO'S STATE-DESIGNATED NATURAL AREAS

(In the order of their designation)

No.	Preserve (acres)	County	Manager
1.	**Fowler Woods** (133)	Richland	ODNR
2.	**Little Rocky Hollow*** (259)	Hocking	ODNR
3.	**Caesar Creek Gorge** (463)	Warren	ODNR
4.	**Adams Lake Prairie** (26)	Adams	ODNR
5.	**Cranberry Bog*** (13)	Licking	ODNR
6.	**Seymour Woods*** (106)	Delaware	ODNR
7.	**Highbanks** (206)	Frank/Del	Columbus MP
8.	**Eagle Creek** (441)	Portage	ODNR
9.	**Shallenberger** (88)	Fairfield	ODNR
10.	**Blackhand Gorge** (980)	Licking	ODNR
11.	**Rockbridge** (100)	Hocking	ODNR
12.	**Knox Woods** (30)	Knox	ODNR
13.	**Gahanna Woods** (51)	Franklin	ODNR
14.	**Hueston Woods** (200)	Preble,Butler	ODNR
15.	**Sheick Hollow*** (151)	Hocking	ODNR
16.	**Stage's Pond** (178)	Pickaway	ODNR
17.	**Marie J. Desonier** (491)	Athens	ODNR
18.	**Irwin Prairie** (187)	Lucas	ODNR
19.	**Tinkers Creek** (786)	Summit/Port.	ODNR
20.	**Kiser Lake Wetlands*** (51)	Champaign	ODNR
21.	**Mentor Marsh** (647)	Lake	ODNR
22.	**Edward S. Thomas** (319)	Franklin	Columbus MP
23.	**Goll Woods** (321)	Fulton	ODNR
24.	**Christmas Rocks*** (208)	Fairfield	ODNR
25.	**Headlands Dunes** (16)	Lake	ODNR
26.	**Greenbelt*** (97)	Hamilton	Hamilton MP
27.	**Newberry*** (50)	Hamilton	Hamilton MP
28.	**Spring Beauty Dell*** (41)	Hamilton	Hamilton MP
29.	**Trillium Trails*** (23)	Hamilton	Hamilton MP
30.	**Lake Katharine** (1,850)	Jackson	ODNR
31.	**Old Woman Creek** (572)	Erie	ODNR
32.	**Cedar Bog** (428)	Champaign	OHS
33.	**Kyle Woods** (82)	Mahoning	ODNR
34.	**Sharon Woods Gorge** (21)	Hamilton	Hamilton MP
35.	**Walter A. Tucker** (55)	Fairfield	Columbus MP
36.	**Conkles Hollow** (87)	Hocking	ODNR
37.	**Siegenthaler Esker** (37)	Champaign	ODNR
38.	**Hach-Otis** (80)	Lake	ODNR
39.	**Dean A. Culberson*** (238)	Clinton	ODNR
40.	**Bigelow Cemetery Prairie** (1)	Madison	ODNR
41.	**Crooked Run** (78)	Clermont	ODNR
42.	**Portage Lakes Wetland*** (6)	Summit	ODNR
43.	**Lou Campbell*** (170)	Lucas	ODNR
44.	**Morris Woods** (104)	Licking	ODNR
45.	**Sheldon Marsh** (435)	Erie	ODNR
46.	**Clifton Gorge** (269)	Greene	ODNR
47.	**Gross Woods** (49)	Shelby	ODNR
48.	**Brown's Lake Bog** (80)	Wayne	TNC
49.	**Dupont Marsh*** (114)	Erie	ODNR
50.	**Compass Plant Prairie*** (16)	Lawrence	ODNR
51.	**Jackson Bog** (6)	Stark	ODNR
52.	**Springville Marsh** (161)	Seneca	ODNR
53.	**Owens Fen*** (18)	Logan	ODNR
54.	**Prairie Road Fen*** (95)	Clark	ODNR
55.	**Gott Fen*** (45)	Portage	ODNR
56.	**Triangle Lake Bog*** (61)	Portage	ODNR
57.	**Frame Lake/Herrick Fen** (110)	Portage	TNC/Kent State

58.	**Mud Lake*** (25)	Williams	ODNR
59.	**Miller Nat. Sanctuary*** (88)	Highland	ODNR
60.	**Smith Cemetery Prairie** (1)	Madison	ODNR
61.	**Erie Sand Barrens** (32)	Erie	ODNR
62.	**Drew Woods*** (15)	Darke	ODNR
63.	**Ladd Natural Bridge*** (35)	Washington	ODNR
64.	**Kent Bog*** (42)	Portage	ODNR
65.	**Zimmerman Prairie*** (4)	Greene	ODNR
66.	**Chaparral** (67)	Adams	ODNR
67.	**Springfield Fen*** (91)	Clark	ODNR
68.	**Vermilion River*** (82)	Huron	ODNR
69.	**Allen F. Beck*** (2,234)	Hocking	Columbus MP
70.	**Pickerington Ponds** (406)	Frklin/Frfld	Columbus MP
71.	**Tummonds SR Preserve*** (86)	Portage	ODNR
72.	**Little Beaver Creek*** (454)	Columbiana	ODNR
73.	**Sears Woods*** (99)	Crawford	ODNR
74.	**Goode Prairie*** (28)	Miami	Miami Cty. MP
75.	**John & Emma Pallister*** (85)	Ashtabula	ODNR
76.	**Carmean Woods*** (39)	Crawford	ODNR
77.	**Swamp Cottonwood*** (21)	Medina	ODNR
78.	**Boord*** (89)	Washington	ODNR
79.	**Milford Center Prairie** (7)	Union	Dayton Power
80.	**Johnson Woods*** (193)	Adams	ODNR
81.	**Emerald Hills*** (74)	Belmont	ODNR
82.	**Audubon Islands** (170)	Lucas	Toledo MP
83.	**Greenville Falls** (79)	Miami	ODNR
84.	**Lakeside Daisy*** (19)	Ottawa	ODNR
85.	**Whipple*** (187)	Adams	ODNR
86.	**Halls Creek Woods*** (278)	Warren	ODNR
87.	**Davey Woods** (103)	Champaign	ODNR
88.	**Betsch Fen*** (35)	Ross	TNC
89.	**Evans Beck Memorial*** (10)	Portage	TNC
90.	**Flatiron Lake Bog*** (68)	Portage	TNC
91.	**Kitty Todd*** (36)	Lucas	TNC
92.	**Rothenbuhler Woods*** (44)	Monroe	TNC
93.	**Strait Creek Prairie*** (75)	Pike	TNC
94.	**Clearfork Gorge*** (29)	Ashland	ODNR
95.	**Mantua Bog*** (63)	Portage	ODNR
96.	**Crane Hollow*** (1,112)	Hocking	Crane Hollow
97.	**Crabill Fen*** (32)	Clark	ODNR
98.	**Marsh Wetlands** (152)	Portage	ODNR
99.	**Karlo Fen*** (15)	Summit	ODNR
100.	**Stratford Woods*** (95)	Delaware	Stratford Cnter
101.	**Wardner-Perkins*** (27)	Hamilton	Audubon Society
102.	**Kendrick Woods** (159	Allen	Appleseed MP
103.	**Baker Woods*** (47)	Mercer	ODNR

TOTAL ACRES: 19,066

The beside the site name means the preserve is not open to the public. Permission from the managing agency or owner is required for visitation. Some sites marked* may be open to the public temporarily.*

The owner of the site may differ from the managing agency. Check with the site manager to determine ownership.

- *TNC is the Ohio Chapter of The Nature Conservancy.*
- *Columbus MP is the Metropolitan Park District of Columbus and Franklin County.*
- *Hamilton MP is the Hamilton County Park District.*
- *Toledo MP is the Metropark District of the Toledo Area.*
- *OHS is the Ohio Historical Society.*
- *Appleseed MP represents the Johnny Appleseed Metropolitan Park District.*
- *Miami Cty is the Miami County Park District.*
- *Dayton Power is short for the Dayton Power & Light Company.*